"Be still and know that I am God."

Psalm 46:10

*Disclaimer: If you have a serious mental or physical medical condition,
please continue with your doctor's prescribed medical regimen and seek
clearance before beginning the mediation practices herein.*

For information about this title or to order other books
and/or electronic media, contact the publisher:

Two Sisters Writing and Publishing
18530 Mack Avenue, Suite 166
Grosse Pointe Farms, MI 48236
www.atkinsgreenspan.com

ISBN
978-1-945875-44-1 (Hardcover)
978-1-945875-19-9 (Paperback)
978-1-945875-20-5 (eBook)

Printed in the United States of America

Cover and Interior design: Van-Garde Imagery, Inc.

Front and back cover photos: © Clarence Tabb, Jr.

Dedication

I'M DEDICATING THIS BOOK to all the women and men in whose bodies my spirit dwelled during past lives. Each incarnation of my spirit has provided lessons on how to cultivate and teach a spiritual life. This dedication also celebrates every ancestor who contributed to my evolution. Whether they helped or hurt me, they shall also be exalted for preparing me for this and future life missions.

Acknowledgments

WORDS CANNOT CONVEY MY immeasurable gratitude to God, Jesus, Mother Mary, the Archangels, the angels, my ancestors, my spirit guides, my power animals, the keeper of the Akashic Records, and every loving being in the spiritual realm that has helped me learn, write this book, and teach. I also have infinite gratitude for:

My father, Thomas Lee Atkins, an extremely powerful entity who lives in the spirit world guiding and protecting us, and assisting God in orchestrating our steps.

My mother, Judge Marylin E. Atkins, who exemplifies woman-power, intestinal fortitude, and divine service in a spirit of generosity, humility, caring, and love.

My sister, Catherine Marie Atkins Greenspan, who is a most loving angel blessed with a literary gift that is entertaining and inspiring people around the world.

My son, Alexander Thomas, whose "old soul" wisdom awes me, and who is anointed as an exemplary citizen and leader destined to uplift countless people during this lifetime.

My family and friends.

Dr. Rama, for teaching me how to meditate and guiding me on this spiritual journey.

Lori Lipten, founder of Sacred Balance Academy for Healing Arts, for teaching me so much about spiritual empowerment and how to use it.

Foreword

ELIZABETH HAS SOMETHING THAT many people want, but they don't have it, because it's not available in the market.

You can't buy it, even by giving a million dollars.

What is it?

Peace, joy, love, and purpose.

How do you get it?

By connecting to God.

This is possible for everyone.

In this book, Elizabeth is teaching how to do it, by sharing her story of spiritual awakening and the lessons she has learned.

"When the student is ready, the teacher will appear," Buddha said.

I pray you are ready to learn information that can dramatically change your life.

Elizabeth began as my student; now she is teaching how to use meditation and other practices to connect with the Divine. Elizabeth shares many miraculous and celestial experiences resulting from her extraordinary connection to God.

"This is not possible!" some may say.

Others may laugh, or ask: *"Is this a hallucination?"*

No, no, no, this is the real thing. You have so much power in meditation, it's unbelievable. You can see and do whatever you want with your astral body. You must experience it for yourself to understand.

And you can enjoy spiritual growth when you devote time to learning what Elizabeth is teaching in this book. In the first section, she tells her life story, and how she became a student of the Divine. In the second section, she teaches what she has learned.

She keeps it very simple, so that even if you have never had any spiritual lessons or experiences, you can now learn how to incorporate them into your life.

The goal is to enjoy love, peace, and bliss—and to know your life's purpose so you can be fulfilled and make a positive contribution to people and the planet.

These practices can also heal the mind, body, and spirit, as Elizabeth describes through her own life story. She has overcome many struggles, including overeating, being overweight, suffering from asthma, enduring conflict from her former spouse, and feeling depressed.

God always intervenes and brings us the help we need. He does this through synchronicities that are anything but coincidences.

This is what happened when I met Elizabeth's mother, former Chief Judge Marylin E. Atkins of Detroit's 36th District Court, while standing in line to renew my driver's license. We began chatting, and I invited her and her family to a spiritual program where they met my wife, Aruna.

Years later, Marylin and Elizabeth came to our home near Washington, DC, and Elizabeth was eager to learn how to meditate and connect with the Divine.

As founder of The International Society for Spiritual Advancement, and leader of devotional programs in the United States and India, I recognized that Elizabeth has a crystal-clear heart and a very evolved soul. And so I taught her how to meditate, and here is the secret to success:

She went home and meditated every day. Spiritual practice is called "practice" because it's something you do repeatedly. Just as a tennis player practices her swing to become a champion, seekers of

God's light and love must pray and meditate every day to cultivate the clearest connections to the spiritual realm.

Elizabeth has done that. As a result, she began to experience fantastical experiences that she is revealing for the first time on the pages of this book. They are above and beyond the ordinary, yet God has told her to share them and to teach, and she is following that calling, being an obedient servant of God.

Her father Thomas Lee Atkins did the same, as a deeply devoted spirit who recognized his daughter's anointing to lead others on a path toward peace and love.

It is my greatest honor to encourage you to read *God's Answer Is Know: Lessons From a Spiritual Life*, by my beloved family member, Elizabeth Ann Atkins.

> Dr. Rama S. Dwivedi
> Founder
> The International Society for
> Spiritual Advancement

Introduction

"Now go, write it before them…
and note it in a book,
that it may be for the time to come for ever and ever."
Isaiah 30:8 NKJ

"YOU'RE GOING TO BE REBORN!"

That's what Spirit declared as I looked up at churning gray clouds over the wind-whipped lake. I just stood there—silent and stunned—as waves crashed on rocks near my feet.

"You're going to be reborn!"

Over the next seven years, I cried a lot. Felt sick and stuck. Struggled. Got depressed. Thought about suicide.

All the while, I was like a caterpillar undergoing metamorphosis within the dark confines of the chrysalis. With hard work, courage, and divine intervention, I cracked the stifling shell, and emerged to fly into the infinite possibilities of a spirit-powered life. Through this awakening, I released fears, struggles with food and fat, and many other conflicts, to soar into a life of self-love, peace, and purpose.

"Elizabeth, you must teach!" Jesus told me. "You must testify loudly and fearlessly as your expression of gratitude for these miracles."

Yes, I've experienced miracles amidst extraordinary two-way communication with Jesus, God, my father's spirit, angels, ancestors, and other divine beings. This may sound fantastical. But it's real, and you also have this power that gives you access to the cosmic energy field of life-changing knowledge.

In this book, I'm teaching you how to access it, activate it, and apply it to heal, prosper, love, experience peace and joy, thrive, and be a positive influence in the world. It starts with my life story, which shows how I changed. Then I show how to *Ascend: 8 Steps to an Infinite You.*

Back when I was struggling with food and fat, fears, divorce, racial identity issues, depression, and career disappointments, I wanted to empower myself on a spiritual level. But some of the information I encountered was hard to understand.

So, this book is for you if you're eager to learn how to embark on a spiritual journey.

This book is for you if you've never meditated—or if you've tried and failed—or if you've never heard of a chakra, or don't know that what you eat and drink can either deepen or dull your intuitive powers. Or maybe you know a little, but want to learn more.

This book is for you if you're "spiritual, not religious." Though I reference Jesus and the Bible, the messages are presented with universal application for everyone, as expressed by Mahatma Gandhi: "I am a Muslim and a Hindu and a Christian and a Jew and so are all of you."

This book is about cultivating unconditional love and peace within yourself, so that you can "Be the change that you wish to see in the world," as Gandhi said.

This book—along with my in-person and online workshops, workbooks, and speaking events—can help you be that change. One simple sentence summarizes how to do that:

"Be still and know that I am God."

Psalm 46:10 starts with "Be still." Get quiet, go within, and explore your mind, heart, and soul. That's the triple gateway to connecting with the infinite power of God that's already inside you. Your express pass through this gateway is meditation, which activates two-way communication with the spiritual energy field that's within us and around us.

Just as you trust your cell phone's invisible wi-fi to connect you with information and people everywhere, you can use your spirit power to access information, guidance, and insights that elevate your "believing" to a new level:

Knowing.

And what will you know? "That I am God."

You may interpret "I am God" as an entity outside of yourself. And you may envision God as a male figure looking down with a scrutinizing, scornful, even punishing temperament. Please allow me to share how I encounter God in my meditations, as I am often led by my own father's spirit. My father died in 1990, but remains very much alive in spirit.

"Come," my father said, taking my hand. In the spirit realm, my father is very tall and powerful, and wears long robes and glows with pure love, peace, and wisdom.

"I'm taking you to God," he said as a floaty sensation fluttered through me and I ascended into the fifth dimension where I was no longer conscious of my body.

First, I saw a golden throne. Rather than witnessing a bearded man in a white robe, or any human form, I was overwhelmed with blissful peace and knowing that I was with God. And God is pure energy that appeared as an infinite, golden glow that flowed in vast streams and swirls, engulfing and permeating everything, everywhere.

Beside this indescribably huge, warm glow of love, was Jesus, who first appeared to me in 2011, and is now a constant presence in my meditations and my life.

In this one, the pure golden energy that is God emanating from the throne suddenly rolled toward me. This golden flow tapered to a point that entered the center of my abdomen, and the God energy poured into me, fusing with every cell in my body, setting me aglow from the inside out. Then this God energy exploded inside me, spraying gold sparkles brilliantly and beautifully in every direction. Like I was at the center of an exploding star.

As this occurred, I absolutely knew that I am one with Source.

God was showing me that *I am* the God energy.

And you are the God energy.

God is within us.

My life's divine assignment is to teach how to allow God's light and love to set you aglow from the inside out. This will help you attain inner peace, and feel fulfilled and prosperous by discovering and living your life purpose.

What's the goal in doing that? To serve humanity and Mother Earth so that love and peace prevail everywhere. God is pure love. God is the Source of all creation and all being.

Our souls are individual starbursts of this God energy that is the pulse-giving life to our human bodies. If you doubt what's keeping your heart beating, remember that a person suffering cardiac arrest is brought back to life with an electric jolt from a defibrillator.

That electricity is a starburst of God energy, which is your soul. Your soul is your true identity. Not your name, your appearance, your family's history, your education, or your job.

When you cultivate a spiritual lifestyle, you can activate that starburst of God energy within. You can expand it, strengthen it, utilize it to maximize your potential on every level: health, love, joy, relationships, career, wealth, and what you contribute to the world.

Unfortunately, the human condition is such that fear breeds hatred; we're taught that we're different, superior, inferior, and separate. We ignore our intuition and our soul's calling, and instead shape our lives on the external expectations, rules, and restrictions of our families, religions, and society.

This makes it easy for forces of evil to hijack our lives and stop us from fulfilling our divine purpose. I speak from experience; I've been writing this book for 16 years. Many distractions derailed my focus, leaving this book as nothing more than an icon on my computer screen for a file called, "God's Answer Is Know."

It sat unfinished, because the devil's answer is "No."

By the devil, I mean negative forces—including people, situations, and our own blocks, such as fears and bad habits—that distract us from our God-given missions to do good things for ourselves and for humanity. We have the power to eradicate war, hatred, famine, disease, discord, inequality, and injustice. We have the power to heal Mother Earth and make peace prevail.

But first we have to find it within ourselves. I am your guide on that journey, as my father baptized me and asked God to make me a Princess of Peace. Then, 44 years later, the Prince of Peace came to me and began teaching what became a spiritual curriculum that I now present to you.

As you step into your spiritual power, you will be awed by seemingly miraculous synchronicities, psychic flashes, inner peace, vitality, and better health. The light of God glowing within you will burn away your old self, and you will feel reborn with the power to serve as a change agent to help yourself, humanity, and the world.

I pray that *God's Answer Is Know: Lessons From a Spiritual Life* helps you ascend into an infinite you.

Elizabeth Ann Atkins
Co-Creator
Two Sisters Writing and Publishing
Atkins & Greenspan Writing
PowerJournal.Life

Contents

Princess of Peace

I WAS BORN INTO the bold and brave union of a 20-year-old black woman and a 45-year-old white man who was a former priest.

Back in racially turbulent 1966, Marylin Elnora Bowman and Thomas Lee Atkins sparked a scandal of race and religion by defying the restrictive conventions of the day to marry across the color line. All while breaking a centuries-old rule that Roman Catholic priests were forbidden to marry. The Bishop excommunicated them, which meant they were banished from receiving soul-cleansing communion during Mass.

It also meant they were damned to hell.

And my parents believed that.

Yet their love was heavenly, as was the gift of their first child. Back before technology could reveal a baby's gender, they thought I would be a boy.

"David," the nurse wrote with a magic marker across my mother's pregnant belly. As you probably know, young David in the Bible slayed the giant Goliath with only a slingshot and a rock, and went on to become the King of Israel and a forefather of Jesus.

Well, I wasn't a boy.

Shortly after I was born on July 11, 1967, my father named me Elizabeth Ann, after Queen Elizabeth II of England. He nicknamed me "Eli," which means "my God" and "ascended" in Hebrew.

The next day, Daddy—who still had his priestly powers—baptized me in the hospital room in Saginaw, Michigan. He chronicled it in a hand-written passage in his journal. Here is an excerpt:

It has been a full day. Most significant event was the baptism and confirmation of the baby.

At 8:30 p.m., I asked permission of the nurse in the nursery to Baptize the baby. She in turn asked her supervisor. She in turn asked the floor supervisor. Finally I persuaded them to say ok. I scrubbed and put on a gown and mask and cap. The nurse got a few "cc's" of distilled water in a small beaker.

I had Chrism (baptismal oil) ready and so—muffled by the mask—I said aloud as I poured water across Elizabeth's forehead… "I confirm you Ann, in the name of, etc."

Meanwhile my big hand covered her entire head even down to the scapula. And it was my intention not only to give my daughter these sacraments but also to give her membership in the family of David that she might become an instrument of—a literal Princess of Peace and into the royal priesthood of God so far as my power to convey this in these sacraments.

She was born on the 365ᵗʰ day of the year in which I gave Marylin my typed and signed formal engagement. And I admitted Elizabeth into the Church on the exact anniversary of giving this paper to her mother. I have been mindful all day, yesterday and today, of my very strong and oft repeated prayer to God for this child…

At the time, the world definitely needed a Princess of Peace. As Daddy was speaking those words, a deadly rebellion was exploding in Newark, New Jersey, killing 26 people, injuring hundreds more, and deepening America's racial divide. Then, 12 days after I was born, as the Detroit insurrection claimed 43 lives amidst looting, fires, and the National Guard, a death threat prompted my parents to retreat with me to a motel room with a rifle.

Thankfully, we returned to the safety of our home in Saginaw, where we lived with an elderly family friend. My mother worked the night shift at a bank and my father worked in a flower shop.

While my parents were extremely happy, and my sister Catherine Marie was due to arrive just a year and six days after my birthday, my devoutly Catholic grandmother wanted nothing to do with her defiant son, his pregnant black wife, or their biracial baby.

But my parents wanted Alphonsine Marie LaLonde Atkins to know her granddaughter. So they drove from the mid-Michigan factory town of Saginaw where they lived, up Interstate 75, for the 90-minute trip to Daddy's forest-shrouded hometown of West

Branch. They went to the house where he grew up with brother George and sister Mary. My grandmother now lived there with Mary, her husband, and their eight children.

My father had traveled such a long and arduous road to arrive at this happy point of his life. If only his family could embrace and celebrate his joy.

But my grandmother, who attended daily Mass, had set her heart on having a son as a Roman Catholic Priest. That seemed imminent when her first son, George, was attending seminary. But he was drafted into the Marines during World War II, and her dream crashed into a nightmare when George disappeared at the bloody Battle of Tarawa. George Joseph Atkins is inscribed in the wall of 28,808 missing soldiers in Honolulu, Hawaii.

At the time, my father was a US Navy ensign in the South Pacific. He had graduated with a bachelor's degree in English Literature from Notre Dame University, and earned a master's degree in philosophy from American University. Whatever his career ambitions were, they died with his brother's disappearance, which thrust the family's aspiration for a priest onto the next son.

My father was sent to Sacred Heart Seminary in Detroit. He was ordained in June of 1951 at St. Mary's Cathedral in Saginaw. He served as a Navy Chaplain on ships around the world, then led Mass in English and in Latin at several parishes, finally arriving at Sacred Heart, whose parishioners were a mix of Mexican and black people.

During that time, his yearning for a wife and children intensified. He was also becoming increasingly disillusioned by the scurrilous and sometimes criminal activity occurring behind church doors: alcoholism, pedophilia, and secretive tactics of hiding priests' crimes. He was deeply disturbed that priests who confessed crimes were relocated to other parishes, rather than prosecuted. And he was not allowed, by church law, to report the crimes to authorities.

In 1965, he became one of 100,000 priests who have since left the Catholic Church. At the same time, he was falling in love with church organist Marylin Elnora Bowman, whom he described as "The Queen" in his journal entries.

He was 44 and white. She was 19 and "Negro." On December 19, 1966, they demonstrated radical courage by defying the bishop's damnation. All the while, my father's mother agreed with the Bishop that my father was being disobedient. At the same time, my mother's mother accused my father of unscrupulous intentions.

Despite this opposition, my father wanted to make peace with his mother. Little did they know, that his baptismal prayer over me would manifest in a magic moment that shocked them both, as my mother describes in her book, *The Triumph of Rosemary: A Memoir* by Judge Marylin E. Atkins. She granted permission to share the following excerpt, in which she refers to my father by his middle name, "Lee."

Meeting Alphonsine

Sometime during my eighth month of pregnancy, my dear husband decided that it was time for his family to meet us, so we planned to make a trip on the upcoming Sunday. Not a shred of communication had come from his mother, Alphonsine Marie Atkins, since his October 6, 1966, note to her telling her that he had found peace within himself. He had not heard from his sister, Mary, either. Lee always believed that his sister should not have raised her eight children in the same house under the ever-watchful eye of their grandmother.

Lee hoped Mary did not allow the sexually and psychologically repressive atmosphere that permeated his house while growing up to engulf his nieces and nephews. His brother-in-law, Sterling, had always been friendly toward him. He brought balance to the house in Lee's eye. He loved his nieces and nephews, and wondered what his mother and sister were telling them about their Uncle Tom.

West Branch, Michigan, with a population of about 2,200, was situated 88 miles north of Saginaw. Before the drive, I dressed Elizabeth in a pretty pink dress. Her big blonde curls bounced all around her head. Once again, I was as big as a house, and I dressed in my nicest maternity suit.

When I told my parents about our trip, my mother assured me that after all this time, it would be fine. They would be accepting and loving.

Lee responded, "Billie does not know my family like I do."

We started out at noon, arriving in West Branch in the early afternoon. Lee pulled up in front of his childhood home. By this time, we both got cold feet.

"Do you want to go in?" he asked.

"No," I responded.

We pulled away, drove to Bay City which was on the way, picked up some fresh peanuts at the peanut store, ate lunch at a nice restaurant, and drove back to Saginaw. When we arrived home, I called my mother and told her that we chickened out.

"Next Sunday," she directed, "you drive to that woman's house. Put her granddaughter in her lap! If she drops her, call me, and I'll come and take care of her! This is ridiculous!"

Wow! I was not expecting that response.

I told Lee what she said, and he responded, "For once, I agree with your mother. We will go back next Sunday."

The following Sunday, we arrived at Mary's house. This time, we parked the car out front and walked up to the door. We were both very nervous. Lee held Elizabeth. He knocked on the door.

A woman a little older than Lee opened the door, and I immediately saw the family resemblance. This was Mary. For what felt like an eternity, but was probably just a few agonizing seconds, she just stood there staring at us with no smile or other emotion on her face.

"Hello, Mary," Lee said.

"*Well,*" Mary said in a flat tone, "*since you drove all this way, you may as well come in.*"

This is going to be a cold afternoon on a sunshiny day, I thought. I was doing this for my husband. For me personally, I never had to meet his sister, or his mother, even though this 86-year-old woman was our daughter's grandmother.

We stepped inside. The living room was neat and tidy with furniture that had obviously been in the family a long time. Mary directed us to sit on a couch directly across from the chair where their mother was sitting.

You mean this tiny, frail-looking lady was the boss of everybody? Alphonsine could not have weighed more than 90 pounds, and though she was sitting, I doubted she stood more than five-foot-two. The resemblance between Lee and his mother was striking. (But later when I saw a photo of his father, Samuel Merritt Atkins, who died in 1945, I was awed that Lee so strongly resembled his dad).

Once on the couch, Elizabeth became fidgety on Lee's lap, looking around at these strange surroundings. Two children, a boy and a girl, appeared in the door to the kitchen.

"*Hi, Uncle Tom,*" they said in unison, then disappeared.

No one introduced them to me. Was I the first black person they had ever seen? I was sure I was the first ever in this house. Okay, Marylin, you can get through this, I thought.

Lee's mother just stared, her eyes moving from Lee to Elizabeth and then to me, again and again without saying a word. She was sitting about six feet away from us.

Finally, a friendly voice said, "Hi, Tom!" as a man I guessed was Sterling, Mary's husband, came into the living room. His tone cut through the tension with its joyful, glad-to-see-you sincerity. Sterling bent down and gave Lee a hug, and introduced himself to me.

He touched Elizabeth on the chin, and asked affectionately, "And who is this little one?"

"This is our daughter, Elizabeth Ann," Lee said proudly, "and we have another on the way."

"I see!" Sterling replied as he glanced at me, careful not to look directly at my protruding stomach.

This man is a saint! I thought.

He sat down and asked, "Tom, how are you getting along, workwise?"

He and Lee talked for a bit. Although Sterling had broken the ice, the tension in the room was still very thick and icy stares continued in my direction from his mother and sister.

They must be thinking, "So, this is the girl who corrupted our priest!" I thought. I wonder if Mary is afraid to talk to her brother in front of her mother?

About 20 minutes had passed. We were not offered a glass of water, or asked if we needed to use the bathroom. Sterling was great. I always loved him for making us feel at home. (He died in April of 1986 after a recurrence of leukemia. A good man).

Just as I was about to say, "Lee, let's leave," Elizabeth began to squirm on her father's lap. Lee put her down on the floor. To my utter amazement, she crawled straight toward Alphonsine. When she reached her grandmother, Elizabeth pulled herself up to her feet by using Alphonsine's long dress for assistance.

Lee and I looked at each other. Was he thinking what I was thinking? My mother had said to put Elizabeth on her grandmother's lap…

Alphonsine reached down and put her hands under Elizabeth's armpits to steady her. Elizabeth, whose back was to us, must have grinned at her grandmother. To my surprise, a smile came over Alphonsine's face as she looked at her granddaughter.

We could tell that Elizabeth wanted to sit on her lap, but the old lady could not lift her. Lee stood, crossed the room, and lifted our daughter onto his mother's lap. Alphonsine's smile grew bigger, and she even kissed Elizabeth on the cheek.

Is this really happening?

Elizabeth touched her grandmother's long, pointed nose as she reached for her silver glasses.

Mary, my dear sister-in-law, whether she liked it or not in that moment, spoke for the first time since letting us in the house. "She has such beautiful blonde curls! And look at those big green eyes!"

Elizabeth now wanted to get down, so Lee stood, took her in his arms, and returned to his chair.

"We need to get back to Saginaw," he said.

On the drive home, we talked about what transpired. Lee was happy with his mother's interaction with Elizabeth. If either of us thought that the visit would open the lines of communication between Lee and his mother and sister, however, we were wrong.

Lee wrote a nice note to his mother and sister thanking them for the visit. He received no response, nor did we receive an invitation to return. I had expected as much, and understood. They were both still angry over his departure from the priesthood, and that was not about to change. I was not mad...

I consider this my first act as a Princess of Peace. That afternoon set the stage for slow but dramatic change toward love and harmony in our family.

Our Haunted House, An Exorcism, And Proof Of Supernatural Power

The sound of footsteps ascending a wooden staircase that no longer existed in our house sent a shiver of fear through my mother. She held my tiny body—swaddled in a blanket—closer in her arms, as heels on hardwood creaked the floor above us. This invisible entity was upstairs, traversing the empty second floor, which was impossible to access without a staircase or ladder.

It's the ghost, my mother thought.

Despite her previous disbelief in the supernatural, she knew the footsteps were the spirit of the former lady of the house. Daddy saw this lady in the morning, sitting at our kitchen table. Turns out, she had conducted séances—ceremonies involving communication with the dead—in the large, wood-frame house that had stood vacant for decades.

The run-down house was all my parents could afford as newlyweds. They were so poor when they moved in, that a neighbor strung extension cords across the lawn to reach a plug in his house, so a light could be turned on in the otherwise dark house.

Our home had one bathroom next to the kitchen, which led to a living room whose walls had no drywall; the two-by-fours and the wooden slats held together by cement were exposed. The "shotgun" floor plan led to another room that led into our parents' bedroom. Beside that was a small room that, after Catherine and I outgrew the bassinet and crib, became our bedroom with bunk beds.

At the center of the house was the unfinished "No-No" room where a stairwell no longer existed to reach the doorway to the unfinished second floor. We were not allowed in this space where Christmas presents were hidden, along with terrible opportunities for splinters on the old wooden walls. My parents spruced up the home's exterior with white paint and black trim.

After they purchased the house in a low-income neighborhood of Saginaw, lights with no apparent source would flash on the kitchen walls. The strong smell of garlic would suddenly fill a room. The temperature would become very cold, even during the summer.

One hot summer night, after my parents had left the windows open, some entity closed and locked them, and yanked the fume-carrying furnace pipe from the living room wall. Another time, while they were sleeping, the headboard on their bed—a gift from a woman whose spirit apparently clashed with the one in the house—disintegrated into sawdust in the middle of the night. The particles were so small, my parents swept them up with a broom!

While most of the haunting seemed innocuous, these last two incidents scared my parents into thinking the entity had malice toward our family, which now included Catherine—born on July 17, 1968.

Finally, Daddy summoned his priestly powers and exorcised the house with Biblical incantations and holy water. I later learned that the prayer that priests use to exorcise evil spirits calls in the power of Archangel Michael, Jesus, Mother Mary, and saints. It worked; the ghost, the garlic, the footsteps, the cold spells, and the other incidents immediately stopped.

But, as I grew up and heard my parents' hair-raising accounts of ghostly activity—and Daddy's ability to exorcise it from our home— convinced me that the supernatural was real. It could be evil. And it could be defeated through a human invoking the power of God.

Cash Poor, But Rich With Love

Daddy drove a delivery truck for a flower shop; our mother worked nights at "Big Bank" downtown Saginaw. When her six-week maternity leaves ended for both me and Catherine, Daddy drove us as infants to the front of her building so she could breastfeed us. This schedule enabled them to avoid hiring a babysitter.

Later, Daddy worked as a job counselor with the Michigan Employment Security Commission (MESC). He left for work in the morning, wearing a jacket, tie, and cufflinks that we selected. He carried a briefcase. Our mother, just arriving home from the bank, was asleep. She locked us in the bedroom with her so we wouldn't get into anything.

When we were old enough, we watched TV in the living room. I vividly remember running to wake our sleeping mother, shaking her and exclaiming, "Mommy, you have to come and see what's on *Sesame Street!*" She just wanted to sleep!

Our parents lavished us with affection, encouragement, and intelligent conversation. They had little money, but we were rich with happiness. And they loved cultivating a peaceful home that neither of them had enjoyed as kids.

Catherine and I loved when Daddy gave us rides in his wheelbarrow in the front yard, or let us stand on his slightly bent knees, holding our hands, as he twirled us around. He also built us a sandbox and taught us to swim before we could walk at "Big Beach" on Saginaw Bay.

Our mother was really fun, always making us laugh. In the car, we sang along with songs on the radio. And we loved playing dress-up in her clothes and going shopping with her at Federal's department store, where she treated us to big bags of aromatic popcorn.

"Whose kids are you babysitting?" strangers asked. These people—black and white—at the grocery store, the laundromat and other places, thought our mother was our nanny.

Because we looked like two little white girls and our mother looks like a blend of her Italian birth mother and her biological father, who was black. Our mother was beautiful, with caramel-hued skin, big brown eyes, and a soft, wavy aura of black hair. Daddy had silver-streaked, dark hair, white skin, and hazel eyes that radiated gentleness and love.

Likewise, our beloved Uncle Percy, who was dark-skinned, said he would never take me and Catherine—who had big, blue eyes and wavy, brown hair—anywhere until we were old enough to tell a police officer that, "Yes, this is our Uncle Percy, and we adore him." He called me "the Big Swede."

Later, Catherine and I had so much fun at daycare, playing in the table-level sandbox, eating celery sticks filled with peanut butter, and napping as the teachers rubbed our backs until we fell asleep under the soft, pink quilts that our father's mother, whom we called "Grandma UpNorth," made for us. By this time, his family had reconciled and accepted his new family. For Easter, Catherine and I were photographed in *The Saginaw News* playing with bunny rabbits at daycare.

When I started kindergarten at Trinity Lutheran School, our

mother drove us up Cherry Street in her dark purple Buick Skylark with white vinyl interior; we sang along with the radio and loved it.

Teasing Inspires Empathy

The lights were dim in our first grade classroom. Mrs. Mosley let us watch *Sesame Street* on television. I joined my dozen classmates—who were all brown-skinned—in a circle, wearing a jumper-style dress with a ruffle-collared blouse, and tights. I was extremely pigeon-toed, and my medically-prescribed shoes were supposed to correct how I walked with my feet turned inward.

I loved watching my favorite program. Most of the time, the show's star characters, Bert and Ernie, bantered as puppets, with their bodies visible only from the waist up. But on this day, the segment showed them from head to toe. They were suspended and controlled by strings, marionette style. And Bert was very pigeon-toed.

"Look!" exclaimed a boy who mispronounced my name. "He walk just like Lizzabit."

The whole class turned to me—and exploded with laughter. I hated being ridiculed for a physical abnormality—something I couldn't control. Though I didn't know the word "empathy," I was overwhelmed with a strong desire to never hurt another person's feelings the way mine were making me cry.

I was not teased amongst the neighborhood children. Catherine and I were the only white-looking kids in our mostly African American and Mexican American neighborhood, and we all played together in our sandbox, on bikes, and in each other's yards. One day, an elderly black family friend drove past and saw me and Catherine playing with our friends. The woman called and asked:

"Marylin, why do you let your girls play with those pickaninnies?"

Speaking of mean, I didn't like my mother's mother, Billie Alice Bowman. We called her Grammum, and she was always making our mother cry. You can read about the physical and emotional abuse she inflicted in *The Triumph of Rosemary*.

In contrast, our grandfather, Clyde James Bowman, was kind and gentle. He had served in the segregated troops in the US Army in Italy during World War II. We loved when Grandpop read Uncle Remus stories to us. It was really sad when Grandpop died when I was five years old.

Flash To The Future

One day, our mother was watching me and Catherine play on the floor in our living room. She glanced at Daddy, who was reading the newspaper on the sofa. Suddenly, she calculated that when we reached college age—Daddy would be retiring.

"I realized that if we were going to send our daughters to college," she has said many times since then, "it was on me, because Tom was not making much money at the time."

So our mother—who had attended Aquinas College in Grand Rapids for one semester until her father had a heart attack and she came home to take care of him—returned to school to earn her bachelor's degree in psychology from Saginaw Valley State University.

With her degree, she was hired at MESC as a claims examiner, helping people file for unemployment. Meanwhile, Daddy also worked at MESC, leading job trainings and counseling Vietnam veterans.

Our Second Home: Aunt Ann & Percy's House

When our mother returned to college, Aunt Ann took care of us. She was Grandpop's sister, and having no children of her own, was like our second mother. She and Uncle Percy were some of the most fun, loving people we've ever known.

They had come from Keokuk, Iowa so Uncle Percy could get a good auto industry job at the GM plant called Saginaw Malleable and Iron. Uncle Percy's salary enabled them to live in a nice, yellow aluminum siding ranch home with three bedrooms. Their all-black neighborhood epitomized the comfortable middle class lifestyle afforded by blue-collar jobs in the auto industry.

While Uncle Percy drove a forklift, Aunt Ann picked up me and Catherine after kindergarten and first grade. She took care of us until our father left work or our mother finished classes or work. We also spent weekdays with her during the summer.

Every afternoon as Catherine and I watched cartoons on the giant Curtis Mathis TV console in the front room, Aunt Ann cooked dinner. It would be ready for Uncle Percy when he arrived home from the plant. One of her specialties was fried pork chops, which she served with peeled, boiled potatoes, and sauerkraut. I used to mush the sauerkraut into the potatoes, then spear a piece of the golden-brown meat, to create one bite of perfect taste and texture. It was mush, meat, salt, and grease. Oh my goodness, it was so good!

Mealtime was fun at their round, faux-blue marble table, with turquoise pleather chairs that had mod 1960s-style, cone-shaped backs, and they rotated from side to side.

When Aunt Ann served French fries, Uncle Percy pointed across the room and said, "What's that?" If Catherine and I turned to look, he'd grab a few of our fries, and we'd crack up. He made us laugh all the time. He had an "outie" belly button that was like a quarter-sized dome. We used to push it like it was an elevator button, and say, "Third floor, please." Other times he'd extend a finger for us to pull, and he'd fart. We roared with laughter, over and over.

Time with Aunt Ann was an adventure; she took us to such diverse places as "the egg lady" who lived on a farm on the outskirts of town and sold fresh eggs. Every year for our birthdays, Aunt Ann went to "the cake lady" and brought us beautiful cakes. Once mine was shaped like a pink house with a peaked roof, a door, and windows.

My sister had a cake shaped like a dress with a big blue and white skirt around a real Barbie sticking up from it.

Aunt Ann also took us to the butcher for meats that were stored in their huge freezer in the basement. It wasn't far from the tall bar and stools, behind which stood a refrigerator. Inside—a box of live worms for fishing! They showed us how to hook the worms when we went fishing along the Saginaw River. Uncle Percy's 20-foot Chris Craft, parked on a trailer beside the one-car garage, became our fortress for playtime with the neighborhood kids.

Aunt Ann, who once drove a taxicab, kept a police scanner on the stand next to their bed. Throughout the day, we constantly heard electronic crackle punctuated by the dispatcher's updates. Things really got exciting when a man robbed a bank and hid in a house down the street.

The police scanner was an example of how they always had the latest gadgets and technological advancements. Their living room television was always getting bigger and better. They had the first video games for us, which involved hooking up a box to the TV so we could play black and white "tennis" with cursor-like rackets controlled by knobs that lobbed a circle "ball" back and forth.

They were the first to subscribe to HBO, get a microwave oven, and buy gadgets like a "hot dog cooker." Its two rows of metal spokes speared each end of a hot dog. When we closed the clear plastic dome, the hot dogs cooked fast.

The cookie jar stayed stocked and the freezer had a good array of popsicles. Christmas at their house was awesome. One year they gave us a play organ (we still have it). They also gave us dolls, games, and walkie-talkies. As we got older, they took us to county fairs, movies, and restaurants, and on trips. All the while, they reinforced the good values that our parents were teaching us.

Once I said, "I hate such and such."

"Don't say hate," Uncle Percy said immediately.

The Numbers Man

Every afternoon, while Catherine and I were watching TV, and Aunt Ann was cooking dinner, a man opened the front screen door and stepped inside.

"Hey, how you doin'?" Donald said with a friendly nod. He was dark-skinned, wore casual clothes, and walked with a limp.

"Hi," we answered as Donald stood at a little table by the door, gathering the dollar bills, coins, and slips of white paper on which Aunt Ann had written her "numbers" for the day.

If her sister Ada Mae were in the hospital for "sugar" or Grandpop were hospitalized for heart problems, Aunt Ann played their room numbers. Or if she dreamed about a dog or a boat, she'd sit at the kitchen table in the morning—smoking cigarettes and drinking coffee—consulting tattered paperback books that told her to play a certain number based on her dream. Sometimes she "hit the numbers" and won money, which Donald delivered the next day when he picked up her new numbers. Meanwhile, Catherine and I thought the Numbers Man came to everybody's house.

An Inexplicably Insatiable Appetite

I felt so happy as my father opened the big peanut butter jar adorned with three munchkins. Then he dipped a spoon in, scooped out a salty-sweet swirl, and handed it to me as a treat.

"Thank you, Daddy," I said, savoring the sweet, creamy taste. When I finished, I said, "Can I please have some more?" Apparently I loved peanut butter and everything else too much. I always wanted more!

"Eli, if you keep eating everything in sight," Daddy said, "I'll have to put locks on the cabinets."

He said he knew a man who had installed locks on the kitchen cabinets to stop his son from devouring everything in sight. My parents never did that, but my appetite never diminished either. This threat, however, only made me want to eat more. As a result, I was slightly plump.

"Fatso!" my grown cousin taunted in my grandmother's kitchen during a holiday dinner. I was five years old, and she continued to call me that on the handful of occasions each year when I saw her throughout my childhood. "Fatso! You're fat!"

Food Is A Happy Focal Point

I loved our family trips to Mooney's Ice Cream, where I enjoyed a giant scoop of Blue Moon ice cream. Family outings took us to Sullivan's for fried shrimp and fries, and to the Bavarian village of Frankenmuth, which specialized in fried chicken. Other times, I loved eating King Vitamin cereal, cake, cookies, hamburgers, Aunt Ann's deep-fried tacos, and my mother's egg noodles with chicken, peas, and gravy.

"My butt's too big," my mother declared one day while Daddy was taking pictures of her in the backyard. Wearing a long, blue halter dress, she was going to a wedding, and she looked beautiful. But if her butt was too big, and my five-year-old body had the same shape and proportions, then surely my butt was also too big.

"I'm going on a diet," she declared.

Did that mean I needed to go on a diet, too? I wasn't sure what that meant, but it sounded like something bad in response to being too fat. As a result, I began to believe that I was fat, that I needed to lose weight, and that I never would, because I loved to eat.

Fear Of Fire

"Wake up," my parents said, scooping me out of the top bunk as they took Catherine from the lower bunk. "We have to go over to the neighbors' house for awhile."

It was the middle of the night. I was four years old; Catherine was three.

I smelled smoke. Sirens screamed outside the window. Red and blue lights flashed into our pink bedroom.

"The house next door is on fire," our father said. The wall beside our bunk beds was just 10 feet from the burning house. Our parents carried us across the street and tucked us into our neighbors' beds. We were safe.

Physically. Emotionally, however, the fire terrified me. A short time later, when the fire alarm went off at school, my whole body shook as I joined a dozen classmates outside the white wooden church and attached, two-story brick school. Waiting outside on the sidewalk with our teacher, Mrs. Schultz, during this fire drill made my stomach hurt. When we were told it was "safe" to go back inside, I was so scared that Aunt Ann picked me up early.

"Please God, Don't Let Him Kill Me!"

I was five years old, and all I wanted to do was play outside until my family was ready to leave for the funeral. On this warm summer evening, I walked around our front yard, past the sandbox and blue plastic swimming pool. I didn't dare get wet or dirty—not in my new dress, black patent leather shoes, and white lace anklet socks. And I didn't want to mess up my hair; Mommy had just styled my golden ringlets into two ponytails. Now she was doing Catherine's hair while Daddy got dressed.

As I stood on our corner lot, the teenaged brother of one of our playmates showed up, and lured me into their run-down house nearby. Suddenly I found myself in their bathroom, where he laid me on my back on the wet, dirty floor.

My heart hammered with terror.

I have to get out of here!

I looked around. There was a bathtub, and—

A giant knife glimmering on the sink! Panic shot through me.

"My mommy's calling me!" I cried. She was not calling me; she didn't even know I was there.

He is gonna chop me up and kill me!

"My mommy's calling me!" I cried.

He lifted my legs up in the air.

God please don't let him kill me!

My dress fell, exposing my panties and thighs. With eyes wide with fear, I looked up at my black patent leather shoes and white lace anklet socks. How could I escape?

"My mommy's calling me!"

I don't know if I knew about rape, but I knew about intercourse. It was for grown-ups who were in love. This was not how it was supposed to happen. Nor was it something for kids. So whatever this guy was thinking was really bad.

"My mommy's calling me! Please let me go home! My mommy's calling me!"

I imagined my parents coming outside to get me, so we could go to the funeral. But they would not find me. And they might never know where I was. I had seen news reports about people killing kids and throwing the bodies in the river or in the woods. No! I had to escape!

Time seemed to drag on forever.

"Please let me go! My mommy's calling me!"

What was he going to do? He did not remove his clothes, nor did he touch me.

Finally, he let me leave.

I ran home. Terrified, horrified, relieved.

But silent. I didn't tell anyone what happened. I was sure that Daddy would storm over there and kill that guy. Then Daddy would go to prison, and I wouldn't have a father.

So I said nothing. I just went home, thanking God for saving my life, while simultaneously replaying those terrifying moments when that guy could've done terrible things to me, snuffed out my young life, hidden my body, and left my parents with an unsolved mystery for life.

After the funeral, we visited Aunt Ann and Uncle Percy. I went in the bathroom. From my vagina I pulled something with a sort of peanut skin consistency, only crispier; it was clear and amber brown. Maybe it was cockroach wings. Maybe on that nasty floor, a roach crawled into my panties, and its wings were my disgusting souvenir.

Still at Aunt Ann and Percy's house, I left the bathroom and joined my family in the living room. And I said nothing about what the neighbor had done.

But the heart-pounding terror replayed in my mind over and over and over that night when I went to bed—and *every* night for the rest of my childhood.

Moving Doesn't Calm The Fear

I was so excited to have my very own my pink bedroom, decorated with a ruffled bedspread and curtains that matched my white headboard, nightstand, dresser, and desk. Adjacent to my room was Catherine's, which our mother painted yellow, and decorated with a yellow- and red-patterned bedspread and curtains and white furniture.

"We love our new house!" Catherine and I exclaimed in November of 1974, when we moved from Saginaw to the Detroit suburb of Oak Park.

Daddy had applied for a transfer to MESC's main office on Woodward Avenue and West Grand Boulevard in Detroit's New Center Area. Our mother transferred to a nearby MESC branch.

"Momma, you ain't listenin'!" I exclaimed one day in Saginaw. Using correct English was imperative in our home, but I was echoing my playmates' diction. Sadly, teen pregnancy, crime, school drop-outs, and drug use were major traps for kids in our neighborhood.

"It's time to move," Daddy said.

Our parents wanted good public schools for us, along with a safe neighborhood in a racially integrated community where kids focused on academics and achievement. They found that in Oak Park, which had one of Michigan's best public school systems.

They rented a three-bedroom duplex near Oak Park High School, one block from the city's huge recreation area where Catherine and I took tennis lessons, ice skated with our friends, and spent every summer afternoon swimming and socializing in the sunshine at the Oak Park Pool. We also enjoyed the public library and classes offered by the Community Center, including bus trips to a local ski hill where Catherine and I took lessons.

Our home was cozy. Our mother hung jazzy black and red wallpaper in the gray-tiled bathroom. They put a mural of a pretty stream in nature on the living room wall, which complimented the green shag carpeting and velvet brocade sofas, a brown velvet armchair, and an upright piano. Under a small chandelier in the dining room, we enjoyed meals together, and loved when our mother made cinnamon rolls covered in frosting. She also made us an awesome, carpeted play area in the basement.

Oak Park was mostly Jewish at the time. Many of our neighbors were Orthodox. One nearby family built a sukkah hut outside their home for an annual celebration of God giving shelter to Israelites after the Egyptians freed them from slavery.

Across the street from our home lived Norman Blitzer, whose accent grew heavier with sadness as he showed us the numbers that Nazis had tattooed on his arm. Catherine and I had never heard of the Holocaust, but received a real-life lesson during the many occasions when we sat on his sofa with our parents and he talked about surviving a death camp, but losing his beloved wife. After World War II, he reunited with their two daughters who survived thanks to hiding with a Catholic family in France.

After Mr. Blitzer died, we "sat shiva" with his family, who invited us to join their traditional mourning ceremony. We also attended his funeral a few days later, learning that Jewish people do not embalm; they bury the dead in pine boxes.

We also learned about Middle Eastern culture from our Chaldean neighbors who were Christian and had fled persecution by Muslims in their home country of Iraq. The women often picked wild grape leaves from vines covering the fence between our complex and the high school.

Our neighborhood also included people who escaped oppression in Cold War Russia. Many of the women were plump, pale-skinned, and wrapped in layers of fabric of mixed patterns. Caucasians and African Americans also lived in Oak Park.

And together we attended Albert Einstein Elementary School. Catherine was in first grade; I was in Mrs. Becker's second grade class, where I met Louise, who would become a cherished, lifetime friend.

Playing Apartment With Barbie & Ken

Catherine and I—along with our friends when they came over—loved dressing our many Barbie dolls in stylish clothes and high-heeled shoes, then taking them for a spin in the pink convertible chauffeured by Ken. They'd pull up to our three-foot-tall, furnished Barbie townhouse, which set the scene for creative vignettes with Barbie, Ken, and Growing Up Skipper, who went from a flat-chested pre-teen to a full-blown, large-busted teenager with a twist of her plastic arm.

Louise also had a large Barbie collection. We often used her smooth-tiled fireplace to create all kinds of cosmopolitan scenarios amidst furniture we made from little boxes and pretty fabric set into the cubby holes in the hearth.

"Tornado!" I exclaimed. Exploding with laughter, Louise and I swept our hands through the fireplace condo, making furniture, dolls, and Barbie accessories fly everywhere.

"Now let's play Apartment," Louise said, which meant pretending we were grown, throwing a party with sophisticated friends in her living room. We made mock cocktails by pouring 7UP into her parents' wine glasses, and dropping in a maraschino cherry. Then we'd make up conversations as if we were hosting handsome, fun guys in our downtown apartment.

Louise and I were certain that someday, we'd be living the real Apartment life, and chillin' like Barbie in cool high rise condos—minus the tornadoes. Another favorite activity was raiding the remains of bagels, cheese, and fruit after her parents' book club guests departed on Friday nights. We also played a "Hang Ten" surfing game in her backyard swimming pool.

Joining her family to light Hanukkah candles and celebrate Passover, while Catherine did the same with her friends, was a joyous blessing that taught us about Jewish culture.

Meanwhile, our parents did not force us to attend catechism or confession or Sunday School. We did attend church on some Sundays with Daddy, either Shrine of the Little Flower in Royal Oak, which had a unique round sanctuary, or Our Lady of Fatima in Oak Park.

"I'm Going To Law School"

When I was in third grade and Catherine was in second, our mother told us that she was going to begin University of Detroit School of Law in the evenings, while still working full-time at MESC.

"Your father will be with you in the evening while I'm at school," she said as our family sat in the living room.

"I'll make dinner," Daddy said, "and take you to piano lessons, ice skating night with your friends, and swim lessons. I'll also make sure you get your homework done."

Catherine and I knew this was unusual, as most of our friends had stay-at-home moms; adding law school to our mother's full time work status only made her more unique back in 1976. But we didn't like the idea of her driving home alone up the Lodge Freeway through Detroit at 10 or 11 o'clock at night.

However, we revered our mother for her ambition, and her really fun personality that often found us dancing in the living room to the latest 12" disco singles, sharing robust laughter while "window shopping" at Northland Mall, and simply snuggling together to watch TV.

"My time will be limited," she said, "but the time we do spend together will be good." She also remained committed to attending our piano recitals, parent-teacher conferences, and even my field trip to Greenfield Village, where my class spent the day in a one-room schoolhouse. She even sewed a long, plaid dress and matching bonnet so I could look like an 1800s-era schoolgirl. I was so grateful that she took the day off work to create one of my fondest childhood memories with her.

Catherine and I appreciated every moment with our mother. We understood—without it being said—that our responsibility in our family's new plan was to continue good behavior, academic excellence, and cooperation. We knew that the short-term struggle and sacrifice during our mother's ambitious quest was for the long-term betterment of our family. Money was sufficient but not abundant; we grasped that she wanted to become an attorney to finance two daughters in college at the same time.

"I didn't become a lawyer to save the world," she said many years later. "I became a lawyer to save my family."

"Is Your Mom Black?"

My hair, when released from braids or a bun, exploded into a giant yellow bush of frizz.

"You look like you stuck your finger in a light socket!" a boy teased. Kids said similarly mean things to Catherine, whose hair was dark, longer, and even frizzier.

Though our school was diverse, Catherine and I knew no other white-looking, half-black kids or adults. The only biracial people we knew were our cousins in Ohio. We saw them in the summertime at our cottage in the northern Michigan resort town of Idlewild and at Thanksgiving at Aunt Reoma and Uncle Joe's in Flint; we would hold up our forearms side-by-side to compare our complexions that ranged from milky white to butterscotch.

Back then, there was no President Barack Obama, Halle Berry, Tiger Woods, Mariah Carey, or Derek Jeter. Catherine and I had no such role models, nor did our peers. As a result, we were sometimes singled out.

"Is your mom black?" a kid asked as a half dozen others clustered around me while we were supposed to be working on a project in Mrs. Sugarman's fifth grade class. My cheeks burned, my heart pounded, my hands got clammy. I dreaded being singled out and being questioned about race.

"Yes," I answered, terrified that they would stop being my friends.

One friend invited me to attend her Lutheran summer camp for a week. We had a great time. But a black girl threatened to come into our unlocked cabin at night and cut off my ponytail.

At school, my fears of being rejected were unfounded. I had many friends who came to play at our house, joined us for birthday parties, and invited me to theirs. This included my major crush; he and I were on the safety squad, wearing orange cross-body belts while helping kids walk safely through the hallways.

Lunchtime in the cafeteria was very social with my six girlfriends. I ate from my metal lunchbox containing the ham and cheese sandwich, fruit cup, and Hostess cupcake or Twinkie that our mother prepared every morning. Chocolate milk from the vending machine washed it down.

Catherine and I excelled at Einstein. I always aced the spelling bees, and loved reading and writing. Sometimes at lunchtime, I filled in for the office receptionist, Mrs. Waterstone, by answering phones for the principal, Mr. Dietert. My teachers were great, and I loved Mrs. Barbara Gross, my third grade teacher who lavished me with love and encouragement.

At recess, we played Wonder Woman, spinning like Linda Carter on the popular TV show. We always dominated the boys in play battles. Playing Wonder Woman made me feel strong and powerful against the dangers of being a little girl in a scary world.

David John, Holy Angel, David John, Pray For Me…

On school nights, Daddy led me and Catherine in saying *The Lord's Prayer* before turning off the lights in our bedrooms and playing soft classical music on the living room stereo to help us fall asleep.

Then he headed to the dining room table; behind him hung two large, wood-framed paintings of St. Peter and St. Paul. There he journaled about his day by hand-writing in spiral-bound notebooks.

Meanwhile, he had no idea that I was lying awake in terror, staring wide-eyed into the shadows created by the nightlight and the ruffled curtains in my pretty pink bedroom. All the while, my mind's eye replayed a filmstrip of that frightening time in the neighbor's nasty bathroom when I could have easily been raped and killed.

Now I had something extra to worry about: our mother driving home alone on the freeway between downtown Detroit and home at night. I didn't want to go to sleep until I heard her key in the back door, and felt her coming into my room to kiss me good night.

Overwhelmed with fear, I got up and tiptoed to the dining room, never wanting to leave my father's gentle, protective gaze.

"What's wrong, Eli?"

"I can't sleep."

He took my hand, walked me to my room, where I got back under the covers. He stroked my forehead with his palm and sang at my bedside: "David John, Holy Angel, David John, pray for me. David John, Holy Angel, protect my fam-i-ly."

Only then would I feel safe enough to fall asleep. But the ordeal would repeat the next night, and the next, and the next. I never told Daddy that I was terrified, or why, even though we had moved far away from the scene of that crime. Soon, that would not be the only terror tormenting my young mind.

Native American Heritage and Northern Michigan
Family & Fun

On the weekends, Daddy took us on adventures while our mother studied at home. Before we left, we gave her lots of hugs and kisses and wished her luck with the giant law books and yellow legal pads that surrounded her while studying.

Then we went to Saginaw to visit relatives or to Bay City, where our father served as President of the Saginaw Valley Indian Association. We attended "Indian Meetings" with men, women, and children who had long black hair, turquoise jewelry, and beaded barrettes and belts.

I loved being amidst their super gentle, kind spirits, and witnessing the loving rapport between them and my father. But I was saddened by the poverty and alcoholism that people discussed about loved ones who were in distress.

Everyone loved Daddy, who wore a big silver belt buckle adorned with a turquoise thunderbird. He also wore a necklace whose pendant was a jade Star of David, a symbol of Jewish faith.

We loved attending Pow Wows that featured Native dancing by men, women, and children wearing feathered headdresses, fringed moccasin boots, and beaded jewelry. The drumming, singing, and dancing made my spirit soar.

While in Saginaw, we visited St. Francis Home, where our father's mother lived until she died at age 100. Grandma UpNorth wore a rosary and spent a lot of time praying in the chapel.

Other times, Daddy took us to his hometown, where he owned a square mile of raw woodland that we called "Big Woods." En route up I-75, we always stopped at McDonald's at the Birch Run exit, where I got my favorite fish sandwich, French fries, orange pop, and apple pie.

When we finally reached Exit 212 for West Branch, we visited Aunt Mary and Uncle Sterling, in their cape cod style house. Most of the kids were grown and gone, but we saw cousins—who had a race car track in the TV room—and we talked about *Donny and Marie* on Sunday nights and my crush on Donny Osmond.

Aunt Mary resembled Queen Elizabeth, attended Mass every day, and gave us a subscription to *Ranger Rick* magazine. She was super sweet, often asking: "Girls, how are you doing in school? Would you like some milk and ginger snaps?"

Weekend Adventures In Big Woods

As soon as Daddy pulled his beige, Ford 100 truck into the gas station and general store across from Clear Lake, we dashed to the pay phone to call our mother.

"Hi, Mommy," Catherine and I said excitedly. "We're here! We're buying stuff for the woods."

"I love you girls," she said. "Be careful."

Inside the little store, Catherine and I helped our father gather essentials for our weekend stay in the woods: hamburger, hot dogs, buns, baked beans, big bags of cheese popcorn, a brick of cheese, and giant chocolate bars.

Then while Daddy and the store owner, Mr. Archer, caught up on news about forest fires and local news while filling the truck with gas, Catherine and I glanced longingly across the road at the beach, and the lake where our cousins lived on an island accessible only by boat or a private bridge. Sometimes we boated or water skied with them.

"Daddy, when can we go swimming?" we asked during a pause in his conversation.

"Tomorrow," he said.

After that, we accessed our property via a dirt road that cut for miles through state-owned forestland. When we arrived at the wood-and-wire gate that Daddy had built, and he unlocked it, our truck rumbled further into the woods, until we saw the camper and campfire pit surrounded by benches hewn from logs.

Catherine and I couldn't wait to leap out of the truck and play in the dirt, run around, and go exploring with Daddy. First, we had to unload the truck and settle into the six-person-sleeper camper, which had no running water or power. Daddy's friends owned it, and we used it in exchange for allowing them to hunt deer.

Daddy cooked hot dogs on the campfire grill and heated up baked beans from a can. At night, the three of us played gin rummy by a kerosene lamp in the camper while enjoying our chocolate, cheese, and popcorn snacks.

Then laughing fits that Daddy called "the giddies" made me and Catherine laugh so hard our stomachs ached! Sometimes, after the lights were out and all we could hear were crickets, Daddy's snoring at the other end of the camper, and the *whip-poor-will* birds in the woods, we laughed ourselves to sleep.

The next day, we hiked up the big hill to "the jiggle tree"—a giant tree that had toppled at an angle. Catherine and I climbed up it, held onto branches, and bounced, grinning and laughing.

"There was a fire here," Daddy said, pointing down at a churned-up swath of sand, dirt, and ferns amidst charred-black trees with curled-up branches, as we walked through the woods. "The Michigan Department of Natural Resources has a tractor that churns up the dirt to create a barrier to stop the fire from spreading."

The thought of fire blazing around us terrified me. I felt better as our walk continued into a super lush part of the woods where we filled jugs of water from the picturesque stream surrounded by emerald green moss. It was an adventure! When we walked, Daddy carried his big shovel like a walking stick, sometimes swatting away a snake that appeared on our path.

Catherine and I loved playing in the dirt in an area that Daddy called "St. Jude's Circle," which he carved on a tree. One day, we were wearing our one-piece Speedo bathing suits featuring a star spangled banner design to celebrate America's bicentennial in 1976 when I was nine and Catherine was eight.

For some reason, we thought it would be fun to fill our bathing suits with sand. We stuffed the fronts and backs, creating giant bellies and rotund backsides. Dirt smudged our arms, legs, and faces. Wearing these fat suits made of sand, we rolled around in the dirt, laughing hysterically. (Recently, when asked to recall our happiest childhood memories, we simultaneously thought of that dirt-fest.)

"You girls need a bath!" Daddy exclaimed when he saw us. So we drove to Clear Lake, ran into the water, frightening away the minnows that hung out in the shallow water, and splashed ourselves clean in Mother Nature's bathtub.

During the winter, when the camper was warmed by a propane tank, we ice skated by moonlight on the frozen beaver ponds! Daddy didn't skate, but Catherine and I—thanks to lots of practice at the Oak Park Ice Arena with our friends—glided joyously over the ponds lined with sticks gnawed and strategically placed by the beavers.

During the day, Daddy and his friends used chain saws to topple trees that were cut and split into firewood that we loaded into the back of the truck, then delivered to families back home who purchased it for their fireplaces.

Fear Of Fire Strikes Again

I just wanted him to stop building that bonfire whose red and orange flames were shooting toward the black sky. Would it spread to the surrounding woods? Would the dry brush on the ground catch fire? Would the trees blaze? Would the flames close in around us? Would we be dead?

"Daddy! That fire is big enough!"

"I need to get rid of the brush I cleared from around our camping area," he said, hoisting yet another branch onto the bonfire that was as tall as he was. It crackled. Red sparks danced upward.

I scanned the dark woods. We had no running water. The nearest road was miles down the dirt road. Cell phones didn't exist. We had no way to call for help.

Catherine and I were too small to drive the truck to escape the fire. *Whoosh!*

The wind blew. Flames grew. A flash of heat blazed toward my cheeks.

I ran toward the cool, moonlit dirt road.

I hated those bonfires. And I hated being scared.

The fear didn't end inside the camper. I was always hearing news reports of carbon monoxide killing people inside campers. So after Daddy and Catherine fell asleep, I stayed awake, terrified that the heater was filling the air with deadly fumes. Standing on the blue plaid cushions, I cranked the windows wide open, even though it was cold outside.

Terrified By The Threat Of Supernatural Evil

A girl whose head spun around 360 degrees... who spoke in a deep, demonic voice... vomited green stuff and levitated over the bed... and was possessed by evil that defied exorcism by priests.

When I was eight years old and in third grade, everyone was talking about the 1973 film, *The Exorcist*. This included our really cool babysitter who attended Oak Park High School and watched me and Catherine every day after school until Daddy (and our mother on Fridays) got home at 5:30 p.m.

Our babysitter, who had long brown hair and wore trendy platform shoes with bell-bottom jeans, had an assortment of fun, teenage friends who taught us all kinds of inappropriate words. She listened to cool rock music like Led Zeppelin, The Rolling Stones, Bob Seger, Boston, and Chicago.

Well, our babysitter had seen *The Exorcist.* So had Daddy. They were reading the book, and spoke about its graphic depiction of a 12-year-old girl possessed by the devil.

It sounded terrifying—and fascinating. I really wanted to read the book. I also wanted to see that movie starring Linda Blair. Remembering my parents' stories about our haunted house and Daddy's exorcism in Saginaw, I knew that supernatural evil was just as real as the protection that our guardian angel David John cast around us every day.

"Can I please see *The Exorcist?*" I asked.

"No!" my mother said. "It's rated R."

But I really wanted to see it! Meanwhile, I found the 340-page novel on Daddy's many bookshelves in our basement family room and read the whole thing.

Sometime later, the film—which *Entertainment Weekly* named the scariest film of all time—aired on HBO at Aunt Ann and Percy's house (we didn't have HBO), and I watched it. During that time, my parents also permitted me to read *The Amityville Horror* and watch the film about a house haunted by evil spirits.

This based-on-a-true-story nightmare filled my head with spine-chilling images and ideas. Now when I went to bed, visions of super-natural evil churned in my mind along with the molester, his knife, and that terrifying memory.

So, after saying *The Lord's Prayer* with Daddy, I laid there scanning the shadows as my heart hammered with fear. My fingers dug into the sheets in anticipation of the devil snatching me up into the air to levitate over the bed. I stared with wide eyes at the door, fearing it might slam shut so nobody could rescue me from his evil. I scanned my white dresser; would a demon make the drawers open and shut?

I fled to Daddy, and a short time later felt safe as he ran his palm over my forehead and sang, "David John, Holy Angel, David John, pray for me. David John, Holy Angel, protect my fam-i-ly." Finally, I slept.

Oakland County Child Killer Instills Terror

"Another child's body found," the TV news anchor said, "and police fear the Oakland County Child Killer has taken yet another victim."

Reports about the boys and girls who went missing, then turned up dead, were all over the front page of *The Detroit News* that my parents received every morning.

"You kids be very careful when you're outside," our parents warned. "Don't go near anyone's car. Run, scream, kick. Just get away if anyone comes after you."

A short time after, Catherine and I and a few other kids were standing at the bus stop, across the street from our house at Kenwood and Parklawn, like we did every morning after our parents left for work. A car stopped in front of us. All of us froze as a man leaned out the window and asked: "Can you kids tell me how to get to—"

Fearful, we silently backed up. He drove away. What relief to get on the bus! At school, we told the principal, who drove us back to the bus stop to look for the man's car. He was gone. Police investigated. Nothing happened.

But that didn't make it any less scary when, starting in sixth grade, I walked home from Clinton Middle School with a female classmate. A crossing guard guided us across busy 9 Mile Road, which led into nearby Ferndale, home to one of the Oakland County Child Killer's victims. As we passed the synagogue on the corner, two Hasidic Jewish men passed us, wearing black from head to toe, with long, curled locks dangling in front of their ears.

Thankfully, we came to Kenwood, where some Russian ladies were walking past our house and admiring the giant sunflowers that Daddy was growing near the front window. Across the street, behind Mr. Blum's house, our father had a garden full of tomatoes, cucumbers, squash, and other vegetables.

"See you tomorrow," I told my friend as she turned toward Elaine

Court. I ran up on the porch we shared with the Korean family who lived in the other half of the duplex. The sun reflected off a giant glass jar of kimchi sitting on the porch beside their door, allowing the spicy cabbage condiment to ferment.

I reached inside my shirt for the single key hanging on a white string around my neck. I unlocked the big wooden door, hurried inside, and locked it. Then I turned the bolt, confirming that it was inside the wall by staring at the glimmer of metal between the door and the door frame.

A short time later, Catherine arrived home via the school bus. She was still at the elementary school in fifth grade. Then I felt safe for the next two hours that we were home alone, starting when I was 11 and Catherine was 10.

The world was always bombarding us about bad things happening to kids. I knew, because I loved reading *The Detroit News*. One day, I sat on the dark green shag carpet in the living room, with the paper spread out as I looked at little black and white square photographs of dead boys and young men. They had been raped, killed, and buried under the house near Chicago by John Wayne Gacy, who dressed as a clown. I read every word of each article, the hairs on my body raising with fear the entire time.

That could have been me!

Yet even then, as news reports continued about the Oakland County Child Killer striking again, I did not tell my parents what the neighbor did when I was five years old. By the way, I'm not a fan of clowns.

Asthma Attacks At Age 10

I couldn't breathe. We were outside school, and the gym teacher was making us run a mile for some kind of Presidential Fitness evaluation. I felt like a giant fist was squeezing my chest, and I could hardly inhale. Yet I still had to keep running, and I was far behind my classmates.

Running was one more physical education activity that I failed. I could never climb "the rope" up to the gymnasium ceiling, either.

But that embarrassment paled in comparison to the urgent need to breathe right now. I didn't know what was going on, so somehow I kept running and finally sat down, praying that my lungs would open up and I wouldn't faint.

My first asthma attack was induced by exercise. From then on, every time I sneezed, it was like flipping a switch that squeezed my lungs and caused wheezing. My parents got me an over-the-counter inhaler, which opened my lungs, but made my whole body jittery and upset my stomach.

Family TV Night: The Love Boat & Fantasy Island

"Hurry, it's starting!" I exclaimed as our family gathered on the sofa in the basement family room for two hours of TV bliss: *The Love Boat* at 9:00 p.m. on ABC and *Fantasy Island* at 10:00 p.m.

Daddy brought the big bowl of popcorn, which he had prepared the old fashioned way: heat oil in a pan on the stove, drop in the kernels, let them pop, then drizzle melted butter. A hearty sprinkling of salt made it so delicious.

We loved watching cruise director Julie McCoy, bartender Isaac, Gopher, Doc and Captain Stubing help the guests resolve their romantic dilemmas. The fun continued when white-suited Ricardo Montalbán narrated the dramas as each guest arrived on *Fantasy Island* after Tattoo announced the plane's arrival.

As we watched, crunching popcorn, our mother sat on the couch, arms raised over her head, brushing small sections of her freshly-washed hair, dabbing them with blue Ultra Sheen, then wrapping them around curlers. Catherine and I loved this Saturday night tradition with our parents. Since our mother was working and attending school during the week, every minute with her was precious. We also

Princess of Peace

enjoyed family outings to Dairy Queen and the sit-down Little Caesars restaurant in Ferndale, where we were just happy to be together.

Watching *The Love Boat* inspired us to nickname our mother "Captain," for her take-charge personality. We later shortened it to "Cap," and that's what we call her to this day.

"How Did You Get So Heavy?"

My mouth was watering as I pried open the stiff taco shell and drizzled ketchup over the fried ground beef. Biting into the salty-sweet-greasy-crunchy combination was pure bliss. As I held each taco at an angle to crunch the top end, grease and ketchup dripped from the other end, forming a red-gold swirl on my plate alongside bits of lettuce and tomato.

"You girls want more?" Aunt Ann asked, holding a tray of her amazing tacos as Catherine and I ate from TV trays facing the big wooden TV console.

"Yes, please!" we exclaimed, filling our plates. "Aunt Ann, you make the best tacos!"

"There's plenty more," she said, heading back to make more taco magic in the kitchen. She did it with fresh, handmade corn tortillas from a Mexican bakery. She filled them with browned ground beef, sealed the pocket of meat with a wooden toothpick, then laid the half-circle in a pan of bubbling grease.

One after another, she filled the pan with tacos; Catherine and I could hear the grease sizzle and pop as we watched *The Flintstones* in the front room. When each taco was fried to crispy perfection, Aunt Ann lifted it from the grease and drained it on a plate layered with paper towels. Then she removed the toothpicks, and stuffed the tacos with chopped lettuce and tomato.

"I ate ten tacos!" I boasted, clueless that I had probably just downed a week's worth of calories and a cholesterol nightmare.

37

I was only 10 years old.

Then I was reminded that what you eat in the living room shows up at the swimming pool. This happened when Catherine and I took our first trip to Florida with Aunt Ann and Uncle Percy. Their bowling league participated in championships every year in cities across America, and they took us to their tournaments in Washington, DC; Orlando, Florida; Saint Louis, Missouri; and Baltimore, Maryland. Our parents could not afford such vacations; they took us on lovely driving trips in Michigan to see the Mackinac Bridge and Mackinac Island, as well as to Niagara Falls and Toronto, Canada to visit my mother's brother.

Thankfully, Aunt Ann and Percy enabled us to see the Smithsonian museums and landmarks of our nation's capital, and so much more. So, when the tournament was in Florida, they asked our parents if they could take us to Disney World.

Riding in the plush back seat of their big, burgundy Pontiac Bonneville was great fun. Aunt Ann and Uncle Percy both smoked cigarettes, but back then, nobody talked about second-hand smoke being harmful. Also silent were the piercing stares from strangers as this black couple in their late forties drove through the South with two white-looking girls.

When we reached our beachside hotel in Florida, Catherine and I immediately put on our swimsuits; my yellow bikini had gold metal circles on the hips. As we hurried across the patio toward the pool, a woman from Saginaw who knew our family was approaching. She stopped in her tracks; her jaw dropped as her eyeballs raked up and down my body. Then with a scolding tone, she blurted:

"How did you get so heavy?!"

Her words felt like a slap. But the sting soon dissipated as I jumped in the pool with Catherine and the other bowlers' kids.

Another slap came later that night, when we all ordered burgers in a restaurant with Aunt Ann and Percy and a group of their bowling friends. The white male waiter brought Uncle Percy's burger. It was raw inside. Disgust and hurt flashed over his face.

"It's not done," he told he waiter with a steady and assertive tone. "I need you to take it back and have it cooked right."

I had a feeling that he thought it was a deliberate act by the waiter and/or restaurant. It was a bad feeling that I'm glad I didn't fully understand as a 10-year-old because as an adult it makes me cry.

After School Nausge-fest

Every day after school, when the grandfather clock in the living room said 3:15, Catherine and I had two hours and 15 minutes to indulge our favorite activities: eating and watching TV.

"Hi, Cap, we're home," I told my mother on the phone in the kitchen.

"Hi, honey, did you have a good day?"

"Yes, I won the spelling bee."

"Great! Remember to fold the laundry and put it away. I have class tonight. And practice for your piano lesson."

"Okay," I answered, thinking about the homework that I also had to complete.

"Have some soup or ravioli, and do your homework," she said. "Your father is here. Hold on. Love you!"

"Love you too!"

"Hello Eli," Daddy said. "It's no coincidence that I just happened to be in your mother's office when you girls called. We were telling everyone about the excellent report cards that you and Catherine just brought home."

By then, Cap was working in the MESC "Big Office," just two doors down from Daddy's office, both on the sixth floor.

"Let me talk!" Catherine demanded.

"I thawed hamburger for dinner," he said. "We can have Uncle Ben's rice and green beans with it."

"Okay," I said. "*Cassrin* wants to say hi. Love you!"

Neither of us pronounced each other's names correctly. We were *Lizbath* and *Cassrin* to each other.

"I love you too," he said before I handed the phone to my sister.

Minutes later, we hurried to our rooms, changed into "play clothes," and dashed down to the basement pantry. The hairs on the back of my neck stood up as I creaked open the wooden door to the three-by-four-foot, windowless room that had a cement floor and wooden shelves.

While reaching in to pull the cord to turn on the light, I was terrified that the red-eyed pig in *The Amityville Horror* would be staring back from the corner where we stored large bags of onions and potatoes. Even with the light on, I felt chills as Catherine and I scanned the shelves stocked with cans of ravioli, soup, chili, vegetables, and more.

"I want Spaghettios," I said, grabbing a can. "What do you want, Cassrin?"

"Cheese ravioli," she said.

We raced up the stairs to the small landing lit by the sunshine pouring in from the window on the back door. Up two steps, and we were in the kitchen that our mother painted sky blue.

When we were at Trinity Lutheran, kids shared a story about a ghost named Mary Lou who lived in the closet. So Catherine and I teased each other all the time by racing up the basement stairs, turning off the light switch, and calling, "Mary Lou!"

Catherine was equally freaked out by *The Amityville Horror* and *The Exorcist.*

Within minutes, our parentally condoned after school snacks were bubbling in pans, then steaming in bowls on TV trays as we sat in two big chairs facing the TV. We devoured the food while watching drama unfold on *General Hospital.* During a commercial break, we dashed up to the kitchen, where we could still hear the TV in the basement. We put our dishes in the sink, then flung open the cabinets and refrigerator.

"Let's nausge!" Catherine said, grabbing a half-gallon of chocolate ice cream from the freezer.

The clink of a blue glass as I set it on the yellow tiled countertop was like an exclamation point after her words. I poured a glass of milk and reached into the stocked cabinet for Pecan Sandies—buttery, round cookies with flecks of nuts.

"Look what Daddy bought!" Catherine exclaimed, her blue eyes growing wide with delight as she held up a giant Hershey's chocolate bar that had been nestled in the cabinet amongst popcorn, potato chips, toffee candy bars, peanut butter, and much more.

"Nausge!" I exclaimed as Catherine returned the chocolate to the cabinet, then scooped ice cream into a bowl.

"Triple nausge," Catherine giggled, licking the spoon.

We made up the word "nausge"—pronounced "nawsh" with a sort of "j" sound at the end. Our Jewish friends said "nosh" for snacking. But our word stems from "nauseous," because that's how we felt by dinnertime.

Nausge is a verb: "Let's nausge!"

It's an adjective: "That looks nausge."

And it's a noun: "Let's have some nausge."

Now, as I glimpsed the package of raw hamburger on the counter, I knew I would feel nauseous after eating a real meal on top of the nausge that Catherine and I were about to scarf down. But I was so excited to eat cookies and ice cream that I pushed that out of my mind, along with thoughts of practicing piano, doing homework, and folding laundry.

"Hurry!" Catherine said as theme music for *The Brady Bunch* began to play.

We dashed downstairs just in time to watch Mike, Carol and Alice cope with the daily dilemma that Marsha, Greg, Jan, Peter,

Cindy, and Bobby had created. Other days, we watched *Lost in Space*, *The Jetsons*, *Gilligan's Island*.

"Let's make popcorn before *The Flintstones*," Catherine exclaimed, standing up, empty ice cream bowl in hand.

We ran upstairs, set the pre-packaged popcorn on the stove in its pie-pan container that had a metal handle attached. As the corn inside popped, the tin foil covering rose like a silver dome. Then we romped back down the stairs, parked in front of the TV, and laughed as Fred, Wilma, Barney, and Betty tried to resolve the conflict *du jour*.

During a commercial, a news anchor came on the screen: "Up next: an update on the Oakland County Child Killer who remains at large—"

Catherine and I stared in silence at the TV. I envisioned the front door, remembering how I had set the bolt after we came inside. Then I thought of the back door, which had a glass window that could easily be shattered so someone could reach in, unlock the door, and come down the stairs to "get" us.

"And investigators in Chicago say they have a new development in the gruesome John Wayne Gacy case," the anchor said. "Stay tuned, we'll have more at five o'clock."

Minutes later, I was dipping a spoon in a brand new jar of peanut butter. I closed my eyes, savoring the salty-sweet, creamy bliss. Then I dragged the spoon over the smooth expanse of peanut butter in the jar. I ate some more while Catherine unwrapped a brick of Colby cheese and pulled the cheese slicer from the drawer.

"Biss, let's go," she said, heading downstairs. "*Gilligan* is starting!"

Catherine made up the nickname "Biss" for me when my friends started teasing her about this.

I put the peanut butter away, then followed her and the cheese downstairs.

As we watched the antics of Gilligan, the Skipper, the Professor,

Maryann, Ginger, and Mr. and Mrs. Howell while stranded on a tropical island, Catherine shaved off thin pieces of cheese that we savored, one by one, too many times to count.

"I'm illin'," Catherine announced, slumping back in the chair and casting a woeful stare down at the much smaller brick of cheese on the TV tray.

"Me too," I said, pressing a hand over my distended stomach.

Who was the little girl who'd fallen victim to The Oakland County Child Killer? Had she been out riding her bike or skateboarding or roller skating or walking to the park like Catherine and I always did, when she was kidnapped and killed? What were her parents thinking? How would her friends handle the news? And who was the killer going to get next?

Despite the heavy feeling in my body, I went upstairs and made sure both doors were locked. The hair on the back of my neck stood up as I thought about how it would be dark soon—before Daddy got home from work.

"Biss," Catherine said with a worried tone as we both cleaned up the kitchen. "We have to fold laundry and practice!"

My heart pounded. If Daddy got home and the kitchen was a mess, our chores weren't done, and we hadn't practiced piano, we would hear it from him and our mother. Worse, if this were a day when she didn't have night school and came home after work to discover that we'd neglected our chores, we risked a scolding, a spanking, and not getting our allowance.

My stomach cramped with "I'm in trouble" anxiety.

"Hurry!" I exclaimed. Catherine and I shifted into turbo speed, doing dishes, folding clothes on the laundry table downstairs, hauling everything to the bedrooms and putting it in drawers and closets, then plunking down at the piano to practice just enough to get through tonight's lesson. We sighed with relief as we heard Daddy unlock the back door.

"Hello, girls, I'm home!"

We ran to hug him and he kissed our cheeks. While he cooked dinner, we continued to practice piano and do homework, until it was time to set the table and eat.

The first few bites of dinner were delicious. But when the big hamburger patty, green beans, and rice washed down with milk began to churn on top of the afternoon's nausge, I wanted to heave. Catherine and I shared a shameful glimpse across the table.

"Is something wrong?" Daddy asked with a concerned expression.

"No, I just have a math test tomorrow that I have to study for," I said, which was true.

"You'll have plenty of time after piano," he said. "Now let's finish dinner so we can get there on time."

I picked up my fork, scooped up some rice, and prayed that my stomach would stop aching.

Starving To Become Skinny

Standing in the hallway beside my locker with a half-dozen girl-friends, I watched with envy as they pulled little combs from the back pockets of their skinny designer jeans, and fluffed their "feathered" hairstyles inspired by Farrah Fawcett.

A poster—taped inside a boy's locker—drew my attention to the image of her in a red bathing suit and popular blond hairstyle. Oh how I wished I could "feather" my hair like the *Charlie's Angels* actress or like girls who were sporting the Dorothy Hammill, another fluffy hairstyle inspired by the Olympic ice skater.

Instead, my tight corkscrew curls remained in braids and buns—and when unleashed, they exploded into a yellow aura around my head.

"I love your new Calvin Kleins," exclaimed my friend who was wearing Gloria Vanderbilts amidst a cluster of designer-labeled denim.

I was acutely aware of my no-brand pants—that my parents had put on layaway for our back-to-school shopping; I was very grateful for the one pair of Levi's that my parents had saved up to buy me as a treat.

Now that I was 11 years old in sixth grade, I longed to fit in and feel as cool as my friends with their feathered hair, expensive jeans, and skinniness.

My mother had lost 30 pounds in law school by not eating all day, then—when she arrived home at 11 p.m.—having only a small beef hamburger (no bun) or baked chicken and vegetables left over from our dinner.

"Marylin, you're so skinny!" people praised. "You look fantastic! How did you do it?"

Her confidence sparkled, she ran for miles on the nearby high school track, and she bought beautiful dresses and suits that showed off her slim physique. Clearly, being skinny was the secret to happiness. So, in order to be skinny and admired and happy like her—and to have a body as slim as most of my friends—I emulated my mother's diet plan.

I skipped the instant grits or shredded wheat cereal that Catherine and I usually ate for breakfast. For lunch, I packed a single red apple—or a Tupperware container full of plain iceberg lettuce, no dressing. That's it! I ate in the cafeteria with my six girlfriends, most of whom were enjoying pizza, tater tots, and peanut-butter-and-jelly sandwiches followed by ice cream.

Fortunately, my friend joined me in my starvation regimen. The lunchroom monitors often came by our table to chat and laugh, but didn't seem to notice that I was eating dry lettuce for lunch back before anyone knew the words anorexia or bulimia.

After school, I did homework and practiced piano to keep my mind off eating. For dinner, I ate a tiny hamburger (no bun) and some salad. I restricted my daily caloric intake between 300 and 500 calories; a typical adolescent girl needs 1,600 to 2,000 calories per day, according to health.gov. I was eating a fraction of the calories that my 11-year-old body required.

"Elizabeth, your waist is so tiny!" a girlfriend marveled as she stared at my belt-cinched waist. I was wearing my mother's size-four pencil skirt with a tucked-in blouse while attending another girlfriend's bat mitzvah at a synagogue. Several girls gathered around me, gawking at the dramatic change in my body.

"How much weight have you lost?" one asked.

"Thirty pounds," I said, beaming with accomplishment and finally feeling good about how I looked now and in the skinny jeans that I wore to school.

"Want to dance?" asked one of the cutest boys in school at the party following the ceremony to celebrate my friend's 13th birthday. I grinned the whole time that we danced to the first rap songs. I felt like a new person, and I wanted to stay that way.

After Starving, Stuffing…

After school, when my stomach was flat, and I felt so empty and light, I opened the cabinet for a snack. The peanut butter jar stared back. My mouth watered.

Just one spoonful won't hurt…

The sweet, creamy indulgence led to another spoonful. And another. Oh how I had missed my favorite treat! Then I glimpsed the breadbox. I had not eaten toast for months. Warm toast with butter, sprinkled with cinnamon-sugar. I made two slices…

Delicious didn't begin to describe the melted butter and chewy, warm bread dancing on my taste buds. Just like the cheese and cookies and ice cream that followed… as I slid down a sugary slope into a dreaded place, feeling so out of control and afraid that I would pack on the pounds just as quickly as I'd lost them.

I'll get back on my diet tomorrow. But I didn't. I spent weeks stuffing myself to make up for all the starving. Bloated, puffy, heavy, and ashamed, I retreated to my bedroom to cry. I felt totally unable to stop eating like tomorrow was the end of the world. Food made me feel better, but I'd wake up feeling even fatter and more depressed. In a matter of weeks or months, I was even fatter than when I started.

At school, I wanted to disappear when all the people who had praised me in the skinny skirts and jeans glimpsed my ever-growing body now squeezed into my much bigger jeans or hidden under baggy shirts. They said nothing, but their disappointed and sometimes mocking expressions said everything that I was already thinking.

That I was a big, fat, out-of-control whale.

Thus began my descent into "yo-yo dieting" hell that destroyed my ability to eat like a normal person. I envied my skinny friends who could eat two slices of pizza, feel satisfied, and simply stop eating. They did the same with one candy bar or one cookie. They felt no attachment to the food, whereas I had the feeling of always wanting more, but never getting enough.

I wish a genie would grant me one wish: eating as much as I want of any foods, and staying skinny.

The reality was that my self-esteem and my self-worth were measured by the size of my jeans and the number of calories I had—or had not—consumed that day. If I had been "good" by sticking to my starvation diet, then I felt euphoric and excited to keep the momentum going the next day, until I lost the 30 pounds I had recently gained. If I had been bad, then I was usually in a terrible mood, felt sluggish, and admonished myself for "pigging out" yet again.

Despite this, I had lots of fun with my girlfriends. To celebrate my 13th birthday, seven of my friends—as well as Catherine and two of her friends—packed into the covered back of Daddy's truck and rode up to Big Woods for a weekend with our parents. We had so much fun hiking, swimming at Clear Lake, and telling stories around the campfire.

Uncle's Death Sparks Revelation About Knowing God

Uncle Percy drowned.

And now I can't breathe. It feels like a giant fist is squeezing my lungs. Like I can't suck down air to save my life. I'm coughing. Air goes out. The fist squeezes tighter. My lungs are like empty balloons that won't fill back up.

"Biss! You ok?" my mother demanded from the front seat.

"Eli, should I pull over?" Daddy asked while driving us through farmland toward Saginaw, to Aunt Ann's house. Uncle Percy wouldn't be there. He jumped in the river to save his friend who fell off the boat while fishing. The friend survived. Uncle Percy didn't.

"I need my inhaler," I wheezed.

"Biss!?" Catherine exclaimed with an alarmed tone. Sitting on the back seat beside me, she snatched the L-shaped plastic inhaler from my tote bag on the floor. "Here, Biss!"

Our mother peered back with panic in her eyes. Daddy glanced at me in the rear-view mirror while steering up I-75.

I held the plastic tube to my mouth, and pressed the canister to deliver a spray of medicine that would hopefully open my lungs. As I tried to inhale the bronchodilator, a squeaky, wheezy sound escaped my mouth. I sucked down as much medication as possible.

God please help me breathe!

Just an hour ago, Catherine and I had been enjoying her 12th birthday celebration with her friends at the playground near our home. Until Daddy walked over and said, "We have to go to Saginaw. Uncle Percy drowned."

Now, I coughed, trying to imagine the medicine seeping through my bronchial tubes, forcing that evil fist to stop squeezing them shut. One minute later, I took another puff of medication. Finally, the fist eased its grip. I coughed up phlegm that accumulates during an asthma attack as the bronchial tubes constrict. Then, I could inhale, and my family sighed with relief.

A few days later, I refused to approach Uncle Percy's open casket in the funeral home to look at his dead body. Instead, I stood in the carpeted vestibule of Elsie Black's—where unfortunately we went often for family hours and funerals. I wanted to remember Uncle Percy as the fun, loving, silly man who let us pull his finger to make us laugh when he farted.

"It's too bad he never found God," a relative said after the funeral.

My mother exclaimed, "Church affiliation has nothing to do with whether someone was a good person." Uncle Percy had illustrated the ultimate God within by sacrificing his life to save another. He had unequivocally earned his golden ticket through the Pearly Gates.

From Diversity To Homogenous Affluence

I felt like an alien in the classroom amidst affluent white students wearing preppy monogrammed sweaters, khaki pants, and Docksider boat shoes.

"Everyone say hello to Elizabeth Atkins," said Mr. Williams, my eighth grade English teacher. "She has a sister named Catherine in seventh grade, and today is their first day at Kinawa."

We had left Oak Park six weeks into the school year, because our mother—who passed the Bar Exam on her first try—began her legal career with Michigan's Legislative Service Bureau. We were so proud to watch her walk across the stage to receive her law degree, and now apply her knowledge in the state capitol. Daddy worked in offices in Lansing and Detroit, so the transition was easy for him.

But not for me and Catherine. Going from the diversity of Oak Park to this wealthy white enclave of Oldsmobile executives, Michigan State University professors, and stay-at-home moms was pure culture shock. The social strata included the "popular" cheerleaders and male athletes among extremely studious students.

They lived in big houses. We lived in a rented townhouse in an apartment complex. They returned suntanned from holiday vacations and spring break trips to Aspen, Mexico, and the Caribbean. Catherine and I had never been on an airplane. They listened to Bruce Springsteen and REO Speedwagon. Our house often pulsed to the beat of R&B and pop music hits.

Most of the kids had homemaker moms; Cap worked full time and was active with civic and political organizations. Our classmates' dads golfed at country clubs; our silver-haired father drove a pick-up truck, gardened, led Indian Meetings, and competed with the local chapter of U.S. Masters Swimming.

So why did our parents choose Okemos? Because it had one of Michigan's best public school systems. And the stable suburban community was safe for raising children.

Our school was predominantly white, except for a handful of black students, along with Asians and Indians. Going to a new school is terrifying, especially when you feel different. Catherine and I were quiet and studious; we wanted to make friends and be accepted.

"Another A-plus," Mr. Williams said, handing back my homework for diagramming sentences. I loved identifying nouns, verbs, adjectives, gerunds, and participles.

I thrived in every class—math, science, French with Mrs. Sledd, home economics, and typing. At parent-teacher conferences, our parents heard only praise for our citizenship and academic excellence. Catherine and I both made friends, enjoying play dates at their homes or going to the movies and the mall together.

"Play it again!" Lara exclaimed while dancing around the living room with me, Catherine, and our mother. I dashed toward the stereo to replay the 12" disco version.

"It's the Captain!" Lara announced playfully, as her dark hair bounced and she snapped her fingers. Her bulky purple sweater over matching stretch pants complimented her olive complexion. "We're jammin' with the beat!"

My mother danced and laughed with us while the scent of garlic and tomatoes wafted from the kitchen where Daddy was making spaghetti from scratch.

"I love to dance!" Lara said. "It's the passionate Italian in me!"

I had fallen in love with Lara's exuberance and nonconformist personality the moment we met in school. She became my best friend, and we spent a lot of time at each other's homes. Her mother also worked full time.

"Bissy!" Lara said as her jazzy black boots clomped on the shiny school hallway where we were constant companions. "Let's go to Meridian Mall this weekend." Lara and I were kindred spirits and continue to enjoy a beautiful friendship today.

Moving Into A Big, Pretty House

In 1981, our parents purchased a five-bedroom house on a pretty street.

"This room is so big!" I exclaimed, twirling in my new bedroom in the split-level house on an Okemos street lined with shuttered colonials. The brick and white aluminum-siding home had a foyer, a split staircase leading to the living room, dining room, kitchen, full bath, and three bedrooms upstairs. The lower level had a paneled family room with a fireplace, a big laundry room where we put a pool table, two spacious bedrooms, and a full bath. Catherine and I loved having our own level.

Daddy tilled a large swath of the huge back yard to create a garden. He was so happy growing giant beefsteak tomatoes from plants taller than him, along with squash, corn, cucumbers, herbs, and green beans.

"These tomatoes are delicious," Cap exclaimed as Daddy served them sliced with pepper and fresh chives at dinnertime. He also grew sunflowers that stood six feet tall, along with roses.

During the winter, Cap made blazing fires in the fireplace, and we'd all sit on the couch watching TV.

Our mother was steadily moving up the career ladder as a lawyer. Once, when she had a business trip in Chicago, she took me and Catherine for a really fun weekend. We shopped on Michigan Avenue, visited Shedd Aquarium and the Museum of Natural History, and walked along Lake Michigan, having a ball!

Active with the National Urban League, our mother campaigned statewide for the election of Michigan Governor Jim Blanchard. She was surprised and delighted when her dedication was rewarded with an appointment to the Michigan Worker's Compensation Appeal Board. The Governor soon promoted her to Chair—the first woman of color in that position—overseeing 35 lawyers who successfully resolved a huge backlog of cases under her tenure.

Many days after school, before our parents were home from work, Lara came over, and we watched the latest music videos on the new and very popular MTV. We knew all the vee-jays and the words to songs by Madonna, Duran Duran, David Bowie, Billy Idol, Janet Jackson, Prince, and so many more 80s artists.

"Let's go pick up Lara!" I exclaimed as Catherine and I snuck out of the house at night while our parents were sleeping. We got in the silver Ford Granada that our mother had given us to drive to school, put it in neutral, and let it roll down the driveway. On the street, we started the engine, drove to Lara's house, then headed to East Lansing. Burger King near the MSU campus was the cool teen gathering place. We'd get something to eat, park, and hang out amongst kids we knew. We didn't drink alcohol or smoke or have sex. We just socialized and loved feeling independent and mischievous. Our parents never knew we were gone, and thankfully we always got home safely.

"These nachos are so good," I exclaimed, crunching on chips with melted cheese, refried beans, beef, and salsa. Catherine and Lara nodded as they devoured burritos while Mexican music played. Chi-Chi's restaurant was one of our favorite hangouts where we consumed large amounts of calories topped off by "fried" ice cream.

Tasting The Bitterness of Racism

Boys were one of our favorite topics. I had a huge crush on a fun guy from school. We went on a few dates, and when he phoned, I grinned and glowed like a lightbulb.

"Hey, Elizabeth, I heard your mom's a n******." His words shot through the phone and felt like they slapped my cheek.

I didn't know what to say, and I never spoke to him again. A few months later, a cute blond guy from a nearby town took me on a fun date, brought me home, met my mother. Never heard from him again.

"There will always be people who don't like you because you're biracial," my mother said during one of many weekend trips to Detroit so that I could hang out with my friends who were mostly black and Jewish. "That's just the way of the world. Racism has nothing to do with what kind of person you are. It overrides everything. It's just something you have to deal with in life, and you can consider someone doing you a favor when they reveal their hatred, because you don't want to keep people like that in your life, anyway."

She was 35 and had very clear, confident understanding of this reality. I was 15, and hated that someone who looked just like me could like me one minute, then disappear forever when they learned something that made me suddenly unacceptable.

Apple Fritter Bliss Sweetens The Bitterness

The sweet scent of apple fritters wafting through the parking lot lured me and Catherine into the Meijer store near our home. At the bakery, we bought a bag of the doughy, soft-ball sized confections covered in white glaze. We also bought donuts and cookies. Then we hurried home, plopped in front of the TV to watch *General Hospital,* and delighted in the decadent oblivion of every sugary, greasy bite.

I loved the thrill of tasting the food, feeling a physical and emotional high from it, like a euphoria that kept us giggling out of control, followed by a super mellow state of just laying back on the couch, vegging out with whatever we were watching on TV. The guilt and worry about the weight gain that would follow this binge was easy to offset by thinking about what to eat next.

"Don't you want to be skinny?" my mother asked after finding a one-pound bag of M&Ms in my closet full of clothes that no longer fit.

Of course I did. But I felt so bad, I just kept eating. Peanut butter remained a favorite indulgence; I would just lose myself in opening the jar, smelling it, staring at the tiny puddles of oil in the little grooves where a knife had been, and spooning up a dollop of pure heaven.

If peanut butter were a drug, I was addicted. And I wouldn't stop eating it until I felt sick. Then I'd remember that every tablespoon of peanut butter had 120 calories, and I had just eaten 10 spoonfuls! Guilt attacked my senses, making me spiral into a panic about overnight weight gain.

"I hate this!" I sobbed, standing in front of my closet the next morning, unable to zip my jeans. I stared at the clothes that were now too small. My heart pounded with panic because I had to find something to wear and get dressed, or we'd be late to school.

Binge eating made me feel "puffy" in my face, fingers, and belly from water retention, especially if I consumed high-sodium foods like potato chips or fast food. So I would sneak into my father's medicine cabinet and take half a "water pill," his prescription diuretic that was part of his medical regimen for high blood pressure. Pretty soon—during bathroom runs between every class—I'd be peeing out all the excess fluids, loving how the "puff" was deflating.

"That smells so good, Daddy!" I exclaimed, walking into the kitchen as he stirred a bubbling pot of spaghetti sauce and meatballs made with all fresh ingredients. The garlic and tomato aroma filled the house, tantalizing me for hours while doing homework.

One day, he served me a hearty plate. I felt so guilty, because all my declarations about getting and staying skinny were empty words. Shame made the spaghetti taste even better because it was soothing my hurt feelings and my own sense of failure for not staying as slim as possible. Disappointing myself triggered a wicked cycle that I didn't know how to escape.

The best way to feel better was to eat ice cream. This perfect elixir highlighted a frequent family outing to the Quality Dairy store near the MSU campus. They were famous for serving multiple scoops inside giant Styrofoam cups.

One day, I thought I had discovered my wish-come-true: eating to my heart's content while staying skinny. I had read about this stay-slim-secret—a "disorder" called bulimia—in newspaper and magazine articles. So, the next time Catherine and I went to Quality Dairy with our father, I gorged on Praline Pecan ice cream, then dashed to the bathroom. I leaned over the toilet, sticking my fingers down my throat. I was so excited to purge all those calories from my stomach.

I gagged. My eyes watered. Weird pressure on my face made it turn red. But I couldn't throw up. I tried and tried. The ice cream stayed in my stomach, and later filled my fat cells.

Feeling Déjà-vu In A French Church

Inside the famed Palace of Versailles in France, my pulse raced with excitement. We had studied this home of General Napoleon Bonaparte in French class as I had earned all A's and served as president of the French Club. After selling fancy tins of nuts to neighbors, family members, and my parents' co-workers to finance the trip, I was finally on a 10-day voyage to France with our teacher, Mrs. Kate Marsh, and about a dozen OHS students. I was 15, taking my first airplane trip from Detroit to London, then to Paris.

I couldn't wait to see the famed Hall of Mirrors. The photographs of this chandeliered, gilded space were so enchanting in our textbook. But standing there, jostled by shoulder-to-shoulder tourists, as a cacophony of languages echoed off the dull, dingy mirrors, I was super disappointed. I hadn't considered that the mirrors were 300 years old!

I went outside, sat on one of the terraces, and wrote about it in my journal that contained my reflections on our prior stop in Paris, the scene of another disappointment: the pastries. Our tour bus stopped at La Patisserie, and all 12 of us loaded up on pretty *pain au chocolat, biscuits* and *tarte aux pommes.* Each chocolate croissant, cookie, and apple tart looked enticing—but they were dry and crumbly.

Similarly, after all our classroom talk about the great vineyards and wineries in France, stepping into the musty cave to watch the wine-making process made me have an asthma attack. We had lots of fun, however, walking around Paris, shopping for fun clothes, eating melt-in-your-mouth croissants for breakfast, and people-watching.

I shivered with déja-vu inside Notre Dame Cathedral in Paris, completed in 1260. I knew I had been there before in a past life. I was overwhelmed with awe at the age of it, thinking about how many countless people had prayed under its spectacular stained glass and cement arches.

Goosebumps of déja-vu also danced on my skin as we visited the Mont-Saint-Michel monastery off the Normandy coast. Walking through the archway-lined courtyards of this fortress named for Archangel Michael felt hauntingly familiar. As did the enormous, Gothic Cathédrale Notre-Dame, completed in 1220, in Chartres, where we purchased hand-made lace. Another amazing moment happened outside the museum at the Normandy D-Day Beaches.

"Botticelli!" exclaimed a petite, gray-haired Italian lady as women circled me, chattering in Italian.

"Uffizi!" one lady said, staring with wide eyes as the ocean breeze blew my hair in the evening light. Then they said in French that I look like the *Birth of Venus* painting by Sandro Botticelli, housed in the Uffizi Gallery in Florence, Italy. It depicts the goddess Venus emerging from the ocean on a giant seashell, naked with long, flowing hair.

While I loved Botticelli's celebration of her curves and strength, I was excruciatingly self-conscious and self-loathing over the fact that my natural body shape and size were more like the voluptuous beauties in Renaissance paintings than the x-ray-thin fashion models who set the standard of beauty in the 1980s.

Putting My Muscles To Good Use

Shortly after the France trip, I developed a newfound pride in my thick leg muscles and natural athleticism, when I attended Diving Camp at Michigan State University with a classmate. She invited me to join the OHS Swim Team, and we attended the camp with Coach John Narcy, where we worked on trampolines with belts attached to wires secured to the ceiling.

After learning to dive, pike, twist, and flip, I earned the Most Improved Diver award! During daily swim team practices at 7:00 a.m. and after school, swimming laps and diving toned my muscles, kept my weight down, and built awesome shoulder and arm strength. This was my first and last team sport, and I loved our spaghetti dinners before meets and state competitions.

Being nude in a locker room with athletes, as well as walking around at meets in a bathing suit, was a huge motivator to maintain a healthy weight. I often admired a teammate who was overweight and popular. I marveled at how she was so upbeat—even in a bathing suit in front of crowds! At the same time, two girls succumbed to anorexia, wasting away to skeletons.

My relationship with food and my body was as sick as theirs. I was always thinking about food, and evaluating whether I felt fat or thin, which influenced whether I felt bad or good. After practice, I attacked the peanut butter jar, bricks of cheese, and bowls of ice cream. But it didn't show because of our grueling hours of swimming and diving twice a day.

Loving Creative Writing Class

"Someone in this classroom is going to be a superstar writer someday," announced Mrs. Marsha Tanner, my super fun Creative Writing teacher in tenth grade. I loved her class, as she talked about writing poetry, novels, and short stories.

While walking through the aisles between our desks, handing back papers, she stopped and handed me my paper marked with "A+." I had spent hours composing the story, losing myself in the joy of my imagination.

"This is excellent, Elizabeth," she said, smiling. "Your narrative is crisp and vivid, and your command of dialogue is authentic. Great job!"

I grinned.

So did the handsome European guy at the next desk. He was one year older than me, spending his junior year at our high school. He had dreamy blue eyes, a fun personality, and a brilliant mind. I loved that he spoke multiple languages, and I was intrigued by his account of life in Europe. He was among many exchange students at our high school; Catherine and I made many friends from Spain, Belgium, England, and Colombia; our family even hosted a Scandinavian student during our senior year.

As for my European Romeo, he was soon visiting our house, enjoying Sunday dinners with my family, and playing volleyball in our backyard. He shared polite, intelligent conversations with my parents, who welcomed him on many evenings and weekends.

"I want to become a doctor," I told him. "I'm studying cadavers through a Michigan State University program for high school students who want to attend medical school."

Then he told me about the great business opportunities that awaited him back in Europe, after college. I also loved telling him about the discussions about Henry David Thoreau and Transcendental Meditation in Mrs. Anita Hammerle's English class.

"Elizabeth, don't get married and have babies before you do something meaningful with your career," she warned one morning after a spirited classroom discussion about a woman punished for an affair with a married man who is not penalized in *The Scarlet Letter* by Nathaniel Hawthorne. Mrs. Hammerle's unconventional advice affirmed my ambition to attend college and become Dr. Atkins.

Meanwhile, my European Romeo took me to the prom. I wore a pink taffeta dress that I designed and sewed myself in Mrs. Baker's Home Economic class; it was off-the-shoulder, with a white lace overlay and fabric-covered buttons down the back. With pink roses and baby's breath in my hair, I felt like a princess as we rode in a luxury car to dinner with other couples, then to the dance. My beau was super attentive and romantic.

"I'm sorry, Elizabeth," said the note stuffed into the slats on my locker at school. "I can no longer date you because you are mulatto."

The handwritten words on the half-page of notebook paper

blurred through my tears. I couldn't believe it. I tried to talk with him, but he said his host family had learned that my mother is black, and had made this decision for him.

Fortunately, he rejected their racism, and continued to visit our home. When he returned to Europe within a few months, he carried with him the wonderful memories of our teenage romance, and the stinging lesson on American racism.

My own lessons would continue, like when my friends took me to a party at their friend's luxurious home. Some guys were on a sofa, drinking beer, while the girls stood nearby, talking.

"The n*****s at my job are so lazy," one guy exclaimed angrily.

His comment roused more racist commentary. Fear gushed through me like ice water. *Do they know I'm black? Would they hurt me if they found out now? God please get me out of here safely... and fast.*

Losing Weight & Finding Love

The big numbers on the scale at the weight loss clinic made me want to burst into tears. *What have I done to myself? Why am I so fat and unhappy?* I was only 16, a high school junior, and missing out on so much fun, especially dating, because I felt so awful.

"We're going to help you do this, fast," the nurse assured me.

All I had to do was starve for several months and the weight would melt off. Breakfast and lunch were a packet of protein powder mixed with water. Dinner was a tiny portion of lean protein and vegetables. But the terrible hunger and even worse moods were rewarded by frequent weigh-ins with dramatic results. In just a few months, I dropped 40 pounds!

Also, something happened during my mid-teen years where my hair texture became less frizzy, more corkscrew-curly.

"I love your hair!" girls exclaimed. "I spend so much money on perms and still don't get curls like that! You're so lucky!" I began to feel grateful for my unique hair and no longer wished for a Farrah Fawcett style.

Feeling and looking like a new person, I embarked on the summer before my senior year vowing, *I'm going to stay skinny forever!* I was amazed at the person looking back from my bedroom mirror in skinny jeans, shorts, mini-skirts, and bikinis. I even wore a svelte, mermaid-cut, red taffeta dress that I designed and made in sewing class to the Oak Park High School prom. My date was an African American senior whom I'd met through a friend.

Back in Okemos, I was preparing for another adventure: studying French in Québec, Canada through an MSU program at Collège de Rivière-du-Loupe. A few nights before the trip, I wore my favorite blue jumpsuit to "Teen Night" at the Outer Limits, a nightclub near Michigan State University where Catherine, our friends, and I danced to the latest hits.

"Want to dance?" asked the most beautiful guy I'd ever seen. He was tall with broad shoulders. Casting an enchanted look at me, he held out his hand, and everything became a blur as I danced with this Adonis. It was love at first sight, and we went on a date that Saturday night in June of 1984. He picked me up in his red sports car, we went to a Mexican restaurant, saw a movie, and shared our first kiss in the flower-filled MSU Arboretum.

The night was magical. We shared an unspoken understanding and comfort as mixed-race people in mostly white environments. One year older than me, he had just graduated from a local high school. Best of all, he made me laugh until my stomach hurt.

I just met the love of my life, and I'm leaving town!

Speaking French and Falling In Love With Maple Sugar

The next morning, I flew with my OHS classmate to Quebec City, and took a bus to a small town 895 miles from Okemos. We each had a pretty bedroom upstairs in a big white farmhouse with the Pelletier family.

Every morning, Madame Claire Pelletier, a plump, happy woman who wore flower-print dresses and aprons, prepared big breakfasts for her husband, Maurice, who worked in the fields and raised cows, pigs, and horses.

She spoke no English, but we understood her French. She made thick crèpes and taught us to sprinkle them with chips that she shaved off a big brick of maple sugar! Then she showed us how to roll the hot crèpes, causing the maple sugar to melt. Every hot, sweet, doughy bite was divine!

I fell head over heels in love with maple sugar! The Pelletiers put it on everything, including ham and ice cream. Sometimes I would chip off a piece and just suck on it. Then I discovered maple-leaf-shaped sandwich cookies, which seemed like Canada's answer to Oreos. My taste buds went wild over the maple frosting sandwiched between two maple-flavored, shortbread cookies. I couldn't get enough!

Fortunately—despite these indulgences—I stayed skinny, because every morning we walked into town to the school where we studied French. In the afternoon, we trekked home for lunch—another big meal to feed Maurice before he headed back to the fields. Then we joined our friends for an adventure, often hiking up the nearby mountains along a picturesque stream.

I exchanged letters with Catherine, who was having an amazing summer adventure in Sweden with a similar exchange program. I also kept in touch with First Love back home. Meanwhile, a cool guy from Toronto captured my attention by making me laugh a lot. Once, Madame Pelletier caught us kissing in the barn, and she scolded me in French about how the girl always pays the consequences of behaviors like that with boys. I kept seeing Mr. Toronto, but never did anything to cause the kinds of consequences that worried her.

Farm life was fascinating. I even watched a baby horse being born. And I absolutely loved being immersed in a French-speaking environment. How thrilling to apply what I'd learned in classrooms to speaking with real Francophones and having coherent, two-way conversations! Our group visited Montréal and Québec City, where we toured the famed Chateau Frontenac Hotel. I concluded the stay feeling excited for another French-speaking adventure in Québec or France.

"Your Butt's Too Big!"

Back home, when I saw First Love, it was on! For the rest of the summer, we were inseparable. Our attraction was electric, and I loved to just stare at him because he was so beautiful.

Throughout my senior year, we enjoyed an epic teen romance. He had a good job and was attending a local college. Every Friday, he bought me flowers. We went to dinner, movies, sporting events, and on trips with each other's families.

The ominous cloud rumbling into this sunny picture was my monstrous appetite. When I was with my boyfriend, I was "good"— eating salad or something low-calorie. But away from him, I got my fill of ice cream, peanut butter, cheese, and all my old favorites. I was so ashamed that I had met First Love looking and feeling my best, but now I just couldn't stop stuffing my face and blowing up.

"Your butt's too big," he said.

I stopped eating.

Starting Monday morning, I set my alarm for 6:00 a.m., went in the bathroom and drank water with No-Doz caffeine pills, then hopped on the exercise bike in our laundry room. After riding for an hour, I'd get ready for school, then drink Diet Coke for breakfast to get through my classes. It was easy to avoid food at my after school "co-op" job at a small company where I learned accounts receivable. Then I spent most evenings with my boyfriend and family.

All I wanted was to wake up, weigh myself, and see a smaller number on the scale. That would make me feel and look better, and shrink my butt back down to an acceptable size.

So I ate nothing. By Saturday, after my sixth morning of vigorous exercise, I felt dizzy. I ate a few tomato slices, but that didn't stop the ringing in my ears. So I laid on my bed. And everything went black.

I woke up later and ate a healthy dinner, vowing to lose weight in a healthier way. By summer, I was looking slim and great. But my guilt, shame, and self-disgust made me paranoid that First Love would dump me for a naturally skinny girl who would join him to eat all the pizza, burgers, and French fries she desired. Once, when I questioned him about another girl, he said:

"You can't believe that I love you, because you don't love yourself."

Those words haunted me for years. Because he was right. And I didn't know what to do about it.

Pursuing My Doctor Dream

I was a stellar student throughout high school. During senior year, I was earning A's in Advanced Placement Biology with Mr. Purvis. AP classes are college-level; they enable you to bypass the entry-level class as a freshman. I loved this class!

When we talked about technological advances in human reproduction since the first test tube baby born in six years before in 1978, I was so fascinated, I decided that my goal was to become an embryologist, studying what has evolved into artificial insemination and in vitro fertilization. I was on track throughout high school, earning A's in chemistry, algebra, calculus, English, French, physics, and history.

But at times I was spending so much time with First Love, I was bombing AP English.

"Elizabeth, what are your thoughts on this character?" Dr. Collar asked during discussions. My cheeks burned with embarrassment. I could not respond because I had not read the book. And I blamed no one but myself. (Today I often warn young women to stay focused and not allow themselves to get distracted from schoolwork by a boyfriend).

In September of 1985, I moved into the all-girls dormitory, Stockwell Hall at the University of Michigan in Ann Arbor.

When my roommates from wealthy suburbs of Chicago and Boston mentioned being on a "wait list," I realized how lucky I was that my high school guidance counselor had submitted only one college application for me: to the University of Michigan, and that I was granted admission right away.

My roommates were really fun, and we celebrated our first night on campus by attending a fraternity party where we drank neon-green punch spiked with who-knows-what kind of alcohol. All the handsome guys, the pumping music, and the excitement of being away at college, were just as intoxicating as cup after cup of that green stuff served in giant metal tubs on the floor.

We had a ball! But as soon as we staggered back across campus to our dorm room, I dashed to the bathroom and puked up a whole lot of neon green.

When my four classes started in the College of Literature, Science, and the Arts, it was exhilarating to walk across the beautiful campus in the "city of trees" amongst 40,000 students from around the world. I was so excited to begin my pre-med classes, make new friends, and stay slim. Feeling good about how I looked, I loved meeting people in class, at parties, and everywhere around campus. This was the face and body that I wanted to maintain and present to the world.

I began Chemistry 123, the required introductory course for pre-med students. Two times per week, I joined hundreds of students in an auditorium where a professor lectured about organic chemistry.

Then twice a week, we attended a small class "section" with a teaching assistant who spoke little English. I was in a constant panic about Chem 123, and sought help from tutors and classmates. Still, I bombed the midterm and final exams, which accounted for most of my grade.

Meanwhile, having placed out of regular freshman English, I earned A's in Shakespeare 125. I loved the class, and often sat with a fun new friend and fellow pre-med student, Sam Hess. Despite my struggles in Chemistry, I was confident that I could retake the class and pass, and someday write "MD" after my name.

College Is A Food Lover's Dream And Nightmare

One night, I almost swooned when my roommates ordered the cheesiest, most delicious pizza. This giant rectangle of chewy dough under a thick blanket of melted mozzarella cheese was nausge to the max! I savored a slice or two with my roommates, thinking, *I can't wait to get my hands on a pizza like this and devour as much as I want!*

Fortunately, solitude was not a common occurrence with three people living in one room. But it was easy to eat bagels and cream cheese, candy bars, cookies, and fast food around campus throughout the day. I was flirting with "freshman 15," the notorious weight gain that afflicts a good portion of college teens, thanks to dorm food, late-night pizza, and study snacks. Campus life was rigged with countless opportunities to trip on caloric explosions. Like Steve's Ice Cream.

"Vanilla with chocolate chip cookies, please," I said over the counter. The server laid a big scoop on a marble slab and mashed cookie crumbles into the creamy blob, using two metal spatulas to continuously fold the crushed cookies into the ice cream, before plopping it into my cup and handing it over with a spoon. Heavenly!

Thin and determined to stay that way, I balanced all this nausge with big salads at mealtime in the dorm. I felt like an alien as my roommates and friends came to our table with trays holding dinner entrees of baked chicken, rice and vegetables, or spaghetti, or meatloaf and potatoes, along with a small salad, and a single-serving dessert. They ate normal, balanced meals. I never ate entrees; it seemed totally foreign. I was either eating a salad or pigging out on fattening food outside of normal mealtimes. I wrote about my struggles in pretty, cloth-covered journals. Here's an excerpt:

Food—I've gained weight. I hate being hungry. It's depressing. I'm constantly having what-should-I-eat debates in my head. All Day. Here's the daily dialogue inside my head:

"I need to be thin so I'll feel good and people will like me."

"I'm hungry."

"Be really skinny."

"If I don't eat anything, I'll be tired and my metabolism will slow down, then when I start eating again, I'll gain weight really quick."

"Why are all the girls/women on campus so thin?"

"Wow, she's so fat. Do I look like that? It wouldn't take me too long to lose weight, just 20 pounds to look and feel good."

"I have to be thin. So I can wear anything. And jeans are so sexy."

"What's for dinner? Wait, what have I eaten today?"

"Am I hungry? Puffy? Look how my thighs spread in the chair. Gross. And my jeans feel so tight. My stomach is bloated. I feel so gross."

"I want to be a knockout."

"(The guy I'm dating) will look at my butt and legs and think, 'Wow, she's gained weight.'"

"I hope I don't have to eat with anyone in the cafeteria."

"None of my skills as a writer or compassionate human being mean anything when I feel fat."

"A double chin is forming."

"Well, I'm not physically hungry right now so I won't eat. That way, I'll be able to eat when I truly am hungry."

"The cafeteria lady will think I'm a pig if I go get a bagel."

"How can those skinny girls eat that fattening food? I only want it if I can have large amounts. But I can't do that in the cafeteria so I'll just have cereal."

"Biss, just face the fact that you'll never be able to eat as much as you want. If you did, you would accomplish nothing, not be able to function, and probably kill yourself in a fit of hysteria."

"But feeling full is so gross—bloated, can't breathe, just want to sleep. Fear of waking up in the morning and facing tight clothes."

"Wow, I really weigh a lot."

(On a day that I went home for the weekend) "Haven't Daddy and Cap noticed I've eaten two giant bowls of Cream of Wheat and spaghetti tonight? They didn't see the cookies or the frozen yogurt with syrup I inhaled in the car. I feel sick."

These thoughts and others echo through my head all day. They push out—or take up the space of—productive, happy thoughts. They force me to tune out in class and make me realize I didn't hear a word the professor said. They make me crazy and afraid.

Tears welled in my eyes as I walked across campus after a late-night binge. All that sugar wreaked havoc on my mood. My body hummed with anger at myself for being so out of control.

I'm going to starve the rest of the day to compensate for the caloric chaos.

The Face Of Which Race?

The frat house was packed with people, the music was blasting, and the drinks were pouring as I danced amidst a sea of white faces. With me was my "big brother," a blond-haired, blue-eyed guy named Jeff who was really fun and smart, and who had invited me and my girl-friends to become "little sisters" at the fraternity.

That gave us entrée to all the parties, and we had a blast!

But the racist boogie man of decades past always lurked in the shadows of my mind. With long blond curly hair, suntanned skin, and green eyes, my multiracial mix was invisible to most people.

"If guys think you're white and like you, but find out you're black, they might become enraged and rape you," warned an elder family friend who was African American and attended U of M during the 1950s.

Underscoring this fear was the scene in the 1959 movie, *Imitation of Life*, when Sara Jane's white boyfriend attacks her when he finds out she's keeping her black mother a secret and "passing" for white; my family had watched this tragic film countless times.

Thankfully, my experiences attending frat parties were always fun and I always felt safe and respected, and remained friends with Jeff throughout college.

I had hoped to find a college social scene where people of every race hung out together, but gatherings were usually black *or* white. In class, I was often the only black person—and nobody knew! At the time, I was not vocal about it, but never kept it a secret.

"Elizabeth, you should come to the frat party tonight," said one of the black male students whom I had befriended along with students who were Jewish, Indian, Asian, and Greek. He and other African American men and women were extremely friendly toward me in the dormitory and around campus.

That night at the all-black fraternity party, most people were welcoming and I had fun. But some women who were not my friends glared at me as if I were an intruder. And when they were watching, some of the guys who'd been so friendly around campus were suddenly cool and distant.

A Triple Dose Of Sadness
Aunt Ann was dying from liver cancer—and suffering from a painful, experimental treatment at the University of Michigan Hospital, a five-minute walk from my dormitory. When I visited her, she was in agony. And when she died, we were devastated.

At the same time, my dream of becoming a doctor was dying in Chem 123. I was about to flunk this required pre-med class for the second time!

Compounding my angst: I was breaking up with First Love. After a few months of a long distance relationship, we agreed to go our separate ways.

Living A California Dream

The hot sunshine, the exotic cornucopia of people, and the mesmerizing peace of the ocean captured my heart and soul during my first trip to Southern California.

"I want to live here," I told Louise as we walked along Venice Beach, marveling at a tattooed man with a snake around his neck, street performers and artists, vendors with cool sunglasses and beachwear, buff guys lifting weights at Muscle Beach, and more mixed-race people than I'd ever seen in my life.

Then, as we sat on the sand near waves crashing on the beach, I gazed at the Pacific Ocean for the first time, and was absolutely enchanted.

"I'm so excited to spend three weeks here with you, Louise," I exclaimed.

Louise had moved to Los Angeles after high school graduation to study modern dance at a renowned studio, and she invited me to visit during my summer vacation.

That day on the beach, I met a handsome gentleman who picked me up in his sports car the next day and took me to dinner and an oceanside stroll on a boardwalk. He soon joined our gatherings.

"Now we're really playing Apartment," I told Louise as our friends danced in the living room of her cool apartment in North Hollywood.

"Just like when we were in middle school," she said, clinking her glass against mine for a toast. We laughed, loving that we were grown up, following our dreams, and celebrating our lifelong friendship.

"Happy birthday to you!" Louise sang, presenting a cake decorated with maple candies for my 19th birthday celebration with her sister and friends. "Want to stay for the rest of the summer?"

That was a no-brainer! I called Kelly Services and took secretarial temp jobs at local companies a few days a week to earn money to help pay rent. The rest of the time, we went to the beach and a 24-hour gym to work out and sit in the Jacuzzi.

I wasn't skinny, but I wasn't huge. When Louise and I weren't eating salads, we were indulging in burritos at her favorite Mexican place. We also ate frozen yogurt almost every day.

It was love at first bite when I tasted Middle Eastern food for the first time while we hung out with some Israeli men who lived in an apartment above us. They served us hummus, tabouli, and stuffed grape leaves, and I ascended into food bliss with every new flavor and texture. All the while, they shared stories of living in a commune-style kibbutz and serving in the Israeli Army. They also became aware of how I was obsessed with calories and weight loss.

"She is always battling her weight," one man told his friend as they walked behind me. I assumed that his friend had commented about my derrière.

I loved southern California so much, and felt so natural and free, I vowed to return to live there as soon as possible.

Back On Campus, A Secret Strategy For Staying Slim

I returned to campus for my sophomore year looking like the quintessential California girl—slim, toned, and tan. The sun had bleached my hair super blond, and I was getting a lot of attention from guys, including a handsome graduate student who was super intelligent and fun.

I felt amazing—determined to keep off the 20 pounds I'd lost since the end of freshman year. Thankfully, I'd discovered a new secret to gorging on delicious, fattening foods—without gaining weight.

Even better, my lifelong nausge partner was now on campus! Catherine lived in the co-ed South Quad dormitory; we each had single rooms in all-female hallways separated by a guy's hall—a gauntlet of pizza boxes and hilarious hijinx amongst the football players such as our friend Leroy Hoard, who later played for the Cleveland Browns.

It was really fun when Catherine began her first year at U of M. Of course I introduced her to the steamy, dreamy indulgence of various pizza places, as well as Steve's Ice Cream, Stucchi's frozen yogurt, and other campus delights. I never told her, however, what I did after eating to my heart's content.

I would pop a few pink pills from a box that said Correctol. *What a great name!* Because they sure did correct my ridiculously high caloric consumption.

The next morning, I loved waking up with the urgent need to rid my body of the offending food. The discomfort of cramping was a small price to pay for the wonderful results. I'd dash to the bathroom, and relish the idea that *boom!* it was gone. Those little pink pills had ushered thousands of calories right into the toilet. My hips and butt were spared a sudden growth spurt. My face and fingers would not feel "puffy" from the water retention from all that salt in the pizza. And my stomach would be flat, too!

This feeling was especially intoxicating one sunny September day in 1986, as I walked across campus feeling super thin in a pair of billowy shorts that cinched my waist and exposed a good portion of my legs that I no longer felt ashamed of.

The thrill of winning my battle with the bulge was so great, it negated my rational knowledge that laxative abuse was a form of bulimia, and that it could be very harmful, physically and psychologically.

The Invisible Black Girl Speaks Up

Hot, prickly waves of anger shot up through me as students in my English class continued to make inaccurate and stereotypical comments about black people. Our professor had initiated this discussion amongst the 30 students based on a book we were reading.

But as one student after another spoke, further veering the conversation into offensive territory, I had to say something to set the record straight on behalf of all black people. I looked around.

I was the only student of color in the room—and no one knew it!

My heart hammered in my chest. My mind was a tornado of terror:

They think I'm white...

I could be attacked and raped if people feel "tricked" after learning I'm black...

Sarah Jane's classmates in Imitation of Life ridiculed her when her black mother showed up to class to deliver her lunch, thus "outing" her... and her boyfriend beat her up.

High school guys dropped me like a hot potato because I'm "mulatto."

So what, I have to speak up!

My pulse was pounding... my whole body was trembling.

I raised my hand.

"Yes," the professor said, pointing to me.

"I need to clarify what was said about the black community," I said. "First—"

I spoke, the professor nodded, and it was over. Sweat prickled all over me. My pulse kept racing. But at least I'd found the courage to speak up.

Others were also speaking up. Loudly.

My gaze fell to a copy of *The Michigan Daily.* The full-sized campus newspaper had more headlines about how racist incidents on campus— including an offensive flier posted on the door of a black student's dorm room—were inspiring a rally by students who were also demanding that the university recruit and retain more students of color. Every day, a new edition of *The Daily* had stories about campus racism.

Tension was palpable as I walked amongst throngs of students across The Diag, a vast square of trees, grass, and sidewalks cutting diagonally across a large cement square marking the center of campus. Every hour on the hour, between classes, it was a sea of shoulder-to-shoulder students, walking, talking, stopping to chat, meeting friends on the cement benches, or sitting on the Graduate Library stairs.

"We're having a rally tomorrow at noon," announced a black student leader with a megaphone as other students erected a banner across the top platform of the Graduate Library stairs.

As I walked amidst the stream of students, a guy whose skin color was the same as mine blurted to his friend: "What do the black students want now? They're always protesting about something!"

I headed to class, wondering why people lacked the ability to see that rallies were triggered by problems that needed solutions. My best elixir for sweetening this bitterness was a giant Snickers bar or two. Yes I felt really fat and out of control, but the thrill of the moment as the sweet creamy salty nausge melted in my mouth and gave me a sugar buzz was too intoxicating to resist.

That night, I went to a black fraternity party in the cafeteria of South Quad. The music was pumping, it was packed, and I was excited to see my male friends who were always so happy to see me around campus. Several called often to ask me out.

But right now, some black female students were glaring at me, like I had invaded their turf. One whispered to another, and they cast mean looks at me.

I glanced at the cluster of guys I knew; no recognition or warmth registered on their faces as they made eye brief contact with me. The women were watching how the men would react to me, and that apparently mattered so much, my friends treated me like a stranger.

Suddenly overwhelmed by a sense of rejection, I turned around and walked out of the party. When I reached the elevator, alone, I burst into tears and ran to my room, where I flopped on the bed and sobbed.

Facing Failure, Being Fat, Never Fitting In

The steak knife was too dull to slice through the skin on my wrist. The blade just glided across the blue-veined whiteness, leaving the same harmless trail as a fingernail might.

Standing in my dorm room, I looked up in the mirror at my red-rimmed eyes.

My childhood dream of becoming a doctor was dead. Killed by flunking Chem 123 twice, and bombing Physics and Algebra. Why had I been an A-student in these subjects at my college-prep high school, and a failure in college?

Showing my report card to my parents was simply devastating. My mother was paying tuition and dormitory fees for both me and Catherine, all by herself. We received no scholarships, no financial aid. I remembered that her motivation to become a lawyer had been to make enough money to put us through college after Daddy retired.

Now here I was, flushing thousands of dollars in tuition down the toilet.

I'm a failure! If I can't become a doctor, what will I be? I feel so fat... obsessed with eating... failing yet again at staying slim...

Sobs wracked my body. I felt so alone and misunderstood. Would I ever make peace with food and my body? Would I ever find peace in a racial place of my own? Would I ever feel confident to speak up and out—all the time—about race? Why did God create me as such an enigma?

When would the gloominess within me crack the bubbly blond veneer that I showed to the world? When would I stop feeling profoundly guilty that I had even a moment of angst in the context of my extremely blessed life that included a loving family, excellent health, intelligence, a unique appearance, and the opportunity to attend the University of Michigan?

When would I stop fearing that scary men were lurking at every turn, while I was walking on campus alone at night, or getting up in the middle of the night to go to the communal bathroom where a rapist could be hiding in the showers?

When would I stop stuffing myself so full of pizza, that all I could do was lay there and wait for it to digest down, like a snake that swallowed a rat. As soon as some space opened up in my stomach, I filled it with ice cream. Then I'd spend the rest of the evening eating chocolate and cookies, downed with coffee, while studying and writing papers.

I would feel horrible, my senses deluged with sugar and caffeine, guilt assaulting my mind, and dread creeping through me at the thought of waking up feeling really fat, bloated, and angry at myself. (Thankfully, when I almost fainted in the bathroom and cried out to God for help, I stopped abusing laxatives. I also thank God to this day that He never enabled me to make myself throw up after a binge. That would have been a fast track to a really bad place).

When would I stop spending hours running endless laps around the track in the Central Campus Recreation Building (CCRB), to burn off all those calories before they stuck to my legs, hips, and behind?

These questions overwhelmed me with hopelessness. I tried to pray, but felt really stupid that maybe God thought I was being melodramatic and ungrateful. That consumed me with more guilt that I was—for some inexplicable reason—sabotaging myself from feeling, looking, and being my best.

Sobbing uncontrollably, I called my mother. My angst gushed out in sentences punctuated by slobbery sniffles and cries.

"If you hurt yourself," she said, "they'll have to put me in the ground with you."

That was the most sobering sentence I'd ever heard. I called the campus counseling center. The receptionist said: "We don't have any openings until—"

"By then it will be too late," I told her.

She scheduled an appointment immediately.

Meeting My New Love: Journalism

I changed my major to English Literature, and began earning A's on papers and exams. I even got an A+ on the 10-page paper I wrote about *The Color Purple* by Alice Walker.

I loved my English classes, and especially enjoyed those focusing on literature by women and people of color. I even had an entire class on Richard Wright. The few authors who wrote about biracial characters cast them as the "tragic mulatto" stereotype: too white to be black, too black to be white, and relegated to a life of rejection, confusion, and tragedy.

Was I a tragic mulatto? On one hand, it seemed that I was. But deep down, I knew that God had a good reason for making me this way, and for giving me this life experience. When would I figure it out? What would I do with it?

Even though I loved reading and writing in English classes, I felt sick to my stomach every time I saw the female students whom I had befriended in pre-med classes. They were passing the required courses that I had flunked. My insides roiled with anger, resentment, and disbelief at my academic failure.

One day, I was lamenting the downfall of my doctor dreams to my friend Sam, who was excelling in pre-med classes. He asked:

"Elizabeth, have you ever considered writing for *The Daily?*"

I had not, but I regularly read the student-run newspaper that was provided at no cost in bins all over campus. Students and professors routinely picked up a copy and carried it to class, and the papers were a common sight on classroom desks and cafeteria tables.

One day shortly after Sam's question, I walked to the Student

Publications Building, loving its gothic architecture. Inside, I ascended the dark, worn stairwell, noticing the distinct scent of dusty books, ink, and students who had eaten garlicky pizza. Upstairs was a landing with pop machines. To the right were the Art room and the Editorial Board room. To the left were open double glass-paned doors leading to a cavernous newsroom.

Straight ahead between two long, wooden counters was a desk, behind which stood the editor as machines hummed and noisily printed old-school, dot-matrix style "wire" stories from the Associated Press, United Press International, and Reuters. Behind the editor's desk and the machines, a wall of stained glass windows peaked at the vaulted ceiling, flooding the huge room with natural light.

On one side of the newsroom, behind a long wooden counter, students worked the phones at desks in the advertising department. On the other side, behind the other long wooden counter, sat a row of Macintosh computers on a desk where editors and reporters huddled in lively dialogue about stories.

The feeling in the newsroom was electrifying!

"How can I apply to write for *The Daily*?" I asked the woman standing at the editor's desk.

"I'm the dayside editor," she said. "I can help you."

We chatted, and she assigned me to write a story about a shortage of campus housing. She gave me the number of a University official to call for statistics and comments about the problem. The topic sounded really boring, but I did the reporting, wrote the article, and was thrilled to see "By Elizabeth Atkins" published above the article in *The Michigan Daily*.

The day it was published, I was walking to class in a crowded hallway when a female student said to her friend: "And I read in *The Daily* this morning that the student housing shortage is a huge problem on campus. The article said—"

She was talking about my story! I wrote something to highlight a problem, and now someone was talking about it!

In that moment, I became absolutely enamored with journalism. I realized that it was the ticket to making a positive impact on the world by using my writing skills. So I continued to write for *The Daily* as a reporter. Once, an editor assigned a local story relating to a situation in Russia. I was totally unfamiliar with it.

"You have to stay informed about current events," she admonished. "You can't write for a newspaper and be unaware of what's happening in the world. That's part of your job. If we have breaking news, you don't have time to go research information that you should already know."

She didn't have to tell me twice. I committed to reading the local and national newspapers and news magazines.

Awakening To Women's Power and Lack Thereof

After I demonstrated an ability to report and write stories on time, I was promoted to cover a beat: Women's Issues. I loved this, as it corresponded with my Women's Studies classes that sometimes overlapped with English courses.

Learning about the unjust and often brutal treatment of women throughout history around the world infuriated me. I was especially disturbed that at one time, women were not allowed to read and write. Those who were bold enough to do so in Europe were called "scribblers." They often published under masculine pseudonyms—such as George Eliot—because male authors were celebrated, but female authors were not.

These courses provided a historical backdrop for covering some of the modern issues affecting women, such as equality and personal safety. One of my sources for commentary on stories was Julie Steiner, the first director of U of M's Sexual Assault Prevention and Awareness

Center, which opened in February of 1986. Its mission to create a campus environment where women felt safe resonated with me, as a new report was always coming out about a rapist on the loose in Ann Arbor, and I was very careful about taking a shuttle back to my dorm at night as opposed to walking alone.

Writing about Women's Issues for the paper felt like a valuable contribution to the campus community. And taking Women's Studies classes was awakening me to social and political dynamics that often infuriated me. "The personal is political," was a phrase used by feminists in the 1960s to talk about how everyday interactions with people are microcosms of the greater political realm in which women had very little power. When I viewed life through this lens, I was furious!

I awakened to how it played out in nuances and blatant ways between men and women. For example, I revered one of my professors for his wit, knowledge, and presentations about old English authors. Except, one day after class, as I stood with him and male students engaging in a spirited discussion, our professor only made eye contact with the male students as he talked! This continued for many minutes. As if I were invisible!

So I spoke up, and made them all look at me.

"The personal is political," I thought when shaving my legs, putting on makeup, and realizing that I sat with my legs crossed to be "ladylike" which really means—according to a theory in one class—to take up less space. As I learned about the feminist movement, and viewed marriage as a construct designating women to play a certain role, I vowed to stay independent.

"I never want to get married," I wrote in my journal.

All the while, my mother was my greatest role model as a powerful woman. She had courageously pioneered her own way, defying the Bishop as a 19-year-old woman who wanted to marry the man she loved. She struggled and sacrificed to attend law school while working full time. Then her hard work and integrity fueled her ascent up the ladder of her legal career. She was active with the Wolverine Bar Association, and co-chaired the annual Barrister's Ball, the organization's glittering gala. My mother always looked stunning in sparkling gowns, and I was so proud to serve as a teen volunteer who helped take tickets at this huge extravaganza attended by the mayor, the governor, and other dignitaries amongst 3,000 lawyers and judges.

Learning "A People's History"

The enslavement, lynching, and oppression of black people... the slaughter of millions of Native Americans... and the stereotypes and inequalities that persisted into modern times...

All of this came crashing down on me as I took many ethnic studies classes, most of which were through the Center for Afro-American and African Studies. One course was all about South Africa, and how apartheid had started and was now inspiring the ubiquitous "End Apartheid" signs around campus, as well as protests and calls for sanctions against corporations doing business with South Africa, whose government system run by whites oppressed blacks and imprisoned Nelson Mandela.

Another class explored the roots of racist messaging and symbolism that remain pervasive today, including Aunt Jemima on pancake mix, blackface, and images of black children eating watermelon.

One course required reading *A People's History of the United States* by Howard Zinn. It chronicled how the European take-over of America resulted in the slaughter of millions of Native Americans, later implemented slavery, and imposed domestic terrorism by lynching blacks thereafter, while confining Native Americans to deplorable conditions on reservations.

While the content was extremely disturbing, it bothered me that this was not taught in public school. I learned it in elective classes in college. Just over a third of Americans have a college degree, and of those, the majority probably did not take ethnic studies or women's studies classes.

So the truth about American history remains buried under the feel-good stories about the Pilgrims sharing Thanksgiving dinner with the "Indians"—people wrongly labeled because Christopher Columbus at first thought he had landed in India.

The angst that gnawed at my soul as I learned all this made me want to do something for positive change. How could I work to promote justice, equality, and peace among people of every race and gender?

Campus Current Events Make National News

Bigoted jokes on the campus radio station... racist fliers... complaints about the racial climate from faculty... and other incidents inspired rallies and protests on campus.

Students staged a sit-in of the administration building, demanding that the University work aggressively to raise the percentage of black students from 4.7% to the 10% that school leadership had promised in 1970 during protests inspired by the death of Dr. Martin Luther King, Jr. The goal established by the Black Action Movement went unattained, provoking BAM II protests in 1975 and BAM III demonstrations in 1987.

This time, Reverend Jesse Jackson, Jr., came to campus and led a march down the major campus thoroughfare of State Street. This, and the racial unrest on campus, made the national news.

I experienced the racial tension and demand for change from a unique vantage point. First, as a white-looking person of color. Second, as a journalist, because one of the ethical rules of journalism is objectivity. Reporters and editors *cover* the news and are prohibited from participating in it. That is an inherent conflict of interest and makes objectivity impossible.

So in a sense, I was hiding behind the headlines, hunkering down in the Student Publications Building and helping to bring the news to the campus, but I was not participating in it directly. All the while, racial tension on campus only exacerbated my sense of aloneness.

Finally Finding My Place In A Multiracial Space

In the midst of this, I read an editorial in *The Daily* written by Karen Downing, a biracial librarian who was apparently caught in the same battle zone between black and white. She was announcing a meeting for mixed-race students to come together and talk about it.

When I walked into that room in the Michigan Union to see dozens of male and female students whose complexions ranged from white chocolate to butterscotch to chocolate brown, and whose hair showcased the whole straight-curly-wavy-kinky hair range, my heart raced with excitement.

"I always feel so alone and misunderstood," one young lady said after Karen had introduced herself and explained the importance of calling this meeting. "I feel like I'm too white to be black and too black to be white and either nobody wants me or they keep me at arm's length because they don't trust whose side I'm on."

Tears welled in my eyes. She was expressing exactly how I felt. As we went around the room introducing ourselves and explaining why we were there, goosebumps danced over my skin. Male and female students were echoing my experience, and mirroring my appearance. This was the first time that I had ever heard other mixed race people express this.

Now suddenly I felt that this unprecedented kinship was awakening something inside me.

"My name is Elizabeth Atkins and I can't believe how much better I feel after just a few minutes of seeing all of you and hearing you talk," I said. "I feel like you're telling my story, but I've been on campus all this time and had no idea anyone else was going through the same thing."

In that moment I realized that the simple act of coming together and talking about this was tremendously therapeutic and healing. Courage surged within me to talk about something that had been so taboo and difficult.

"I'm a writer at *The Daily*, and I've really been hiding behind the headlines as all the protests with black students have been happening," I said.

Then it clicked. I had the power to write about things and influence how people were thinking and behaving. But would I have the confidence to write about this?

Fortunately, the race consciousness on campus roused by rallies, protests, and sit-ins were inspiring the leadership at *The Daily* to diversify the staff and the topics we covered. Our editor who oversaw coverage of the protests was an Asian male student; I was the only "black" staffer, and most people walking into the newsroom assumed I was white.

Once, when my parents visited campus and I gave them a tour of *The Daily*, a staffer asked a few days later, "Is your mom black?"

"Yes," I said.

Becoming A Newspaper Editor

It was 8:00 a.m., and I was standing behind the desk of the newsroom as sunshine streamed in, phones rang, the newswire machines hummed, and student reporters hurried in for assignments.

"David, make sure you get good quotes when you cover the meeting today," I told a young reporter. "And remember to bring back a copy of the report they're publishing today."

"Okay," he said enthusiastically.

It was Monday, and I had no classes; I'd arranged my schedule this way when elected as one of five dayside editors who ran the entire paper for a full day every week. It was nonstop action, and I loved it! It was exhilarating to know the latest news about everything, and having the privilege of packaging it and delivering it to help and inform the campus community.

In addition, every week I worked two "nightside" shifts from 4:00 p.m. until midnight.

To end my dayside or to start nightside, I attended our daily story conference at 4:00 p.m. in a small room off the newsroom. The dayside Editor shared what stories had been covered, and we discussed what would be the lead, as well as where every other story would be laid out on the front page and interior pages. After the meeting, the nightside staff edited the stories, and sent them down to "Lou," the older man in the production room on the first floor. He wielded a boxcutter-type-knife as he stood in front of the pages on easel-like display boards. He spent hours pasting every headline, byline, article, and photograph onto the true-to-life-sized templates for the next day's paper.

Though Lou was a very kind man, he could be rather gruff if we didn't get things right. Nobody wanted to run down the back staircase to report a problem to Lou, and this further motivated the spirit of excellence, passion, and commitment that distinguished *Daily* staffers.

For dinner during nightside, we had food delivered; this introduced me to my favorite college meal: "a chipati" from Pizza House. A chipati is a round, whole-wheat loaf, maybe seven inches in diameter and one inch high, sliced open and filled with salad, and accompanied by spicy-creamy dressing. I always ordered a chipati during nightside, and introduced Catherine to the sheer delight of eating the chewy bread that becomes saturated by the dressing. (I still know the Pizza House phone number by heart). Some of my fellow *Daily* staffers ordered pizza during nightside, and the scent of garlic often wafted through the newsroom.

The long hours and intense concentration of editing stories on deadline was a huge time and energy commitment that I believed was laying a foundation for a great career in journalism after graduation.

So it was with great concern that I attended our many meetings about diversifying the staff. Reporters and editors engaged in passionate debates about how to recruit and retain students of color. I wholeheartedly supported this endeavor led by Editor-in-Chief Rebecca Blumenstein, who is now Deputy Managing Editor of *The New York Times*. Students of color were soon joining *The Daily* to write stories, and it was delightful to witness the paper's progress.

Catherine, The Boss

Catherine's excellent work ethic and leadership skills at her part-time job in the Michigan Union food court soon earned her the title of manager. She oversaw employees and the operation of the ice cream counter, a salad bar place with coffee and muffins, a pizza spot, and a burger joint.

The surrounding wooden tables and booths were a popular place for students to eat, socialize, and study. It was a five-minute walk from *The Daily*, so every Monday after dayside, I went to see Catherine. I usually hadn't eaten all day amidst the hustle-bustle of the newsroom.

So, Catherine made me the most delicious salads, heaped with spinach, sprouts, cheese, broccoli, and sunflower seeds, all drenched with ranch dressing. She also gave me a giant banana nut muffin. Those were great dinners!

At the time, we shared an apartment on Church Street. Sometimes Daddy made spaghetti, drove to Ann Arbor, and delivered it—still warm! And we were so grateful, during spring break, to take a family vacation to Disney World with our parents. Taking fun photos while trying on hats from around the world at Epcot Center was an especially memorable time.

Two Sisters Taking A "Living Authors" Class

Now that we were both English majors, Catherine and I often had classes together. My hours at *The Daily* made it impossible to read the stacks of books required for our classes, so Catherine read the books, then told me about them so I could participate in class. This was especially hilarious in English 434: Living Writers with Professor Nicholas Delbanco. Every week, we read a book, then the author visited our class to speak and answer questions.

On more than one occasion, thanks to Catherine's verbal summaries, I asked poignant questions of the authors that made it sound like I had read the books. One day, novelist Francine Prose visited our class and talked about life as a writer:

"The only reason to bother is because you'd rather do that than anything else," she said. "It's like a religious thing."

When she took questions, I raised my hand and said, "My biggest fear about becoming a writer is how I would support myself. And about time."

"No matter what," she replied, "there will always be things that you'll feel like you should be doing—like taking care of kids or whatever. But if you really want to write, write."

That night, I recorded her words in my journal, along with my own: *"And that's what I do every day. I love to write. Or else I wouldn't do it. And it's SO therapeutic. Monday when I felt so bad, I felt tranquil after writing in the computer center. It was encouraging to hear her say that."*

Another day, author Tim O'Brien spoke about how imagination and reality weave the fabric of life. How daydreams are based on reality. How often we daydream. And I had been doing just that during the lecture about his book inspired by his traumatic memories of serving in the Vietnam War.

Catherine and I later attended his reading at Rackham Auditorium, which was excellent. Then Catherine made a poignant observation about the difference between being the reader and the writer of disturbing content: "It was moving and great material for an author to draw on. We can say that and leave Rackham and forget about the descriptions of war's gore. But Tim O'Brien has to live with those thoughts constantly. He has no escape."

Another memorable moment as an English Major was hearing Maya Angelou speak at Hill Auditorium.

"Okay, we have the next 12 hours to write 10 pages," I told Catherine at 8 p.m. as we hurried into the campus computer center in Angell Hall. The giant room contained row upon row of long tables equipped with Apple desktop computers (the first rendition, as this was the mid- to late-1980s, when we had never seen a laptop, nor was it customary for most students to own a computer). Here we learned how to use computers for the first time, and we wrote our many English papers, stored them on square plastic disks, and printed them onsite.

We chose two side-by-side computers, plunked down our book bags, cups of steaming coffee, and stashes of chocolate, then got to work. The pressure of pulling an all-nighter to compose a paper that was due in the morning gave us an adrenaline rush. Sometimes by 3:00 a.m. we were so wired on caffeine and sugar that we got "the giddies." We just couldn't stop giggling for comic relief while working under the fluorescent lights amidst throngs of other students in the vibrant scene of humming printers, chatter about assignments, and expressions of fatigue and anxiety from our bleary-eyed peers.

"Done!" we exclaimed at the crack of dawn, printing our papers just in time for class. With relief surging through us, we dashed across campus to turn in our assignments, vowing to get an earlier start next time, but knowing we'd be spending many more high-pressure nights together, giggling as two sisters writing English papers at the University of Michigan.

The Meaning Of Life Is Love

Research and writing are in our DNA, as Daddy and his sister, Aunt Mary, had traced our family tree back to Rouen, France, identifying the earliest relative as a man born in 1340. At some point, our ancestors named LaLonde migrated to Québec, Canada to work as furriers, then came to Michigan as loggers, and dispersed to other parts of America, including Rhode Island.

One branch of the family tree produced Ephraim Danes, who served on General George Washington's security detail during the American Revolution in 1776. This lineage earned Daddy and Aunt Mary membership into the Sons of the American Revolution and the Daughters of the American Revolution. (Catherine and I are qualified to join).

Daddy proudly served as a state Chaplain for the Michigan chapter, which required him to attend meetings that included a regional conference in Chicago. It was on a weekend, and I rode with him in his little blue Ford truck, reading *Portrait of a Lady* by Henry James for one of my English classes.

On this particular day, I was consumed with angst over a common theme in the novels and classroom discussions: the meaning of life.

"Daddy, what is the meaning of life?" I asked as he drove on the Dan Ryan Expressway leaving Chicago for the four-hour ride home.

"Love," he said immediately. "Enjoying the love you give to people, and enjoying the love you receive back from them."

Journalism Bliss In New York City!

Visiting New York City for the first time and seeing TV news superstars at the National Association of Black Journalists convention was one of the most exciting times of my life.

It was the summer of 1989, and I was an intern at *The Lansing State Journal*, then owned by Gannett in Michigan's capitol. My byline appeared above the news stories that I wrote and were published in the daily newspaper, and it was thrilling.

As was attending NABJ. This highly respected organization's annual convention provided networking, informative workshops, awesome speakers, and an outstanding job fair featuring recruiters for newspapers, magazines, radio stations, and TV stations across America.

My mother's friend, a lawyer named Leslie Graves, had suggested that I join, and I loved it so much, I helped fellow student journalist Sheala Durant, to co-found the U of M NABJ student chapter, thanks to the support of John Matlock, PhD, Vice Provost-Academic Affairs and Executive Director of Multiracial Initiatives.

So it was exciting to attend my first NABJ convention at the New York Hilton on Avenue of the Americas. I must have spent a half hour in a phone booth near the lobby, telling my mother back home about all the famous journalists I'd seen and met.

The National Association of Black Journalists convention drew the who's who of the industry. In addition, the host chapter laid out an impressive array of receptions, tours, and entertainment. This included a private reception at the MET and a private A Train ride to the Apollo Theatre in Harlem for the annual awards ceremony.

Making the experience even more fun was that Catherine checked into the New York Hilton after a visit with a friend didn't work out. I made many friends, including TaRessa Stovall, then communications director at Spelman College.

At the jobs fair, I saw the baby blue table cover for Columbia University's Graduate School of Journalism, and I stopped to chat with a very upbeat, Caucasian man with short brown hair and cheerful eyes. His name was George Philip Sheer. He gave me a blue pencil with the school's name imprinted in gold, and described the nine-month program.

He, like many people at the NABJ convention, cast a puzzled look and asked what had brought me to this event. I told him about myself, and we clicked. He encouraged me to apply to Columbia. The idea of living in New York as a student while studying journalism sounded like a dream!

Next, I saw Angelo Henderson, a *Detroit News* reporter who would later win the Pulitzer Prize for *The Wall Street Journal*. He introduced me to Managing Editor Mark Hass at the *News'* table in the jobs fair. I asked about summer internships, and Mark said I was already on track to qualify.

In journalism, hands-on experience in a real newspaper counts for everything. That summer, my *Lansing State Journal* internship was enabling me to amass quality "clips" to impress those who selected interns. It was a plus that Gannett owned that paper as well as *The News*.

I also met an editor from *The San Diego Tribune*, George Dissinger, and he told me about their internship program. Moving back to Southern California sounded thrilling, so I put a star on his business card with the goal of sending him my clips. I also chatted extensively with the recruiter for the graduate journalism program at the University of California at Berkeley.

Meanwhile, I met so many people! Several worked at *The New York Times,* including: Features Editor Angela Dodson; Reporter Tom Morgan who would later become NABJ President; Senior Editor Paul Delaney; and Metro Editor Gerald Boyd, who would become Managing Editor.

Everyone was friendly and kind—except a group of young women who surrounded me in the hotel lobby, demanding to know: "Why are you here?"

Their ensuing comments suggested that I was a white person crashing a black conference, to abscond with the good summer internships at the job fair, or network for jobs that they wanted. People who question me like that would be equally furious if they discovered I were "passing for white." Whether I owed them an explanation or not, I explained that I am biracial and that I had co-founded the student chapter at the University of Michigan.

I would soon experience a similar sting at the Howard University Communications Conference in Washington, D.C. Again thanks to Dr. Matlock, Sheala Durant and I obtained funding for several U of M students to attend the job fair and workshops. I was excited, and prepared copies of my articles and my resume to distribute at the job fair. Just like at NABJ, I made my way from booth to booth, talking with representatives from different media outlets. When I sat facing a woman at one particular booth, eager to show her my articles, she quipped:

"This program is for minorities only."

Stunned, I walked away, confident that despite being misunderstood by some, I was embarking on a career to encourage racial harmony.

Senior Year Journal Entries: Food, Fat, Fear, & Family

If only I could foster harmony within myself. My journal entries during my final semester in college provided a snapshot of my inner chaos. On September 14, 1989, I wrote:

I'm going off. Constantly thinking about whether I'm fat or thin or disgusting or OK or happy or sad or ugly or pretty or fun or a bitch or black or white or considerate or selfish or smart or dumb or sophisticated or mature or stable or insane or evil or nice or stressful or at peace or hungry or preoccupied or what. I'm confused.

The thing is, nothing in life is cut and dry, black and white.

Especially people. Especially me.

A few days later, I wrote that I was taking antibiotics for a kidney infection, and: "Diuretics abuse since middle school probably fu##ed me up. When will I learn to eat right?" The next day brought good news about a freelance writing job:

I'm having a happy day! I got the job at The Ann Arbor News! Studied in Union, to class, back for dinner—great salad and broccoli. I've had 1400-1500 calories today, have walked a lot, and feel sane. I cut out a quote by (CBS News Anchor) Dan Rather: "I do get scared. I know that fear can freeze you. I conquer my fears by keeping a laser-beam focus on what I want to accomplish." The things I want to accomplish are: 1) Happiness; 2) Health; 3) Lose weight/have a sane relationship with food and my body; 4) A successful career: a) LSAT & GRE in December; b) Acceptance to Columbia; 5) Work in France. Laser beam focus!

On September 19, I wrote: "I'm keeping my laser-beam focus on myself, especially when food thoughts enter my head." And the next day: "I feel so good. My brain and senses are sharp. I don't want to lose this. I feel like I can do anything. Thank you God." But days later, on September 20, after eating chipatis with Catherine, I wrote:

...somehow my "Eat Everything" Button got pushed. We talked about going to Meijer's or Stucchi's frozen yogurt and my brain cells spun in circles: "What can I have that's not too fattening?" Fear. Anxiety. Thinking how I'd feel tomorrow. Thank you God I didn't do it. Thank you. Went to bed and the tension and insanity and fear slowly drained from me so I went for CCRB walk. Cap called; The San Diego Tribune called, so I called George Dissinger and left a message. Shower. My themes for today's thinking: "Why do I want to go to law school? And am I rejecting the white part of me?" Every day I have a theme. Yesterday was "going to France, never settling down, being a savvy Parisienne." Now I need to study. Thank you God for life, love, opportunities, health, and happiness. Please don't let me sink into the slimy abyss of depression. It only takes a few minutes and it's really scary. Amen.

On October 3, I wrote: "God please help me get accepted to Columbia. Amen. I want it so bad." The next day, I applied to the Columbia University Graduate School of Journalism. I attached recommendation letters from: Jennifer Carroll, my former editor at *The Lansing State Journal* who would become a Gannett executive; Norman Sinclair, an award-winning reporter at *The Detroit News* who became a mentor thanks to a family friend; and one of my English professors, Dr. Robert Chrisman, founder of *The Black Scholar* magazine.

I spent the following weekend with my parents. In 1987, they had moved into a three-bedroom townhouse near downtown Detroit. I journaled: "PMS-induced anxiety, crying at home while Cap hugged me. It felt so good in her arms, because she's the mother and I'm the daughter and everything's OK. I stuffed my face all weekend, so I walked two hours tonight at the CCRB. Always thinking about my future, as usual. Today I decided not to go to law school. I really want to go to Europe."

One morning the following week, I was awakened in my dorm room at 5:40 a.m. by an obscene phone call from a man. I had to go to the bathroom, but was too scared to leave my room until I heard other women in the hallway an hour later. I journaled, "I called Daddy this morning; he made me feel better. I want to be happy."

I enjoyed the following weekend, October 14th and 15th with my parents at our cottage in Big Woods. I chronicled the time in my journal:

I love my life, my family, the woods, men, friends, my hair. I'm very happy. The weekend at the woods in our beautiful cabin was great—just me and the parents and the trees. On the way up, Cap and I talked about everything, especially men. I described my virgin/whore scale philosophy (about how women are unfairly judged) and my total strong woman attitude toward men. She thinks it's great. Then at the woods, we walked to the beaver ponds and both parents took their guns. They taught me how to use them.

"Pretend it's the obscene caller," Daddy said as I aimed his rifle at a big stump. I blew a big chunk off—got the bastard!

Then I read, slept in Daddy's flannel shirt that smells like him, while Cap and Daddy shot at targets and listened to the game. Then we went to Forwards (restaurant). It was fun.

Back to cabin—the moonlight is so beautiful. Slept great.

This morning Daddy made biscuits, then I read and slept and they gathered wood. I got up and went outside awhile, then all of a sudden it got really dark, in minutes. It didn't seem real. It blew over. Then they shot. I read. Later to Forwards again, then Cap and I left and Daddy went back to the woods. It was like there was love and joy in the air—we'd just smile or Cap and Daddy would hug. It was cute.

Graduation & Beyond

Wearing a black cap and gown on graduation day, I stood in a sea of students feeling very alone. I was grateful that Catherine and my parents were in the audience inside Crisler Arena for the commencement ceremony. And I was proud that I was receiving my bachelor of arts degree in English Literature from the University of Michigan on that snowy day in December of 1989.

I was graduating a semester late, due to changing my major and taking a reduced class load to work at *The Daily*. That was my tribe, as were members of the multiracial group, whose affirming monthly meetings I had attended since its inception. Throughout my four and a half years on campus, I had invested my time in either studying or working at *The Daily*, not cultivating a social network.

So now, as other graduates clustered with great excitement amidst their tribes—fellow sports team members, fraternity brothers, sorority sisters, etcetera—I thought: *I'm a lone wolf.* When I saw a biracial woman whom I knew casually and who also appeared to be sadly solo in this sea of festivity, we sat together.

It was a thrill to walk across the stage and receive my diploma. A wonderful family celebration dinner followed at The Gandy Dancer, a nice restaurant inside the historic train station.

After that, I moved home with our parents. Daddy, who was 68, and had retired, was diagnosed with kidney failure, and was on a waiting list for a donor. Doctors would not consider me or Catherine, ages 22 and 21, as donors, because we were so young.

He opted for a type of dialysis that is administered at home: peritoneal dialysis. It required suspending clear IV-type bags of fluid that entered the body through a port, detoxified the blood, and drained out for disposal. While this afforded our father the opportunity to avoid spending hours in a dialysis center several days each week, it also resulted in frequent infections.

Once, when he was not feeling well, I took him to a doctor's appointment at Henry Ford Hospital. He was weak and winded, forced to sit on a ledge near the hospital entrance to rest, looking pale and sad. Then I helped him inside, praying, *God please make Daddy feel better and get a donor kidney...*

Praying Away The Taste For Pastries

It was Fat Tuesday, and the trademark "poonchki" pastries were everywhere.

"I don't want any!" I declared to my co-workers at my temporary office job at Blue Cross Blue Shield of Michigan.

At the time, I was having such a tough struggle with food and fat that I began attending meetings for a 12-step program for food addiction. It was deeply spiritual, which inspired constant prayer. That blessed me with the ability to abstain from sugar and binge eating.

But the world was always tempting me—especially on Paczki Day when people ate giant pastries stuffed with custard or jelly as their pre-Lent indulgence before giving up sweets until Easter. Bakeries in the Polish enclave of Hamtramck produce masses of them, and people line up before dawn to buy boxes of Paczkis, taking them to schools, homes, and offices.

This included the office where I was working. Since I had no car, Daddy drove me to work and picked me up every day. It was fun to hear his observations about people as they entered and left the office building; he was deeply intuitive and would tell me stories about each person's life and feelings.

Well, on Paczki Day, the sweet scent wafted over desks and through cubicles as my coworkers downed these massive calorie bombs. And every time I went to the restroom or the copy machine, someone put a pastry on my desk! Annoyance prickled through me as I moved it each time. I was grateful for the ability to pray away the desire to indulge.

Paris Is Calling

Confident that our father would get better, I dreamed of spending a few months in Paris, working a temporary office job while practicing the language, enjoying the City of Lights, and immersing in French culture.

So while sitting at my desk in Detroit, I was fantasizing about sipping coffee and writing French poetry at Parisian cafés. I wanted to flirt with handsome, intelligent, European men. I wanted to feel worldly. I wanted to satisfy a voracious hunger for living and learning and writing about everything.

Paris, graduate school in New York or California, or a summer internship at a newspaper in another city—could all satisfy this yearning. So this period at my parents' house was all about applying and praying for good news about one or all of the above.

My contact at Kelly Services in Detroit helped me write to her Parisian counterpart, requesting a job assignment, as I'd done in Los Angeles. Now I couldn't wait to get home and check the mail, eagerly awaiting an approval letter from Kelly Services in Paris. Finally, a letter came. Due to high unemployment in France, they could not offer me a job.

I was so disappointed! Working an office job during the dreary Detroit winter seemed the antithesis of my Parisian dream.

Murder Taints California Adventure

I was overwhelmed with joy and excitement to return to Southern California for a five-month internship at *The San Diego Tribune*, starting in April of 1990.

A newspaper employee invited me to rent a room with a private bathroom in their apartment in a picturesque complex bursting with pink and orange hibiscus flowers and lush foliage around two swimming pools. It was so close to the newspaper in Mission Valley that we could walk to work, passing through an outdoor shopping mall filled with flowers, fountains, and colorful tiles. It was paradise!

But fear followed me there. Days after my arrival, an 18-year-old Okemos woman was killed in a nearby apartment complex! On spring break visiting her brother, she was the third young woman stabbed to death since January. Her murder made me vigilant about safety.

At the newspaper, my desk faced the mountains. The California native at the next desk was a veteran reporter who shared stories about boogie boarding in the ocean. Once, she invited me to a Vietnamese restaurant where we ate vegetable soup from giant bowls. I'd never seen anything like it!

Whenever I saw the editor who hired me, I expressed profuse gratitude.

After work, I loved to drive to La Jolla, where I sat on big rocks, journaling, listening to waves crash, and watching the sunset. "Listen to the ocean!" I told my parents through a payphone as waves crashed on jagged rocks. I also explored Coronado Island, downtown San Diego, and oceanside neighborhoods.

I drove all over San Diego County to report stories that were published in the paper several days each week under my byline. After awhile, I was assigned the "beat" of covering eastern suburbs that included Lemon Grove and El Cajon. I worked in a "bureau"—a newspaper satellite office—with a man and a woman.

The murder of the teenager from my hometown haunted me. As did my weight and appetite.

"You're in California," a young male doctor said with a callous tone when I visited a clinic for a minor stomach upset. "People here wear shorts year-round. Lose some weight."

I did eat pretty healthy, and loved jogging on Mission Beach. But I was never thin enough by skinny California girl standards.

A Scary Brush With Fire

One sunny day, while driving to work, I saw a wildfire along the highway. I thought, *Wow! I can be the first reporter on the scene and the editors back at the paper will be impressed!*

So I kept driving on the highway; it had two lanes going one direction, with a wide median of sand and desert shrubs next to two lanes going the opposite direction.

Pretty soon, traffic slowed amidst fire trucks and firefighters. The fuel tanker truck ahead of me crept along. Smoke thickened and darkened the air. To the right, fire blazed up the side of the mountain.

My heart hammered with fear. I focused on the red taillights on the truck ahead, wishing it would move faster. Soon it got darker and darker. Red dots—embers!—rained down on cars around me.

That truck full of gasoline is going to explode and kill us all!

My right leg started shaking so hard that I could barely press the accelerator. The firefighters were directing traffic to continue—further into the black smoke where it was raining fire!

Somehow, I turned around and drove on the shoulder in the opposite direction. The firefighters were yelling at me. But my teeth were chattering with terror. And I drove out of the smoke and into the light. So much for being the first reporter on the scene.

Daddy At Catherine's Graduation

In May, I flew home for Catherine's graduation from the University of Michigan.

As we sat in the stadium seats inside Crisler Arena, proudly watching Catherine receive her diploma for her bachelor of arts degree in English Literature, I glanced over at Daddy. His normally tanned cheeks were chalky; his hazel eyes were weary. He looked deflated inside his beige wool overcoat. Daddy looked sick and weak. And I started crying.

Receiving Good News In The Newsroom

One day while I was at my desk in *The San Diego Tribune* newsroom, my mother called to read a letter that had arrived from Columbia University.

"Dear Ms. Atkins: On behalf of the Admissions Committee, we are pleased to inform you that you have been admitted to the Class of 1991 at Columbia University's Graduate School of Journalism. We welcome you to what we hope will be one of the most engaging, invigorating, and challenging learning experiences of your life."

The letter included information about a security deposit and housing, and concluded by saying, "Congratulations on your achievement. We look forward to seeing you next Fall." It was signed by Judith Serrin, Director of Admissions, and George Philip Sheer, the Admissions Officer whom I had met at NABJ in New York.

I was elated!

Things only got better when my mother came to visit the week of my birthday. I had a ball showing her around San Diego, and her childhood friend from Saginaw, Grant McArn, a hospital vice president in Los Angeles, came down and we visited the Wild Animal Park, Sea World, Tijuana, Mexico, and other attractions. We had so much fun!

On the weekends, I frequently took an Amtrak train up to Los Angeles to stay with Grant, who showed me all around Beverly Hills, Rodeo Drive, West Hollywood, Venice Beach, and Marina Del Rey, where we ate at The Cheesecake Factory. Other weekends, I enjoyed fun stays with Louise.

Even more good news, the NABJ convention was held in Los Angeles at the Century Plaza Hotel in Studio City. It attracted the top people in journalism and celebrities. I was thrilled to attend as a working journalist, and to meet people whom I'm proud to call friends today.

"Keep A Stiff Upper Lip"

The weekend before I was supposed to leave Detroit for New York, Daddy had a stroke. We visited him daily at Henry Ford Hospital, and constantly told him, "I love you."

"Do you still want me to go to New York?" I asked.

"Yes," he said immediately. "Get your education."

I started to cry.

"Keep a stiff upper lip," he said.

I interpreted that to mean carry on, keep your composure, and focus on achievement. So a few days later, I made an early-morning stop at the Intensive Care Unit to say a tearful goodbye to him, then flew to New York.

I lived in a small, single room in International House, a dormitory housing 700 students, scholars, and researchers from more than 100 countries. A cacophony of languages filled the elevator, hallways, and dining room. Located on Riverside Drive at 123rd Street, my room overlooked General Ulysses Grant's Tomb in Riverside Park, the Hudson River, and New Jersey. My daily walks to and from campus took me past Union Theological Seminary and Riverside Church.

I was so excited—and somewhat scared—to live in New York City.

"Always keep at least $20 on you in case you get mugged," the director of campus security said at orientation in The World Room of the Journalism School at 116th and Broadway on Columbia's campus in

Morningside Heights, between the Upper West Side and West Harlem.

"A person on crack could get enraged and make things worse if you don't have any money." I had heard so many stories about people getting robbed or worse in New York; my imagination went wild with scenarios every time I stepped onto the sidewalks or the subway platform. That was a daily occurrence, as our classes required covering stories all over Manhattan, including Harlem, as well as the Bronx, Queens, Brooklyn, and Staten Island. That meant walking, taking the bus, and riding the subway.

That was so much fun with my classmates, as our classroom assignments enabled us to cover stories that included Security Council Meetings at the United Nations during the Persian Gulf War!

As an international reporting major, I was 23 years old, standing beside reporters from the BBC and CNN, reporting on UN Secretary General Boutros Boutros Gali's updates! It was so exhilarating and exciting to be at this epicenter of world news. I was also learning from my classmates, who had lived and worked all around the world.

Being a student at the world's top-ranked journalism graduate program with New York City as our classroom was amazing. We were watching technology revolutionize journalism before our very eyes.

"Sometime in the near future," said Professor David Klatell, who led our intensive broadcast news workshop, "you'll see one-person news crews all around the world, as you take a tiny, hand-held, 'high 8' video camera and report from anywhere on the planet."

Now, of course, we can do that with our cell phones. But this was 1990 and 1991. When the Persian Gulf War started, we witnessed an epic TV news moment as CNN correspondent Wolf Blitzer reported live from under a table as a light show of missiles showered on Baghdad.

Back then, our TV news class divided into crews of three students: the talent/reporter, the camera person, and the sound person. We rotated constantly, and I loved working alongside Suzanne Malveaux, who became a CNN correspondent; Jonathan Dienst, now a WNBC investigative reporter and NBC News contributing correspondent; Jeff Rossen, a Today Show investigative journalist; and Keith Brown, senior vice president of programming at HLN at CNN.

All the while, I loved hearing Professor Klatell impart his Boston-native wisdom with his super witty, hilarious, and brilliant expertise and experience as he led our newsroom-style classroom. We each got assignments, then headed into New York's five boroughs, to cover real stories that included press conferences at City Hall with Mayor David Dinkins.

We lugged our large TV camera in a black case, along with another case carrying a large sound machine. We also carried a microphone, cords, and lighting equipment. Imagine trudging up and down busy New York streets—in sunshine, rain, snow, and slush—on and off buses, up and down subway stairs, onto and off of crowded subway cars.

Every week, we edited our stories on video editing machines, then did a live newscast, with the anchor positions rotating to provide each student with that opportunity. It was so exciting!

One of my print classes was taught by a *Wall Street Journal* writer; we met in a conference room at their offices in the World Trade Center. We also took a First Amendment class taught by Professor Floyd Abrams in the Columbia University School of Law. For a hot minute, I contemplated a joint journalism-law degree.

Meanwhile, I kept in touch with the many accomplished and kind people whom I had met at the NABJ convention. Paul Delaney, senior editor at *The New York Times*, facilitated my attainment of employment as a part-time "copy clerk" in the newsroom, then located off Times Square.

At *The Times*, I loved being amongst so many intelligent people at the pinnacle of global journalism. When correspondents returned from the Middle East, they held talks with the staff to share their experiences. Rotating assignments took me to the Book Review department, where I pushed giant bins on wheels overflowing with books. More bins brimming with more new books arrived every day. My job also entailed answering phones and sorting mail. I met so many nice people, and my co-workers even gave me rides home, 80 blocks away.

I loved it there so much, I hoped to one day return as a *New York Times* reporter.

One of the coolest things ever was that the super-thick Sunday edition of *The Times* was placed in big stacks on the outdoor newsstands throughout New York—on Saturday night!

The first time I saw that, I stopped in my tracks. Reading the Sunday paper on Saturday night? Journalism heaven! Now, nearly three decades later, I still treat myself to reading the Sunday *Times* on Saturday night. The digital version still feels like a treat to peek at tomorrow's news today.

Then, as now, my favorite section is *Weddings & Celebrations*. I love reading about how couples met and fell in love, along with all the details of their ceremonies. Even during my most jaded phases about romantic relationships, I've found these stories uplifting and entertaining. This remains one of my favorite activities of the week.

My *New York Times* job paid $10 an hour, which I really needed. I had enough money to eat frugally, as well as pay my phone bill, subway and bus fare, and incidentals. Thankfully, Catherine sent frequent care packages containing soup, trail mix, and other goodies.

International House offered many dinners, dances, and other events that celebrated global cultures. I made a good friend from Kuwait, which I had never heard of until the Persian Gulf War. And I loved hearing people speak multiple languages in the elevator and hallways.

Daddy's Spirit Speaks In a Dream

When the phone rang at 7:30 a.m., I knew something was wrong.

"Daddy died," Catherine said.

"No!" I shouted. I'm certain everyone on the floors above and below me in International House heard me. "No!" I cried, over and over, gripping the phone in my dorm room.

The resident assistant, a very warm woman from Syria, came to comfort me while several women gathered in the hallway.

It was September 13, 1990, and Daddy had died of cardiac arrest. He was scheduled for open heart surgery that day. The night before, my mother, Catherine, Aunt Mary, and others, had enjoyed a beautiful gathering around him where much love was expressed. Our mother eloquently recounts the evening in her memoir.

But my final memory was seeing him in the ICU, his legs in plastic leggings that stimulated circulation, his eyes filled with weariness and sadness, and the red letters on the digital clock on the monitors saying 7:12 a.m. Now 10 days later, I was in New York alone, riding the subway, staring into space. The car was nearly empty as I took the 9 train down to Grand Central Station to board a shuttle bus for LaGuardia.

That night, as I slept in my bedroom in Detroit, I "dreamed" that Daddy was sitting on the edge of my bed in the darkness.

"Eli, everything is going to be okay," he said, stroking my back above the blanket like he did when I was afraid as a little girl.

The next day, a helmet of pain gripped my entire head as I approached the entrance to the funeral parlor in West Branch. The body in the casket looked like Daddy, only waxy. His straight, silver hair sprouted up and out of his prominent, usually suntanned forehead, and I kept stroking it.

The night before the memorial service at Steuernol Funeral Home, I wrote a poem in the hotel room. Somehow, I recited the poem for the standing-room-only crowd that included family members, friends, priests, and even a man who said he had been an altar boy who worked with my father as a priest.

"You Can't Be Scared In New York! You're from Detroit!"

My whole body was trembling with fear as I walked alone down Flatbush Avenue in Brooklyn. It was 7:00 a.m., and I had just taken the subway here, and was following hand-written directions to reach the police precinct for my assignment.

God please get me there safely...

As horns honked and brakes screeched on the busy street to my left, I hated that to my right, metal security gates were still locked over storefronts. No people were around, so I had nowhere to run for help should I need it.

How ironic that my destination was the police station to do a "ride along" with officers and write about whatever happened on their patrol that morning. Finally, I swung open the police precinct door and dashed in.

Thank you God that I'm here safely! My teeth were chattering, and every cell in my body was jumping with anxiety.

"That was such a scary walk," I told the officers behind the front counter.

"Where are you from?" they asked.

"Detroit."

They burst out laughing, and I giggled with comic relief as they playfully teased, "You're from Detroit and you're scared in Brooklyn?"

"Yeah, but in Detroit, we're in cars all the time, with the doors locked," I answered. "Here we're so exposed and vulnerable."

I especially felt that way one day during an assignment that required a subway trip to the Bronx with my classmate, a native New Yorker. He was totally unfazed by the fact that we couldn't find our destination on this desolate block with crumbling, graffiti-covered buildings. My whole body buzzed with fear.

"This way," he said, leading me into the bodega to ask for directions to where we had to interview someone. I didn't feel any safer inside, because the employees were behind thick plexiglass. After we finally reached our destination and conducted the interview, my body hummed with anxiety as we stood on the raised subway platform. I had the feeling that anything could happen, and we had nowhere to run, and nobody would help us.

To distract myself, I talked a mile a minute with him about any- and everything, and my voice was quavery and high-pitched. This also happened while walking at night with classmates on residential streets where no other people were around or no businesses were open. Thankfully, I felt my father was a guardian angel, keeping me safe.

Slipping Into a Spiritual Sanctuary

Sadness overwhelmed me as I left the Columbia campus after a full day of classes.

Daddy is gone... I'm so tired... I have so much work... Cap and Catherine are so sad at home...

As I trudged up Broadway, and took 120th Street over to Claremont Avenue past apartment buildings, toward the back door of International House, my thoughts churned over the huge task of interviewing everyday people and experts across America about the history of race-mixing for my master's thesis.

On top of that, Columbia's extremely challenging program included all-day classes for my focus on broadcast news and international reporting. Plus, I was playing catch-up for assignments I missed while in Michigan for the funeral. My instructors, including Professor Klatell, were extremely compassionate. Professor Mary Ann

Giordano blessed me with the amazing experience of covering the New York City Marathon for Reporting & Writing 1.

Sadly, reflections of my father were everywhere, especially on the face of a man with silver hair at a senior citizens home as I interviewed people for an assignment. His image triggered tears that wouldn't stop, and I had to leave.

Now, as I walked home, consumed with sorrow while passing the open doors of Riverside Church, a voice within me said, "Go in." As I stepped past the reception desk and security station, and up the stairs, serenity washed over me like a warm wave.

Daddy is here... I opened heavy wooden doors to enter the sanctuary. The scent of incense hung in the warm air as I walked up the long aisle past empty pews. I marveled at the stained glass windows, the soaring stone arches, and the spectacular gothic architecture.

Joy and peace overwhelmed me.

Thank you God for leading me into this spiritual sanctuary.

I slipped into a pew and prayed. Then in my mind, I heard my father's voice: "You're going to do just fine in the program. You are very talented, Eli. Just do your work and you will succeed." Even more powerful than the words sounding in my mind, his presence was strong and comforting.

Riverside Church became my oasis. I would slip into the empty cathedral before and after class to pray and feel my father's spirit empowering me to get through the intensive program while mourning his loss in the physical world. How was it possible that I felt closer to his spirit now than when he was in human form?

I Am Triumphant, Not Tragic

The Columbia program required that I compose a Master's Thesis. I chose the history of race-mixing in the United States. I interviewed people across the country—mixed race men and women, scholars, and interracial couples who were advocating that the government add a "multiracial" category to the U.S. Census questionnaire and other documents for education and employment that required people to "check one" race box.

Many of these couples were leading support and social groups for mixed-race individuals and interracial families, such as the Los Angeles-based Association of Multiethnic Americans.

Writing my master's thesis about the history of black-white race mixing in America was therapeutic and inspiring. I learned that some states had laws stating that if you were 1/32 black—from a great, great, great grandparent—you were black. Period.

When my parents married in 1966, interracial marriage was illegal in 16 states until June 12, 1967—just a month before my birthday—when the U.S. Supreme Court struck down those laws in *Loving v. Virginia*. I interviewed mixed-race people—ranging from college age to seniors—about their personal identities. Experts on race and sociology shared their perspectives and research about this topic. Here's an excerpt from my 51-page report:

Growing up in an interracial family has given me a unique perspective and sensitivity to physically, socially, and politically blur racial lines. And I feel it's my place on Earth to use that ability to help create more harmonious race relations...

In a society where race is either a privilege or a problem, embodying both Black and White sets the stage for personal turmoil and societal scorn. Before biracial and multiracial people can use our intrinsic understanding of two or more races to fight racism, we must understand love ourselves. And as more of us are born and speak out, a trend of self-affirmation and pride is boosting our confidence. For many, that means choosing a life of activism.

I also interviewed parents whose interracial unions had produced children like me; they were lobbying the U.S. government to add a "multiracial" category to the U.S. Census questionnaire in 2000. The parents were inspired to push for this change by their children being forced by school bureaucracies to "pick one"—black or white, which made children feel that they were choosing one parent over another.

That conversation always veers into the reality that a brown-skinned person is perceived as black and must deal with certain issues as such. Thus, my thesis explored the many fascinating and far-reaching tentacles of this topic rooted in the horrific history of people "owning" people and raping African women who then birthed mixed-race children who were also considered human property.

As I interviewed people across America and wove their comments and conclusions into my report, I felt that I was looking into a mirror that sometimes felt warped or smudged or cracked or even shattered. Many mixed-race people of older generations were given no space to contemplate race; they were shunned by white relatives and society at large for being part black, and ostracized by their black relatives and community for having lighter skin, blue or green eyes, curly or straight hair, or "talking white." Many of their experiences were, indeed, tragic.

But I saw that we live in a new day, a new age, when it was safer to speak up and out about who we really are. That it was ok to declare that embodying multiple races is a blessing, not a curse. And that because interracial births had quintupled since the civil rights movement of the 1960s, we had power in numbers to change the way we were counted, categorized, and valued in society.

I am not a tragic mulatto, I concluded at my desk in my room in International House. *I'm a triumphant mulatto!* I didn't love that word, which derives from "mule," but I couldn't resist the word play.

Here I am, blessed with the gift of writing, and this unique, dual perspective as both a white person and a black person, with our Native American, Jewish, and Chaldean influences along the way. I'm supposed to do something with this. Something big. Very big. But what, exactly?

My life purpose was beginning to crystallize: using my God-given gift of writing and our family's unique heritage to cultivate human harmony with the written and spoken word. I felt something shimmer in my soul as this epiphany began to provide answers to the "whys" that had puzzled me for so many years.

This is why God created me to look, feel, and experience life from a never-fitting-in perspective; He placed me on a solitary perch to view the world through a unique lens, and He rerouted my medical school quest into a writing journey that was unfolding in fascinating ways.

Why the fear, food, and fat issues? Plus, what would I do after graduation?

"There are no jobs!" my classmates panicked, because we were about to graduate during a recession under President George W. Bush. They lamented, "We're spending all this money on grad school, and there are no jobs!"

I coped with this anxiety, the grief over my father, and the pressure of our program, with my favorite comfort: food. New York bagels are famously delicious, plus they're cheap, so I ate them often and in abundance. My favorite lunch from the deli across from campus was a sesame seed bagel sandwich filled with sliced provolone cheese. Pure bliss. The little store also sold fresh-baked bread; nothing was better than a loaf of sourdough smeared with butter. Simple pleasures, glomming on hips forever.

Running for hours in Riverside Park or at the student recreation building's indoor track helped burn the excess calories. At one point, however, I became so plagued by binging and exercising that I attended 12-step meetings for food addicts. All the while, I trusted that God would ultimately illuminate a purpose for my struggles.

Meanwhile, I channeled my mental energy on researching and writing my thesis. I shared it with Paul Delaney, who referred me to *Times* Features Editor Angela Dodson, who asked me to extract a portion about the growing number of mixed-race support groups on college campuses, including Harvard and Stanford. That article was published in *The New York Times* on the front page of The Living Section with my byline on June 5, 1991 under the headline, *When Life Isn't Simply Black or White*.

This was a big deal, because people were not talking about or writing about interracial identities or issues. The names Barack Obama, Tiger Woods, Derek Jeter, Halle Berry, and Mariah Carey were not known or synonymous with being biracial.

But America was ready to talk about it! It was a hot topic! I was flown to Washington, D.C. for my first national TV appearance: "Our Voices with Bev Smith" on BET. Next, The CBS Evening News with Dan Rather flew a crew to Detroit to interview me. Appearances on Good Morning America Sunday and other shows followed. During each interview, I explained how I was giving voice to a taboo topic rooted in a painful aspect of American history: slavery.

Meanwhile, despite the recession and dearth of journalism jobs, I was extremely blessed. *The Detroit News*, whose Publisher Bob Giles was a Columbia Journalism School graduate, and whose Managing Editor Mark Hass, hired me as a summer intern. What a thrill to cover everything from fires to funerals to features about good things happening in the community. That summer, I attended the NABJ convention in Kansas City.

The internship enabled me to return home with my mother, who was in deep mourning. She had shared more than half her life with our father. Catherine had spent the past 10 months with her, and was eager to move away and ultimately earn her master's degree in Writing from the University of San Francisco.

Thankfully, *The Detroit News* hired me as a full-time reporter and, after a stint as a general assignment reporter, offered me the new "race relations" beat. At the time, Gannett 2000 was pushing to diversify both the staff and leadership in newsrooms, as well as the coverage of people, experts and issues on the news pages. I was fortunate to visit Gannett's headquarters in Virginia to discuss diversity, and to participate in a huge *News* project about the Civil Rights Movement. It was an exhilarating time, on the cutting edge of such progressive journalism!

Becoming NABJ Chapter President & An Impactful Reporter

In 1992, Detroit hosted the NABJ convention, and it was exciting to serve as host! George Sheer attended for Columbia, as did many of *The New York Times* editors. The publisher, Arthur Ochs Sulzberger, Jr., whom I had met before, attended, and I had the honor of introducing future Detroit Mayor Dennis Archer to him in the lobby of the Renaissance Center where the convention was held.

Another honor came the following year: I was elected president of the local NABJ chapter. In addition to running monthly meetings, we hosted special events, such as a Q&A for journalists to chat with mayoral candidates. We also taught a journalism class at Butzel Middle School in a low-income neighborhood on Detroit's East Side every Tuesday morning.

That year, *The News* sponsored my attendance at the NABJ convention in Houston, which featured a tour of NASA and a big barbecue party in a barn. The paper also paid for me to participate in the 1994 NABJ convention in Atlanta. It was called Unity—a joint experience with the national Hispanic, Asian, and Native American journalists' organizations. The opening ceremony was a spectacular display of music and dancers representing each culture; I shivered with awe and joy amidst this melting pot of people committed to using the written and spoken word to make a positive difference in the world.

While there, I was invited to a group dinner at an Italian restaurant with *New York Times* Metro Editor Gerald Boyd and other leadership from the paper. I was one of several writers whose progress they were tracking with the intention of possibly hiring me in the future.

Also encouraging was the feedback I received about my articles on the race relations beat, which I wrote under the brilliant guidance of my editor, Patricia McCaughan, who would later become an Episcopalian priest and move to California. Pat was deeply spiritual, and we often went to lunch and talked about God, angels, and other divine topics. She was also an excellent teacher, providing constructive criticism on how I could improve as a reporter and writer. I believe that our articles were nominated for The Pulitzer Prize.

I wrote many stories, and was thrilled to interview author Toni Morrison, when she became the first African American to win the Nobel Prize for Literature in 1993. In college, I had studied her novels, including *The Bluest Eye, Beloved,* and *Sula.* Speaking by phone from her hotel room in Oslo, Sweden, she answered my questions, then I wrote an article.

Another memorable story was about "the wall of silence" between the races, how the topic of race was so sensitive and politically charged, people chose not to talk about it out of fear of offending someone.

"Your story about the wall of silence between the races is having a big impact here," a veteran reporter said to me on Writer's Row, an open space in the newsroom where reporters' desks were placed in rows. "It's getting the staff talking about something that nobody talked about before. Good job!"

"Thank you, that means so much!"

I was elated, because my stories were making a difference! I was also doing that on a personal level, by inviting black and white employees who otherwise sat separately to join me at one table in the newspaper's cafeteria. One day a short time later, I walked into the lunchroom and stopped in my tracks. My black and white colleagues whom I had introduced were now sitting together, talking and laughing. Workplace lunchrooms can be notoriously segregated, but I had bridged the racial divide.

Gratitude overwhelmed me in moments like that and for being in a position to write about a very difficult topic in a city where the bloody 1967 rebellion killed 43 people and caused epic damage as U.S. military tanks rolled down the streets. How awesome that my work was inspiring healing dialogue and socializing amongst my peers. If it were having that effect inside the newsroom amongst hardboiled journalists, then certainly it was doing the same in other settings across the highly segregated metropolitan Detroit area.

My writing was expanding far wider, as a contributor for *New People* magazine, created by *News* Features Editor Yvette Walker, who was interracially married and founded the national publication to celebrate mixed-race individuals, couples, and families. I wrote many articles and was honored to pose on the cover of a wall calendar that she created featuring the photography of Monica Morgan. My photo also appeared for the months of July and August with a quote: "Being biracial is both a blessing and a burden… I dream of a world in which people can live where the races cross without concern."

"The World Is Your Oyster"

We were sitting on the front of a luxury boat, drinking cocktails, listening to jazz, and watching the sun glow over the city skyline. That, and the shimmering river around us, mirrored our euphoria.

"It's your world," my date said, clinking his cocktail against mine. As we toasted and sipped, I savored the feeling of meeting a man who celebrated my ambition and seemed to want to help me achieve my dreams.

We had met at a formal event a few months before, and soon we were enjoying dates that included dancing at Flood's Bar and Grill, one of Detroit's most popular nightspots. He lived in a cool bachelor pad in a high-rise building overlooking the city.

He traveled often for work, and took me to Fort Lauderdale, Florida. We stayed at a beachfront hotel, drove a Mustang convertible, hung out at cool hotspots, and had a ridiculously fun time. We drank champagne and enjoyed amazing meals at waterside restaurants.

That set the tone for frequent trips to Chicago, Los Angeles, New York, Miami, and Fort Lauderdale. In Detroit, our social calendar included parties and black tie events where I wore sparkly dresses, enjoyed cocktails, ate delicious food, and socialized with fascinating people.

"The world is your oyster," he often said.

I believed that, and was certain that all my dreams—personally and professionally—would be served up on a diamond-studded platter. I was on top of the world!

Enchantment Leads To Engagement

"Will you marry me?" he asked on his knee at 1940 Chop House, a chic restaurant owned by Kronk Gym Founder Emanuel Steward. My mother, his parents, and other relatives were sitting at the table around me. He presented a diamond engagement ring.

"Yes!" I answered as our families applauded.

A short time later, we moved into an apartment overlooking a pretty park. Our 21st floor corner unit offered spectacular views through floor-to-ceiling windows. During the day, the blue river sparkled as sailboats and freighters passed; at night, the city lights were dazzling.

The apartment had high ceilings and a giant living room where we hosted "fight parties," inviting friends to watch pay-per-view boxing matches. When the Hudson's department store was imploded, we hosted a gathering to witness a giant cloud of dust rolling toward us and engulfing our building. Our annual June "fireworks parties" for our friends and families featured a great view of the North American International Fireworks.

We took evening and weekend rides on our friends' boats. Went dancing and drinking into the night, often ending up at Bert's Jazz

Club in Eastern Market, indulging in fried chicken wings at two in the morning.

"You're living like a movie star, Biss!" my mother exclaimed one day as she helped me arrange artwork in our master suite that included a king-size canopy bed, a seating area with black leather furniture, and a dressing room and vanity. We each had a full bath, and the second bedroom was my office. I was loving it!

One evening, I was home alone, sitting on the sofa. Suddenly I heard a loud, raspy male voice in my head ordering:

"Get out!"

Chills crept over my skin. *Who or what was that?* I remembered the ghost in our house in Saginaw, and the demonic energy in *The Exorcist*. So I grabbed my keys and left, fast! Then I went to my mother's house, not returning until my fiancé got home.

The Monster In My Head

The helmet of pain struck while I sat at a computer in the midst of the usual buzzing beehive atmosphere of phones ringing, reporters and editors having spirited debates, and intense-looking people hurrying about, trying to finish their own stories before the 5 p.m. deadline.

My headache throbbed.

Light from the ceiling and computer screen hurt my eyes as a tiny hammer of migraine pain throbbed behind them. The scents of coffee, cologne, and cigarette smoke on someone's clothing nearby made me want to vomit. And weird muscle spasms along my jaw felt like my face was jumping around.

God, please make this pain go away... I have to finish my story! I had done the reporting, and no one else could decipher my hand-written notes or compose all the information into a cohesive article. But all I could do was close my eyes, clasp my head in my hands to massage it, and pray. It felt like a monster was inside my head, punching behind my eyeball, squeezing tentacles around my skull, and tormenting my jaw muscles.

I just wanted to cry. But I had to write! Even though the pain caused brain fog, making it nearly impossible to focus on writing a story fast, or at all. Somehow, I slogged through it, emailed the story to my editor, and went home.

There, with the light as dim as possible, I laid on the bed and injected a needle into my thigh. The Imitrex migraine medication was supposed to alleviate the pain. I also had 800-milligram Motrin tablets, and muscle relaxers for the spastic jaw muscles. Then I laid in the darkness, praying for God to relieve the throbbing, nauseating pain.

The Monster in My Head, I wrote in a poem by that name, was born on a fun Friday night in September of 1993, as music pumped through the hip nightclub that my fiancé and I often frequented.

Bam! Something hard hit me in the head. Liquid poured through my hair and down my face. Stunned, I cowered low, pressing my fingers to my scalp.

Am I bleeding? What was that? A beer bottle rolled near my feet. In a flash, I knew that someone had dropped it from the balcony over the dance floor.

In the Emergency Room, I was diagnosed with whiplash and a closed head injury, which set off terrible pain for years. I filed a lawsuit against the club, alleging negligence for failing to protect customers by placing a net or chicken wire along the balcony and for serving in glass bottles instead of plastic cups.

My injury triggered painful "TMJ" spasms that radiated up my temples and around my head; a jaw specialist treated it with tiny electric shocks. A migraine specialist prescribed a plethora of painkillers.

"Make sure you exercise," he said, "because it releases endorphins in your body that help relieve stress that can trigger migraines. Your natural body chemicals released during exercise can actually combat pain."

I exercised daily: running and walking outdoors; and doing cardio and weight lifting in the fitness center of our apartment building. I also avoided migraine-triggering foods such as wine and blue cheese.

Chronic pain changed my personality. I was always fearful of a migraine, whose horrific hammering pain could put me out of commission for days. I was diagnosed with "divided attention;" if you spoke to me while the TV was blaring, or some loud commotion were occurring, I couldn't concentrate on what you were saying because I'd get so agitated.

I hated that this was happening. I hated the pain in the eyes of my mother and my fiancé when they saw me suffering. The Monster in My Head was stealing my joy and slowing me down. Somehow I had to kill it.

My Mother Becomes A Judge!

Our mother's upward career trajectory continued during the 1990s. First, she was appointed a magistrate in Detroit's 36th District Court, one of the biggest and busiest courts in the country. Then in 1994, she was appointed by Governor John Engler and she became a judge.

Her investiture ceremony in the auditorium in the City-County Building was one of the largest the legal community had seen. Our family, including Aunt Mary and many of her children, attended. I wrote a poem and recited it at her reception. It was a beautiful day, and we were beyond proud that our mother was now a judge.

Obsession: A Book Is Born

My career was booming. My articles about race relations continued to attract local and national media attention and invitations to speak at events such as the Multiracial Americans of Southern California's conference in Los Angeles.

I decided to expand my master's thesis into a nonfiction book, and met with a literary agent on how to write a book proposal that could be presented to publishers to attract a book deal. I interviewed several people across America, then wrote an outline, sample chapters, and other materials required for a formal book proposal.

The agent shopped it to New York publishers. They said that the people whom I interviewed weren't delving into the pain and struggle of the unique brand of racism and personal angst as black-*and*-white individuals in a black-*or*-white world. I knew that struggle and could articulate it, because I was living it.

"So I'm going to write a novel instead!" I declared. I called the book *White Chocolate*, about mixed race TV reporter Taylor James who's on a mission to fight racism with her dual heritage and journalistic skills. She's engaged to a TV executive, and her first love, TV entertainment reporter Julian DuPont, who's also biracial, comes back into her life, begging for a second chance.

The more I wrote in my home office, the more obsessed I became about creating a phenomenal story to *edu-tain* people. Entertained by a provocative, suspenseful story. And educated about this oft-misunderstood and taboo issue so close to my heart.

To achieve any goal, you need a plan. So one day during my lunch break in the cafeteria at *The Detroit News*, I wrote on a yellow legal pad: "10 Steps to Getting Published."

This included making a commitment to work on the book four to five hours each week, and to finishing the first draft within a year. To do this, I got up at 4:00 a.m. to write before reporting for a full day's work as a reporter. I wrote at night and on weekends. My fiancé praised my ambition and dedication when I preferred to stay home and write.

I frequently visualized myself sitting in Borders Bookstore, autographing books for long lines, and picking up my book from the New Releases table. I *knew* this dream would come true.

My first intention was to debunk the "tragic mulatto" stereotype and write myself into contemporary American literature as a "triumphant mulatto." As mixed-race kids, Catherine and I had had zero role models of high profile, biracial people. As English majors, we had read no books or stories about confident, successful mixed-race characters. My books would begin to provide literary balance.

My second intention was to cultivate a career as a novelist to simultaneously merge my passion for writing, my desire to inspire healing conversations about race, and my fascination with the magic of love and romance.

Meanwhile, I researched everything I could find about writing and publishing. This was before the Internet, so I read books and magazines. I joined the local Romance Writers of America chapter and attended monthly meetings to learn from members who shared information about agents, editors, and publishing industry trends. I even attended an RWA conference in Chicago, and later became the editor of the monthly newsletter for the local chapter.

My dream was to become a romance author using the *nom de plume*, Elizabeth Lavender, living a lavish lifestyle and traveling the world promoting her books. She would own a yacht and a Caribbean island, and her philanthropy would help writers connect with resources to tell their stories.

In my office, I posted inspirational notes, including *Essence* magazine Editor-in-Chief Susan Taylor's monthly column from September 1993 entitled, *There's Magic in Believing*. I still have it in a box with my journals. I listened to inspiring songs by Mariah Carey. And I hung pictures of what I wanted, including a heart-shaped diamond ring in a Harry Winston ad that I had ripped from page two of *The New York Times*, which I read daily. Someday, I promised myself that I would have that ring to celebrate my success.

In many ways, I was already living the Elizabeth Lavender lifestyle, which epitomized accomplishment and opulence, passion, and purpose, and of course love and romance. Unfortunately, nothing is perfect, and every story needs conflict.

Those debilitating migraine headaches often stopped me from writing for days. Sometimes I was so desperate to keep working that I wore sunglasses so the light from the lowest setting on the computer screen's brightness didn't make my eyes ache.

In addition, I discovered something about my fiancé that was very worrisome, and he promised to resolve the problem. I believed him.

Then I focused on all that was good, especially the dream of Elizabeth Lavender writing books about love and romance. And what could be more romantic than planning my own wedding?

The Wedding Is A Lavender Dream

My Godfather, Grant, walked me up the aisle under a white tent adorned with purple and white flowers. Under it sat 250 of our closest friends and family members. As I reached our officiant, Michigan Court of Appeals Judge Myron Wahls, I beamed, glancing at Catherine, my maid of honor, and the four bridesmaids who included my childhood friend, Louise. They wore sleek lavender gowns, while the groomsmen sported gray tuxedos.

Behind them, the sun sparkled on the blue river. Our guests fanned themselves in the 90-degree humidity with lavender programs printed with an excerpt from Daddy's journals. When Catherine and I were toddlers, he had written about how he would play wedding with us, often wondering if he would still be alive on our wedding days.

He wasn't. But his sister Aunt Mary was looking like Queen Elizabeth's twin with her soft, white-yellow hair and flowery purple dress. Her children, my cousins, were there, and her granddaughter was a flower girl, as was my fiancé's niece.

After the ceremony, a white limousine took us to The Roostertail for a sit-down dinner reception for 400. Then we took a moonlight boat cruise on the Detroit River with the wedding party.

During our 10-day honeymoon at a luxury resort in Jamaica, the problem I had been worried about regarding my fiancé came to my attention. I wasn't happy. But it was easy to forget about it while splashing in the turquoise water, jet skiing, and climbing a waterfall.

Back home, I loved being married. After a great day at my job that I loved at *The News*, I would hurry off the elevator, dash down the hallway, grinning with excitement that he was waiting for me on the other side of the door. We traveled often to New York, LA, Miami, Chicago, and Las Vegas, and enjoyed a robust social life in Detroit, often attending black tie events or dining in nice restaurants with friends and family. "You're such a happy couple," people said often.

Catherine Earns Her Master's Degree In Writing

In the spring of 1996, Catherine earned her master's degree in writing from the University of San Francisco. My mother and I flew out for the ceremony, along with Aunt Mary; my cousins; and Grammum.

We had a wonderful trip, riding streetcars, taking a sightseeing boat to Sausalito, and riding in rickshaws along Fisherman's Wharf. We also rode the ferry to Alcatraz Island, a former prison in San Francisco Bay. The tour has sound effects that make it feel real. Our mother loved hearing stories about the prisoners who were notorious gangsters during the Al Capone days.

Mostly, we laughed and loved being together to celebrate Catherine's accomplishment. For her master's thesis, she completed three Young Adult novels, inspired by her adolescent experiences as a white-looking biracial girl whose long hair went from curly to super thick and frizzy.

She called this The Veronica Series, and named the novels *Veronica, I Heard Your Mom's Black, Veronica Talks to Boys*, and *Race*

Home, Veronica. Her goal was to secure a literary agent and sell the books to a New York publisher.

I was really proud of my sister for moving to the other side of the country and excelling in academics while also working and supporting herself with a cool apartment and a white cat named Owen.

Writing Dreams: Rejected!

I finished *White Chocolate* in four months and sent it to the literary agent.

Rejected!

"The editors are looking for a 'big book,'" my agent said. "So you need to do more work." I shelved it for awhile. As much as I'd heard about rejection at Romance Writers of America meetings, it really stung.

So I kept plugging away at my job at *The Detroit News*. But I was starting to dislike the inherent confrontationalism of journalism, where reporters have to question people who don't want to be questioned. I didn't like going to neighborhoods alone, knocking on strangers' doors. My new editor was very critical, often expecting me to stay late into the evening to rewrite articles.

That, and disappointment about not selling my novel, cast gloom over my career. As did the newspaper union strike in July of 1995. My colleagues on the picket lines wanted to shut the paper down, and stop delivery trucks driven by "scab" drivers, the people hired to replace the strikers. I wanted no part of that. I walked the picket lines for a few weeks, then officially left the paper.

Finally, A Book Deal!

All I wanted was to become a published author. I took a temporary office job at a downtown bank, and continued working on my book.

Over Thanksgiving weekend in 1995, thanks to family friend Jeff Wardford, my first book contract arrived in the mail from New York. *White Chocolate* would be published by St. Martin's Press' Tor/Forge imprint.

"Conflict is the engine that drives your story," said editor Natalia Aponte, instructing me to read several books about scene development and dialogue. I devoted tremendous time to rewriting my book and creating a high-conflict love triangle. I expected the book's release within 18 or 24 months, and eagerly awaited news from my editor. Finally, she said, "Your release has been pushed to May of 1998." That seemed like forever and a day away. I was so disappointed!

Breaking News: A TV Job & A Baby!

God's divine timing would soon be evident. First, the delay led me to my first TV job as a writer at Detroit's Fox 2 News. I am forever grateful to Huel Perkins for his recommendation.

I demonstrated my worthiness while writing stories for the anchors to read during the five, six, and ten o'clock shows. Once, News Director Neil Goldstein brought in Melvin Mencher, author of *News Reporting and Writing*, one of the textbooks that I studied at Columbia, for a staff-wide writing workshop. Professor Mencher had us do a writing exercise.

"Don't put your names on the papers," he said. "I'll collect them." Then he reviewed our writing samples and read one aloud. "This is excellent. Who wrote it?"

"I did," I said, beaming and making our news director very proud.

Meanwhile, I loved working in the newsroom. I met so many accomplished, fun people who became longtime, dear friends, including: anchor Micah Materre, now anchor at WGN Chicago; reporter Al Allen; cameraman Rodney Ferguson; Huel and his wife, Priscilla; writer Sean Lee and her husband, morning anchor Alan Lee; anchor Monica Gayle; Kim Harry who trained me; and many more people!

One day I was sitting in an edit bay with a video editor, who was using the script that I wrote to create a news "package," a compilation of video, voiceover by a reporter or anchor, and sound bytes. A coworker introduced a new reporter who had just come from New York.

"Hi I'm Lee Thomas," he said, smiling.

"My father's name was Thomas Lee," I told this person who would become my dear friend.

At the time, I was celebrating personal news: I was pregnant! The baby's gender did not matter as I prayed, *God please bless us with a robust baby.* My meticulous self-care included healthy eating, sleep, prenatal vitamins, and going to all doctor's appointments.

I worked from 2 p.m. until 11 p.m. I was a vegetarian—so repulsed by meat that I wouldn't walk past meat at the grocery store. One day, a craving for pot roast overwhelmed me while working at my desk in the newsroom. I called my mother, and after we stopped laughing, she prepared one for me.

After that, I couldn't get enough meat, or anything else. My favorite pregnancy meal was fried chicken with Frank's hot sauce, macaroni and cheese, greens, corn bread, and peach cobbler from Franklin Street restaurant. I ate with wild abandon—and gained 70 pounds! At one point, when I packed on 16 pounds in one month, my doctor suspected I was pre-diabetic. The tests were negative.

When my healthy baby boy was born, my doctor said playfully, "Congratulations, you've just given birth to a toddler. He's ten pounds, thirteen ounces."

Robust, indeed.

From The Bliss Of Birth To Barely Breathing

I could hardly breathe. My temperature was 104 degrees.

Just a week after giving birth, I had to leave my infant at home and return to the hospital with my annual winter bout of pneumonia. Whenever I caught a cold, it worsened into bronchitis and pneumonia, requiring antibiotics, inhalers, and steroids.

Now, the infection was constricting my airways and making me wheeze. Sucking medicated steam through a tube barely helped. Clammy sweat covered my body; my cesarean cut felt like a knife lodged in my gut. During my five days in the hospital, my mother spent the night with Alexander while my husband's mother took care of him during the day in our apartment.

Cravings for raw tomatoes overwhelmed me. My mother brought me bags of them; I sliced them on a plate and devoured tomato after tomato. That was all I wanted to eat. I concluded that tomatoes must contain something that heals the lungs.

Thankfully, I finally went home, still wheezy and fatigued. It would be months before my lungs felt back to normal.

The 100-pound Challenge!

I stared in disbelief at my naked body in the mirror.

I am enormous! What did I do to myself? My book is coming out in three months, and I'm not going to do TV interviews and book signings looking like this and feeling this bad!

Plus, becoming a mom made me want to stay healthy. If I had been pre-diabetic during pregnancy, I wanted to quit sugar binges and cultivate wellness and longevity.

Despite the limitations of my health, winter weather, and having a newborn, I got exercise any way possible, including "power cleaning" by mopping, and washing our many windows. Later, I bought a "baby jogger"—a stroller designed to safely hold a baby while I ran.

All the while, I wrote in my journal about the joy of being a new mother, as well as what I ate and how I would feel at my goal weight. I composed vignettes about walking into a store and purchasing a pair of skinny purple leather pants. I journaled about feeling liberated from cravings. I detailed how I would look and feel great during book signings and media interviews.

Then I practiced what I had read in Shakti Gawain's book, *Creative Visualization*—allowing my written vignettes to play out like mini mind movies as if they have already manifest in 3D form.

But sometimes I looked in the mirror and cried. *What have I done to myself?* My body was heavy and bulky. My thighs rubbed together. My stomach jiggled as I walked. It was easy to dwell on how bad I felt. At the gym, my reflection on the mirrored walls made me think: "You're such a fat, disgusting cow! It'll take forever to lose all this weight! Why bother?"

I prayed to find compassion toward myself. "I am healthy, I am strong," I repeated with every step as I power-walked, then jogged. "Size six. Sleek and strong. Size six."

In my journal, I composed a new script for my thoughts: "I look in the mirror and smile," and "I love Elizabeth." After composing a long passage about celebrating myself and believing that I could achieve my goals, I recorded these words in a microcassette recorder, and listened to this tape every day while driving, exercising, and falling asleep. I was reprogramming my brain by providing it with a new script. It worked!

Within one year, I lost 100 pounds. Then I walked into a store, tried on a pair of skinny purple leather pants, and bought them—along with a black pair.

Going Gluten-free Cures Asthma

To expedite weight loss, I removed starches from my diet. No more toast, pasta, cookies, cake, pie, pizza crust, pancakes, waffles, or anything else made with flour. As my lungs began to recover from pneumonia, I realized that I was no longer coughing or wheezing. Did starchy foods cause asthma symptoms?

I went online and searched for a possible correlation between asthma and diet. That's when I learned the word "gluten." While the "gluten-free" label is ubiquitous and even vogue now, it was not well-known back in 1998. Nor were food allergies understood or respected as they are today.

When I returned to my awesome pulmonologist for a check-up and x-rays, I asked, "Do you think there's a connection between eating flour and having asthma symptoms?"

"Possibly," he said, "but you should take this preventative inhaler every day."

Instead, I banned gluten from my diet and had no asthma symptoms. The following year, I was speaking on a panel about race in media coverage at Columbia University. The catered lunch featured delicious-looking roll-up sandwiches.

If I eat one, will I wheeze? I ate it, and sure enough, I sneezed, which triggered wheezing. Full-blown bronchitis followed, requiring antibiotics, an inhaler, and steroids. That was the last time I knowingly ate food containing gluten. And that was 20 years ago.

A Baby, A Book, and A Big Check

Wearing a black lace dress over my shrinking body, I autographed 290 hardcover copies of *White Chocolate* for friends and family in the International Marketplace in Detroit's Greektown.

"I'm so proud of you, Biss!" exclaimed my mother, who hosted the party in May of 1998, when my book was distributed to bookstores across America. Apple Book Center handled sales, landing my book on *The Detroit News* Bestseller List.

"I can't believe this is Elizabeth's first book," one family friend said. "It's very well done."

Reviewers agreed. "This book will tempt you with solid writing, a good old-fashioned romance and steamy sex scenes," *The Detroit News* wrote in a review. "Once this romantic thriller takes off, the story really heats up," *The Detroit Free Press* wrote.

"A well-formatted summer read," *The Reno News & Review* said. "It's got all the necessary elements: a long lost love, a sleazy new one, a heroine who must fight for what she believes in and, at its core, a hot button societal topic… Oh, and there's some really steamy sex scenes as well."

My literary dream was manifesting in glorious reality as I prepared for media interviews and book signings around Detroit and in surrounding states.

"Elizabeth, here's your check," a messenger said during the book party, handing me an envelope. I had won a lawsuit against the venue where the beer bottle dropped on my head. The divine timing of this windfall enabled me to stay home with my son. My fantasy was that I could write books while at home with him. But I soon learned that the reality of a new baby means you're lucky to take a shower, much less write a sentence.

Then when he was crawling, climbing, and walking, he wanted in on the action at my desk, banging on the keyboard, playing with the mouse, and squirming all over. Thankfully, our Aunt Mimi came to babysit while I was writing at home, and they had a ball out in the park feeding nuts to the squirrels. Other times, it became routine for me to pull all-nighters, then sleep during the day when he napped.

So many people had warned, "Cherish every moment because they grow up so fast!" that I tried my best to stay present in the moment when playing, rocking him to sleep, reading books to him every day, and watching him grow and learn. He loved healthy foods! He would sit in his high chair, pinching one garbanzo bean at a time, eating it with gusto.

Returning To NABJ As An Author and Mother

I had skipped a few years of attending NABJ conventions, and since leaving the newspaper, I was no longer on *The New York Times'* prospects list. But I believed in my future as an author, and attended the 1998 NABJ convention in Washington, D.C. to promote *White*

Chocolate. I took my mother, my husband, and six-month-old Alexander, and it was exciting for my colleagues to meet him. The following year, we attended another Unity conference in Seattle, my last NABJ convention for 19 years.

"You Could Pass For White"

Chills crept over my skin as I stood in a plantation house in Virginia, knowing that I would have been enslaved "property" had I lived there at one time. It wasn't far from Monticello, where Thomas Jefferson lived with Sally Hemings, who was enslaved and bore seven children with him, three of whom died.

The "mistress" of former U.S. President Jefferson—who wrote the Declaration of Independence yet "owned" people—fascinated me, as did the hierarchy of skin color and associated "privileges" during slavery days, which continue to taint dynamics amongst black people today.

Similarly, I loved Alex Haley's book about his mixed-race grandmother, *Queen*, which became a TV miniseries starring Halle Berry, and showcased the difficulty of light-skinned slaves.

"You could pass for white," people often told me. That meant living as a white woman and hiding my black heritage. I never considered that, but I wondered, "What if?"

That inspired my second novel, *Dark Secret.* It's about two sisters raised by a single black mother in a rough Detroit neighborhood. Their white father abandoned them with their mother, who mistreated white-looking Sharlene and doted on caramel-hued Karen. Sharlene moves to New York, changes her identity to Camille Morgan, and becomes engaged to the son of a conservative Congressman whose family lives in the 300-year-old Virginia plantation where they once enslaved African people.

Meanwhile, back in Detroit, their mother is dying. Karen tracks down Camille at her luxurious Manhattan home, and begs her to save their mother by donating a kidney. As the only genetic match,

Camille refuses, and Karen seeks revenge that sparks a scandal of race, sex, politics, and money—that could kill them both.

A plantation house became the setting for the home of Camille's father-in-law, the Virginia Senator. To accurately portray him, I ventured to Washington, D.C., thanks to U.S. Senator Carl Levin, who allowed me to observe his day in the life of a Congress member. It was delightful to visit his office, ride the trolley in the underground tunnel, and attend a Congressional hearing with him. I thanked him on the acknowledgments page of *Dark Secret*.

"Let's go to the cottage so you can finish your book," my mother suggested. "I'll take a week off work and entertain Alexander while you write."

During my pregnancy, she had renovated the four-bedroom house that she helped build as a 10-year-old during the 1950s. Back then, segregation banned blacks from vacationing in most places; Idlewild, Michigan became a mecca for black summer vacationers after the Branch brothers in 1912 began selling cheap parcels of raw forestland around several picturesque lakes. Black people built cottages, hotels, and nightclubs that would attract families from across America.

Performers who entertained them in the glamorous Paradise Club and other venues included Count Basie, Louis Armstrong, Duke Ellington, Della Reese, and the Motown greats—before they were famous. Along with world heavyweight boxing champion Joe Louis, entrepreneur Madame C.J. Walker, and Chicago heart surgeon Daniel Hale Williams, Harlem Renaissance writers including W.E.B. DuBois, Langston Hughes, and my beloved Zora Neale Hurston—traveled to Idlewild for rest, relaxation, and writing!

As a writer, I discovered that their genius energy crackles like a jolting current of creativity that whispers in the rustling treetops, in the chirping birds, in the warm sunshine, in the earthy scent, and in the far-away sanctuary feeling of this Black Eden. It strikes me like lightening, as I go there to plug into the brilliance of our literary forebears. My spirit sings, my synapses fire up a storm of storytelling, and my fingers dance over the computer keyboard to compose it all.

All while fueled by walking, biking, and running on our road called Heavenly Way, eating the delicious steaks and chicken that my mother grills outdoors, laughing with family and friends on our deck, and sleeping serenely under heavy "crazy quilts" stitched together with scraps of clothing and curtains long ago by my grandmothers.

"We have all the comforts of home!" my mother proudly declares, after painting, re-furnishing, installing heat and air conditioning, updating the kitchen, and adding a second full bathroom. "My father would be amazed!"

Grandpop purchased our property and built the cottage with bricks and wood that he and his friends received in exchange for tearing down a housing project in Saginaw. He and my grandmother, my mother, and her brother, Sonny, chopped down trees to clear the land, then built our cottage. Now my son is the fifth generation of our family to enjoy it.

While integration inspired many families to abandon their properties, and crumbling hulks of houses remain as blight, the magic of Idlewild is its pristine beauty and the invisible energy of the ancestors. This energy is still so electric—nearly six or seven decades after Idlewild's heyday of the 1950s and early 1960s—that it rouses goosebumps; you can feel the happy energy of an oppressed people who—once they arrived—exuded profound joy, liberation, and celebration so far away from the harsh world.

What better place to weave a torrid tale of race, history, and romance into my novel *Dark Secret!* While I was writing, my mother entertained 18-month-old Alexander on a playscape that included a swimming pool, a wagon, and a swing. They had a ball, I cherished break-time to join the play, and I did some of my best writing ever!

On my birthday in 2000, my mother hosted a book party for

the hardcover release of *Dark Secret* from the Tor/Forge imprint of St. Martin's Press. This time, I autographed more than 300 copies for friends, family members, and fans at a table adorned with orange roses in front of a marble waterfall.

"Elizabeth, where's your diamond?" a woman asked as I signed her book.

The prongs on my wedding ring were empty; the diamond was lost. As was the sparkle from my marriage, due to a recurring problem. My new book, however, gave me great hope that my literary star was shooting.

"Packed to bursting with steamy romantic intrigue, fatal illness, race and class strife, murder, kidnapping, rape, and high-level politics… provocative," wrote *Publisher's Weekly* in a review.

"So deliciously convoluted is (Atkins') tale, filled as it is with schemers, liars, and villains who all but twirl their mustaches (and that's just the women!)," wrote *Booklist*, "readers will have a hard time tearing themselves away."

That's what happened when my friend was reading *Dark Secret* on an airplane. It landed, the passengers departed, and she kept reading. "Ma'am," a flight attendant said, "we're going to have to ask you to leave the plane."

"Just a minute, I have to finish this scene," she said.

Dark Secret spent five weeks on *The Detroit Free Press* Bestseller List, and the paperback edition was published the following year.

The Thrill Of Twilight

"Billy Dee Williams wants to write a romantic novel and is looking for a collaborator," my literary agent Susan Crawford said in early 2000. "Are you interested?"

I flew to Los Angeles in a heartbeat. My mentor had told me to read *Think and Grow Rich* by Napoleon Hill, so on the airplane, I immersed in this life-changing message.

I had spoken with Billy by phone, and we arranged to meet at his favorite Italian restaurant. I arrived first, and was seated on an outdoor terrace near a trickling fountain amidst an ivy-covered brick wall, Italian music, and the delectable scent of garlic and tomato wafting through the stylish crowd. Then he walked in—handsome, suave, and wearing amazing cologne. I was a little nervous, but we clicked immediately, and our creative synergy popped.

"I want to write a book set in Brazil," he said, "to showcase the multiracial mélange of people, and I want a lush romance exploring the delightful complexities of love and relationships." I started taking notes immediately.

We shared a piece of flourless chocolate cake. I didn't know such a thing existed, but with the first bite of its gluten-free, chocolate-fudgy decadence—in this beautiful setting with a movie star as we outlined a book together—I was in pure bliss.

After I flew back to Michigan, we spoke by phone. He shared ideas and I did the writing about a love affair between a movie star and a judge. We worked in person when he came to town for events, and Alexander was excited to meet "Lando Calrissian," the character Billy plays in *Star Wars*. A few times, Billy and I were both in Chicago, so we worked there, too.

We named the book *Twilight*, inspired by a quote from poet and *Les Misérables* creator Victor Hugo: "…day must join with night to bring forth the dawn and twilight which are more beautiful than they."

Book Promotions Across America

I was in author heaven, inside the Ritz Carlton in Marina Del Rey near Los Angeles, autographing copies of my books in a ballroom with Moses! Actually it was Charleton Heston, the actor who played Moses in *The Ten Commandments*, and as well as the lead role in the classic film, *Ben-Hur*, one of my mother's favorite movies.

We were so excited to shake his hand at this book fair that my Godfather, Grant McArn, helped organize. I participated twice, also meeting then-TV talk show host Montel Williams. I talked with him about being on his show to talk about biracial identity, and he put me in touch with his producer!

"You are so sweet and humble," said a lady who was assigned to help me at another author book fair at the Ritz-Carlton in St. Louis. "I meet so many authors and you are just shocking me with your lack of ego and arrogance. You don't have a diva bone in your body!"

I loved the author life!

I was a guest on *The Ananda Lewis Show* twice, including a time with Catherine. The show flew us to New York, and during the taping, asked the audience to guess our race and/or ethnic heritage.

"Jewish!" people exclaimed about Catherine.

"Swedish!" people guessed about me.

The Rob Nelson Show flew us and our mother to Los Angeles to talk about our interracial family. A BET Show called *Oh Drama!* with actress/comedienne Kym Whitley also brought us to LA to talk about being mixed. I was interviewed on NPR, locally and nationally.

I also wrote a book about Grammy Award winning rap artist and producer *Sean "Puffy" Combs* for the Black Americans of Achievement Book Series, which would be published in 2003.

Thanks to Pam Nelson at Levy Home Entertainment, I participated in two Romance Author Bus Tours around Midwestern states. It was a blast to join a bus full of authors from across America, as we made many stops at bookstores and other venues for mass book signings. We stayed in hotels, enjoyed dinners at nice restaurants, and talked about the writer's life.

At one point, Pam invited me to a luncheon for young people in Chicago who had won a writing contest. I gave a speech about being different as a biracial girl, and how never fitting in can make you a leader, not a follower. The students gave me a standing ovation!

I believed that I was on course to achieve great success as a novelist whose provocative stories inspired human harmony. Success to me meant: topping the bestseller lists; getting lucrative book and film deals; cranking out new books for readers eagerly awaiting my next release; and being a sought-after speaker and media commentator.

"These books should be movies!" people constantly told me.

One friend even brought a Hollywood producer to my *Dark Secret* book party, and we talked about the possibilities for a book-to-film production. My agent sent books, letters, and treatments to representatives for actresses whom we believed were perfect to star in film versions of *White Chocolate* and *Dark Secret*. Those who replied declined.

Still, I kept the faith, believing at the right time, influential people would discover these books and make them films. I was certain that my magic moment of being "discovered" by someone with the power to anoint me as the next "It Girl" in the publishing and film world. I was constantly seeking, writing, hoping, wishing, and trying creative approaches.

Once I wrote a sparkling letter to Nike Founder Phil Knight. I shared my weight loss success story, asking if I could be featured, get sponsorship, or somehow be involved in using my story to promote fitness. He wrote me back, and we talked about possibilities, but nothing happened.

Still, I remained determined to keep writing and promoting. Someday, I just knew that my books would entertain and inspire people around the world.

Meanwhile, readers were loving my books. In fact, my friend Ormandy Singleton liked *White Chocolate* so much, she asked her girlfriends to read it and meet with me, thus beginning Cover to Cover book club. They also read *Dark Secret*, and we enjoyed fun discussions as well as an annual Christmas party with spouses.

"This is Elizabeth," said another book club president, leading me into her dining room where members were sitting.

"Oh my God, I loved your book!" one lady gasped, shocked that I was at their meeting. I loved talking with book clubs in homes and restaurants as members spoke about characters I created as if they were real people.

Being a guest at book clubs was wonderful because the members loved speaking one on one with the author of that month's selection. One club's members baked a white chocolate cake and served it with a meal that's in my book.

Catherine's Courage With A Brain Tumor

Her head was shaved, and a nurse was inserting an IV in her arm to anesthetize her for surgery. Catherine was cool and confident, but our mother and I were a crying mess. My little sister had a brain tumor, and we were praying that it would be removed successfully, with no residual problems with thinking, talking, or walking.

This had all started after Catherine collapsed in a store beside her future husband, who called our mother. A CT scan revealed a meningioma, a golf-ball-sized growth in the lining of the brain at the top of her head, between the lobes.

"If you're going to have a brain tumor," Catherine repeated what her doctors had said, "this is the best kind to have."

She was confident after selecting a surgeon who said, "I love tumors."

So, praying constantly, we sat in the hospital waiting room with her husband for hours and hours, entertaining Alexander with toys, books, and snacks.

"The surgery was successful," her surgeon told us.

We stayed in her apartment in Reno, Nevada, and helped her recover, which meant caring for the 21 staples holding her scalp together to heal the L-shaped incision. We accompanied her to get the staples removed. Some people come out of this surgery with impaired speech, challenged thinking, seizures, and restricted physical abilities. Instead, Catherine had a perfect recovery.

She even wrote a cover story for *The Reno News & Review* where she was the office manager, called "My Summer Craniotomy." Now 18 years later, Catherine continues to be blessed with clean MRIs. And we couldn't be more grateful.

September 11, 2001: Shattered Security

On September 10, 2001, I snuggled with three-year-old Alexander under his colorful Noah's Ark comforter as I read bedtime stories. I felt especially overwhelmed with gratitude that we were healthy, safe, and living in abundance.

The next morning, I drove him to The Giving Tree Montessori School, where he was having an excellent experience that included learning Spanish. While driving home, I got the sudden urge to turn on WWJ News Radio 950. The announcer said an airplane had struck the Twin Towers in New York. I arrived home in time to see the second plane strike the second tower on live TV. Then came the report about something hitting the Pentagon.

Was America under attack? I called my husband. Went back to pick up Alexander. Called Fox 2, where I was now working part-time. They said come in. I took Alexander to his grandmother's house, then went to the station to write stories for the five, six, and 10 o'clock news.

That day, and the way it shattered our sense of security, made me hug my loved ones harder and appreciate our blessings of safety and love. With my heart aching for the victims and their families, I prayed that peace would prevail.

Journaling My Way Onto The Oprah Winfrey Show

At the time, Oprah's Book Club was a global phenomenon, and I dreamed of her selecting one of my novels. So in my journals, I described being a guest on *The Oprah Winfrey Show*. I even wrote about feeling my fingertips on the smooth leather of the big, banana-yellow chairs on her set. I visualized this often, as if it were a real memory, not an imaginary wish.

I also mailed my books to Harpo Studios in Chicago; they were returned. One day on her website, I saw that her producers were looking for "weight loss success stories."

I submitted my story. Would the producers even read my email amongst so many others? Much to my shock, a producer called to ask more questions and request that I mail in photographs. I did, and they called again—to invite me onto the show!

The night before I was scheduled to fly to Chicago, Alexander spent the night at my mother's house, so I was free to pick my outfits, pack, and head to the airport early in the morning. My mind whizzed with excitement that I would meet Oprah and share my weight loss success story. Unfortunately, that night something happened with my husband that expedited the demise of our marriage.

The next day in Chicago, a limousine picked me up from the airport and took me to the Harpo Studios where I was videotaped exercising in its gym, and journaling at a desk. During a rehearsal, I sat on the stage and had an amazing moment: my fingertips were touching the smooth leather of the big, banana-yellow chairs—exactly as I had written in my journal.

I wrote this, and it happened!

The difference was that I had written about being on the show for my books, but was a guest for weight loss instead. I trusted that God had a plan.

The next day, while taping with a live studio audience, I stood backstage and heard Oprah call my name. As I walked out, it felt like a dream. She touched my arms and said, "You look great!" The segment showed pictures of me jogging in a bikini on the beach on Martha's Vineyard where my family had gone in 2000 for my *Dark Secret* book signings at Cousen Rose Gallery and Bunch a Grapes bookstore.

"Yeah, baby!" Oprah exclaimed as the photo appeared. This was one of the most exciting moments of my life.

Demise Of My Marriage

Unfortunately, my gut burned with angst when I thought of my husband at home. Deep down, I knew it had a divine purpose, because when Alexander was three years old, he announced that, "I looked down from heaven and chose you and Dad as my parents."

Our child is an "old soul." Years later, I would learn that our souls choose our human experiences to learn lessons and evolve.

I prayed that things would get better. I knew nothing about how to get a divorce and told no one what I was thinking or feeling. That was on my heart as my husband travelled with me to New Orleans for my *Twilight* book signings (without my co-author) at the Essence Festival.

While I felt perfectly comfortable at this event celebrating black women, many pairs of eyes questioned: "What's that white girl doing at the Essence Festival?"

At one point, I met a man whose national radio program was really hot. He was with other authors whom I knew, and when they told him that I'm black too, he doubled over in loud laughter. I couldn't believe this man was laughing at me. Not with me. At me. Hello?!?! We were in New Orleans, which has some of the whitest-looking black people due to its "Creole" heritage and generations of race-mixing.

Again, I wondered if this individual would lambaste me on his radio program if I were passing for white and were somehow outed. The bottom line is, you can't please everyone, and by embracing and celebrating all sides of me, I was showcasing my authenticity.

The Twilight Book Party, The Party of the Summer!

Jazzy music from a live performer on an electric fiddle greeted more than 600 people as they streamed into the two-story ballroom. To the right was a lavish seafood buffet amidst ice sculptures. To the left was a stage where I sat with Billy Dee Williams and stacks of our new hardcover novel, *Twilight*.

"What's your name?" Billy asked a woman who stood before us, beaming as he scrolled a note in her book.

She said her name, then asked, "Will you please say the line from *Lady Sings the Blues?*"

Billy chuckled, then repeated his famous line to Diana Ross in her role as singer Billie Holiday in the 1972 film. The woman swooned, as did many of the friends, family members, and fans who stood in the long line around the perimeter of the bustling ballroom, waiting to get their autographed books.

This was one of the most fabulous experiences of my career thus far.

I am forever grateful to my mother for hosting this gala book party. Billy and I autographed more than 600 hardcover copies of this lush love story set in Brazil and Los Angeles. People still talk about this party of the summer! I was extremely grateful, and expressed it in a poem on the Acknowledgments page of our book:

May the soft blossoms of gratitude sweeten the lives of those who care,
Enabling me to live this dream through the gifts they share.
First and foremost, eternal thankfulness to God up in the sky,
Along with my father's protective spirit, beaming down, nearby.
Then my mother's dedication and sacrifice to show how wishes come true,
Her words of wisdom are cast in gold; her helpful acts speak volumes of
*   virtue.*
A husband who understands the goal, the hours, the fantasy of creation,
"Darling, can I get you some tea? It's 3:00 a.m., isn't your brain aching?"
A cherubic smile and big, happy eyes saying, "Mommy, can I write, too?"
Yes, anything you like, because the message in this book is for you.
A sister who knows just what to say in a mellow, calming tone,

142

Far more brave and graceful in the face of fear than anyone I've ever
  known.
A network of family and friends whose love and support are always there,
Whether it's to celebrate or cheer me on or just say they care.
An editor whose expertise and enthusiasm are icing on the cake,
An agent whose vision predicted what a cool project this would make.
A romantic hero and intelligent man who charmed me from page one,
Creating a lush drama with progressive themes until the work was done.
The mentors and advisors sitting at the table around a lavender wish,
Believing that the magic is as real as Sonny and Simone's first forbidden kiss.

In *Twilight*, Simone doesn't know her racial background because she's never met her father. When she meets him, and learns she's biracial, she questions her identity. All while having a secret affair with Sonny.

Billy and I really enjoyed talking about these racial dynamics during TV and radio interviews and book signings throughout the Midwest. In Chicago, Pam Nelson arranged an elegant, supper club-style event at the Regal Theatre where Billy and I sat facing people at tables and talked about the book. We stayed at the swank Peninsula Hotel downtown, rode in a limousine, and dined in delicious restaurants.

An accomplished painter, Billy Dee Williams is a brilliant, worldly man who can talk about anything from his prolific passion for art, to the Byzantine Empire. He was always a perfect gentleman and we continue to enjoy a friendship today as he prepares to again play Lando Calrissian in the upcoming *Star Wars* film.

Meanwhile, it was so fun watching how *Star Wars* fans of all ages and races revered him at our book signings. And I loved witnessing his impact on women who viewed him as a romantic icon. Once, as we rode in a limousine downtown Detroit en route to a book signing at Borders in the Compuware Building, we stopped alongside a lady standing at a bus stop. Billy rolled down the tinted window, looked at her, and said, "Hello."

"It's Billy Dee!" the woman shrieked. Then she literally fell out on the sidewalk! It was hilarious!

Reviews for our book were also enthusiastic: "A richly detailed story—pulsing with the passion we expect from the original ladies' man himself, Billy Dee Williams… *Twilight* reads like a screenplay, filled with expressive dialogue and visually rich description," wrote *Black Issues Book Review.* "Readers looking for a racy, entertaining romp full of plot twists, scandal and exposed secrets will not be disappointed."

Romantic Reviews Today wrote: "Starts with a bang and simply keeps going at death-defying speed until the final climax… Rich and complex."

An Undercurrent Of Angst

Despite the fanfare, I was plagued by an undercurrent of angst about my marriage. One night when I was working on the screenplay to transform *Twilight* into a film, another conflict arose with my husband.

As I contemplated divorce, I thought about the upheaval and unknown negatives of "a broken home" for our child, who was four-and-a-half years old. One night, I was giving him a bath, and we were laughing and playing as he splashed around.

His dad came home, and that recurring issue arose. My energy sunk. Then I saw that our child's expression mirrored my angst. If I had any doubt that I should stay, that moment erased it.

Staying for the sake of the child is not good for the child, I concluded. (Alexander's college professor would later tell me that he wrote a poignant paper about that moment when he witnessed the "sparkle" in my eyes extinguish).

Praying For A Solution On Heavenly Way

The following month in Idlewild, I went in the woods and prayed and prayed and prayed for a solution to leave the marriage. My mind spun in a million directions as I rode my bike in circles for hours along the dirt road by our cottage that I named "Heavenly Way." It's beautiful, peaceful, and seems to extend into an infinity of forest.

I have to get a divorce. I gazed up at the canopy of tree branches and leaves forming a green lattice against the blue sky. *Please God, help me figure out what to do and how to do it.*

The idea of divorce terrified me. Didn't know who to call. Or how much it would cost. But I knew it was time.

Book Dreams Coming True?

I knew I was about to jump, and what better parachute than a book deal? I had yet to secure a fourth book contract, and felt that it was time to change literary agents.

Then I read an article about an agent at one of the world's most powerful agencies. He represented the kinds of books I was writing, and he seemed like a perfect fit. I called him, and within 48 hours, I was sitting in his office in New York.

We went to lunch in a Manhattan restaurant. I was elated, talking with a literary agent about my books and my future, and him seeing my potential as an author. Plus, his agency had a film department in Los Angeles, and we talked about book-to-film deals.

We discussed transforming my father's journals into a book—a fictionalized version of my parents' interracial love story and the religious scandal that it created. So I went home and got to work.

A Baptismal Prayer About The Princess Of Peace

I started reading my father's journals, one by one, from a box that I retrieved from my mother's home. Hand-written on spiral-bound notebooks, they began in 1965 before he left the priesthood, and concluded with a passage he wrote shortly before he died in 1990.

Sitting at my desk in my home office, it was amazing to flip through the pages and read his innermost thoughts. Then I read the July 12,

1967 passage about how my father baptized me in the hospital and asked God to make me a Princess of Peace.

Daddy had never told me this! Ever! Chills danced over my skin as I realized:

I have become a Princess of Peace as a journalist, author, speaker, and citizen!

My soul had organically found its purpose and a path to execute it by creating a "literary ministry." This included three books featuring characters and stories that "edu-tain"—educate and entertain— by celebrating colorblind love. As a journalist and guest on TV and radio programs, I was sharing this message about human harmony. I read my father's passage over and over, studying each word and how these words had manifest in my reality.

"And it was my intention not only to give my daughter these sacraments but also to give her membership in the family of David that she might become an instrument of—a literal Princess of Peace and into the royal priesthood of God so far as my power to convey this in these sacraments."

My mind whirled. What did this mean for my life? My life that, unbeknownst to anyone, was haunted by the secret demise of my marriage. I prayed to find answers on the pages of Daddy's journals.

I tried to connect the dots: Jesus is the Prince of Peace, emanating pure love for everyone. However, I felt zero resonance with Jesus. Never had. Next, my father used the word "literal" when he asked God to make me an "instrument" of his "royal priesthood."

Instrument? My physical make-up—as a genetic blend of sometimes clashing cultures and races—is a teaching tool. My white-looking blackness, and my black-thinking whiteness, force people to question their own beliefs about race.

Instrument? A pen is a writing instrument. English author Edward Bulwer-Lytton first said in 1839, "The pen is mightier than the sword." Meaning, words and communication are more effective at winning battles than physical violence. My instrument is indeed the pen (and the computer keyboard). Likewise, the word "literal" echoed literary, my chosen vocation.

All this stirred my soul as I yearned to know what I should do about it.

Déjà Vu

That warm Saturday in October of 2002 was déjà-vu: I was about to see Oprah Winfrey in person, and was confronted by the same marital problem as the night before going to Chicago for her show. Now, it weighed on my heart as I heard Oprah give a motivational talk at the Fox Theatre in Detroit. Wearing red patent leather boots, she electrified 5,000 people in the sold-out theatre.

Then she talked about how God warns us with whispers, but if we ignore them, the whisper becomes a shout, and if we ignore that, we find ourselves barreling toward a brick wall that ultimately crumbles to a devastating mess that could have been avoided if we had just acted on God's first warning. Well I felt I was barreling toward a brick wall, and needed to do something before catastrophe struck.

"Pray ceaselessly," she said, "and have faith as sure as the sunrise."

Oprah talked about having the courage to make big changes to "live your best life." After her talk, I stood on the rooftop parking deck overlooking the bright lights of the marquis and traffic below on Woodward Avenue. Suddenly something surged up within me and I decided: *The next time this problem comes up, I'm leaving.*

The following day, I ran and walked by Lake St. Clair for two hours, praying on her message. "When I got home I cried and cried and cried… the tears that had wanted to come as Oprah spoke," I wrote in my journal, "and realized what I had to do."

Within a week or two, I left with our son, who was three months shy of his fifth birthday. That night, my soon-to-be-ex-husband made a positive change for himself. Thankfully, he remained a very hands-on father, spending a lot of time with our son, coaching his sports teams, taking him to family events, amusement parks, movies, restaurants, and Detroit Pistons games.

But he became so verbally abusive toward me that I would have— over the next 14 years—four restraining orders to prohibit him from having any contact with me.

"God please help me!" I seemed to pray constantly.

Life During Divorce: Faith, Family, And Fitness

Alexander and I moved in with my mother, who was an absolute angel from the moment I told her why we were leaving. It shocked her and everyone else. No one had a clue, because our life had looked so stable and happy.

My son loved being at Gramma's because she made him pancakes and bacon for breakfast, had Nerf sword fights with him, and took him to The Disney Store whenever he wanted.

I was grateful beyond words that she was so supportive and protective during this very difficult time. Meanwhile, I was confident that I would land book deals that would enable us to move into our own place in a matter of months.

So I worked hard on two book proposals for the literary agent. First, I was reading my father's journals and composing a fictional drama around my parents' story. It was amazing to read how he chronicled the mundane details of family life, such as having meatloaf for dinner, to the magnificent observations and revelations about the depth of love he felt for our mother, Catherine, and me, as well as for God and Jesus.

The second book proposal was called *The Divorce Workout*, showing how to use faith and fitness to endure the process of ending a marriage. I wrote two sample chapters, along with complete workouts based on what I was doing to stay more trim and toned than ever.

While my mother was at work as Chief Judge of Detroit's 36th

District Court, and Alexander was at school, I worked diligently. At the same time, I took aggressive action to come through the divorce looking and feeling my best. My daily self-care regimen included: praying, journaling, eating a healthy diet, exercising, using mantras, and reprogramming my thoughts. Though I called the divorce "the harmonious resolution" in my journal entries, it wasn't playing out that way in reality.

"You Are Goddess"

I coped by going to PowerHouse Gym, where I burned off stress on the cardio machines. One day while pumping my legs on the elliptical machine, his angry words reverberated relentlessly in my mind.

"God please help me!" I prayed.

"You are Goddess," announced a voice inside me.

Then a silver box, like a transformer, appeared in my mind's eye. The box was in the middle of my mind, directly between my ears. I "saw" a stream of his vile words coming in one ear, flowing through the transformer, and coming out the other side as empowering words like Queen and Goddess.

I knew God was talking to me, and showing that my mind has the power to transform negative messages into positive ones. The word "Goddess," I understood at the time, was that the power of God was within me, in female form. He didn't say, "You are *a* goddess." He said, "You are Goddess." Like God, with the female suffix.

So from then on, whenever negative thoughts came to mind, or my soon-to-be-former-husband glared and insulted me, I thought, "I am Goddess." That mantra was like flipping a switch to call in the strengthening, shielding power of God that was already within me.

In addition, I created mantras, such as: "The divine light and goodness of God are radiating from my heart," and I would imagine a golden glow of safety and serenity delighting everyone around me. I repeated these mantras while jogging or exercising at the gym.

All the while, I kept hearing that strength training was the key to true fitness, so I ventured into the weight lifting area, intimidated and clueless about how to use the machines.

"Can I help you?" asked a deep voice.

I jumped. The trainer taught me how to use dumbbells and weight lifting machines. In no time, I was sleek, toned, and more fit than ever. One day while doing squats on the Smith machine, I was consumed by worries about my mounting legal bills. I glanced in the mirror, and froze.

Is that me? I wondered. *Is that the same person who used to look in this mirror and scowl with disgust at chipmunk cheeks, a bloated belly, and bulging thighs? How did I chisel my shoulders into those rippling muscles and sculpt my hips and legs?*

I thanked God for helping me look and feel great under duress—and for showing me the kickboxing dummy—a man-sized, rubber figure on a weighted stand. I bought red boxing gloves and whaled on that thing to my heart's content, several times each week. Some days my hair and sweat flew all around as I grunted and even drooled. It felt so good to release anger! I wanted to tell all women that this was a great way to relieve stress.

"Can I show you something before you hurt yourself?" a trainer asked. "You're going to injure your wrist or throw out your shoulder if you keep this up." He showed me how to properly punch and kick, and I loved it!

I became so fit that I ran 18 miles in the Detroit Free Press Marathon—without training! I was registered to participate on a relay team to support the National Council on Alcoholism and Drug Dependence. I committed to run the first seven miles, and my first marathon was exhilarating. First, everyone's adrenaline electrifies the air. Then, being surrounded by countless pattering feet and muscular legs—all while racing in the middle of a street with no cars—is thrilling!

Even better, running over the huge Ambassador Bridge—above the Detroit River and under the bright blue sky—with the treetops of Canada ahead and the Motor City's skyline to the left—was glorious. I was supposed to pass the baton to the next relay team member in Windsor, and I did. But I kept running! Through the waterside park, into the Detroit-Windsor Tunnel under the river, down Jefferson, around Belle Isle Park.

While collecting my medal and celebrating alongside marathoners inside Ford Field where the Detroit Lions play, I stretched, then ate the best banana ever. After that, I ran in the Susan G. Komen Race for the Cure a few times, as well as the Thanksgiving Day 10K Turkey Trot. A few years later, I ran Detroit's half-marathon, and was thrilled when Alexander (with his dad) joined me at the finish line to celebrate amidst a sea or runners wrapped in silver thermal capes.

Reprogramming My Brain Through Faith & Fitness

Just like with losing weight and getting toned during the divorce, I had to reprogram my thoughts to replace negativity with a Teflon bubble of optimism and faith. I did this by writing in my journal. My passages were prayerful and praiseful. They made me feel peaceful.

Here in the creative safety of my journal, I wrote a detailed script for how I would speak, think, act, eat, exercise, and feel during the divorce, and how my son would feel loved, be safe, and thrive. I read this "New and Improved Elizabeth" script into a microcassette recorder. Every day for seven months while the divorce was pending, I listened to the specific terms and conditions that I wanted, including the best case scenario for our son to spend lots of quality time with his father. I even wrote out scenes detailing exactly how that would work—with calm, cooperation, and composure. I believed that ultimately, we would have a resolution that was, indeed, harmonious.

At the same time, I scripted my fitness objectives, and how I would feel the day of the divorce. The recording also provided a detailed description of my career aspirations that included securing book and film deals, meeting Mariah Carey to collaborate on a creative project, and being a guest on *The Montel Williams Show*. Every day while exercising, driving, and falling asleep, I listened to the recording, allowing my voice to brainwash me into knowing that I could manifest them all.

"I have to work out," I told my mother after a contentious exchange with my soon-to-be-ex. As I drove to the health club, I realized that the fat and frightened Elizabeth of just a few years ago would be speeding to the grocery store for ice cream and cookies. She would sedate herself with sugar and go to sleep. In the morning, she would dread waking up to confront her puffy face, bloated belly, and the emotional chaos of a sugar crash. All the while, the lumps of fresh fat on her thighs would spark such guilt and self-loathing that she would forget the problem that had driven her to pig out and feel horrible. So she would eat more. Gain more weight. And stay trapped in that miserable cycle.

Instead, I was slipping into the swimming pool for 30 minutes of freestyle laps. With every underwater exhalation, I imagined that the bubble of air shooting from my mouth contained my anger and anxiety, floating away, dissolving. *Out with the negative*, I thought, in rhythm with my strokes and breathing. Then, turning my head, I sucked in fresh air, thinking: *in with the positive*. Kicking, pumping my arms, letting the water soothe me.

During the swim, I thought not about burning calories or how my body looked. Instead, I focused on the therapeutic and preventive power of swimming. Then, drying off, I felt light, limber, and relaxed.

Later, at home, after a dinner of baked turkey and spinach salad, I called a spiritual leader who asked God to finalize this divorce so that I and my husband could live peacefully for the rest of our lives. He also prayed that our son would be happy, healthy, safe, and strong.

The result? My body felt swathed in a tingly energy field that was purely positive. Optimistic. Confident.

The next day, we signed the divorce papers. At the courthouse, a crowd blocked the elevators. So I took the stairs—all 18 flights!—wearing black stiletto boots. It was hard to believe that five years earlier, I was 100 pounds heavier, wearing size 26 jeans, with legs so swollen that I could not cross them.

"Elizabeth," a friend said, "if you're stressed, it doesn't show one bit. In fact, you look five to 10 years younger. And you have peace glowing in your eyes."

Novel-Writing Career Sputters After Divorce

It felt like everyone had abandoned me. My literary agent. The businessman who was supposed to ink a deal and write me a big check. My girlfriend who cancelled our lunch date. My personal trainer.

And all the prominent people across the country who had enthusiastically offered to help me secure book and film deals, speaking engagements, and media interviews.

But I was alone, in my room. Ears ringing in the silence. Eyes boring holes through my non-ringing phone. Fingers pounding the keyboard to escape the cybervoid where people had not returned my emails.

I can't believe I'm stuck in this spot in my life.

I thought as soon as I got through the divorce... did a great interview on Montel as the TV author/expert... celebrated my weight loss success on Oprah... got into a speakers bureau... sent my film proposals to the entertainment moguls I met... got a new literary agent who shopped two book proposals around New York...

That the sky would open up, music would play, and fame and fortune would be mine. I would move out of my mother's house, support myself with my little boy, and pay for his private school education.

My career had seemed to come to a screeching halt as a flurry of legal bills threatened to bury me in financial oblivion. Not to mention, with no health insurance, I was a medical bill nightmare waiting to happen.

What was I doing wrong? Why had all the projects and proposals that had seemed like such a sure thing fizzled into disappointments? Why hadn't the decade of hard work that I'd invested in my literary career catapulted me to the next level?

When I tried to get a job, people knew me as an author said they wanted me to remain free to work on my books, while others said they suspected I would leave the job as soon as the right book opportunity came along. I applied for writing grants and reconnected with another literary agent (who flaked out on me), and continuously reached out to agents, editors, and anyone who could help me secure a book deal.

Protected From Harm Despite Naiveté

I was sitting beside an entertainment powerhouse at a banquet in Detroit, telling him about my books after a prominent family friend seated us together.

"I can help you get your books made into movies," said this man who was lauded in the media as a family man and humanitarian. "Bring them to the hotel tonight. Here's my room number and cell phone number."

I went home, retrieved the books, and returned to the hotel. While my naivete sounds unbelievable in hindsight, I was so focused on the Hollywood dream that I did not consider that he had any other motives.

With an armful of books, I walked across the upscale hotel lobby, en route to his room. However, there he was, walking toward me in the lobby with his entourage, and they were heading for the front door. So I handed over the books, and he said he'd be in touch. Over the next weeks and months, I made several follow-up phone calls that did not result in further dialogue or meetings.

Thank you God that I never went to his room, I prayed years later, when many women shared chilling accounts about being sexually assaulted by him. I had shared their starry-eyed trust in his stellar image. *There but for the grace of God go I.*

I profusely thanked God for orchestrating that divine timing. Perhaps he had no other motive than to help. Perhaps he *did* try to help me. I'll never know, but I remain grateful that nothing happened.

Appearing On The Montel Williams Show

Flying to New York... checking in to the famed Waldorf-Astoria hotel... and going to the TV studio for an interview on *The Montel Williams Show*...

I was elated as Montel said my name and, wearing a slim black suit, I walked onto the stage as the Author/Expert for a segment called "Racism: Within Your Own Race." During the October 2003 interview, I said that God created me this way, and blessed me with writing talent, to serve as a messenger about colorblind love. The uplifting show aired and inspired an abundance of praise.

While in New York, I took a jog on Fifth Avenue. When I came to the Harry Winston jewelry store, I remembered the heart-shaped diamond ring that I had posted by my computer while writing my first books. I tried on the two-carat ring! It sparkled so beautifully on my finger, with its F-clarity and baguettes on a platinum band. The perfect heart-shaped diamond was so pure and symbolic of love.

Someday I'll return to get this ring! For myself!

Later, I headed up to Columbia to visit David Klatell, my broadcast news professor. I always visited him when in town, and was honored that he displayed my books on his shelves. I also dined with George Sheer, who had become my "spirit brother," and my friend Michelle Miller, the CBS News correspondent and anchor whom I met at NABJ in LA in 1990.

My national TV appearance on *Montel* shortly after divorcing was encouraging. I remained devoted to exercising and eating healthy. I stayed slim, but was often dizzy with hunger. But I felt confident, in control, and ready for the opportunity to finally get discovered by the right queenmaker.

Coping With Verbal Abuse

My ex-husband's verbal abuse prompted me to seek court-ordered arrangements for him to pick up our son from a trusted relative's home, so we had zero physical contact. Going to court was extremely stressful. One time, I hyperventilated in the lobby. Legal bills, anxiety, and disappointment consumed me. I never wavered in my belief that I had done the right thing—despite many people asking, "Are you *sure* you want a divorce? Are you *sure* you don't want to reconcile?"

In the midst of conflict, I chose the high road with a turn-the-other-cheek response. This infuriated many people who thought I should lash back verbally. I did once, and it made the problem worse. After that, I imagined a Teflon shield over myself, making words and glares simply roll off like droplets of rain on a freshly waxed car.

Angst Inspires Prolific Poetry

Angst is an amazing Muse. After a decade of being part of a couple, who I was as an individual? My quest for answers inspired prolific journal-writing, composing fiction, and creating poetry that included my autobiographical poem:

WHITE CHOCOLATE By Elizabeth Ann Atkins

Don't be fooled by the vanilla hue of my skin,
It doesn't even hint of the chocolate shades of my kin.
Blond hair? Yeah, it comes from England and France.
But questions arise, when I turn around, and you see the way I dance.

Green eyes emphasize this genetic potpourri
An exotic mix of Italian, African American and Cherokee.
I'm like sweet white chocolate fondue in the American melting pot,
Decadent, unique, but bitter, I'm not.

But you wouldn't believe some of the ridiculous questions I hear
From haters, who want me to cringe and fear.
Is this some kind of *Imitation of Life* you're tryin' to perpetrate?
Denyin' half yourself that you loathe and hate?
What color do you prefer when looking for Mr. Right?
Do you ever deny you're black and pass for white?
I can't recite all the crazy questions I get.
But to tell you the truth, I'm tired of this sh*t.
When I'm with a gorgeous black man, women cut their eyes,
The same way some men glare and despise…
What they think is jungle fever,
But they're wrong, so let me make it clear.

We come in all colors, from milky white to black as licorice,
Getting this point across is my lifelong wish.
What's more beautiful than the spectacular spectrum of cashew, but-
    terscotch, and coffee bean brown?
Redbone, blue-black, high-yella, just look around.
Everybody's got somethin' stirred in their mix.
It's time for our minds to stop playin' wicked tricks.
Hatin' on a sista for lookin' a certain way.
Seein' her with a brotha and havin' something sassy to say.

But the tripped-out thing is, soon as I say "I'm black, too,"
Everything changes and they're saying, "I love you."
Like at the Essence Festival in New Orleans in July.
This woman came up and asked me why

I was in the author tent, autographing books.

It happened on a day full of curious stares and looks.

I'm white and black, here's my book *Twilight,* I wrote it with Billy Dee,

All of a sudden she smiled, gave some love, and hugged me.

That's ok, go ahead and laugh at me,

Because Montel found it intriguing and invited me on TV.

As the author-expert whose goal is to unite the races,

To inspire close-minded folks to rise up from ignorant places.

My father ask God to make me a Princess of Peace,

To create a literary ministry, to cure us of this racism disease.

So I use my Malibu Barbie looks to shock and surprise,

Make folks realize that we love with our hearts and our minds,

Not our skin, but how God made us within.

So bring it on, ask me why I'm here.

I've gotten over the embarrassment and the fear.

This is my purpose, my passion, to educate and entertain

To use my White Chocolate sweet stuff, to heal the pain.

I performed this poem at many spoken word events, including: the Harlem Book Fair; jazzy Detroit nightclubs; programs in Los Angeles; and Poetry in the Woods in Idlewild with New York poets and tap-dance performer Savion Glover.

Also during this time, I enjoyed freelancing for *HOUR Detroit Magazine, HOUR Bride,* and *HOUR Home,* thanks to my former *Detroit News* colleague Rebecca Powers, who became HOUR Editor-in-Chief. Her many awesome assignments included writing a biography of Rosa Parks for the program when she received the Presidential Medal of Freedom from President Bill Clinton in 1996.

I was tremendously grateful that Alexander and I lived with my mother. Each day I drove him to school, where he was thriving. We had so much fun going to Detroit's Riverwalk, where he splashed in water spraying up from the cement amongst a mini United Nations of children shrieking with joy under their parents' adoring gazes.

More fun followed at our cottage, where we searched for bugs, played in the sand, swam in Lake Michigan, and took bike rides with him pulled behind me in a covered trailer. Our favorite pastimes included perusing the children's section and reading books at the Borders bookstore in Grosse Pointe and the Compuware Building downtown Detroit.

We also cherished wonderful and frequent visits to the Detroit Zoo. Walking hand-in-hand to observe otters, alligators, tigers, and exotic frogs, I savored the feeling of being a million miles away from the cares of the world, and conflict with my ex-husband. While watching Alexander run and climb on the playground, I was overwhelmed with gratitude that the Zoo provided this sanctuary of pure joy.

Writing & Reciting To Manifest Goals

Napoleon Hill's instructions for success in *Think and Grow Rich* said to write your "definite chief aim in life." So I did, in three parts:

"For myself: Exercise and superior nutrition are keeping my mind, body, and spirit strong so that I may savor inner serenity, indulge my passion for writing, speaking, expressing myself in creative ways, live every second of this glorious life to the fullest, suck every drop of the delicious maple syrup drizzling over this most decadent life of mine."

Next, I wrote my intention for my family: "Be the most loving, gentle, nurturing, educational mother to raise Alexander into a happy, healthy, confident, creative, fulfilled, productive man. I am also an exemplary daughter for Marylin Atkins, sharing love, laughter, success, and fulfillment with her, making her proud, and taking care of her with the utmost love and attention. I am a loving, listening sister for Catherine, sharing laughter and guidance." It concluded by saying, "We live in this precious, magical glow around us and our family."

After that, I wrote my "definite chief aim in life" for the world:

"Grounded in gratitude and love, my newfound inner sense of peace elevates me to a galactic height of creativity, passion and productivity. I am sharing through my unique lens of sensitivity and desire to heal others, a message through the written and spoken word—in books, novels, articles, advertisements, screenplays, speeches—a vision and angelic energy that uplifts and inspires people across all lines of color and culture, all around the globe."

I recorded all of the above, and much more, into my microcassette recorder, and listened while driving, exercising, and falling asleep. This habit was inspired by Hill's chapter on Autosuggestion, which I interpreted as reprogramming your brain. When you listen to your own voice describing what you want as if you already have it, in a spirit of gratitude, your mind believes it and activates something inside you and in the universe that helps it become reality.

In addition, I conceived my dream home, Sea Castle, to build someday on my private Mermaid Island in the Bahamas. Thanks to years of studying floor plan books, and spending hours on the living floor drawing home designs as a girl, I drew a floor plan for Sea Castle. Then I typed five, single-spaced pages describing the home, including its Moroccan lounge. I knew that someday I would build Sea Castle and call it home.

Visiting Catherine In California

For Thanksgiving of 2002, my mother and I and Alexander visited Catherine in San Francisco. We returned a year later to see her and attend the swearing-in ceremony for former Detroit Mayor Dennis Archer, who was elected as the first person of color to become president of American Bar Association, which had 400,000 lawyers across America and the world and which once banned black members. We met Mayor Willie Brown, and attended receptions celebrating this historic event.

Highlights of the trip included eating at The Stinking Rose, a restaurant featuring garlic in every dish, including ice cream. We visited Alcatraz, shopped, ate Thai food, and visited the Exploratorium. A major highlight was the amount of time we spent laughing and having ridiculous fun as we walked around the city and trudged up the steep sidewalks.

Dating Inspires Provocative Trilogy About Women & Love

When I first divorced, after 10 years of monogamy, I did not want to remarry or have a serious relationship. I just wanted to enjoy myself. But it didn't take long to realize that dating was a big disappointment. Sure, it was fun, and I met some really awesome men.

The long list of negatives, however, soon made me withdraw from the whole scene altogether. Instead, I channeled my energy into writing books, teaching community college, and most importantly, being a mom to my elementary school-age son. This detachment enabled me to observe the modern state of marriage, romance, and relationships.

First came the harsh realization that the mushy-gushy dreams of wedded bliss can spiral into an abyss in divorce court. Then you don't just sign papers and step into the perfect life. Divorce takes a terrible toll; it requires time to recover emotionally and financially.

Meanwhile, I wondered: Is true love a lie? How can all that euphoria during courtship, engagement, and the newlywed years just—*pouf!*—go away?

Is monogamy a myth?

Do I know any long-term married couples who are truly happy? Do I know any men whom I believe are faithful to their girlfriends or wives? Why should they be? Dating apps place a catalog of cuties at your fingertips. If you're not available at the moment, the next girl is… Or if he wants daily variety, voilà. And since technology re-programs us to get everything instantly—and forgo delayed gratification—why should a guy wait until tomorrow to see me, when he can text Suzie and hook up now?

All the while, I was encountering married men who tried to date me by lying that they were single, while single men who pretended I was the only one dropped big clues that I was one of many. Why all the lies? Why couldn't they just be honest?

Men are biologically hardwired to spread their seed to ensure survival of the human race. Women have traditionally been socialized to commit to one man for life; these unions have given men dominion over women while rendering us virtually powerless.

Today is a new day, and many of us reject that relationship template. We want power, we want pleasure, and we want peace. My obsession with this idea, inspired me to write a screenplay about a Detroit-based company called Husbands, Incorporated that goes global by providing legal, one-year marriages that enable women to experience their wildest fantasies with wonderful men who pamper them in every way.

"Where can I sign up for this?" many women ask.

"It's fiction," I say, "but the issues are real." The four main couples in Husbands, Inc. burst open a Pandora's box of conflicts about monogamy, relationships, self-image, and society's expectations. As I composed the screenplay, I attended a three-day seminar in New York City with Robert McKee, author of *STORY: Substance, Structure, Style, and the Principles of Screenwriting*. He played a cameo role as himself in the 2002 Spike Jonze film, *Adaptation*, starring Nicolas Cage.

Robert McKee taught this intensive course as I sat in an auditorium with several hundred writers from around the world. The course concluded with us watching *Casablanca*, whose genius literary devices he had frequently referenced. It was fabulous!

"To Elizabeth: Write the truth!" Robert McKee wrote in purple ink above his autograph in his 467-page hardcover book that I purchased. I went home determined to transform *Husbands, Incorporated*—and my novels—into blockbuster films.

Ask and It Is Given

With Hollywood dreams dancing in my head, I still needed to make a living, and had always wanted to become a college professor. Efforts to secure a teaching position at my favorite university had failed. Still, I prayed, "God to please help me teach college." One Saturday, I told my mother I would pursue local opportunities the following Monday.

Well, God works faster than that. That evening, we attended a performance at the Fox Theater. Seated nearby was Wayne County Community College District Chancellor Dr. Curtis Ivery, whom I had met well before this.

"Hi Dr. Ivery," I said. "I'd like to talk with you about teaching at WCCCD."

"Call my office Monday morning," he said.

A short time later, I began teaching creative writing and Women's Literature at the downtown Detroit campus. The student population is predominantly urban, and many of the men and women are single parents who work full time. Some take the bus—sometimes multiple buses in a city where buses were notoriously late—in the snow and frigid temperatures.

Teaching Women's Lit was glorious! We used *The Norton Anthology of Women in Literature*, and followed a chronology from 17th Century English Writer Aphra Behn up to contemporary writers, including myself, as students read and discussed *Dark Secret*.

Our lessons roused flashbacks to my Women's Studies classes at the University of Michigan when I was furious that women writers were historically oppressed. Now, how would I help urban students relate to women writers in 1600s England? I assigned them to write a paper comparing historic women's poetry to contemporary music lyrics.

One woman wrote a brilliant paper comparing Aphra Behn's poetry to L.L. Cool J songs! I was over the moon that she described how they were both singing about the same love and longing, centuries apart!

That was so satisfying, as were our many spirited discussions about works by Louise Erdrich, Virginia Woolf, Gloria Anzaldula, and Zora Neale Hurston, whom I absolutely loved for her brilliant ability to weave eloquent narrative with Southern black colloquial dialogue. We studied each author's life, and I admired their unconventional, independent spirits when most women were relegated to doing housework and having babies.

Teaching there was amazing. One student had memorized *The Color Purple* by Alice Walker. She recited lines as her comments during classroom discussions! I remain in contact with many students, including filmmaker Malcolm X. Johnson. I'm so proud when they see me in public and call me "Professor Atkins" and say they learned and were inspired my classroom.

Moving To A New Apartment and Starting A New School

Moonlight and the glow of the city skyline poured into the floor-to-ceiling windows as I laid on the new carpeting in my very own living room.

"Thank you God for my own apartment!" Tears of joy and gratitude streamed down my cheeks. My income from teaching, as well as a book deal to write two novels, enabled me to move in January of 2005.

Alexander's room had a spectacular view of downtown. My mother painted the walls blue to match his Spiderman bedspread, and she built shelves to hold his toys and TV. We decorated his bathroom with a shimmery blue shower curtain displaying colorful fish that matched a metal wall hanging, soap dish, and towels.

My peach room featured an ornate copper headboard and crown with gold tulle, and my own full bath. In the living room, a red suede sectional, zebra print rugs, big plants, and chrome-and-glass tables matched the dining room set. It was chic! I worked at a desk in one corner.

I felt safe there, as visitors had to pass through questioning by a guard at the security gate, as well as a doorman/security guard at the locked lobby door. The building also had a swimming pool and was located on the grassy expanse of a park.

During this time, I was determined to find the best school for Alexander, who was in first grade. Since Detroit's public schools were not excellent, I visited local private schools.

The first moment we entered University Liggett School in Grosse Pointe Woods, I was overwhelmed with love and peace. In the lobby, Admissions Director Denise Deane and Lower School Director Sheila Chaps made us feel at home.

"Mom, let's go in there!" Alexander said, pulling my hand toward the open double doors revealing high school theatre practice in the auditorium.

Dr. Phillip Moss and the teenage actors stopped to talk with six-year-old Alexander, who watched with wide-eyed fascination as they practiced on the student-built set. They invited him to return after our tour of the school. I was very impressed by the authentic interest that the students and Dr. Moss showed for my excited little boy.

Likewise, the teachers were enthusiastic, emphasizing good citizenship, participation in sports and other activities, and individualized attention in classes of 14 students or less. The tuition bill was huge for second grade, but this was an investment that I and his father believed was worth every dime.

"Are you buying a house?" the bank teller asked, when I requested a cashier's check for his first tuition payment. Thankfully, this would become the best small fortune that we've ever spent. I would need 10 Thesauruses to describe my gratitude to God and to the school for this priceless blessing.

One morning in my son's classroom, an adorable little girl told me, "My mom gave me a hundred dollars because I won a bet with her!" Then I drove to the college. A paper was due, and as students turned them in, one young man whispered, "Ms. Atkins, I couldn't print my paper because our electricity got cut off last night." I gave him an extension, feeling chilled by the socioeconomic discrepancies between people's lives who lived just miles—but worlds—apart.

"It Sounds Like Angina... A Heart Attack"

Grief wracked my body as yet another report flashed on TV about the horrors inflicted on the people of New Orleans by Hurricane Katrina. I couldn't stop sobbing when an old black man stood in a flooded intersection, pointing to the direction where water had swept his wife out of his arms, disappearing and presumably drowned.

Through my tears, I couldn't see the newspapers spread out in front of me on the coffee table, along with an empty bowl that had held several scoops of ice cream. It was August of 2005, and I could not look away from this nightmare. I empathized with the plight of the men, women, and children suffering in the stadium.

"Alexander, let's take a donation of clothes and other things to a drop-off spot," I said. When we returned, I plunked back on the couch to immerse in my media vigil, praying for those suffering, and for help to come soon. This came on the heels of a very stressful writing project.

The following week, Alexander started his new school, and I was facing deadlines to write two, 100,000-word novels while beginning a full-time teaching schedule. While grateful for these blessings, I was anxious.

One afternoon, while I was sitting at my desk writing a syllabus for one of my four classes, tension burned in my neck, shoulders, chest, and down my left arm. I called my doctor.

"You're young, but it sounds like angina," he said.

"What's that?" I asked.

"A heart attack. You should go to the ER and get it checked out."

My mother drove me to the hospital. In the ER bay, she said, "You need to get a grip on your stress!"

"I'm fine!"

"That's why you're hooked up to a heart monitor!" she exclaimed.

We both cracked up. Thankfully, my heart was fine. It was "just" stress. I had to find peace, but didn't know how.

"What Brings *You* Here?"

The cab driver glanced at the African American professionals in front of the Cleveland Convention Center. Then he turned his puzzled face to me as we pulled into traffic.

"So," he said, "what brings *you* here?"

He echoed a black woman in the bathroom that afternoon during the 2005 PowerNetworking conference. As my reflection contrasted with the ladies around us in the mirror, I knew she was wondering, *What's this white woman doing at this black event?*

Well, as PowerNetworking CEO George Fraser often begins his speeches, I could have exclaimed, "Yes, I *am* black."

But sometimes I just don't feel like explaining. Sometimes I like to see what happens if folks take me at face value—and deal with my spirit, rather than all the question marks they see dancing in my green eyes, over my white skin, and through the curls of my blond hair. Sometimes I enjoy watching them try to figure it out.

But it's not fun when a cold blast of hate gusts from their eyes, their faces, their actions. Like the black woman who checked me into the hotel. I knew it wasn't personal. It was about pain she had endured in a racist world. So I responded with my antidote—super-sweet politeness—to show that good comes in every color.

As for the taxi driver, and the woman in the ladies room, I said, "I'm biracial. Half black, half white, and I write books about it, to help people think and talk about race in a new way."

"Oh," they said, intrigued.

I attended PowerNetworking conferences for several years, at the invitation of George Fraser, whom I helped write *Click! 10 Truths to Building Extraordinary Relationships.* (McGraw Hill, Jan. 2008). I conducted my How to Write a Book and Get Published seminar to standing-room only crowds.

During one workshop about the entertainment and sports industry, a panelist with blond hair, blue eyes, and white skin spoke with an African American inflection. After the presentation, I talked with him, and neither of us believed that the other was black. He stared at me, I stared and him, and we both shook our heads. It was hilarious. I've called him "my white chocolate brother" ever since.

Speaking French At LAX

After a trip to Los Angeles to visit friends and network, I was standing in a long security line at the airport, when I heard a man speaking French. He was very upset, as was his wife, as they argued with a TSA officer. But the officer was speaking English and the couple understood nothing.

I stepped toward them and, in French, asked if I could help. The couple, in their sixties, looked at me in awe and relief. They explained their dilemma in French, and I relayed it to the TSA officer in English. Then I translated his message to the couple.

Thankfully, their problem was solved. After showering me with an abundance of "thank you's" in French, they hurried away, looking relieved. I tingled with a "Helper's High."

"Nice job," said a Danish man standing nearby.

Celebrating Family Unity At Thanksgiving

During the early 1970s, when Grandma UpNorth Alphonsine was in the hospital, Aunt Mary asked my mother to advocate on her behalf to the doctors who were treating my grandmother. Aunt Mary couldn't be there herself, and trusted my mother in this role.

This inspired newfound warmth that resulted in us being included in family events, such as weddings and graduations. Aunt Mary's eight children are a decade or two older than me and Catherine, and some have grown children and grandchildren.

Together we celebrate Easter and Thanksgiving. In 2006, the family feast that draws at least a dozen and sometimes 20 people representing four generations, included Aunt Mary, who was 88. She sat at the head of the table, and Alexander joined me and my mother. We took pictures, laughed, ate delicious food, and cherished the peaceful, loving day. The following week—on my father's birthday—Aunt Mary enjoyed milk and gingerbread cookies, fell asleep in her own bed, and went to heaven.

We are so grateful for the family unity and harmony as we continue to gather for sporting events and other festivities. Our cousins are extremely supportive and embracing of Alexander, attending his theatrical and sports events.

Obsessed With "The Secret" That Doesn't Work

In 2006, I saw Rhonda Byrne on *Oprah*, talking about *The Secret*, her film and book about how to use the law of attraction to manifest our greatest dreams. I read the book and watched the movie over and over. I even let it play while I was sleeping.

I attempted to use the law of attraction for: book and film deals for the many manuscripts in my computer; speaking engagements through the speaker's bureau; and the perfect romantic partner. It didn't work.

But my life was rich with love and priceless lessons.

My saving grace was my mother, who was indescribably support-ive in so many ways, it would fill 10 books to list them all. No words exist to express the depth of my gratitude for her love and support. Likewise, my sister, Catherine, who lived in a variety of far-away states during this period, was an angel.

As was Alexander. One day after washing several loads of laundry, I dumped them on my bed. While I folded towels, he was batting an empty plastic shopping bag through the air with his hand and laughing. I snapped, "Alexander let's get this done."

Still hitting the bag, he said, "I want to make everything as fun as possible!"

I froze. Why was I so uptight? I joined him in bat-the-bag, laughing and loving how children make us lighten up and enjoy the moment.

Another time, we were in the phone store, which was busy with customers. While waiting for an employee to help us, Alexander and I played peek-a-boo with an adorable toddler hiding under a stool. Her mother noticed, and I said, "She's so beautiful."

The woman snapped, "She so mean!"

Alexander looked perplexed. He glanced at the girl, then at her mother, and said, "But she doesn't have mean eyes."

His wise-beyond-his-years commentary inspired people around the apartment complex to call him, "Mr. President." And in 2008, when then-U.S. Senator Barack Obama was running for President, Alexander and his father attended a rally at Detroit's Cobo Hall, and he was inter-viewed by a local TV station.

Shredding The Bullseye In The Gun Range

As I alternated aiming a Glock and a .38 Special at the man-shape on the paper target, I let 35 years' worth of fear surge up and out into my index finger as I pulled the trigger. In my mind's eye was the neighbor who had terrified me as a child. Each bullet struck the black bullseye. The little holes literally shredded the paper, creating a gaping hole in the chest of my molester. I displayed the riddled paper target on my dining room wall for several years, and I still have it.

Busy Days as Mom and Teacher

My alarm clock jolted me awake before dawn. Chugging coffee, I graded stacks of papers at the dining room table. Then I made a cheese quesadilla and fresh fruit for Alexander's breakfast, before driving him 30 minutes to school.

"Millions of angels are over him," I prayed, staring through the hallway windows outside his second grade classroom as Mrs. McCoy quieted the 14 children in their adorable khaki pants, skirts, and polo shirts. Only when I felt the presence of angels hovering over my son and his classmates and teacher, could I leave the school. I was often the last parent to leave the hallway. (This angel-vision ritual started when he was 2 ½ at Montessori school, until the end of fifth grade, only because he started middle school and it wasn't cool for your mom to walk you into school). Then I drove a half hour to the college.

"The key to great writing is to show, don't tell," I told 30 students in creative writing class. "Don't tell that she's sad. Show that she's sniffling with puffy, bloodshot eyes."

I loved teaching! Standing in front of classrooms and talking for 45 minutes or an hour, several times each day, was a huge energy expenditure. It's actually a performance, to keep students engaged.

Later, I picked up Alexander, and brought him back to campus where he did homework in the back of a classroom while I taught a Toastmasters class about public speaking. After that, we went home and I either made him dinner or he dined during a scheduled visit with his father. In the evening, we played a game or watched a movie, I read to him and put him to bed, then graded more papers. Two evenings per week, I took him to fencing class. On the weekends, I attended his basketball and football games.

Over the course of a few years, I also taught journalism at Oakland University in Rochester Hills, a 45-minute drive from home, and at nearby Wayne State University. I was exhausted!

One day I crunched the numbers: the hours grading papers, preparing for class, driving, and teaching—compared to my pay—was a paltry sum. I stopped teaching, and prayed to earn a living by writing books.

Sharing My Gift Through Ghostwriting

God answered with new ghostwriting clients, including an insurance agent. Corky Gillis flew his small airplane to Detroit to meet me, invited me to Kentucky for research, and I loved writing a suspense novel for him called *The Death Bond Conspiracy*.

I discovered that I am a literary chameleon, blessed with the ability to take on the voice and perspective of another person and write as if I am him or her. This is the key skill required for ghostwriting, which means being hired to write someone else's book. My first ghostwriting project for Detroit real estate developer Anthony Kellum in 2002 had enabled me to discover this skill.

Now, I was always sending out new correspondences and taking trips to meet with literary agencies in New York and Los Angeles.

At one point, my friend invited me to the Soul Train Music Awards in Pasadena, California, where Mariah Carey would perform. As I sat in the theatre during sound checks before the show, the stage manager approached.

"Can you come on stage so we can do a lighting and sound check?" he asked with a laugh. "You're perfect for this. You look just like her!"

I was elated! Back in 2003, my audiotaped goals had included "meeting Mariah Carey." Well, after this show, I was having a one-on-one conversation with her! She was beautiful, tall, and engaging as I talked about being biracial and how her music inspired me.

"I want to write your memoir," I said. She put me in touch with her manager, who invited me to meet in New York. There, my books that I had sent were displayed on a long table with memoirs of famous people whose ghostwriters, I guessed, were also being considered to write Mariah's book. After an excellent meeting with her manager, further communications buoyed my hope that I would be chosen to tell her story. Then—

She had a breakdown. Not a good time to write a book.

Around that time, my friend whom I had met at Fox 2 News, Kristin Schenden, introduced me to Ron and Mike Morelli, who had excelled on NBC's hit TV show, *The Biggest Loser*, and wanted to write a book. I interviewed them, along with wife Becky, and son Max, and composed their story about how they had lost nearly 800 pounds! *Fat Family, Fit Family: How We Beat Obesity and You Can Too* was published by Penguin Books in 2011.

I also contributed novellas to two anthologies published by the Atria imprint of Simon & Schuster in October of 2007 and March of 2011.

"Elizabeth Atkins' 'The Wrong Side of Mr. Right' hits a profound closing note when a pair of old Jamaican wedding slippers inspire a woman to face the reality of her abusive Prince Charming," *Publisher's Weekly* wrote about my story in *My Blue Suede Shoes: Four Novellas*, a collaboration with Tracy Price-Thompson, TaRessa Stovall, and Desiree Cooper. For this Sister4Sister Empowerment Series, each of us wrote about a woman becoming empowered to escape domestic abuse, and *Publisher's Weekly* called it "a moving collection."

Our first anthology was *Other People's Skin*, about women becoming empowered about racial identity in the context of skin color, hair texture, and eye color. My story, "Take It Off!" is about a mixed-race woman who's caught in the crossfire between blacks and whites on a college campus, and covers her coarse hair with a hat. I organized panel discussions in Detroit featuring myself, Des Cooper, and psychologist Gail Parker, PhD. National NPR's Michel Martin interviewed me and TaRessa.

Also during this time, *New York Times* bestselling author E. Lynn Harris, who became famous during the early 1990s with his release of *Invisible Life*, about a gay black man hiding his sexuality while dating women, hired me to edit his books. I had met him around 2003 in Chicago while attending Book Expo America; he invited me and other authors to a reception in his downtown high-rise home. We kept in touch, and he reached out to me to help on the last books of his life. He even mentioned me in the acknowledgments.

One morning, we enjoyed a great conversation about how to proceed with his next projects, which included a book called, *Upon My Demise*. He was heading to Los Angeles, and we would talk soon. The next day, July 23, 2009, I was at a book fair, and during a lull, I checked my *USA Today* phone app. A headline said that E. Lynn Harris died in LA of an apparent heart attack. I was so sad to lose my beloved friend who had pioneered a new voice in American literature.

Also during this period, my ex-husband arranged for me to write a book for his friend, Kenneth Tyson, who was quadriplegic due to a car crash. The Motown native achieved his dream: opening a record company. It was an honor to write his inspiring story, *Coming Full Circle: From Birth to Death to Life* before Ken died in 2008.

At times, in the spirit of wanting a harmonious co-parenting relationship, my ex-husband and I made peace and even took a non-romantic family trip to Disney World. We also held great birthday parties for Alexander and attended events at his school. Many people remarked that we seemed to get along so well that they thought we were still married.

But when a reconciliation didn't happen, his resulting hostility prompted me to obtain another restraining order. With this, and yearning for commercial and financial success for my novels, I became depressed.

"Why do I exist?" I cried on the floor of my apartment, desperate to feel better and thrive emotionally and financially while raising my young son. I literally clung to him for dear life, as I felt such pure love, joy, and gratitude with him. How could I generate that feeling within myself, about myself? I prayed and prayed and prayed. "God please help me!"

I often jogged or biked to the RiverWalk, then stood at the railing, casting prayers for career success, peace and joy, and true love. When I prayed, "God please make my dreams come true," God answered every time: "They will."

I wanted so desperately to stay upbeat that I started a blog called The Bliss Report, featuring snapshots from my daily life that I hoped would inspire others to feel happier.

Attempting Lift-off As A Diversity Speaker

In a sleek conference room in Beverly Hills, the entertainment lawyer clicked a remote to play one of his mega-star client's promotional video on a big screen.

"Elizabeth, you need a sizzle reel," he said. "Like this. To show people who you are and share your message, so they can hire you to speak events across the country. After you wow the crowd, they'll buy your books. This could be very successful for you."

I returned from this trip—like many that I took to meet with literary agents and others in New York and Los Angeles—encouraged that a promotional video would result in paid speaking engagements and book signings.

My friend Lee Thomas created a sizzle reel—a high-energy compilation of clips from my TV appearances interspersed with video he shot of me, telling my story and writing at my desk overlooking the city. I reciprocated our creative synergy by editing Lee's memoir, *Turning White*, about his courageous and inspiring experience with

Vitiligo, a condition that causes skin to lose its color.

After that, I sent the sizzle reel to my speaker's bureau, which represented influential people around the world. They posted the video in their online catalogue. The goal was for me to speak as an author-expert about the biracial experience and human harmony at colleges, conferences, and companies.

I was grateful that the agency booked two speaking engagements: one at a small Illinois college; the other at Beaumont Hospital Diversity Symposium near Detroit. Through my personal and professional network, I was invited to speak at General Motors World Diversity Day, the University of Michigan, Columbia University, the 100 Black Men conference in Orlando, Florida, and the North Oakland County NAACP banquet. My poem, *White Chocolate*, and keynote speech roused a standing ovation from 500 people, who then purchased my books.

As a workshop leader at the annual Oakland University Writers Conference, I met New York editors and agents with whom I kept in touch. For several years at the conference, I taught how to write suspenseful scenes, create engaging characters, and compose realistic dialogue.

"I really liked your presentation," said one attractive white gentleman. "I was thinking about asking you out on a date. But when you said you're biracial, I had to ask myself if I still wanted to date you."

I calmly asked him, "What does it mean about race if you liked me before you heard that label? Doesn't that show that it doesn't matter?"

He looked pensive, then his eyes lit up. "You're right," he said. "Wow. I never thought about it like that."

Another time, a black man said he would not be seen with me because he didn't want anyone to think he was with a white woman. And a respected professional advised me to dye my hair brown and visit a tanning booth if I wanted to do successful business with people of color.

Later, after I wrote an article for *Ebony* magazine about my unique racial space, I was invited as a guest on *Tyra* and was flown to New York for the taping. I also contributed to *Essence*, and enjoyed interviewing Alice Walker's daughter, Jessica Walker, for *Ms.*

I also worked as a diversity trainer for a local law enforcement agency, an auto company, and a local county's human resources office. During this period, I advertised my services as a Book Coach via email, and guided several aspiring writers in Detroit and other states, through the writing process.

In 2008, I self-published a second edition of *Dark Secret*. It was my most popular book, and I needed inventory for book signings and other events. For the cover art, my mother and I had a photoshoot in Idlewild; she took tons of pictures of me, using my father's camera.

This was an example of the many fun times I enjoy with my mother at the cottage. Whether we're talking on the deck swing, watching a movie, or taking a bike ride around the lake, the serenity of Idlewild sparkles with an energy that makes you laugh harder, smile wider, and cherish your loved ones more deeply.

"Magic, Miracles, and Millions Are Mine"

When Alexander was completing fifth grade, we were facing a hefty tuition bill for sixth grade, and I had no current or projected means to pay it. Still, I knew God would make something amazing happen.

Meanwhile, I volunteered at the school's annual spring picnic. For weeks before it, students sold raffle tickets for prizes such as new cars, jewelry, even a boat. This year, the grand prize was one year of tuition, paid in full. I entered, as I had for the three previous years, but had never won anything.

My hopes weren't too high for winning, so I left before the drawing. The freeway was the fastest route home, but I preferred the flower-lined boulevard where mansions overlook Lake St. Clair. The bright blue water extending to the horizon radiates soothing spiritual power. There I pray, cast wishes into the universe, and recite out loud one of my favorite mantras:

"Magic, miracles, and millions are mine, now and forever." I declared this over and over as the sun shimmered on the lake. A spiritual vortex in front of St. Paul Catholic Church often causes cell phone calls to drop. A circle-shaped rainbow frequently appears over this spot, and as I drive, jog, or walk through it, I have often experienced epiphanies, great ideas for writing, and sudden calm.

"Magic, miracles and millions are mine, now and forever," I repeated, driving through the vortex after the picnic. My cell phone rang. It was my friend, another mom at the school, exclaiming:

"Elizabeth! You won! You won full tuition for sixth grade!"

I gasped, cried, and praised God over and over. Shaking, I did a U-turn, and drove back to the picnic, where I was showered with congratulations. I profusely thanked the head of our school, Dr. Joseph P. Healey.

"You deserve it," he said. Several parents phoned, saying, "We are so happy that you won! We can't think of a better person to receive such a gift!"

This gift came straight from God. I share it as an example of knowing that God can always make a way out of no way.

Alexander attended sixth grade at the middle school, which was red brick with white columns, and the entrance hall had a black and white checkered floor, an open staircase, and a chandelier. Nearby, students ate lunch in a carpeted dining room. Most importantly, love and peace permeated this building where Alexander thrived in academics, acted in theatrical performances, and played on the basketball team.

It was an honor to serve as a "Room Parent" with another mom. And I knew he was getting a stellar education when I picked him up one day and he clearly explained something I had never understood:

the Arab-Israeli conflict. I was in awe!

Slipping Into An Emotional Abyss

During the summer of 2009, when I turned 42, I composed a journal entry called "The Abyss." Here it is:

I feel so alone.

I sat staring at the river this Friday evening, sitting on a bench under the warm blue sky as the setting sun cast a cozy orange glow over my skin.

Alexander went to an amusement park with his dad and their friends for the weekend. I've been trying to lose weight, which means eating less, which means even when I try to work—today on one of my screenplays— my brain is dull and my focus is fuzzy.

(The man I was dating was going to come over at 5:30). I took my bike ride for about an hour, along the RiverFront, then freshened up and waited. And waited. And waited. It's 4 hours later and he never even called. He's never done this before. Maybe he had an emergency.

I have gained 30 pounds since this time last year.

I have no (local) friends, I realized tonight by the river.

When Alexander is with his dad, I feel lost. And when I'm sad—this week I've been downright depressed—the writing doesn't flow. It seems like I should have all this time for writing. But to tell the truth, after I finished E. Lynn's book two weeks ago today, it's just been turned off. Do I need the pressure of working for someone else to motivate me? Am I so discouraged that I've given up?

I have four book proposals in my computer, ready for (the latest agent I was speaking with), but none of them excited (the agent). I have this memoir, but the agent said it'd have to be done in a really spectacular way to work, or would be better if I relaunch my career and become really famous and then do a memoir.

The idea of promoting myself makes me cringe sometimes. I think, "Oh please listen to me, please pay attention to me, please, please."

The idea of going to a party makes me cringe, too. The other day when I went to the gym—I rode my bike there—there was a party for the The Detroit Free Press in the lobby and... I was so hoping that no one in the crowd would recognize me or want to talk with me.

Today when I was spaced out and trying to work on The Ghostwriter screenplay, I heard Daddy as if he were speaking to me inside my mind... I glanced often at his picture hanging above my desk.

"Release all the negativity and progress into the future," he said. "Forgive yourself." I concentrated on that, suddenly feeling free. "Everything you've experienced is to prepare you for your greatness that is coming very soon."

It was wonderful.

"You're furious," my therapist said yesterday morning during our weekly, 45-minute session. I owe her about $2,000, but she said she doesn't want to drop me during my darkest hour. She is phenomenal; I gain tremendous insights every time we talk.

I told her that I have felt downright depressed over the past week, and that I have binge eating disorder. "All I want to do is sit on my couch," I said.

"That's classic depression," she said.

When she first said that word a long time ago—I think I first went to her three years ago in March—I couldn't grasp it or apply it to myself. But now I do. "A lot of times I'm just two thoughts away from crying," I told her.

And usually it's in relation to feeling so alone (in terms of adult companionship). I remember going to the movies with Alexander... and I was crying because either someone in the film was in love or someone was alone, and I cried with the fear of never feeling loved by a man again.

So what do I want? On many, many levels, I have everything I want. First, Alexander is healthy, happy, and thriving. He gets so much love from me and his dad.

I love my apartment. The dream of moving to Grosse Pointe is there, but when I wake up in the middle of the night and feel scared, I'm relieved that there's only one door and we live on the 9th floor, so the windows are secure. I like my city girl swag but I love Lakeshore and the lake. I feel instantly serene there.

Otherwise, I am so happy in so many ways.

We are tremendously healthy. I LOVE being Alexander's mother. I kiss him so much on his cheeks and just smile at him while he's sleeping or looking back at me. I stare at him with complete enchantment. I love being with Alexander.

"Look at you and your mini me," a lady in the elevator said yesterday. "He looks JUST like you!" I loved that! Then we cuddled on the couch and watched a movie.

Outside of being an excellent mother, I have no idea who I am, I feel lost, and when I slip back into that wonderful space of being his mom, I am again at peace.

Back in June, when Alexander was with his father for his first of four weeks of summer visitation, I didn't know what to do with myself. While I look forward to that time when I can write and have solitude, the reality of it is that I miss him so much!

Many times in recent weeks I just wanted to sit on the couch and stare trancelike at the TV. I'm grateful that my mother is healthy and helpful; she watches Alexander whenever I ask. I have beautiful pink roses on the desk.

I concluded the journal entry by writing: "The Bliss Report is unplugged."

Glimpsing The Ice Cream Fiend In The Mirror

Ice cream was my favorite elixir. Bowl after bowl of French Vanilla was a temporary sweetener. Sometimes it was topped with caramel sauce, or hot fudge. One day, Alexander and I enjoyed ice cream together. After one serving, he was satisfied. But I kept going back to the freezer, spooning up more, until my stomach could hold no more. I was cold and shivering.

"C'mon Alexander, let's get you in the shower," I said. He followed me into his bathroom, where I usually turned on the shower, got the right temperature, then left.

This time, I glimpsed my reflection in the mirror over the sink. My lips were purple. My teeth were chattering. My face was pale. My eyes were hollow with disappointment that I had just binged on all that sugar. I gawked at the stranger in the mirror, thinking:

I look like an addict.

I glanced down at Alexander and worried, *Does he see what I see?*

"Mom, in the Batman movie—" he said, proceeding to describe what the Joker had done.

I looked into his eyes, feeling pure joy, listening, and vowing to quit ice cream cold turkey.

Flu Pandemic Provides A Good Job "Out Of The Blue"

I was standing in the September sunshine while my son and his sixth grade classmates were digging in the dirt nearby, searching for artifacts on a field trip at Historic Fort Wayne, a U.S. Army fort in Detroit. While it was fun to serve as a chaperone on this field trip, my mind was churning with financial worries.

I had applied for so many jobs: newspaper reporter, newspaper columnist, magazine writer, and more. Somehow I was piecing together enough income to survive with child support, ghostwriting jobs, freelance articles, and teaching a weekly Toastmasters class. I had no health insurance. I just wanted to cry with frustration and fear.

Should I apply for welfare? How crazy is it for me to have degrees from Michigan and Columbia and even have that thought? God please help me...

My cell phone rang.

"Hi Elizabeth, can you send me your resumé?" It was someone

I'd known for a long time, explaining that the Wayne County Health Department had received a federal grant to orchestrate mass vaccination clinics as the H1N1 Flu pandemic claimed lives across America.

"They need a communications professional to help with messaging about the vaccine," he said, "and you're perfect for the job!"

Within weeks, I was earning the biggest salary of my life, with great benefits. I absolutely loved working for Health Department Director Loretta Davis, who epitomized woman power with her intelligence, dedication, warmth, and fun personality. I was blessed to work with many wonderful people, including communications specialist Mary Mazur, who had attended my Billy Dee Williams book party.

Plus, I loved the work, as we vaccinated thousands of people at clinics in gymnasiums across Metro Detroit. As part of the Emergency Preparedness section, I also participated in emergency drills with law enforcement agencies, learned about biochemical warfare such as anthrax, visited the U.S. Centers for Disease Control in Atlanta, and spoke at a Homeland Security conference in Orlando, Florida. It was fascinating!

Keeping My Writing Dreams Alive

It was 5:00 a.m., and I was at my desk, writing an original screenplay called *The Ghostwriter*, later renamed *Redemption*, about a writer and a reformed gangster.

I loved my job at the Health Department, and was extremely grateful for the salary and benefits. But while working in my cubicle, I yearned to be writing. The only time to write was before work and on weekends when Alexander was with his Dad.

"Ah!" I shrieked as a rodent ran through the apartment. That, plus the frequent marijuana smoke wafting from the neighbors, prompted us to move back in with my mother. I kept writing, and when my screenplay was complete, I traveled to Los Angeles seeking representation to shop my script to studios.

Meanwhile, the film industry was booming in Detroit, thanks to Michigan's attractive rebate for production companies. Movie crews and equipment—along with headlines about actor sightings and scenes being shot throughout the city—were constant reminders that my Hollywood dreams were just that. Dreams. Not reality. One day, Alexander and I watched a truck blow up on a downtown Detroit street, for *Transformers*.

Around that time, I found myself stepping over cables and light stands at my gym as I walked past a film set in the hallway outside my Saturday morning spinning class. It felt like the world was taunting me. My dream was happening all around—for other people. When would my time come? In moments of faith, I thought, *God is showing me that this can happen for you, right here, right now.* When fear hijacked my heart, I wondered, *what if my movie dreams, or any of my other dreams for that matter, never come true?*

Spiritual Awakening

When The Student Is Ready, The Teacher Will Appear

I wanted to learn how to develop psychic powers, so I bought a book about how to do it. Sitting on my sofa, I tried to follow its instructions about envisioning a staircase that would take me into another realm to tap into supernatural abilities. The imaginary stairway went nowhere.

This isn't working!

I parked the paperback on my shelf beside books by Deepak Chopra and Wayne Dyer.

I wish I could talk to Daddy about this!

As Catherine and I grew up, he was always practicing his telepathic skills.

"I mentally asked Jimmy to call, and the phone rang," Daddy would say, referring to the Chaldean man with whom he shared a father-son relationship, "because he received my psychic alert." Daddy also had a collection of books by Edgar Cayce, an American clairvoyant whose trance-like meditations provided insights from the spiritual realm about healing illness, world history, Jesus, and guidance about daily life.

Our father also seemed to know things about people in the grocery line. Once, while driving on a cold February night, we noticed a Christmas tree was glowing inside a house. "One of their loved ones was just released from prison and they kept the tree up to celebrate with them," our father said.

When circumstances synchronized in seemingly magical ways, Daddy playfully asked, "Coincidence?" conveying the message that nothing is a coincidence, and everything happens according to a divine plan.

Meanwhile, I often thought of someone and they called, or I heard song lyrics that echoed my thoughts, or I wondered something and the perfect article showed up with answers. In terms of spirituality, however, I didn't know where to start learning. Back then, the explosion of spiritual materials now at our fingertips had yet to hit the Internet.

Little did I know that a man whom my mother just happened to meet while in line to renew her driver's license, would personify that saying attributed to Buddha: "When the student is ready, the teacher will appear."

It happened at the Secretary of State's office downtown Detroit, when my mother began chatting with Dr. Rama S. Dwivedi, a Hindu spiritual leader from Northern India who founded the International Society for Spiritual Advancement. He invited us to gatherings for prayer, music, and vegetarian dinners, and said he and his family meditated together every day.

At home, I tried sitting crossed-legged, closing my eyes, hoping to slip into a soothing stream of serene thoughts and visions. Instead, it felt like 10 television screens were blasting bad channels in my brain. Meditation was frightening. Disturbing. Not something I thought I could master. So I stopped trying.

Then Dr. Rama and his family moved to metropolitan Washington, D.C. He and his wife, Aruna, invited us to visit their home in July of 2010. The immense peace in their house created such a joyous sanctuary that the leaves on their many plants seemed to dance. During the weekend, we enjoyed delicious, aromatic cuisine that Mrs. Dwivedi prepared with fresh herbs and spices that she ground herself.

"We are vegetarians," Dr. Rama said, "because when you eat the flesh of the animals, you are consuming the negative energy of fear and violence that came when the animals were killed."

That made me lose my appetite for animal flesh.

Then, as we sipped tea, my spirit soared as Dr. Rama spoke about meditation, reincarnation, and their spiritual beliefs as Hare Krishnas.

Our souls live many lives, Dr. Rama said, learning new lessons each time, and evolving to a higher state of spiritual consciousness with each lifetime.

He recommended a book: *Many Lives, Many Masters: The True Story of a Prominent Psychiatrist, His Young Patient, and the Past-Life Therapy That Changed Both Their Lives* by Brian L. Weiss, MD, a former Columbia University psychotherapist.

"I want to learn how to meditate," I told Dr. Rama, "but my mind is like a tornado."

"I will teach you how to meditate," he said, leading me and my mother into his meditation room. We sat on pillows facing him beside an altar where each morning and evening he performs devotional rituals and prayers.

"The mind is like a million wild horses running in different directions," Dr. Rama said as Hindu mantra music played softly. "Through meditation, you can tame the horses and find peace and direct connection with God."

Here's how Dr. Rama taught us to meditate:

- Sit with a straight spine and your legs crossed on a blanket, pillow, or yoga mat to provide a barrier between yourself and the floor or the ground.
- Infuse your brain and body with oxygen through *Pranayama*, or Alternate Nostril Breathing. Press your left thumb to close your left nostril. Inhale deeply through your open nostril, as if you're filling your belly with air. Lift your thumb, and press your ring fingertip to close your right nostril. Exhale through your open nostril, until all the air is expelled. Repeat several times.
- Touch the tips of your thumbs to the tips of your index fingers, as if making the OK sign.
- Rest the backs of your wrists on your knees.

- Close your eyes and focus on the end of your nose or the space between your eyebrows—your "third eye."
- Press the tip of your tongue to the roof of your mouth—between your teeth and that hump in the middle.
- Repeat "Om." Say it in a drawn-out way, like "Oooooooooooo hhhhhmmmmmmmmmm." This ancient chant creates a sound-wave of pure God energy that attunes you to your spiritual power. Think of Om as the password for direct, clear access to divine wi-fi.
- Enjoy the vibration through your body, washing over you like a sound bath to purify your aura.
- Repeat Om until you feel deeply relaxed.

I felt such peace! I wanted to remain in that meditative state, savoring the mellowness in my mind and the stillness in my body.

"Elizabeth, you must practice," Dr. Rama said. "Try for a few minutes every day. Soon your meditation will come naturally and will become an integral part of your day. It will keep you connected to God."

Back at home, I became a vegetarian and meditated every night before bed. At first, scary images and sounds barraged my mind. But as "Om" vibrated through me, peace and pureness permeated my mind and body.

In this state, I used my imagination to visualize positive outcomes for specific events, such as a business meeting, or my son's success on a test, or my sister's safe cross-country drive as she moved from Nevada to Michigan. In addition, I concentrated on excellent health, safety, and prosperity for my family. I expressed gratitude for my awesome job. And I prayed that God would continue to bless me with the time, energy, and resources to write books, movies, and speeches to help people everywhere.

Then, while still chanting "Om," I began receiving new ideas for writing, instructions on what to do the next day, and guidance about my life purpose. And somehow, I began to just "know" things.

"How Did You Know That?"

One Saturday morning, I was meditating on the sofa, when my son and his dad called from their weekend adventure at Cedar Point Amusement Park in Sandusky, Ohio.

"I lost my keys," my ex-husband said from the hotel room. He sounded agitated and worried. His key ring held keys to his car and his house.

"When did you have them last?" I asked.

"Last night when we got here and parked the car," he said. The worst-case scenario was someone finding his keys, stealing his car, driving to Detroit, and robbing his house.

"Have you retraced your steps?" I asked, remembering that Cedar Point is huge, with giant parking lots and thousands of daily visitors.

He exhaled, angry and frustrated. "Yeah."

"Let me call you back." I resumed meditation, repeating, "Om." Then I "saw" in my mind's eye, his keys at the hotel reception desk. I called him and said, "Go to the front desk. Ask if anyone turned in keys."

He hung up, then called a few minutes later.

"My keys were at the front desk," he said, amazed and relieved. "How did you know that?"

I smiled and thought, I just *knew*.

Heeding My Internal Warning System

The sudden vision of blood—my blood!—on the marble floor of a man's mansion, was my intuition warning that this new romance was not for me. On the surface, it was lovely, but this ominous feeling was so strong, and the mental vision was so scary, I felt sick. I wanted to run out of his house.

He had said and done a few things that were easy to disregard while he wined and dined me, took me to upscale events, and promised luxurious travel. But I knew that the gentlemanly veneer was masking something sinister.

It's easy to ignore this when nothing in 3D reality substantiates a mental vision or "just a feeling." But it's *not* just a feeling. It's your intuition. It's God warning you. Trust this internal warning system! The proof of its power is what didn't happen, and thankfully I'll never know, because I stopped dating that person.

"Don't go running today," a voice within me warned repeatedly on a beautiful spring day. I really wanted to go running, so I did. After a few minutes, I tripped, flew forward, and rolled. My knee bled. Tiny rocks pierced my palms. Then this voice that was a distinctly higher power ordered, "Go home!" Was the Divine protecting me from stray dogs? An out-of-control car? A malicious person? A fallen electrical line? I'll never know. But now when I hear, "Don't run," I don't run.

Another time, while driving my son from the orthodontist back to school for sports practice, he wanted a snack. I was about to turn toward the corner gas station's convenience store when a powerful voice within commanded: "Don't go there!" *What?* Other stores required driving a distance in heavy traffic; that would make us late. I glanced at the nearby store.

"Don't go there," I heard. We went to another store. A few days later, when fueling up my car at that corner gas station, the attendant said they had been robbed the afternoon that I was warned to stay away! If I had ignored my intuition, my son and I could have walked into a robbery.

Seeing Spirit Messages Everywhere

The license plate on the car ahead of me said "EAA 444." The sign at the bank said 44 degrees. My car's odometer said 4,444 miles. The dashboard clock said 8:44. The grocery store bill was $144. And I sometimes awoke at 4:44 a.m.

Is the Universe trying to tell me that when I turn 44 in a few months, it will be an amazing year?

I learned online that seeing 444 means that "you are surrounded by angels." Many websites explained that Spirit communicates with us through signs and symbols, such as number sequences, feathers, coins, and birds. My father understood this.

"Think of me every time you see a cardinal bird," he said while living. When he was a priest, his desire was to become a Cardinal someday. A Roman Catholic Cardinal is celebrated as a Prince of the Church, and wears a hat and gown that are the same color as the bird.

Human Cardinals serve the Church; cardinal birds are messengers from the spiritual world. After Daddy died, cardinals appeared frequently. Now, a male and female cardinal often visit my backyard, chirping to get my attention. When cardinals flutter past in a flash of red, or perch on the fence, a message pops into my mind. Once, before the four-hour drive home from our cottage, a cardinal flew in front of my windshield, and I heard: "You are safe."

As curiosity sent me online seeking answers, I loved connecting the spiritual dots. The four Cardinal Archangels are each assigned to a cardinal direction: north, south, east, and west.

Archangel Michael leads all angels and protects us with a shield and sword. He's ubiquitous, and comes immediately when we call him for protection. Archangel Gabriel is God's messenger. When I ask Gabriel to help me write and speak, words flow effortlessly. Archangel Raphael heals. Archangel Uriel oversees wisdom. When we request their help, these angels provide guidance and direction.

I first heard the term "archangel" in 1994 when interviewing Detroit radio legend Martha Jean "The Queen" Steinberg for a page one *Detroit News* article. When I visited her Home of Love ministry, we toured her meditation room, passing large mannequins of Archangel Gabriel and Archangel Michael in the halls. At the time, this did not resonate with me. Now, I couldn't learn enough about these powerful beings.

God Works In Serendipitous Ways

Malice glinted in his eyes as he held a giant knife over his wife's terrified face inside a run-down house. Cameras were rolling. And Alexander and I were in awe, watching the filming of *Silent No More*, about women who survived domestic abuse.

After that chilling scene with actors Daniel Lujan and Erlinda Navarro, the photography director Keith Smith—who's worked on major films including those with Pastor T.D. Jakes—showed Alexander how to operate the movie camera. My son was fascinated because he had been acting in his school's theatrical productions since fourth grade with his role as Coalhouse Walker in *Ragtime*. The day was amazing!

The Executive Producer, Pastor Marvin Miles of International Gospel Center in the Metro Detroit community of Ecorse, invited us to the filming, directed by Demetrius Navarro of D Street Films in Los Angeles. Award-winning *Silent No More*, starring Kym Whitley, K.D. Aubert, and Tiny Lister, was released by Nu Trend Productions in 2012.

Meanwhile, Demetrius invited me to email my screenplay, *Redemption*, to him to explore whether he could help me find the right producer. He also suggested shortening it and boosting the suspense and romance. So I resumed work on my script, dreaming of being on my own film set someday.

A short time later, I attended a movie screening in Detroit to ask a famous actor to play the lead role in my movie. I had met him in Los Angeles a decade before at a chic restaurant, eliciting a bow of gratitude when I complimented his most intellectual film. Then I gave him an autographed hardcover copy of *Dark Secret.*

Well, when I saw him in Detroit and expressed my desire for him to play the hero in my movie, he said, "A lot of people say that, sweetheart. Call my agent."

I wrote a letter to his agent at a powerful agency in Los Angeles, then followed up with a phone call. I politely explained to the agent's assistant how this actor had requested my call. The assistant hung up on me.

Tearful Prayers Elicit Movie Magic

A few months later, I was having a meltdown. A hot, heavy sadness melted through me with feelings of failure and worthlessness. I was riding in the backseat of a car with my family (Alexander was with his father), en route to a luncheon. All I wanted to do was cry on that sunny afternoon of July 30, 2011.

At the time, I still had the full-time Health Department job, which I enjoyed and was grateful that it provided income for our comfortable life. We were living in a lovely condo near Alexander's school. At work, I was doing a very good job, helping people get and stay healthy. But commuting two hours a day, and working in a cubicle, made me feel I had failed as a writer. Now I was 44 years old, and yearned to be writing full-time, earning a comfortable living through books, speeches, and films.

What was I doing wrong?

As for being the Princess of Peace, I felt like the Queen of Chaos, questioning and criticizing myself for feeling so stuck and stalled. Especially on this July day in the car. Tears streamed down my cheeks as I gripped my cell phone in one hand and tissues in the other. In my mind, I prayed:

"God, please, please make something happen in my career so that I can share my creative gifts with the world, to help people, and to feel successful."

Ching!

My cell phone chimed with a text message. It was Demetrius Navarro, the movie director in LA. I assumed he was contacting me to offer his critique of my screenplay.

"Elizabeth," he wrote, "I'm going to be in Detroit this week and would love to meet with you." He also said he emailed me a movie script that he wanted me to read.

"Sure," I responded, thinking that he wanted my input as a writer. My Hollywood dreams felt a million miles away, but a tiny spark of excitement lit me up inside. We planned to meet two days later at a restaurant.

Meanwhile, at the luncheon with my family, I went from sad to sobbing. It was awkward and embarrassing. After that, while driving with my sister to her 25th high school reunion in East Lansing, I confided how bad I felt. Then in the hotel room while she took a shower, my phone rang.

It was Pastor Miles. "Elizabeth, what is your acting background?"

"I have an acting 'future' because I'm going to play the lead role in the screenplay that I wrote," I said with a matter-of-fact tone.

"I'd like to consider you for a role in my second movie," he said, adding that Demetrius would tell me more about two possible roles.

I thanked him profusely. A starburst of excitement exploded inside me. "Thank you, God!"

Overwhelmed with gratitude and awe, it hit me: I had prayed for something to happen in my career, and God responded instantaneously. By the way, Pastor Miles said the film was called *Anything Is Possible.*

Even better, Alexander was cast to play the leader of the neighborhood kids.

Demetrius and Pastor Miles, the Executive Producer, blessed me with the significant role of Evelyn Strasser, the mother of a girl who befriends the lead character, played by piano phenom and philanthropist Ethan Bortnick, who has had multiple PBS specials and has performed with Elton John, Céline Dion, and Beyoncé, raising millions for the Children's Miracle Network.

Just *weeks* after my miraculously answered prayers, Alexander and I were on the movie set amidst cameras, lights, and monitors where Demetrius watched the filming. Tears of joy and pride filled my eyes as Alexander aced his lines and actions in every scene. We did not have direct lines together, but we did appear in some scenes at the same time.

"Who's that?!" I gasped, staring at myself in the mirror after stylists straightened my hair for the role. Studying my lines in the screenplay written by Carlos R. Bermúdez and Demetrius Navarro provided a lesson on how writing translates into speaking dialogue on camera.

Remembering my lines amidst the excitement of a film set after Demetrius said "Action!" was surprisingly difficult. But I caught on, and loved shooting scenes with the 11-year-old girl who played my daughter, Fátima Ptacek. At the time, she was the voice of *Dora* on Nickelodeon's *Dora the Explorer* TV series. She has since won an Oscar for her lead role in the 2014 film *Curfew* and now at age 18 is a human rights activist for the United Nations and gender equality.

"Oh my goodness," I gasped, watching a playback of a scene on the director's monitors. "I am really doing this." I blinked away tears as I saw myself on film, interacting with my "daughter."

Our cast and crew created a global melting pot, representing many countries and ethnicities. Comedian/actress Kym Whitley kept us laughing, and I met several other actors: David Haines, body double for Will Smith; Jonathan Bennett, whose film credits included *Mean Girls* and *Cheaper by the Dozen*; and Lacey Chabert, whose résumé included *All My Children*, *Party of Five*, and *Mean Girls*.

The cool thing was that this wholesome, family movie isn't about race. *Anything Is Possible* is about the universal themes of family, love, and hope. We filmed for three weeks in a spectacular house and an apartment building. It was an amazing experience, and everyone got along beautifully.

Jesus Appears At 11:20 p.m. On August 20, 2011

His eyes are large, golden-brown pools of love and comfort. As he casts them upon me, I am mesmerized. His face is angular, with a wide jaw, and sharp nose. His brown hair flows in soft waves over his shoulders. He is stunning, with caramel-hued skin that shimmers as if air-brushed with diamond powder. Around him glows a great, golden light, as if the sun is both rising and setting behind his head.

This warmth, this immense power—electrified my spirit like a million sunbeams pulsing through me. My cells were dancing and sparkling like stardust. And I was overwhelmed with indescribable peace, love, and comfort.

This is what happened when Jesus appeared while I was meditating.

It was 11:20 p.m. on Saturday, August 20, 2011.

It was shocking. Sudden. Totally unexpected.

Because I had no relationship with Jesus Christ. None whatsoever.

Though my father had been a Roman Catholic priest, I had never felt Catholic or even Christian. And the idea of God's human "Son" had never stirred me.

So here I was, a week into filming *Anything Is Possible*, continuing my nightly practice of meditation in the fashion that Dr. Rama had taught. Before I could quiet the cacophony of sounds and moving mosaic of images from the day, the Divine showed me this dazzling image of Jesus.

I gasped. No words could quantify my awe. I marveled at the vivid hues of yellow, warm shades of brown, the chestnut color of his mustache and beard, and those deep, mesmerizing pools of golden-brown that are his eyes. I opened my eyes; the image of Him remained superimposed on the blank, white wall before me. I closed my eyes.

Jesus was still there.

Why I wasn't seeing a darker, brown-skinned Jesus with wooly hair that would be a more authentic appearance for a Middle Eastern man? A man who was a carpenter, with skin weathered by sun, wind, and labor? Overwhelming comfort silenced the questions as I basked in his glorious gaze.

"Elizabeth," He said, "everything you dream of for yourself and your family, is going to be even bigger and better than you can even imagine."

Oh my God! Why is Jesus coming to me, speaking to me?

Part of my dismay was that I had never prayed to him. Ever. In fact, I had often believed I was actually Jewish, because I just didn't "feel" the Lord or Christ. And while taking women's studies classes in college, I had rejected the idea of the Immaculate Conception as extremely sexist.

None of that mattered now as Jesus filled me with a powerful knowing. I felt like the sun was shining in my room. God's Son in fact glowed like the sun, and the two words sound alike. Son. Sun. One and the same in his warmth and brilliance and magnetism.

Just a short while before this, I had felt uncharacteristically lonely while Alexander was with his father for the weekend. I was alone, but Jesus' presence declared, unequivocally, "Elizabeth, I am here for you."

Was this normal? Did this happen to other people? Religious leaders? Had this ever happened for my father?

Oh, how I wish I could tell Daddy about this! Though he had died 21 years earlier, I sensed that Daddy knew what was happening, and perhaps he had helped orchestrate this magnificent blessing. Before he died, I had never spoken with him about Catholicism.

This night, I experienced love at first sight. I fell asleep feeling immense comfort, as if loving arms were around me. I was euphoric, and awoke the next day almost giddy with gratitude. Before I even opened my eyes, I praised God for that divine vision that I knew would change my life forever.

Knowing that Jesus was with me was simply mind-blowing. But I told no one! The only place I shared it was on the keyboard of my laptop computer where I typed the black words on these white pages that remained hidden in my computer until now.

I knew that Jesus' appearance was real. But I didn't want to hear anyone's skepticism or criticism. I had already heard enough cynics ask, "Well, if you have these powers from meditation, then why don't you know the winning lottery numbers?"

Plus, I didn't need anyone to affirm or confirm that Jesus really came to me, or that this was possible or normal or crazy or anything else. It wasn't a question, and it wasn't open for debate. Because I simply knew.

Church: You Are Home

The morning after Jesus first appeared, it was an unusual Sunday because I was going to church. Four months earlier, I had visited Riverside Church in New York, while attending my 20-year reunion at Columbia University. Just as I'd done when I was a student, I slipped into the empty sanctuary alone and savored the serenity.

Today, I was attending because Pastor Miles had invited the cast and crew to International Gospel Center. As I prepared breakfast, put on a favorite dress, and drove 30 minutes, I sang along to *Amazing Grace* performed by the Soweto Gospel Choir. The words, "I once was lost, but now I'm found," gave me chills.

From the moment I entered the church, I was floating on the music and the worshipers' energy. When Pastor Miles spoke, each line of scripture enthralled me. I had never experienced church with such exhilaration. As I stood and raised my hands in praise, tears of joy streaming down my cheeks, my inner voice announced: *I'm home.*

Yet I was suddenly struck by a realization: *I've never read the Bible.*

Embarking On A Crash Course

My fingers danced over the keyboard during yet another online search in my self-styled crash course to answer a flurry of questions.

"What does the Holy Trinity really mean?" I asked, after hearing the term in church. On the screen, I read: "the Father, the Son, and the Holy Spirit."

Shame seeped through me. The Holy Trinity seemed like important general knowledge. My ignorance of Catholicism and Christianity manifested in embarrassing ways, such as not knowing—when doing the sign of the cross—whether to touch the right shoulder or the left shoulder first. The church damned my parents to hell, and they believed it! That made me not believe in its man-made construct of male-dominated religious hierarchy that manipulated two loving people into believing something terrible because they epitomized the meaning of God: LOVE.

Now, however, I urgently wanted to learn the rich, fascinating information about all religions and spiritual beliefs. Perhaps someday I would earn a Master of Divinity degree from Harvard University.

"Now, what did Jesus eat?" I looked it up, and was thrilled to learn that my healthy, natural-foods regimen contained many of staples of His diet, such as honey, walnuts, and fish. Meanwhile, I listened to the Bible on a phone app, and downloaded pictures of Jesus on my computer to experience the instant comfort of gazing at him, especially before going to sleep. The peace and love of His energy consumed me so powerfully that one day during my daily lunchtime walk in a grassy park near the Health Department offices, I said aloud, "Jesus has taken over me."

I also felt protected, as evidenced by little miracles every day. Once, after my one-hour commute to work, I pulled into the parking lot and suddenly the steering mechanism on my car conked out. Not a few minutes before, while I was driving alone on the long stretch of truck-filled, 70-mile-an-hour highway. Not on a street where a stalled car could have put me in danger. No, it happened in the workplace parking lot, affirming that angels were watching over me.

"Thank you, God," I said aloud, before calling for a tow truck from the safety of my desk.

Meanwhile, I felt empowered to help other people feel this euphoria; it was like an electric current pulsing through my body so powerfully, I could illuminate a lightbulb with my fingertip. The following Sunday, I returned to church, where Pastor Miles recited Acts 1:8—"… you will receive power when the Holy Spirit comes to you—"

"Yes!" I shouted, raising my arms in praise. "Yes!" As the church music and the sermon roused fellow worshipers to clap and cry out in praise, Spirit pulsed through me as never before.

I realized that seeing the number 44 meant far more than it being a great year: *I've been seeing 44 because I'm 44 now and this is the year of my Spiritual Awakening!* It was like my second birthday for a whole new, spirit-powered Elizabeth. After Pastor Miles' rousing sermon, the congregation became an electrifying frenzy of singing, dancing, and praising. Sitting in a pew, I was overwhelmed with emotion. I bent over, sobbing into my hands.

That's when I heard God command—very loudly—"I am the Almighty! Banish all fear, worry, and doubt!"

I sobbed harder. Fear, worry, and doubt were the cross that I had been bearing for as long as I could remember, and my highest potential could only be attained by obeying God's edict. I prayed for the power to replace fear with faith, worry with courage, and doubt with knowing. I didn't walk out of church that day. I floated. At home, I wrote long journal entries about my visions and revelations:

Daddy was 44 when he left the Church. My mother was 44 when he died. We celebrated America's racial progress with the election of our 44th President, Barack Obama. In the Bible, God created the physical world on the fourth day, and endowed it with:

Four seasons: winter, spring, summer, and fall;

Four directions: north, south, east, and west;

Four elements: fire, water, air, and earth.

"Oh my God, it's 7:44 a.m." I wrote on October 3, 2011. That evening, I concluded my journal entry like many others: "Thank you for bringing me to this beautiful place of epiphany and revelation on my amazing spirit journey... moving at warp speed right now."

A Magic Moment Secures A Ghostwriting Project

In October of 2011, my contractual position with the Health Department ended. I applied for communications positions with another health department, an automotive company, an advertising agency, a university writing center, and other places. No job offers resulted.

Meanwhile, I asked God to help me apply my literary talent to showcase inspiring people by ghostwriting their memoirs. I hoped that someday my sister—who was longing to return to writing—would leave the financial services industry and join me in a writing business. She could apply her corporate expertise, and we could both write and publish books full-time.

For now, my plan was to solicit prominent Metro Detroiters to hire me to write their books. I composed personalized letters and hand-delivered them to each person's office. Most times, their secretaries or security guards took the large, sealed envelopes from me, promising to deliver them to the intended recipient.

"This is for Mr. Jones," I told the guard at the security desk at the world headquarters for a huge company as I held out the envelope.

"I'll take it," another man said, as his hand intercepted the envelope.

It was Mr. Jones! I just stood there, stunned, with chills. No way would I ever anticipate this top leader in the lobby, much less retrieving his own deliveries at the security desk.

That morning, I had envisioned a lightning bolt of divine energy shooting down through me to magnetize myself to attract the best opportunities to support myself and my son—while paying my half of his hefty tuition bill—with book projects.

Wow, it really worked! What a surreal moment! I had never called his secretary, and he had no idea that I would be there. God truly was orchestrating every nanosecond of my life.

After we chatted for a few minutes in the lobby, that "chance" meeting developed into an amazing ghostwriting job, followed by a second one years later. This, and several other projects, enabled me to interview fascinating people of diverse backgrounds. This also blessed me with the opportunity to travel to beautiful places in other states where I sifted through historic records, explored towns, and met interesting people.

Meanwhile, however, my own books sat untouched in my computer. Three projects in particular danced in my spirit all day and night.

First was *God's Answer Is Know*, which I had outlined many years before. Second was *Husbands, Incorporated*, which had evolved from a screenplay into a book. Each day, my observations about relationships and conventional marriage inspired revelations that would somehow get woven into that novel. Third was *Goddess: Be One*, a guidebook that uses some of my toughest moments to teach women how to find their power. It began as my memoir, inspired by a troubling moment in the wake of filing for divorce. *Goddess: Be One* will be published shortly after this book.

As I devoted time and energy to raising my son and working on the bill-paying ghostwriting projects, I periodically recorded ideas, scenes, passages, and experiences in these three manuscripts on my computer. However, the idea of publishing them triggered terror about revealing my potentially controversial beliefs about relationships and spirituality. I just wasn't ready.

"She Speaks To Spirits For A Living"

Shortly after the magic moment of connecting with my client in his company's lobby, my friend Kristin Schenden called out of the blue.

"I want to introduce you to someone to explore writing a book," Kristin said. "Her name is Lori Lipten, and she's a medium. She speaks to spirits for a living." As creator of Sacred Balance Healing Arts in Bloomfield Hills, Michigan, Lori has a master's degree in clinical psychology and is a professional intuitive practitioner. She helps people by venturing into divine dimensions to communicate with spirits to obtain life guidance and healing for her clients. She also teaches people how to access their own intuitive power.

In October of 2011, I went to Lori's office to meet her, and we felt an immediate kinship and familiarity. In fact, Lori said that we were cloistered nuns together in France many centuries ago. During our visit, she said my father was standing behind me, very tall, and that he was extremely proud of me and our family, and that he was with us, guiding us, protecting us.

Lori exuded warmth and humility, and I was fascinated by her divine calling to use her spiritual abilities to help people love and heal. I wanted to ask her 10,000 questions! Thankfully, she invited me to attend her Intuitive Empowerment Weekend.

Connecting With The Divine

Weeks later, I sat on the soft carpet of the Soothe Your Soul yoga studio in Oxford, Michigan, amongst 25 people, all facing Lori, who perched on a large, ornate pillow.

She explained that her life mission is to teach how to love more, and to instruct everyday people how to amplify our innate intuition, which is the voice of our soul. It's the channel through which we can hear the Divine—God, Source, Universe, Creator, or whichever word resonates with your beliefs. Unfortunately, this voice gets silenced by a world that tells us to only trust what we experience with our five physical senses.

Thankfully, we can heighten our intuition through meditation and other practices that create a clear channel into spiritual dimensions. We hear that channel when we plug in to the highest-frequency energy in the universe: light. Connecting with this light can help us heal and become empowered to manifest our goals, dreams, and life purpose.

"We're going to begin by calling in the light," Lori said, guiding us through a visualization of a light beam coming into the tops of our heads, saturating our bodies, and shooting down to connect with the core of Mother Earth. Then this light expands outward to surround the planet with peace and love, and comes back to us. You can try this in the teaching section of this book, *Ascend: 8 Steps to an Infinite You.*

"Now we're going to clear our chakras," Lori announced.

Our what?

She described a string of eight colorful—but invisible—orbs of light glowing between the tailbone and above the head. These orbs are non-physical organs at the center of the aura around every human being. This "light body" houses our soul, and contains organs of light that regulate the energy for specific aspects of our physical, mental, and spiritual existence.

Each light is a "chakra," an ancient Sanskrit word for "spinning wheel of energy."

Lights... spinning wheels of energy... hhhmmm... As I tried to process this, it seemed that chakras must be like metaphoric ceiling fans that circulate the energy inside us for optimum health in mind, body, and spirit. And these fans have lights attached, and the lights glow as colors that correspond with the rainbow, starting upward from the tailbone: red, orange, yellow, green, blue, indigo, violet, and gold.

This idea brought to mind the image of a prism. When the invisible, pure light from Source/God comes into our bodies, it's like sunshine striking mist: it becomes visible as a rainbow. Smog or pollution in the air will make the rainbow appear dim, dirty, or dingy.

Our goal is to cleanse and clear the light energy in our chakras, so they glow brightly and spin quickly, thus circulating the highest, strongest energy within and around us; this helps us receive more love, joy, better health, and new opportunities. Consider this your spiritual hygiene—like showering, brushing our teeth, and keeping our physical bodies clean.

Just as cholesterol deposits in our heart's arteries, toxins lodge in our livers, and junk food gets stuck in our intestines, our chakras accumulate energetic gunk from stress, anger, pain, trauma, and over-stimulation. Failing to release this negative energy can be toxic, causing emotional discomfort and physical disease that can be deadly.

We prevent this by cleansing and clearing our chakras every day. Clearing chakras involves saying a request or prayer, then chanting a "bija" sound that provides a cleansing sound bath for each chakra. As Lori led us through this practice for all seven chakras, our 26 voice boxes created vibrations that felt powerful enough to blast off the roof. The energy pulsed through my body, and it was electrifying. The eighth chakra above the head—the Higher Self chakra—is already a pure connection to the Divine and does not require clearing.

You can learn how to clear your chakras in the *Ascend* section of this book. For now, here's an example of how to cleanse your sacral chakra. Sitting comfortably with your legs crossed, in a spot where you will not be disturbed, close your eyes and envision an orange sphere of light glowing and spinning in your groin. While you can use many methods to clear your chakras, I was inspired to infuse it with prayer, so think or say aloud:

"God, please cleanse and clear my sacral chakra, to empower my divine right to release guilt, anxiety, and addictive behaviors, and to forgive myself, so that I may enjoy emotional balance, creativity, and pleasure."

The corresponding element is water, so envision clear water gushing through the orange orb, cleansing it of smudges, imprints, shadows, and deposits. I imagined little angels holding bottles of Windex, spraying and wiping the orbs as if they were giant Christmas tree ornaments. You can also "see" Archangel Michael holding a giant vacuum to suction away the dirt and grime of daily life that accumulate as negative energy inside you.

Take a deep breath, and say a loud, "Vam" or "Vaaaaaaaaaa hhhhhmmmm," for as long as possible. Savoring the vibration through you and around you as it cleanses this chakra is very relaxing and helps calm your mind.

Learning A Powerful Meditation Technique

"Who wants to journey?" Lori asked, smiling at us and glowing with a comforting aura.

"Where are we going?" a woman asked playfully.

"You're going to go to the most exquisite place you have ever been," Lori said. "Set that intention."

Lori then taught how to use a meditation technique known as a Shamanic Journey. As a professional intuitive practitioner, she is gifted with the abilities that "medicine men" and "medicine women" have used in indigenous cultures for more than 40,000 years. They would "journey" into the divine realm to retrieve information to help people heal and thrive. The word *shamanism* comes from an ancient Siberian language and means "one who knows."

Now, we have the ability to take Shamanic Journeys on our own behalf, to obtain information that can enhance our health, wealth, relationships, careers, and anything else. To do this, Lori said you can journey to: the Upper World, via a golden light beam that passes through a veil separating the earthly realm from the heavenly dimension; the Middle World, where we live (but this is not recommended for beginners); and the Lower World. The Lower and Upper Worlds are in the spiritual realm, which is comprised of infinite dimensions.

I had never heard of this or other concepts that Lori introduced, such as Earth angels, lightworkers, soul retrieval, and Ascended Masters including Jesus, Mother Mary, Buddha, Kwan Yin, Confucius, and many more. They were once human, then ascended to serve as enlightened beings who guide and protect us when we call upon them.

Rule number one in spiritual work, Lori said, is to "call in the light" and ask for divine protection while venturing into non-physical realms, and ask to encounter only "benevolent" spirits. Dark energy doesn't exist in the Lower and Upper Worlds; these realms are made entirely of love. Any encounter with dark energy signifies something—such as fear—that you're trying to resolve, and you can learn how to infuse it with light to heal it.

I felt anxious. Could I successfully take a Shamanic Journey? Would I just lie there thinking about my grocery list? What would happen? What if nothing happened? If we had to call in protection, was it dangerous? If I stepped through this doorway, could I possibly encounter the awful stuff of *The Exorcist* and *The Amityville Horror* that had scared me as a child? Having no idea what I might experience in this type of meditation, I decided to relax and be open to the experience.

"Set an intention to ask the Divine, 'What will serve my highest good?'" Lori said.

Then, after calling in divine beings to protect us, she began our Shamanic Journey by beating a drum. It created a rhythm that served as a "sonic driver" to help our brainwaves get into a meditative state where the third eye—which sees beyond the physical world—can peer into the infinite dimensions of the spirit world.

"Imagine yourself walking out of your house to a beautiful tree," Lori instructed. I imagined myself at the St. Jude tree on Daddy's property near West Branch. After his funeral, my mother and sister had spread some of his ashes around it.

"The tree becomes magical," Lori explained, adding that a small door or portal appears at its base, and you enter. This exercise launches with a push from your imagination, but suddenly shifts into a place that is totally new and unimagined. The experience is different for everyone. For me, the tree's interior was a golden tube sparkling as if lined with jewels, and I slid down it, into the roots, landing in my "power spot" that would later serve as the exit point.

Lori said you can also experience this by reverting to yourself at age 10. This reminded me of when Jesus said in Matthew 18:3: "Truly I tell you, unless you change and become like little children, you will never enter the kingdom of heaven." Well I sure did see myself, clear as day, as 10-year-old Elizabeth with two braids bouncing on my shoulders as I landed, as happily as if I were really going down a slide.

Then I just sat there, marveling at a lavender forest with giant trees whose branches sparkled as if covered in crystal moss. Everything was pulsing with indescribable vitality and joy—like humming, chirping, vibrating—abuzz with birds, fairies, animals, and beings. I felt the strong presence of Jesus and my father's spirit, both of whom exuded immeasurable love and comfort.

This did not feel like my imagination; it was unlike anything I had ever seen or felt. Nor did it feel like a dream, because I was awake. Part of me was shocked that this experience was unfolding so vividly. It really felt like I was peeking into another realm where many divine beings greeted me and emphasized messages about my life purpose to write and speak about love and peace.

"What will serve my highest good?" I asked.

A Native American man appeared and introduced himself as my spirit guide. He said that he was my husband many lifetimes ago in the Lakota tribe, and that I was killed in front of him as we rode horses while fighting soldiers during the government's "manifest destiny" takeover of Native lands. Now, he radiated indescribable love and comfort as he said, "I'm always with you. My assignment is to teach you to love and to trust."

I also encountered animal spirit guides. Lori had explained that "power animals" may appear in meditation to guide us. A particular animal may show up to inspire you to emulate its characteristics. For example, lions can symbolize your need for courage, whereas bears and wolves represent healing and many powerful qualities in shamanic culture. A plethora of websites offer information about power animals and their meanings. You may be guided by an animal that already fascinates you, such as a shark, an eagle, or an elephant.

During my meditation, a cheetah carried me really fast through the forest that was vibrant with angels and fairies and lightning bugs and animals. We were going and going and all around were dark purple trees glowing lavender.

"What's taking so long?" I asked, slightly scared. "Where are we going?! When are we gonna get there?"

Suddenly we came to this enormous, golden altar, like in a church, but it was outdoors, with no roof. Golden lights twinkled upward for as far as I could see. The lights rose like pews in a church—and it was actually angels, angels, angels—an immeasurable number of them, filling the space upward from the altar, ascending into infinity.

While my spirit was in a divine dimension having this fantastical experience, it felt like I was inside a movie scene, watching everything unfold with complete surprise. None of these images or ideas had ever popped into my mind prior to this. All the while, I was completely aware that my physical body was lying on the floor in a yoga studio with my eyes closed. Lori was still beating a drum at the front of the silent room as everyone laid or sat on the floor.

In the meditation, I experienced a beautiful ceremony.

"I hereby ordain you as the Princess of Peace," said a man in robes with a crown and long white beard. (Subsequent meditations confirmed this was King David). As I sat on a throne, a crown was placed on my head. Then angels put a golden microphone and a golden video camera in my lap.

"What am I supposed to do or not do?" I asked.

They responded, "You already know."

Then Lori changed the pace of the drumbeat to alert us that it was time to conclude the meditation. My animal spirit guide carried me back to my power spot. I thanked all the divine beings, then came back up through the tree and into the yoga studio. My body was extremely still; my breathing and heartbeat were very slow. Lori told us to wiggle our toes and fingers to re-acclimate to the physical realm.

Next, participants shared what they experienced during their journeys. Some people heard and saw nothing. Others had vivid, fantastical experiences. It was encouraging to hear men and women speak about seeing and communicating with angels, animals, spirits of loved ones, and Ascended Masters. It was also fascinating to hear non-Christian people express love for Jesus as a non-denominational being who radiates love and comfort for everyone.

During our next Shamanic Journey to the Lower World, my spirit guide took me in a canoe across a lavender-moonlit lake to a pretty cottage. Inside, I was overwhelmed by inexplicably pure love.

Suddenly angels entered. They were delivering large baskets of gold bricks, and in exchange they were carrying out big baskets filled with books that I had written. I tried to read a book cover, but only saw a brown-striped spine on a beige book jacket. I thought perhaps it was this book. Instead, I was told that the books could only be described as: "Elizabeth teaching people how to live better."

Then someone knocked on the door, and it was a king.

"You must write!" he ordered. "You must speak!"

These experiences left me awestruck. They did not feel like my imagination *at all*. Using my imagination is a deliberate act of taking one idea, then flexing my creativity and brainpower to expand it into a bigger vision. In meditation, it's the opposite; everything unfolds as a surprise. It's like stepping into a video that provides messages to help you.

I think it's something you have to experience to truly understand. That's why I'm sharing some of my meditation experiences: to *show* what it's like. Please try it. In addition to the long list of mental and physical health benefits of being in such a deeply relaxed state, it's like tuning in to your own personal entertainment system featuring interactive dialogue with celestial beings. And it's free!

You can learn how to meditate in *Ascend: 8 Steps to an Infinite You.*

Honoring The Divine Voice Within

We all have a "team" of spirits—guardian angels, ancestors, and other divine beings—who surround us at all times. Imagine when you walk into a crowded place, the air is bustling with every person's spiritual crew.

How do these spirits communicate with us? We "hear" them as voices inside our heads. "Hearing voices" is sometimes a symptom of mental illness, but from a spiritual perspective, you can discern the voices of spirit guides because—unlike our "inner critic"— they are loving and provide helpful guidance.

Spiritual messages come from within, through a voice in our minds. You can call it your inner voice, your higher self, your intuition, your spirit, your spirit guides, God, Source, Creator, the Universe, angels, the Divine, or whichever loving entity you believe is helping you with hunches, insights, instructions, gut feelings, and knowing things without evidence. It's best to use language that resonates with your beliefs.

This divine voice within delivers messages and ideas as immediate responses to prayers—or as unsolicited, spontaneous guidance. These messages align with peace, love, and valuable information. Listening and honoring this guidance can profoundly transform you.

You Can Speak With The Spirit World Through Intuitive Writing

What if you could communicate with God and other spiritual beings as easily as you text a message to someone far away and receive an immediate answer? You can, with "Intuitive Writing." After learning this at Lori's seminar, I tried it at home.

"God, what should I do today?" I typed into a journal entry on my computer. Faster than I could think, answers flashed through my mind, and I knew they were coming from God. So I typed what I was "hearing:"

"Work on your ghostwriting projects until noon. Take a jog to the lake. Then write until after-school pick-up. Alexander will want to meet with his math teacher." I followed the guidance, and sure enough, my son called and asked me to pick him up an hour later than usual.

"Intuitive Writing" or "Automatic Writing" are the spiritual version of "stream of consciousness" writing exercises in high school English class.

To use Intuitive Writing, "call in the light" for protection, allowing only loving spirits to communicate with you. Then get into a meditative state, and set an intention to connect with God, deceased loved ones, angels, and other spirit-beings. You can tell when the answers are not coming from your thinking brain because they shoot into your mind faster than regular thoughts. Sometimes it's just an impression, a "knowing" from the Divine, revealing your deepest truth and guidance for the best possible outcomes.

Intuitive Writing opens a channel to reveal your highest truth, because it bypasses the self-sabotaging landmines of fear, doubt, and worry that rig our thinking minds and shatter our boldest ideas and dreams.

As a lifelong journaler, this was a thrilling discovery. Since I was already recording my spiritual awakening in daily journal entries, I began incorporating this new communication technique and was amazed at the clarity and speed of responses. Then I began tapping into this supernatural flow of knowledge while writing books.

Creating A Daily Spiritual Practice

Now having two meditation teachers and a new repertoire of spiritual practices, I created a daily routine to cultivate spiritual empower-ment. Meditation remained the centerpiece of my daily rituals, and it became so much more than the standard definition as a technique to "quiet the mind." So I wrote my own definition:

Meditation is your personal portal to peace and positive transfor-mation. It's a method to go on a fact-finding mission within yourself and in other dimensions, to discover secrets for your success! It starts with getting still and silent, then disconnecting from the physical world, so you can:

1. Subdue the "thinking mind" and dial into a heavenly zone for two-way communication with God, angels, ancestors, helping spirits, and other enlightened beings such as Jesus and Buddha;

2. Discover your spirit self;

3. Access information about your soul's experiences across all boundaries of time and space; this includes past lives, the present, and the future;

4. Transform energy to: heal yourself and others; and manifest experiences to fulfill your life purpose; and

5. Receive constant guidance to live your healthiest, happiest, most purposeful life.

I viewed meditation as an all-access pass to infinity. So every day I meditated, cleared my chakras, and took Shamanic Journeys. I used guided meditations on YouTube featuring a narrator with a soothing voice, music, and user-friendly instructions to enter the divine realm via a tree, a forest path, or a sacred rock by the ocean. Then in my mind, I asked:

"What will serve my highest good today?"

In response, a spirit guide such as Jesus, my father, my guardian angel Esmerelda, and/or a power animal appeared. These beings provided guidance, and I journaled about each experience. Questions were answered by using Intuitive Writing. Adding creative visualization enhanced this practice; after writing out my heart's desires and getting guidance from these spirit beings, I visualized my goal coming to fruition. For example, I imagined one of my manuscripts transformed into a published book.

Princess Of Peace Videos Bring Blessings

One day, Jesus told me to write Princess of Peace Poems and recite them on video, then upload them to YouTube. I obeyed, composing poems on topics that included blessings for writers, Oprah, President Obama, and world peace.

I began this endeavor to celebrate my father's 90th birthday on

December 4, 2011. On January 1, 2012, I recorded in my journal the following meditation experience:

I went to the rock and asked, "What will serve my highest good today?" and Jesus came and told me that he is endowing me with the discipline and power to achieve my goals.

Then... Oh my goodness... Jesus just told me to do my first public Princess of Peace prayer for sick children in front of Children's Hospital. "Today, today, today," He said over and over and it was not a question, or option. "Today!"

Jesus had said, "You must be obedient." (Fear) tried to jump in and say don't do it. But Jesus said he would calm me. I felt physical fear in my body as I was absorbing the urgency of Jesus telling me to do this today.

I felt His protective, golden glow around me. He said he and my guardian angel will be with me as I do this and that I have nothing to fear. This is my purpose... to serve God as The Princess of Peace. The forecast, of course, is 44 degrees.

It was New Year's Day, and my son, who was almost 14, operated the camcorder on a tripod to shoot the video in front of Detroit's Children's Hospital, where we prayed for sick children to recover with perfect health. Then Alexander and I went to a movie, and I uploaded the video that evening.

Every time I posted these videos, blessings sparkled back. At the time, I was signing contracts for several ghostwriting projects. As a result, during December when I was doing the Princess of Peace prayer videos:

"I made more money in a month than I've ever earned before!" I journaled. "The Princess of Peace is richly rewarded when she is obedient and serves as the human tool for God and Jesus to shine their divine light and love on the world. This is one of the most amazing days of my life."

The Akashic Records Provide Answers About Fear, Food, and Fat

Why was I still troubled by an insatiable appetite and preoccupation with food and fat? Now that I had this new spiritual empowerment, I wanted to finally resolve this problem. But how? I wanted answers, and went searching for them in the Akashic Realm.

"Where is it?" someone asked me.

"It's not a physical place," I said. "It's in the divine dimension."

Also known as the Akashic Records, this archive of the spiritual world contains information about everything that ever was, is, and will be. You can access these records—which include information about your past lives—through meditation and "astral travel," which means allowing your spirit to venture into other dimensions.

Our souls carry the traumas of past lives for generations, even centuries. These traumas can manifest as problems, phobias, and issues in our current lives. We resolve them by exploring what happened to our souls during one of its human experiences, then by forgiving and releasing the trauma, the problem resolves in this lifetime.

This was the message in *Many Lives, Many Masters* by Dr. Brian Weiss, the book that Dr. Rama recommended. It described how Dr. Weiss—whom Oprah has interviewed on *Super Soul Sunday*—healed a patient's fears by exploring her past lives. The Yale Medical School-trained clinical psychiatrist now conducts international seminars that include teaching how to explore past lives to resolve current problems.

I decided to try this, starting with a prayer: "God please help me find answers to forgive, release, and heal my terrible trifecta of food, fear, and fat, by learning about a past life in the Akashic Records."

Then, sitting on the living room floor while my son did homework in his room, I cleared my chakras, called in divine light and beings for protection, listened to drumming music on headphones, and began a Shamanic Journey. As with all meditations, I entered with an open mind, having no idea what I might experience in the spirit world. That's what makes this process so magical and real at the same time; I see, hear, and learn things that I have never heard of or imagined. I described the experience in my journal:

I went to a sacred boulder by the ocean, where I was greeted by my guardian angel, Esmerelda.

"Please take me to the record keeper so that I can find out from the Akashic Records what has blocked me with my career and weight," I said, "so that I may unblock it and live to my highest, divine purpose."

"I must wrap you in my divine light of protection," she said, as her wings came forward and wrapped me in the bright, white-yellow light around her.

Then we ascended. This took awhile.

"You are safe, Elizabeth," she said.

All the while, I was hearing, "Elizabeth, Elizabeth, Elizabeth," and "Astral, astral, astral."

Esmerelda kept telling me, as we rose, "You are safe." First I saw beams of light spilling from a strip of white light within the vast black-ness of space, the same way that sunbeams shoot down through clouds.

I saw the purple flame in the blackness, and lots of faces going by, including my father. Then again I saw the white strip of light in the blackness, and we did a twisting motion upward, into that white light. We came to giant, gold and black gates, and a little pale man came and suddenly I was my 10-year-old self, smiling, with sun-bleached hair and plump cheeks.

Esmerelda spoke: "I have brought Elizabeth Atkins. She would like to access her Akashic Records to find out what has blocked her career and weight, so that she may achieve her highest life potential."

He opened the gate and let us in. The space was black except for a giant table: waist high, made of thick stone, roughly hewn at the edges. On it—a giant, golden book. Esmerelda told him my name, birthdate and time, and the city where I was born.

He flipped some pages and suddenly I was looking at a woman in a French prison, many centuries ago. She was wearing rags, sitting on the dirt floor amidst clumps of hay. On the floor was a bowl of gruel that was her food; it had bugs in it. Her skin was white and she was very dirty as she gripped one of the iron bars.

She was imprisoned because she was a storyteller accused of being a witch. She was taken from her family, her children, and she was jailed and left to die of starvation while afflicted by mental illness caused by infection.

Esmerelda and I showed up in a white glow outside the bars, facing her.

The woman is clasping her hands in prayer, looking up, ecstatic to see us.

Esmerelda tells this woman, "Elizabeth is blessed with the gift of writing and is living a life with your soul, and is writing stories that will be shared with the world."

At some point the conversation turns to French and I am telling her all the countries where the stories will be translated, in French and "en espagnol, et en allemagne, chinois, au Japon, Portuguese, Grece, Africain, partout! Partout!"

The words came to me in French in my meditation. The translation is: "in Spanish, in Germany, Chinese, in Japan, Portuguese, Greek, African, everywhere! Everywhere!"

Then Esmerelda said, "She will share these stories with the world in ways, E, that you cannot even imagine right now."

Then I learned her name: Emille. And I was told to dedicate my book, Goddess: Be One, to Emille to vindicate her death and the deaths of millions of other women who were punished for using their divine gifts as healers and storytellers.

Suddenly a man's face appears. He has reddish hair, a pointed beard, and a mustache. He has sharp facial features and piercing dark eyes that might be hazel. He's wearing a big white collar circling his neck, along with tights and ornate gold brocade clothing.

Then I see and feel myself through Emille's eyes, hauled by mean guards before this king, on the smooth floor facing his throne. She exclaims: "Les mots sont Dieu, par moi. Il parle par moi."

She's telling the king: "The words are God, by me. He speaks by me." She is protesting passionately, on her knees, saying that God speaks through me, and that I am a divine being telling stories, speaking for God. Emille is thrown back into prison, where she dies of starvation.

"You must write," Esmerelda tells me. We return to the record keeper, and she says, "I will tell you much more. We will return, but you must put this knowledge into action before you can learn more. You have much work to do."

We said goodbye to the record keeper and I nodded with my hands in a prayer position under my chin. Esmerelda wrapped me into her light and wings and we descended back to earth on a beam of light. She brought me back to the sacred rock, saying over and over, "Elizabeth, you have much work to do."

She referenced completing my ghostwriting projects, as well as my memoir and related books. Then Esmerelda and my spirit guides showed me on a global TV interview about my books.

"You will achieve tremendous success," they said. "You will avenge the deaths of all these women, especially Emille."

The Harlem Renaissance writer Zora Neale Hurston was starting to enter the picture, but I had the feeling that I would hear from her during a future meditation.

"Do not think about money," Esmerelda said. "Money will come to you from all kinds of sources. You must write and know that you are financially taken care of. You must write and... share these beautiful stories with the world so that Emille's death was not in vain."

When I tearfully came out of this meditation, I thought, "Oh beautiful Emille, I love you." And my heart swelled. "I feel your spirit!" Then I realized, "Your spirit IS me."

Then I went online to learn which king with red hair was

condemning women storytellers as witches. Chills crept over my skin as I found a photo of King Edward III, who looked exactly like the king in my meditation. Turns out, his reign as King of England from 1327 until his death in 1377, included conquering France for a time. He was notorious for the murders of millions of women accused as witches for being storytellers, healers, and spiritual beings.

Then it all made sense. **No wonder I was terrified to reveal my gifts as a writer, as a woman, and as a spiritual being. And no wonder I have always wanted to eat everything in sight!** My soul was still wounded by this past life trauma as punishment for following my divine calling. **For the crime that God was speaking through me, and that I boldly proclaimed that!**

Overwhelmed by these revelations, I sat in silent prayer, thanking God for all the blessings of my life and the freedom to speak and write on behalf of all the people I have been. People who never dreamed of the freedoms that we enjoy today. Freedoms that I must use to say everything that they were killed for saying.

Meeting My Spiritual Writing Team:
The Council Of Women Writers

I was not alone in this quest to give voice to the women who were stopped from sharing their talents and spiritual beliefs during centuries past.

That was especially true when an extraordinary and surprising experience unfolded during a meditative journey on January 2, 2012. Here's what I wrote:

I went to the sacred rock by the ocean and asked, "What will serve my highest good?" My spirit guides appeared and escorted me down the golden cave to the Lower World. My father and other divine beings greeted me with love and celebration. Then a wizard-type man paddled us in a boat across the mirror-like lake reflecting the lavender sky, to the cottage aglow with yellow light.

Inside, I encountered the Council of Women Writers. They were waiting for me at the wooden table. Virginia Woolf was in a corner with a headache. Also there were Louisa Mae Alcott, Aphra Behn, and Gloria Alvarez.

"I loved the way you taught Uncle Tom's Cabin in your Women's Lit classes at WCCCD," Harriet Beecher Stowe said.

Zora Neale Hurston—whose spirit I have felt for many years—was wearing her trademark hat and said, "I knew we'd get together again."

Charlotte Bronte was there because, she said, "When the Divine extends a request to attend, you attend."

My spirit guide and I were standing at the table.

"This is Elizabeth Ann Atkins," He said. "She has the technology to send writing around the globe instantaneously. She's writing on behalf of all of you, and I want you to help her." He specifically asked them to help me write a series of books that I had already begun on behalf of all women.

"I'm delighted to meet you," Aphra Behn said.

Virginia Woolf felt better and joined us at the table. As I sat down, a sparkling, golden glow was over us and around the thick wooden table, where we sat in high-backed chairs made of tree branches fanned together.

"You have to have a writing schedule every day," the women said, as if in unison. Their messages came fast, and I didn't see their faces too clearly. "Write every day. Trust your work."

My dear friend E. Lynn Harris was there, excited that I have access to all this, and he was like, "Girl, these women are gonna help you out! Trip you out! You are so lucky, so blessed."

This experience came as a complete surprise, and reminded me of Napoleon Hill's recollection in *Think and Grow Rich* about how he held nightly "meetings" for many years with his "Invisible Counselors" in a meditative state with the greatest business magnates of his time, to shape his character and emulate them. He describes this in "The Sixth Sense" chapter as he praises the power of imagination;

he was awed at how real these meetings became as the men spoke and behaved as if he were in a real meeting.

I felt the same during my experiences with The Council of Women Writers. The difference is that I did not set a deliberate intention to summon these powerful women, but I was ecstatic that my spirit guides took me to consult with them about once every week.

One day, I took Alexander to a basketball game, made him a homework snack of edamame and fresh blackberries, then put him to bed. It was a happy day, and I expressed gratitude for the love, health, safety, and security that we enjoyed. Then I took a meditative journey, and wrote the following in my journal:

My spirit guide met me at the rock and said, "You're meeting on the beach." He added that he was glad that I am being obedient and doing this daily. It was night. We walked around the rocks and the ladies were sitting around a bonfire.

"You need balance," Harriet Beecher Stowe said. "You need to balance your food and energy because for the past several days, you've been having highs and lows that correlate with food or lack thereof." Then she added, "You need more sleep."

The fire was blazing in the center as we sat on Adirondack chairs on the sand. The full moon was glowing lavender on the waves crashing on the beach nearby.

"Don't ever let anyone make you think that your body isn't good enough as it is," Virginia Woolf said. "You are perfect just as you are. You are beautiful."

Gloria Anzaldúa showed up. "Get your memoir done!"

Zora Neale Hurston expressed awe at the diversity of voices inside me, and said, "Bring them out!" She also wants me to finish Husbands, Incorporated because she loves the themes on love and lack thereof, and feminist takes on relationships with men.

Just as Zora was talking, E. Lynn Harris walked up and everybody was happy to see him. He stood next to my chair holding a fancy bottled water and smiled, and said he was going to help me write one of the books I was working on. The women continued to chime in with advice:

"Spend an hour every day on each project, each book," someone said.

"Only an hour?" I asked.

"The more you do, the more you can do," someone said.

They were telling me I'm really lucky for all that I have available, compared to when they lived.

At the end, I said, "I'm going to take Harriet Beecher Stowe's advice and get some sleep."

The Council of Women Writers told me, "Thank you for representing."

I came out of the meditation and chronicled it in my journal, ending the entry by writing, *"Thank you, God; thank you, Jesus; thank you, Holy Spirit!"*

The following week, during a meditative journey to the Akashic Records, I encountered a woman who pleaded: "Write for us!" The woman was me in a past life, centuries ago, living as an Indian princess. A lion spirit guide took me to the opulent palace where I lived and that I had seen before in meditations. Here's what I wrote in my journal:

The palace is constructed in shades of beige, mustard yellow, and cream, and I'm on an upper level overlooking a dirty square of desert-like sand, where animals are pulling carriages that create a lot of dust.

I am wearing beautiful, ornamental gold around my face, wrists, and fingers. Little tiny coins are draped on a chain over my temples. There's something hanging in the center, a red dot on the third eye, a drapey fabric of beige/gold over my thick, black hair. I wear sandals. I wear thick, black eyeliner. I am beautiful.

My fingernails and toenails are adorned with gold: not necessarily polish, but designs like dots and swirls. I eat sweet fruits with my fingers.

I smell like exotic oils. I feel caged. The patterns of the woodwork and metal grills, and the carvings on the walls are beautiful, but oppressive.

My husband is young and handsome, but not nice. I have visions. People think I'm crazy. I am locked in. I have a bath area with ornate, rectangular, built-in tubs that are dark yellow with four-petaled red flowers in a tile pattern. Beautiful women attend to me. I work with children who are special needs. One girl has thick eyebrows and dark, bewildered eyes.

My mother died on an ornate platform bed surrounded by steps up. My father, an older man, cried out in misery when she died. Children are around us as she died.

This life would ultimately end when a jealous woman poisoned me. This woman who lived a life inhabited by my soul asked me to give voice to the many lives I have lived as women who had no voice, no power, no freedom. As the princess in India, I was not allowed to write in the oppression of my gilded cage.

"Write for us!" the woman repeated over and over. "Write for us, Elizabeth!"

During another meditation, the Women Writers were annoyed that I hadn't been with them and that I hadn't devoted enough time to my personal writing. I was juggling freelance writing articles for *BLAC Detroit Magazine*, as well as many ghostwriting projects, which required scheduling and conducting phone- and in-person interviews, and meeting with my clients.

One was a bariatric surgeon at the Detroit Medical Center, and I donned scrubs to observe him performing surgeries on obese patients. These robotic surgeries used the DaVinci arm, so I watched on a video monitor as Dr. Michael Wood reduced the size of his patients' stomachs using tiny instruments inserted through tubes. It was fascinating! After seeing thick abdominal fat—which resembles melted, orange cheese—I ate a plate of fresh broccoli for dinner.

Devoting Time To Motherhood

In addition, I was planning Alexander's 14th birthday festivities. This included hand-writing invitations for the entire eighth grade at his school for his party featuring basketball, swimming, rock-climbing, and pizza.

The year before, when he turned 13, my mother organized a bowling party for his seventh grade class. As the kids ate pizza, a popular song began to play. To the surprise of Alexander and his guests, a pop star impersonator danced into the party and performed. Then he taught all the kids how to do the dance in one of the pop star's famous videos. It was amazing!

Meanwhile, now that he was in eighth grade, Alexander played lead point guard on the varsity basketball team. Several nights each week, my mother and I and his father attended his games at schools across Metro Detroit.

On school days, I delivered a snack such as a sandwich and Gatorade before he went to after-school practice for basketball or theatre. I always had divine timing; he often just happened to be walking through the school lobby when I arrived, so I could give him the food and a hug. Here's an excerpt from my journal about one such day:

I walked an hour on Lakeshore from 4:30 to 5:30 after the thrill of delivering Alexander's turkey/cheese sandwich that I lovingly made and he was in the computer room and he tore into the foil and took a bite from the center with Colby jack cheese, rolled turkey slices, and soft wheat bread. I love it! Thank you God that I can deliver a sandwich to Alexander and meet with his teachers and school leaders during the day! I love it!

My greatest joy and top priority was always my son. I am so grateful that throughout his education, I went on every field trip, taught an after-school creative writing class with him amongst many children for a few years when he was in elementary school, and spent extra time dropping him off and picking him up each day. In addition, I took him to orthodontist appointments for his braces. I cherished every second of having the freedom to be available for him.

Being a mom and a ghostwriter left little time to write my own books, and I always felt the urgency that The Council of Women Writers and other spirit guides conveyed. So in one meditation, I asked them for help, and they agreed to infuse me with the ability to juggle my responsibilities and focus on my own writing.

"You have so much power," the women said. "You need to fiercely manage your time. Write for all of us."

"Don't eat so much," Harriet Beecher Stowe said.

Virginia Woolf was sympathetic because of her incapacitating depression. Also attending that day were Zora Neale Hurston, Jane Austen, Edith Wharton, and Aphra Behn. Plus I was thrilled to see George Eliot for the first time. Then Daddy was in a wing-back chair near the front door.

"We've been having a great time with your charming father," the women said, "talking about the books you read as an English major at Michigan." Then the ladies faded into the background.

"You can write more," my father said. "You need to elevate into a higher dimension, a higher level of consciousness, and write more. You have so much power."

"You're Radiating Pink Light… Pure Love"

One day, I visited Lori Lipten at her office and expressed profuse gratitude for teaching me so many life-changing practices. I had also attended her group readings as a shamanic medium, during which she shared messages from beyond, often with people who were grieving the loss of a loved one.

"It was so amazing to watch you share your gift to help people find comfort and closure," I told her. "And the guidance you shared with others was really transformative."

Then she revealed what she saw during our first meeting: "You have big white and pink wings. Huge wings of light. You're radiating all this pink light. It's pure love!"

She added: "White light is shooting from your hand chakras in your palms with some from the fingertips." I showed her my business card—whose design I had selected from stock photos at an online store before I knew what chakras were—showing a hand with a ball of light in the palm. We were not surprised. Having once dreamed of being a physician, it was thrilling to discover that healing energy in my hands was infusing my writing with healing power.

Lori also said that earth angels are people whose life mission is to help others awaken their spiritual consciousness; this explained my intolerance for negative, violent, and hateful things. I told her that often during meditation, my guardian angel and I held prayer ceremonies to promote love, harmony, and prosperity for people around the world.

She also said, "You've been a shaman over many lives."

That night, I took a meditative journey to the Akashic Records to discover my past lives as a spiritual healer. The record keeper opened the giant book of the Akashic Records and pointed at something. As if a filmstrip rose from the pages and I stepped into a scene, I saw triangular hats and red soldiers' jackets. They were Redcoats—British soldiers in Connecticut during the American Revolution before America won independence from Great Britain in 1776.

I experienced this meditation through the eyes of the Native American man who embodied my soul. I was running into the woods carpeted by autumn leaves. It was chaotic: many people or bodies were falling into a wide, mass grave. I had a feeling of being thrown head-first, face down. That was all I saw, but I understood that the British soldiers killed me because I was a spiritual healer.

This is a common theme in past lives: being killed for doing God's work as a healer, a spiritual teacher, a writer, and a storyteller. That resulted in being burned at the stake during several lives in Scotland and France, according to meditations that explained my fear of fire. As for asking about past lives as a shaman, sometimes I only saw a flash of gruesome scenes during several lifetimes on different continents.

"You don't want to do this, Elizabeth," my spirit guides said.

"Please take me out," I said, feeling chilled.

After learning this, I asked Archangel Raphael to heal my soul and release these memories. I found comfort in knowing that God is always protecting and shielding me and my family in His divine light and love.

The N-word: Cultivating Harmony

When I picked up Alexander from middle school, the policy required parents to enter the building and sign out their child. Well one day when he was in eighth grade, he was in a computer lab with other students. It was "Twin Day" during Spirit Week for the Liggett Knights, and kids wore face paint and fun clothing.

"We're twins!" exclaimed two girls, standing in front of me and pointing to their outfits. "We're wearing the same hat, outfits, socks, and shoes." They said nothing about how one girl was black and one girl was white. Tears of happiness filled my eyes.

Another day, however, my tears were not joyous. When I picked up Alexander after school, he was doing homework in the library. Our plan was to get him a pizza, then he would go watch the high school varsity basketball game with his dad.

Alexander was happy as we got into the car. The soft evening sunlight was shining as I stopped at a corner amidst pretty homes around the school. That's when he told me that a student called him the n-word.

"I was appalled and outraged and mad," Alexander said. He searched the school for the dean of students and explained what happened. The dean in turn said he was very proud that Alexander reacted in a mature way. Then Alexander said the dean met with the student who had used the n-word.

Still stopped at the street corner, as the golden sunlight illuminated my son's wise-beyond-his-years eyes, it felt like time stood still.

"I'm really proud of how you reacted," I said. "That was really mature. And I'm really proud of how you went and got an adult in an authority position."

I was also extremely impressed with the school's immediate and comprehensive response, as well as its long-term follow-up to cultivate understanding and harmony. That evening, the dean called and described what happened when Alexander first found him.

"He was upset," the dean said. "Our first talk was about the hate of the action and how that would feel. He knew it was okay to feel what he felt at the time. After that, we talked about how to move on. He handled it extremely well. I continue to be amazed at this kid and his growth. He's very wise, Elizabeth."

The dean explained that he and the head of the middle school—who also phoned me that evening—were meeting with the student's parents, and were working with the student to apologize to Alexander. The apology occurred, as did a productive conversation between me and his parents. We even invited the student to the birthday party.

A short time later, the school asked me to speak at a student assembly. I performed my *White Chocolate* poem and talked about never fitting in as a biracial girl, and how kids made mean comments about my frizzy hair, but later my female classmates coveted my curls because they were going to salons to get expensive "perms" to curl their hair. I talked about how our differences are what make us unique and interesting, and that we should all love ourselves as we are, and love each other as we want to be treated.

The next day, the mother of a black female student whose daughter had felt excluded called to say that her daughter felt affirmed by my speech, and that a spirit of kindness had permeated some previously unfriendly girls. Later, I saw the girl in the hallway, laughing and talking, surrounded by a group of white girls who were clearly her friends. A healing truly had occurred, and I hurried away so they didn't see the joyous tears welling in my eyes.

As for Alexander, he was one of six Liggett students selected to attend a national student diversity leadership conference in Washington, DC. And during his high school years, he was part of a student diversity council that worked with the administration and student body to lead meetings and discussions. He also helped brainstorm and implement programs to cultivate kindness and inclusion across lines of race, religion, and ethnicity.

The night of the incident, in meditation, Jesus said: "Alexander is safe. I am with him, along with his crew of angels and divine spirits."

Blessings For Devotion

As I'd been doing for the past decade, I was still trying to find the best literary agent to sell my books—and now my clients' books—to publishers in New York. I went into meditation to ask how to secure representation. Instead, my father appeared, took my hand, and said, "I'm very proud of your hard work and how you've been less critical of yourself."

I felt the presence of Jesus, who added: "You have been honoring writing, so I am honoring you by providing abundant resources to you."

Later that morning, I opened the mail. A letter from Alexander's school said that he was awarded the McGregor Scholarship for the Upper School, which would provide a significant contribution for his tuition for ninth, tenth, eleventh, and twelfth grades.

I cried tears of joy and gratitude all day.

Changing My Prayer Style From Pleading To Praising

During the spring of 2012, I was working to meet a deadline for a major ghostwriting project. As I worked around the clock to tell my celebrated client's amazing story, he kept adding extra people for me to interview.

This put me behind schedule, and I was very anxious about completing the book on time, with the quality of writing that it deserved. Completion would accompany a large check to cover my rent, car note, and other bills. Yes I was making money, but I had paid tuition and some other debts, and as a result, was relying on the income from ghostwriting.

So, as time ticked toward the deadline—and my bank balance dwindled—I was racing against the clock to finish the book and replenish my finances. During the final weeks, I was sleeping six hours per night, just enough to maintain mental focus for my "breakfast 'til bedtime" writing schedule. Aside from taking Alexander to and from school, I spent most of the final weeks sitting at my laptop at the table, working intensely.

My mother, being the angel that she is, often took Alexander to dinner, to a movie, or to a video game arcade on the weekends when he was not with his father. She also delivered groceries, so I would not have to take time to go shopping. Without her, I never would have made it, and I am immensely grateful for her help.

So, finally, I completed the 400-page book. I had interviewed dozens of people, cited countless sources, and the story spanned nearly 100 years. I printed it, put it in a three-ring binder, and proudly delivered it to my client's assistant on a Friday.

I would not get paid until my client reviewed it, approved it, and provided edits for me to make within two weeks. His assistant's first, brief perusal inspired compliments. I was so relieved and exhausted, I went home on that Friday afternoon and slept for 16 hours straight.

Early in the week, my client's assistant called to say he wanted massive changes. Panic shot through me like an lightning bolt. Massive changes would take weeks, and my rent, car note, and other bills were due. She said she'd be in touch, but I didn't hear anything all week.

I was so stressed, I found the first-ever gray hair on my head, which I plucked out and have not seen any more since. By Friday, I was in a full-blown panic. I emailed her, asking for an update. Then I checked my bank balance: $161.

I burst into tears in the middle of my living room, standing in the same spot where I had declared to God that I would serve as a ghostwriter to showcase inspiring people. Now, I clasped my hands in prayer and cried, "God, please, please, please help me."

Then I remembered when I helped Reverend Jim Holley write his memoir called, *Jimmy, This is Jesus*; he prayed by *praising*, not pleading.

After having a stroke and being unable to talk, walk, feed himself, or preach, Reverend Holley said in his mind he praised God for restoring his abilities—before he could do any of the above. He thanked God with the same enthusiasm as if the prayer were already answered. Then one day while sitting in a wheelchair in the hospital, the first thing he was able to do in physical therapy was lift his arms in praise. Soon he was back in the pulpit, preaching Sunday service. Likewise, I'd heard so many metaphysical teachers say that gratitude is the best way to see results.

So in the midst of panic, I changed my prayers from pleading to praising.

"Thank you God for this amazing financial miracle!" I declared. "Thank you God for this financial miracle!" I repeated it over and over, fervently.

As I prayed, the phone rang.

"Elizabeth," said my client's assistant, "can you please come to the office this afternoon?"

A short time later, I was sitting in a conference room with her, a few other people, and my client.

"You did a beautiful job," he said, "and I said everything that you wrote. But I'm not going to have you finish the book."

Panic spiraled through me. I couldn't remember the liquidation clause in the contract. Would I have to call my lawyer, and how long would that take? Nervous sweat prickled over me. I felt sick.

My client reached for an envelope that was on the table and said, "This is for you. It's what was due for completion of the book."

Within hours of thanking God for the financial miracle that I desperately needed, I was holding a significant check that proved the power of prayerful praise.

Moving In With Catherine & Going To California

In the spring of 2012, Catherine found herself living alone in a four-bedroom house in the eclectic suburb of Ferndale. She had moved here in November of 2011 for a job that would conclude her decade of work in large financial services firms.

"Biss, do you and Alexander want to live with me?" she asked.

I felt a bizarre sensation in my heart, like a giant flower blooming fast. It was my heart chakra opening. That was a yes! I'd heard of chakras "opening," and was awed that it created a physical sensation that I had never felt before. Since I had not renewed my lease, we moved into her two-story house.

Then in July of 2012, Alexander and I and his dad traveled to Los Angeles, where Alexander attended Kobe Academy basketball camp at the University of California at Santa Barbara. It began with a ceremony in a huge gymnasium featuring basketball players, coaches, hundreds of kids from across the world, and an inspiring talk by Kobe Bryant.

"Oh my goodness!" I exclaimed as kids swarmed the courts. "Alexander is talking with Kobe Bryant!" I captured this magic moment on video as Alexander looked up at his hero as they spoke for a few minutes.

Alexander stayed in a campus dorm with a roommate he had never met. Prior to the trip, I had to release tremendous anxiety about my child being in a dormitory amongst a lot of boys under the supervision of camp counselors. I meditated on this, and was shown Archangel Michael with my father and my son's other grandfather, all standing outside Alexander's dorm room, while countless angels swirled over the basketball courts and across the entire campus. Alexander also attended John Beilein Basketball Camps at the University of Michigan as well as camps with former Detroit Piston Greg Kelser.

He returned to Kobe Academy the following summer for another awesome experience that included taking pictures and talking with Kobe Bryant. Both times, his dad stayed with a cousin, and I spent several days with Lara and her family.

"Happy Birthday to my BFF!" Lara exclaimed as live music played and lights twinkled over the outdoor terrace at Zaytoon restaurant in Santa Barbara.

"This is so delicious," I moaned, spooning up baba ganoush—Middle Eastern eggplant dip—along with delectable salmon and hummus, as we sat amidst fire pits and a vibrant crowd. We laughed and talked, never wanting the evening to end. One day, Lara brought her kids to visit Alexander at Kobe Academy, and we had a wonderful time.

Back in Michigan, Catherine's house was a 30-minute drive to and from Alexander's school, where acted in the fall theatrical production and played on the junior varsity basketball team.

Each morning, while my sister worked 9 to 5, I focused on my ghostwriting projects in a bedroom converted into my office. One book was especially exciting; my client sent me on research trips throughout New England. I worked hard to complete the manuscript, which was well-received.

All the while, this book, along with *Goddess: Be One,* and *Husbands, Inc.,* sat unfinished in my computer. Profound frustration and sadness spiked my appetite; I was gaining weight, and spiraling into depression.

Still meditating and journaling, I made a large vision board featuring photos of: Jesus, my family, Pope John Paul II, me as super fit, and future bestseller lists topped by my book titles. Next to Jesus is a loving photo of my parents, and a picture of Daddy waving from what looks like Noah's Ark under construction. It's actually his cottage, all pine two-by-fours before windows and siding were applied.

A photo of Lakshmi, the Hindu goddess of wealth and prosperity, is near a photo of my son's quote when he was eight years old: "I think the whole world will think your books are the greatest books in the world!" Another favorite quote on this vision board was spoken by Mahatma Gandhi: "I am a Muslim and a Hindu and a Christian and a Jew and so are all of you."

Voting Dilemma Highlights Biracial Perspective

I love to exercise my right to vote so much, that I usually cry in the booth. Then, glancing at my "I voted" sticker makes me shiver with gratitude for the freedoms that we enjoy as women, people of color, and Americans.

So I didn't mind waiting in a long line at the voting precinct with Catherine, eager to cast our votes in the 2012 primary as President Obama sought a second term.

At the time, national news reports were highlighting efforts by some to block people of color from registering to vote. Our polling place was at a public school, and unbeknownst to those around us, Catherine and I were the only people of color. At the check-in table, the male clerk told me:

"I'm sorry ma'am, you're not in our computer."

"But I changed my address when I moved from Grosse Pointe," I said.

The man checked for my name again, then shook his head. "Your name is not here."

"So how can I vote today?" I asked.

"You can't."

"But I have to vote today!" I insisted. "I live in Ferndale! Here's my driver's license!"

"I'm sorry, unless you're in our system—"

I was furious, thinking, *You just don't want me to vote because I'm black!* Then I realized, *This man has no idea that I'm anything other than a suntanned, blond-haired, green-eyed white lady wearing a floral-print dress.*

Catherine voted, and I calmed down. As we left, it struck me that I view the world through a lens of both black and white, even though the world may only view me through one of those lenses. Sometimes a white lens. Sometimes a black lens.

"You're black!" declared my friend as we sat in a Manhattan restaurant. A cornucopia of humanity streamed along the sidewalk behind him, on the other side of the huge window on which my own reflection mirrored back white skin and yellow hair.

"But you knew my father," I said. "He was white."

"If any part of you is black, then all of you is," insisted this friend who is African American and attended some of the world's top universities. For him, race is a matter of identity and allegiance, not pigment.

Golfing phenom Tiger Woods was criticized when he called himself Cablinasian, a term he created as a child to describe himself as a multiracial blend of his Thai mother's Chinese and Dutch heritage, combined with his African American father's Native American and Chinese ancestry. Sometimes multiracial people are "accused" of claiming their white side or their Native American ancestry as a ploy to abandon their black roots.

And many black people toss up racial litmus tests to assess a mixed-race person's allegiance. They ask, "What race is your spouse? Where do you live? Are you in a sorority? What church do you attend?" Race relations are so complicated by historic injustices, personal pain, and profound distrust, that I understand the questioners' motives.

Once while seated in the crowded waiting area at the Secretary of State, a young woman lamented to her daughter that she had no more parking meter money and feared getting a ticket.

"Here," I said, handing over several quarters.

Surprised, the woman beamed. Will offering parking meter money radically change the world? No, but moments like that can help restore hope that kindness comes in all colors.

Fat, Sick, And Ready For Change

In January of 2013, I was 35 pounds overweight and felt sick, worried about money, and frustrated that my career as a novelist was stuck.

So many things had seemed like stepping stones to a place far better than laying here, crying in bed. Writing books... meeting with high-powered people in LA and New York... doing author events across America... being on national TV and radio shows... writing for national magazines and *The New York Times*... acting in a movie... writing a screenplay... being in a speakers bureau that promised big speaking fees.

As for completing this book—I was caught in that cycle of working on writing jobs that paid my bills as opposed to my own books that had no immediate income attached.

But at 45 years old, it felt like "do or die." I was terrified that God would inflict the Parable of the Talents on me. In that Bible story, the son who used his father's gifts to multiply them and help people, received more. The son who buried his gifts was stripped of everything.

My gifts felt buried under fat, fear, and failure. I had to slay the food and fat demon within, before it killed me. Actually I was going through a "shamanic death," a time of suffering that kills off old ways and strengthens spiritual power to increase the shaman's healing abilities.

"God, please make me feel better so I can finally do this!"

"Let Food Be Thy Medicine"

Thankfully, God answered my prayers immediately, by leading me to documentaries about people using something I'd never heard of— "plant-based diets"—to slim down, heal their bodies, and cure terminal illness.

Lying in bed for a week, I learned about plant-based eating by watching Netflix documentaries on my laptop computer. More programs showed graphic video of how animals suffer in the meat and dairy industries. And other documentaries introduced me to: superfoods; inexpensive herbs like cilantro and parsley that "detox" the body; and the cancer-curing Gersen Diet. The disease had stricken several of my loved ones.

So I embarked on an aggressively anti-cancer, anti-diabetes, anti-hypertensive, and anti-obesity lifestyle. Call it the Hippocrates Plan. It's inspired by what the Greek physician said in 400 B.C.: "Let thy food be thy medicine and thy medicine be thy food."

I began eating fresh vegetables at all meals with only small portions of lean fish and poultry. Already gluten-free, I went low fat, low calorie, low sodium, and low glycemic. I got hooked on chia seeds, which boosted my energy and mental clarity while suppressing my appetite and packing a mighty punch of omega three fatty acids, antioxidants, fiber, protein, and calcium. I was starting to feel better, and lost a few pounds.

My goal was to harness maximum supernatural power to ascend into my best self and most desirable life.

Dedication To Meditation

Most mornings, I cleared my chakras and meditated, often taking a Shamanic Journey to the Upper or Lower World. I did this on a meditation pad that I created from a cushion, blankets, and pillows on the floor of the enclosed back porch outside my office. The meditations were glorious, but seemed incongruent with my physical reality.

"You are extremely rich, Elizabeth," my spirit guides often said. I was extremely rich with an amazing son, an excellent educational experience for him, and a loving family that included close relationships with my sister and mother.

The challenge was to overcome my "human" blockages of fear and perceptions of failure. Could I step into this power and influence?

"Just keep writing, Elizabeth," Jesus and my spirit guides encouraged whenever I worried about finishing my books.

Affirmation came in an email from Tiya Miles, PhD, then-Chair of the Afroamerican and African Studies Department at the University of Michigan.

"There is great interest in having you speak on this panel about your autobiographical experience as a mixed-race individual and as a popular writer who presents these issues to the public in your fiction," she wrote.

I was thrilled to perform my *White Chocolate* poem and speak in the Duderstadt Theatre on this panel discussing race on campus as part of the UM College of Literature, Science & Arts Race Theme Semester, which included the Smithsonian's IndiVisible traveling exhibit about Afro-Native lives and histories.

Attending were Karen Downing, PhD, founder of the multiracial group that had helped me so much as an undergraduate, and Dr.

Matlock, now a mentor. Dr. Miles—who is a Harvard University history professor—is a tremendous inspiration. I had met her when interviewing her for *BLAC Detroit Magazine*, after she won the MacArthur "Genius" Fellowship, which provided a half million dollars to apply to any endeavor she desired.

What an honor that she invited me to share messages that prompted several students and faculty members to say my words influenced their perceptions about human harmony.

A Surprising Instruction From Spirit

I was laying on the living room floor amidst 20 people with pillows and blankets while my dear friend led a meditation.

"We're setting the intention for how we want to create our best lives in 2013," she said, as the January sunshine glowed on snow outside the window. "So ask for guidance on how to accomplish these goals, and ask what your divine assignments are for the coming year."

While clearing our chakras, the energy and volume of our *bija* chants felt strong enough to blow off the roof! This blessed me with several, vivid Shamanic Journeys that provided explicit instructions for the coming year.

"Do not have sex!" my spirit guides said loudly and clearly during meditation.

Whaaaaaat?! Actually, this made sense. I needed to devote all my time to writing, because my spirit guides also laid out a detailed strategy about how to finally complete *Husbands, Inc.* in 2013. It was time to get to work. I knew the year would be extraordinary if I obeyed this guidance.

"Eat Only Plant Food Today"

On February 8, I was about to open a can of white tuna in water, which I usually ate with raw spinach, fresh basil, and a drizzle of olive oil.

"Eat only plant food today," said a voice within that was distinctly a higher power. Still grasping the can and opener, I paused. Then this divine force said, "Don't open this. Eat some lima beans." I did, with fresh garlic, one teaspoon of olive oil, parsley, and a green apple.

"What's going on?" I asked in meditation, and my spirit guides said they wanted to accelerate my weight loss. I was eager to follow directions to make that happen.

That day, I drove my son to his basketball game at a school across town. I loved cheering loudly for him, and he was playing really well. At halftime, I went to the bathroom. After feeling so bad one month ago, looking pale and puffy, my reflection in the mirror now made me gasp.

I look luminescent!

It was Friday, and Alexander would leave with his dad for the weekend. I considered attending a friend's book party. Events like that were a grim reminder that I had no new books, and friends would surely ask when I had another coming out.

"Go home and work on your memoir," said the divine voice within. That night, I enjoyed hours of writing with more clarity, focus, and epiphanies than I'd had on this book in years!

Also that day, dinner was a salad of "super greens," English cucumber, a Roma tomato, fresh lemon juice, lima beans, horseradish, and one teaspoon of olive oil. I shoveled snow, then snacked on blackberries and chia seeds. After the game, I had a green apple and chia seeds.

"My clarity right now is crystal clear," I journaled. "Thank you God for helping me work on my book tonight. Oh my goodness, I have felt so amazing today. I didn't know my energy could be sustained like this, but it can!"

I slept really well, and weighed myself in the morning. I lost *two pounds!* Wow! My spirit soared. *One day* on a plant-based diet meant:

- Looking luminescent;
- Having tons of energy and sleeping great;
- Feeling extra enjoyment at my son's game;

- Receiving constant guidance from the Divine on what to eat, where to go, what to do;
- Being blessed with a writing break-through; and
- Losing two pounds in one day!

I was blessed again—with tons of energy to power through spinning class after eating only a green apple and chia seeds. A few Saturdays later after class, the divine voice within me instructed: "Go to Eastern Market." At Detroit's historic, bustling farmer's market, I bought baskets of: red beefsteak tomatoes for $5; Persian cucumbers for $5; and yellow, orange, and red peppers for $5. I also bought two bunches of cilantro for $1. I spent a few more dollars on yellow squash.

Walking past tables offering fruits, vegetables, and herbs, as the vendors hawked their wares, filled me with joy. The cornucopia of people included chic women with designer eyeglasses and purses walking amongst Indian ladies in sarees, 20-something hipsters, yuppie couples sipping coffee, people sporting a hip-hop look, families, and everyone in-between. At every turn, someone was playing drums, a saxophone, or a homemade instrument.

Walking to my car, less than 15 minutes later, bags in hand, I was elated. I'd spent less than $20 on fresh produce that would have cost double at the grocery store. From then on, I stocked up on the week's vegetables every Saturday morning at Eastern Market.

Manifesting A Miracle To Move

In January of 2013, Catherine announced that she was going to sell her house and move back out west. In meditation, I saw "sold" stamped over the house. Within two weeks, the house was under contract.

Because the announcement was sudden, I had not prepared by saving for a move. I really wanted to live closer to Alexander's school, and was praying fervently for the resources to secure the perfect property for us.

So I wrote over and over in my journal every night: "Thank you God for the financial miracle that enables me and Alexander to move into a condo in Grosse Pointe." Then I scoured the real estate websites for the perfect property, and maintained fervent prayer and belief, often repeating Matthew 21:22: "Whatsoever ye shall ask in prayer, believing, ye shall receive."

I also listed what we wanted: his own room and bathroom, a modern kitchen, safety and peace, and space for me to write and meditate.

Meanwhile, we celebrated Alexander's birthday. I texted him: "Alexander, I am very proud of you as a young gentleman turning 15! You're going to do amazing things in the world!!!!"

For his birthday, his dad took him to the Detroit Pistons game against the LA Lakers, and after the game, they were granted access to the team tunnel in the Palace of Auburn Hills. There, as the Lakers walked to their bus, Kobe Bryant recognized Alexander from Kobe Academy. His dad took pictures while Kobe asked Alexander about academics and basketball. It was an amazing birthday!

All the while, my prayerful praise in my journal activated a miracle in the universe, and I found myself journaling profuse gratitude to God that in March of 2013, we obtained the funds to lease a beautiful, two-bedroom, two-and-a-half bath townhouse near school. In every meditation, my spirit guides confirmed that this was the perfect place for us.

In addition, I asked my spirit guides to show me the "essence"— or the spiritual energy—of the home. First I saw my mother's house, where my father last lived with her; the essence was a solid gold tree, with deep roots, a very strong trunk, and formidable branches. Because Spirit speaks in symbolism, a solid gold tree represents a life rich with love, security, health, and joy. The tree symbolizes family roots, stability, support, and the nourishing base from which we can grow and extend into the world as branches rooted in our family's foundation.

Then I saw the essence of our new home; it was a vortex of baby blue light spinning in the high-ceilinged, loft-like living room and dining room with an open kitchen and a fireplace. This light cast an angelic feeling of peace and love. The color blue represents the throat chakra, which rules communication and speaking our highest truth. Baby blue is also the color of the garment worn by Mother Mary.

In this meditation, I also felt the strong presence of my father, who conveyed that Alexander and I would be very happy and safe in our new home.

When we moved in, Alexander loved his room, which had large windows and natural light, just like his full bathroom, which was spacious and modern. Catherine gave him a large wooden desk where he did hours of homework, and my mother gave him a big, flat-screen TV to watch when his work was finished.

I was tearfully grateful, finding delight in nurturing Alexander. Before school, I made sure his uniform was ironed. Since he didn't eat lunch for six hours into the school day, I served him a hot, hearty breakfast—usually turkey spaghetti, stir-fry chicken with rice and broccoli, or a quesadilla with cheese and chicken, all with fresh fruit such as blackberries, and pineapple juice.

Then I drove him to school, and either picked him up at 3 p.m. or took him a snack before sports or theatre practice, which lasted until 5 or 6 p.m. One day, Alexander was really upset that his team lost the basketball game.

"Alexander, do you know what unconditional love is?"

"Yes."

"It's when someone loves you, no matter what," I said.

"I know," he said.

"That's me, with you," I said.

A Spiritual Retreat From The World

In our new home, I cultivated a daily routine and lifestyle that felt like a spiritual retreat from the world.

Most days, after taking Alexander to school, I cleared my chakras. Then I did Kundalini yoga in our living room with Santa Monica, California teacher Maya Fiennes via YouTube videos. With practice, difficult moves that made my muscles tremble, soon became easier.

Kundalini is an ancient Hindu word for the life force energy that lies dormant and coiled like a snake at the base of the spine; yoga and breathing exercises can "awaken" this energy to empower the mind, body, and spirit for healing and connection to the Divine.

I definitely felt that, as expressed in a journal entry: "I stood up for the end of naval chakra yoga and felt a zillion angels around me and beings and ancestors."

After yoga, I meditated, often taking a Shamanic Journey to the Upper World. Whereas the Lower World is accessed through an imaginary tree portal, you use your imagination to ascend a golden beam—the kind you see shooting down through clouds—to ascend into the Upper World. A spirit guide will appear and escort you up through "the veil"—the barrier between our three-dimensional reality, and the higher, invisible dimensions.

Physicist Albert Einstein said that time and space are an illusion, and that parallel dimensions exist simultaneously. He said "The Veil of Illusion" forms invisible barriers between these dimensions.

During meditation, when you venture into these heavenly realms, it's like when you're in an airplane on an overcast day; the plane ascends through the layer of clouds, and you're suddenly in the bright sunshine of a blue sky that extends to the infinity of the heavens. You land in your power spot, state your intention, and experience what the Divine shows you.

If this sounds fantastical, think of it as a mental exercise for relaxation.

Also please consider that when your mind is whirling a million miles an hour with worries and fears, you are also using your imagination to dwell on worst-case scenarios. Why not enjoy a brief respite from that mental turmoil and indulge a peaceful visualization that could quiet your mind and calm your body? Meditation could even provide insights to solve problems, feel peace and self-love, and improve your health.

This Shamanic Journey method of meditation was bringing more inner peace than I had ever felt, and it was providing a nearly effortless solution to my lifelong struggles with food and fat. Those rewards were a huge motivation to continue this daily practice.

So, after months of celibacy, strict veganism, meditation, yoga, journaling, and a positive information diet, my connection to the Divine became constant and crystal-clear. I felt the strong presence of God, Jesus, my father, angels, ancestors, and other divine beings. As a result, in meditation, I experienced many revelations: some glorious, some gruesome. All provided answers about issues that had been vexing me since childhood.

While some are too personal to reveal, I'm sharing insights with the intention of accelerating and enhancing your spiritual awakening. One such lesson occurred when my father appeared in meditation. First, he showed me a vision of the sun and conveyed that God glows as powerfully as the sun within us. Then my father said, "This is you. God is in you."

And I could hear God saying, "This is you, Elizabeth. Radiate! Radiate love!"

After this, my father used the metaphor of God being the sun inside us to illustrate how God glows within every human being. It's our job to know this, activate it, and use it. This message correlates with the solar plexus chakra at the center of the torso; it's yellow and symbolizes power and action. Here's what happened in that meditation:

"Come," my father said, taking my hand.

"I'm taking you to God," he said as a floaty sensation fluttered through me and I ascended up the golden beam into a meditative state.

First, I saw a golden throne. Rather than witnessing a bearded man in a white robe, or any human form, I was overwhelmed with blissful peace and knowing that I was with God. And God is pure energy that appeared as an infinite, golden glow that flowed in vast streams and swirls, engulfing and permeating everything, everywhere.

Beside this indescribably huge, warm glow of love, was Jesus.

Then the pure white light and golden energy that is God emanating from the throne suddenly rolled toward me. This golden flow tapered to a point that entered the center of my abdomen, and the God energy poured into me, fusing with every cell in my body, setting me aglow from the inside out. Then this golden God energy exploded inside me, spraying gold sparkles brilliantly and beautifully in every direction. Like I was at the center of a bursting star.

This starburst inside us is God.

As this occurred, I absolutely knew that I am one with Source.

God was showing me that *I am* the God energy.

And you are God energy.

God is within us.

Meditations like this inspired lengthy journal entries as I processed the meaning and the message, and what to do with it.

Why was I receiving this seemingly personal counsel from the Divine? Why did I feel that God, Jesus, my father, angels, ancestors, and other spirit-beings were guiding my every step? The Divine is ubiquitous; every person everywhere can tap into this energy simultaneously. And just as it was transforming me in mind, body, and spirit, this power can do that for anyone. Therefore, I concluded that the Divine was using me as a teaching tool so that I could someday share my personal experiences to show you how to access and use this power within.

The biggest lesson at the moment was that our souls are individual starbursts of this God energy that is the pulse giving life to our human bodies. If you doubt what's keeping your heart beating, remember that a person suffering cardiac arrest is brought back to life with an electric jolt from a defibrillator.

The starburst of God energy inside you is your soul. Your soul is your true identity. Not your name, your appearance, your family's history, your education, or your job. And meditation enables you to actually see visuals of this spiritual energy within.

At the time, however, I did not talk about this with anyone. I felt that I had to first fully understand the message—and live it. So I remained an eager and obedient student of the Divine by following the regimen prescribed through the divine voice that spoke within me, providing clear instructions, all day, every day.

Cleansing The Mind, Body, & Spirit

After yoga and meditation, I showered, then moisturized my skin with organic coconut oil.

"Don't use commercial lotion," the inner voice said. "Use natural ingredients or none at all." This included abstaining from nail polish and only wearing make-up for business meetings and special events.

This internal guidance was especially clear and consistent about what I should eat, starting with breakfast in our sunny kitchen amidst the colorful peppers, tomatoes, pineapples, and more of Mother Nature's bounty from Eastern Market.

"Have one cup of edamame, a half-cup of black rice, and a banana," the voice within said, allowing a small portion of healthy fats, such as extra virgin olive oil, coconut oil, and walnuts. Later, for a snack, I was guided to have chia seeds and a green apple or flax seeds and pineapple.

Lunch and dinner were usually beans and grains that included quinoa. Also for dinner, I loved chopping vegetables to make colorful, flavorful salads. I created vinaigrette with lemon juice, herbs, garlic, and olive oil. I ate no meat, fish, poultry, dairy, or food from a box or a can. I consumed no soda pop, alcoholic beverages, chocolate, or processed foods. My gluten-free regimen continued.

Adhering to this menu was easy. So many times in the past, I had ignored my personal knowing about what food was good or bad for me. Then, as now, my inner voice was always providing guidance. Now I was experiencing the transformative power of listening—and obeying.

This created a sort of spiritual autopilot, and the results truly felt miraculous, especially in the context of my past angst with eating and weight gain. Being guided on what to eat alleviated anxieties about food and fat. Extra weight was melting off. A feeling of lightness replaced heaviness; inner peace removed angst.

Most days on this eating plan, I didn't feel that I was missing anything. Except once at a dinner party, when others were enjoying baked brie, I craved the gooey, stretchy cheese.

"Don't eat cheese," my spirit guides said. "Don't eat chocolate."

"Why?" I asked.

"False euphoria," they answered, meaning a sugar high followed by an energy crash. Remembering that bad feeling cured my craving. And recalling how awful I had felt just months ago bolstered my discipline to resist temptation. I wanted to step forward feeling better than ever in communion with God.

Detoxing My Mind

While purifying and shrinking my body with a plant-based diet, it was important to change what I was feeding my mind as well. Since I was celibate, I didn't need any reminders of what I wasn't getting. So in the car, I re-programmed the stereo stations for classical, gospel, NPR, and Radio Canada, to listen to French and study vocabulary. This meant no more hip hop, love songs, or music with provocative lyrics. Nor did I want to hear profanity, violence, anger, or sadness.

This also applied to news. I did not watch TV, and only scanned the online newspaper headlines to stay abreast of current events. When I needed to know something, the divine voice within said:

"Turn on the TV." On December 5, 2013, I followed this directive and clicked on the evening news as the anchor announced the passing of Nelson Mandela, one of the people in world history whom I most admire. It also told me to watch on April 15, 2013, to learn about the deadly Boston Marathon bombings and to pray for everyone involved. These divine alerts occurred regularly, and were reminders to trust my intuition.

All the while, I filled my ears with inspiration. When walking, running, doing dishes, or brushing my teeth, I played YouTube videos of sermons, Bible stories, gospel music, and videos about how angels are always with us, helping us when we ask. While exercising, I listened to fast-paced gospel. If I happened to switch to a radio station playing a sultry song, the voice within said, "Don't listen to this."

Into A Genius Writing Zone

Sitting on a leather stool at the granite-topped kitchen island, my fingers danced over the keyboard of my laptop computer, surrounded by baskets of fruits and vegetables. Sunshine poured into the high-ceilinged, loft-like space; classical music played.

And a symphony of words twirled in my mind, pouring out and streaming across my computer screen as *Husbands, Incorporated* evolved from a single novel into a trilogy. My creativity blazed as I composed this provocative story with a powerful message about women's empowerment in romantic relationships and marriage.

I was doing some of my most genius writing ever, thanks to the solitude and celibacy of this spiritual retreat. Now I finally understood the secret of Sex Transmutation, which Napoleon Hill advocates in *Think and Grow Rich*. When you channel your sex energy into creativity, it surges up into your brain and gives you tremendous energy, clarity, and brilliant ideas—rather than if you indulge it for physical pleasure, which is fun, but leaves nothing to show for it but a good memory (unless you're trying to conceive a baby). And that's the point here, too. Sex energy is the most powerful force in our bodies; it creates life.

So what if you could harness that energy and use it to create literature or paintings or entrepreneurial innovations? Rather than allowing it to leave the body in sexual release, what if you channeled it up to your mind and through your chakra system to connect with the infinite power of Source?

I shivered with epiphany! The sacral chakra just below the belly button rules both creativity and sensual pleasure. So channeling all of its energy blessed me with genius writing to make *Husbands, Inc.* even bigger and better than I had intended in January.

All the while, my entire focus was on taking care of Alexander, devoting time to my daily spiritual practices, and writing, which included freelance and ghostwriting projects for income. Without the distraction of dating or a social life, I created a husbands-for-hire empire where women disillusioned with conventional marriage can finance the perfect relationship. While weaving in my philosophies about love, marriage, and monogamy into the twisted tales of four couples, I brought Sea Castle to life by making it Husbands, Inc.'s world headquarters.

"Keep Yourself Pure!"

Because I did not have a 9 to 5 job with a steady paycheck every week, and by choice I was a writer with sporadic income, I was always crunching numbers to make sure I had enough money to cover tuition, rent, my car note, and other bills.

In the midst of this, a wealthy man offered financial support in exchange for a relationship. I had been celibate for seven months, and was enjoying tremendous spiritual evolution. This was a test! Like when Satan tempted Jesus to create bread from stones while fasting for 40 days in the desert. Clearly, my answer was no.

"Do not sell your body, Elizabeth," Archangel Ariel said during meditation.

"You are not a prostitute," my father added.

"Go write! This is God. You do not need to sell yourself."

"Sweet child," Jesus said. *"Keep yourself pure. You are doing this on your own volition. You are untouchable. Shielded. Protected. Enshrined. Finish your book now. Stay celibate. You are here to write and share your gifts with the world, and when the time is right, we will provide a loving, loyal relationship with someone of your caliber. Your twin. Go write!"*

In my journal, after profusely thanking them all, I wrote: *"Oh my goodness, after that meditation, I had the best writing in weeks!"*

Meanwhile, I viewed everything with extreme gratitude, and mini-miracles happened daily. I'd find hundreds of dollars hidden inside a book. I'd discover something valuable to return to a store for cash. I'd receive gifts out of the blue. And we always had enough.

Then I finally understood what Martha Jean "The Queen" Steinberg once told me: "God is the Source of my supply." Not a job. Not a person. Not a company. God. He always finds miraculous and mysterious ways to deliver what you need, when you need it.

At one point, when my funds were dwindling, a new ghostwriting client was introduced to me by a trusted source via a phone call.

A few days later, I met with this person for the first time. After we talked for about an hour, he wrote me a very large check based on the strictly business terms we had discussed. This was extremely unusual! Typically in a book deal, the check accompanied a signed contract detailing scope of service, timeline, compensation, etc. This contract approval period usually took weeks or even months, due to back-and-forth approvals with attorneys.

This time, God was my agent. No lawyers or paperwork were required.

"You Will Open A Bookstore"

During this time, when Lori Lipten offered a training for spiritual healers, I attended. During one exercise, I was paired with a woman whose task was to connect with my helping spirits, retrieve messages, and relay them to me.

This wonderful woman "saw" my grandmother holding me as a baby, rocking me in her arms, gazing down, and exuding tremendous love and adoration.

"She says you're going to open a bookstore," she said, "and that the writing is on the wall."

With my second meditation partner, her spirit guides shared a message with me to relay to her. It echoed The Council of Women Writers: women and people of color now have freedoms and rights that our ancestors never dreamed of having, and it's our obligation to use our talents in powerful, positive ways to help people.

Celebrating That Anything Is Possible

During the fall of 2013, *Anything Is Possible* premiered at a local theatre, and it was really fun to attend with Alexander, his dad, my mother, the cast and crew, and Pastor Miles and his family.

"Elizabeth, you did a good job," Demetrius and Pastor Miles said, "but Alexander was great!" A short time later, I attended a screening of our movie in Los Angeles, where Lara and other friends joined me with the cast and crew.

Healing With Meditation

The pain was so stunning, I couldn't get out of bed. The slightest movement triggered an excruciating sensation in my lower back. This was my first gym injury, due to adding extra weight to a strength training routine. Home alone, all I could do was lay there, attempting to find a position to swing my legs over the side of the bed and stand up.

But I couldn't move. So I called out loud to God's healing angel: "Archangel Raphael, please heal my back. Please take this pain away."

Amazingly, the pain subsided enough that I could grip the side of the bed and pull myself over with my arms. Finally, I sat up and stood. But every task—going to the bathroom, putting on clothes, tying my shoes, getting in and out of the car—was a painful struggle.

I took an anti-inflammatory, over-the-counter pain killer. It made my heart race. The pain persisted. As I contemplated going to the Emergency Room for an x-ray, I decided to try meditation first, on a rug on the floor, against a wall for support.

Because journaling is my constant companion before and after meditations, so I can record what happens, I used my laptop computer to type my intention for this healing meditation: "Archangel Raphael, please remove my back pain entirely. Thank you, Archangel Raphael, for making my back pain go away."

I placed the laptop on the floor. The acute pain did not allow me to cross my legs; they extended on the floor. Then I closed my eyes, breathed deeply, called in angels for protection as I ventured into the spirit realm, and envisioned myself ascending up a golden beam, through the veil, into the heavenly dimension.

Again, with the voice of my mind, I called out my intention: "Archangel Raphael, please remove my back pain entirely."

I saw him, a giant angel, standing over me as I laid suspended in the air while Native American medicine men danced around me. In beautiful tribal regalia, they were chanting, circling, and aiming their healing hands at me. At the same time, because the Divine communicates through symbolism and metaphors, Archangel Raphael pulled the pain from my lower back; it appeared as a red glob, like those inside a lava lamp.

He tossed it into lavender flames shooting up from a large, shallow, brass dish. The fire resembled the Olympic flame. Archangel

Raphael is a spiritual alchemist, who transmutes hurting into healing with the mystical, violet flame of St. Germain. As Archangel Raphael cast my pain into the fire, it transmuted the negative energy, which crackled upward in a sparkly geyser that arced back down to my body, fusing into me as vitality and health.

"It is done," Archangel Raphael announced. I thanked him, descended through the veil into the physical realm, and slid down the golden beam. I became aware of my body sitting on the living room floor.

"Thank you, God, for this miraculous healing," I wrote in my journal and said aloud all day long. Later, I wrote: "Oh my goodness! Archangel Raphael healed my back today! I got up from meditation with no pain in my back. I laughed out loud, giggling with delight and gratitude."

Moderate pain returned as I sat at my desk, but sitting up straight relieved it entirely. Then I finished the day by straightening up the house, journaling that: "I turned on the radio and was dancing and really happy." From paralyzing pain to dancing!

No medication. Just meditation. So how did I do this?

Lori Lipten taught this during her Intuitive Empowerment Weekend. She said anyone can harness divine healing power to change our bodies on a cellular level. And the process is exactly what I described above.

Except, I added the power of the pen. What evolved from this became my "PowerJournal for Healing" technique, which combines journaling, meditation, and calling upon Archangel Raphael. Only one letter differentiates "meditation" and "medication." For me, they are one and the same. You can do this! Learn how in the *Ascend* section of this book.

Meditation Heals Migraine Headaches

One spring day, a raging headache struck after I did not express my anger during a business meeting. While driving home, I was tempted to stop at the drugstore to purchase over-the-counter Excedrin Migraine, once an effective remedy, but it recently caused jitteriness. Now, as my head throbbed, I considered it.

"Go home," my spirit guides said. As I passed the street to turn to the drugstore, they urged, "Go straight. Go home."

There, the pain worsened. I frantically rummaged through medicine cabinets, my travel toiletry bag, my purse (I used to carry a small container of Excedrin Migraine), and even a bin of travel-sized toiletries in the linen closet. Nothing. I thought about going to the store.

"Stay home," the Divine ordered. "Meditate."

I went to the living room, sat with my legs crossed on the sofa, and typed: "Archangel Raphael, please take this pain away."

I closed my eyes and breathed deeply. The room was silent; my body was still except for deep inhales and exhales. Amazingly, the pain began to subside. Then I envisioned myself floating up the golden beam to meet Archangel Raphael in the heavenly dimension.

"Archangel Raphael, please take this pain away."

In an instant, the pain was gone!

During Thanksgiving week, after another business meeting where I did not express my disagreement, a headache throbbed behind my eyes, making me sick to my stomach. A friend was in town from New York, and I met him briefly at a restaurant. We had a spirited chat, but secretly, I was in agony.

As I drove home in a winter storm, pain hammered behind my eye. I had the urge to vomit. Stopped at a red light, amidst twinkling holiday lights, I prayed, "Archangel Raphael, please heal my headache."

I tried to envision myself floating up to him, but since I was driving downtown and it was snowing, I focused on getting home safely. Amazingly, I connected with the Divine. Almost instantly, the pain diminished.

"Please take it all away so that my head feels normal," I prayed out loud, driving on the dark, snow-blown street. At the same time, I saw a vision of Archangel Raphael pulling a red net from inside my head, saying: "It's your client. Go home. Have chamomile tea, meditate more on the couch, and go to bed."

I suddenly started yawning repeatedly. However, I needed to buy oatmeal and butter for my son's current breakfast of choice. As I walked through the grocery store, the light hurt my eyes. Perfume on shoppers was sickening as I stood in the check-out line.

I came home, set two bags in the kitchen, then hugged Alexander, who was doing homework in his room. After that, I sat on the couch and meditated. Here's what I journaled:

Thank you, Archangel Raphael, for healing my horrible headache that was making me nauseous and was a helmet of pain!

I asked Archangel Raphael to show me what caused it. He said that failure to express myself is toxic. I kept hearing the word "liver." Then he showed me bright blue splinters in my liver—they were like tiny blue light sabers lodged in all directions in the maroon expanse of my liver.

"You have to express yourself," he said. "Or the words, the communications you fail to speak, the thoughts and feelings you keep bottled up inside, become splinters lodged in your liver and they're toxic."

Then, twice, he yanked them out—as if his hands were magnetized and the splinters were nails to a magnet.

I asked him why I had been so fatigued, and he said, "The change of seasons." A few weeks ago, our switch to Daylight Savings Time meant it was getting dark by 5:00 pm, and the colder temperatures meant less time walking and running outdoors, which I did most days during warmer weather.

He also said: don't eat vinegar or coconut oil. Eat a wider variety of organic beans. Organic edamame would be better. Organic everything would be better.

He added that in the morning, rather than my usual half cup of black rice with breakfast, I should have "a hearty bowl of black rice, like a double portion of what you normally eat." Then he said, "Now you may drink your tea and go to bed, Elizabeth."

I woke up the next morning refreshed, pain free, and determined to speak my mind when necessary.

Why was I so afraid to express what I really felt? First, my past life experiences showed deadly consequences for speaking up and doing what I was divinely guided to do. And in this life, I've craved approval. For good grades, for being nice, for not engaging conflict, for doing a good job, for being sweet and agreeable. This Good Girl Syndrome is a disservice that society imposes on girls and women. It brainwashes too many of us so that we don't speak up, we don't argue, we don't disagree, we don't say something that might offend someone. As a result, we tip-toe through life playing nice—and playing small.

"Be louder. Roar!" my spirit guides instructed during many meditations guided by giant lions symbolizing courage. I prayed for the courage and confidence to let Elizabeth roar.

Prayer Stops Pain In Its Tracks

I was shopping when suddenly I felt dizzy. Then my vision was weird. My heart pounded with fear. Because I couldn't focus on the holiday shoppers or the store through a shimmery portal that led to a very bad, painful place.

This portal looked like a silvery pool of light splashing before my eyes, as its frothy edges rippled and bubbled. This seductive, psychedelic vision had come to me many times before. And now, as it showed up more vividly than ever, I was terrified. Lightheaded and afraid I would faint in the busy store, I called Catherine out west.

"I'm having the shimmery aura that signals a migraine is coming," I said, anxiously pushing my shopping basket into a check-out line. "The really bad kind that lasts for days."

"Oh no," she said. "What can you do?"

Tears welled in my eyes as I remembered how I used to give myself a shot of prescription painkiller two decades before when I was frequently incapacitated and forced to bed by migraines that started this way. Now they only struck once or twice a year.

"I refuse to get a migraine!" I declared. "I'm going to my car to PRAY really hard." She stayed on the phone with me for awhile, and I had that weird, light-headed feeling from not eating enough that morning.

"Get something to eat!" she exclaimed.

"I will," I said. "I'm buying bananas."

A short time later, as I loaded gifts and groceries into my car, a helmet of migraine pain was starting to grip my head and throb behind my eye. And the "aura" as doctors call it, was even brighter, like someone had splashed a pool of mercury over my line of vision. The head pain also caused nausea.

I wrote a text to a friend—asking him to pray for me to feel better. But I was so distressed, I did not send the text. Instead, I got in the car, locked the door, and prayed aloud: "Archangel Raphael, please take away this aura and pain."

I prayed with deep knowing that God's healing angel would help me. The day before, he had helped my son quickly recover from the stomach virus that was rampant at his school. And earlier that week, when my dear friend's daughter was in the ER with flu, I asked our Facebook friends and others to pray for her recovery. Heaven heard the outpouring of prayers—from India and Belgium and all across America—and infused healing energy into this girl who sings like an angel. She soon recovered fully.

So on this day, I envisioned Archangel Raphael wrapping me in his giant white wings and filling me with his emerald green light. Then he gave instructions: "Eat a banana."

I ate a banana. The visual shimmer and pain did not slowly subside.

They stopped.

"Thank you!" I exclaimed up to the overcast December sky. "Thank you!"

I called Catherine to report this miracle. Then, as I drove home, God supplemented this divine healing with a big dose of laughter as the best medicine. The friend whom I had started to text—a text which I never sent!—*called*. I never mentioned the headache. Instead, I laughed and smiled all the way home as our upbeat conversation lifted my spirits.

After a healthy lunch, I felt great, as if the migraine threat had *never even happened.* Then I went to the gym for high-energy weight lifting. The icing on this delicious cake was that my son was also feeling much better.

Healing With Mother Mary

One afternoon, I was cutting onions to make tomato-vegetable-edamame soup. The knife sliced through my right thumb nail, into the flesh.

I need stitches! I applied pressure to the stinging pain, then went upstairs to my bathroom to trim the fingernail and wash it.

"Archangel Raphael, please help me!"

I immediately heard, "Don't cut the fingernail."

After wrapping toilet paper around my finger, and squeezing it to stop the bleeding, I closed my eyes and prayed, "Archangel Raphael, please help me!" He showed me a vision of white light going into the thumb. The pain was gone!

"Lie down on your yoga mat," he said. So I did, closed my eyes, and saw blue light. And I felt the presence of Mother Mary.

"You have nothing to fear, child," she said. "You are immensely blessed." She was holding my hand and the pain was gone. "Go put a Bandaid on it."

Upstairs, I found the Bandaids and removed the toilet paper wrapping. The cut was not bleeding. I was about to go downstairs to do yoga.

"Don't go," Mother Mary said. "Lie down."

I laid on the bed for awhile. Then she said, "Go make your food and do yoga later. Much work remains to be done, Elizabeth."

My thumb felt fine and I got back to work, overjoyed and grateful for this healing with Mother Mary.

Healing My Family

One day the school secretary called to say Alexander did not feel well. I immediately picked him up. He was pale and lethargic. In the car, I gave him an over-the-counter painkiller with water. Then I remembered that I didn't need to use medicine, because I can call on Archangel Raphael.

So, as my son laid back in the passenger seat, I stopped at the first stop sign and prayed for Archangel Raphael to relieve his pain. I went through the whole process in a flash, envisioning Archangel Raphael and the Native American healers surrounding my son and making him feel better.

Ten minutes later, as soon as we walked in our house, Alexander vomited up the pill. Then he laid down in his room and fell asleep. I continued to pray for his healing as I sat on the living room sofa, writing on my laptop.

Amazingly, within one hour, I heard robust laughter. I dashed upstairs. He was laughing while watching Jon Stewart on *The Daily*

Show. His eyes were sparkling. His cheeks were pink. I hugged him, then left the room with tears of gratitude to the Divine for making my son feel better. Fast. Free.

Another time, a relative was having severe back pain. I delivered dinner to her, and she could hardly get out of bed. She refused the strong medications offered by her doctor. So I went home, and performed a healing meditation on her with Archangel Raphael. The next morning, I called to check on her. She answered—while riding her exercise bike! The pain was gone!

Healing On A Soul Level

If you took a vow of poverty as a nun or monk in a past life, perhaps you struggle with money now. Or, if your ancestors experienced famine, maybe you overeat today. Our souls can absorb these dynamics from past life experiences, and from our ancestors, bringing them into our current realities to perpetuate the problems.

You can heal and release these patterns by asking Archangel Raphael to perform a healing on your soul. So I asked Archangel Raphael to heal me on an ancestral level of lack, poverty, and powerlessness. As always in meditation, the Divine speaks through metaphors and symbolism to help us visualize and understand the messages.

As this meditation began, a Pegasus showed up as my spirit guide. I felt light as we ascended into the golden glow of the heavenly realm. There, the medicine men around me strained to pull a giant, heavy, red blood clot from my soul, which appeared as a butter-yellow glow.

From their hand chakras, they shot white beams of light, like lasers, to extract the clot. The men danced harder, chanted louder, and finally removed this symbol of lack. They handed it to Archangel Raphael, who put it in the flame. It transmuted into golden sparks that curved down into my body as abundance.

Then came poverty, symbolized by a twisting layer of black net through my being. Again the medicine men worked hard and long, using beams of white light to extract it.

This time as with the prior lack, I asked for the healing back seven generations from Emille. If my math is correct, the seven generations started in 1300-1400 in France. I also saw Emille's daughter, who was courageous, but was also punished.

My relatives had taken a religious vow of poverty, as I had, during past lives as a nun. The medicine men yanked out the black net of poverty and handed it to Archangel Raphael. It transmuted in the lavender flame into golden stardust that came back into me in a great, golden arch symbolizing prosperity.

Lastly, the medicine men removed powerlessness from my body. I felt this great heaviness, because the powerlessness manifest like bowling balls throughout me, literally holding down my soul. It was difficult for the men to remove them, so they danced harder, chanted louder, and intensified the white light beams from their hand chakras.

Finally these heavy black weights of powerlessness were extracted and given to Archangel Raphael, who put them on the fire. The golden sparks whooshed up and back into me so forcefully that I became instantaneously buoyant and joyous as my spirit soared.

"This is complete," Archangel Raphael said.

Healing On A Global Scale

Sometime in 2013, several brutal and sometimes deadly rapes in India were making headlines. One included a five-year-old girl who was hospitalized.

I did a meditative healing with Archangel Raphael for her. Shortly after, I practiced my daily habit of going online to skim the newspapers. The first story I saw said the girl was healing and making progress.

"Thank you God!" The clock on my computer screen said 4:44 p.m.

It's possible to do meditative healings for groups of people in distant places, for Mother Earth, and for world peace. It's simply a matter of focusing your intention on healing and knowing it will work.

Sharing Banana Bread Bliss

The delicious scent of banana bread filled my car as I pulled up to the school just before the Christmas holiday vacation. Then my mother and I carried big boxes of silver foil-wrapped loaves inside.

"It's banana bread day!" exclaimed Alexander's teachers, school leaders, and coaches.

"I'm going to hide it from my husband because last year he ate it all himself," one teacher whispered playfully.

"I'm taking it to share with my family out East for the holidays," an administrator said.

"I like to toast it, smear it with butter, and have it with coffee," a coach told me.

Watching their faces light up as we walked into offices and class-rooms offering this lovin' from the oven was delightful. This tradition began when Alexander was in second grade and continued until he graduated from high school. By then, we were delivering nearly 50 loaves around the school!

My mother was the magic behind this tradition, which she began 20 years ago. She still bakes dozens of loaves of her secret recipe, and delivers them to friends and family—still warm—on Thanksgiving morning, Christmas morning, and random times throughout the year. On a whim, she will have a baking spree, then show up at the grocery store, the car wash, or the soup kitchen, and distribute boxes of these loaves that are so good, people call them "cake."

Delivering her banana bread to the Liggett school community provided a sweet treat to thank the men and women who were bless-ing Alexander with an excellent educational experience.

Lifestyle Strengthens Spiritual Connection

I sat on the sofa in meditation position and felt a powerful spirit with me.

Whoosh! I beamed up through the veil at the speed of light, into the golden infinity of heaven. There, I became a giant swirl of gold sparkles amidst all the more that was God.

This instantaneous entrée into the heavenly realm—and the crystal-clear ability to see myself in spirit form as part of pure God energy—was astonishing.

"You are pure, Elizabeth," Jesus said when I meditated on December 19, 2013, my parents' 47th wedding anniversary. "The reason you are able to communicate with us so clearly is that we have spent this entire year purifying your mind, body, and spirit so that you may continue to evolve into the Princess of Peace... to shine for the world through your physical being, your written words, your spoken words, your teaching, your films, and other multimedia productions."

Oh how I wished I had known this indescribable peace, comfort, and love over the many years when I was struggling with fear, fat, food, and conflict.

The next message that I heard from the Divine conveyed that while our souls can carry past life traumas into the now, they can also bring a wealth of blessings from our ancestors:

"You are inheriting the treasure chest of blessings that contains all the unanswered prayers, hopes, and wishes of your ancestors. Their dreams are coming to fruition through you, and they are cheering you on. They know that you will represent like a sparkling diamond. You will celebrate and honor their faithful service with everything you do."

During another meditation that felt like a family reunion and made the air in my home pulse with love and celebration, my ancestors shared a similar message, and they continually said "represent" to contribute positivity in ways that they never could have imagined during their lifetimes.

Christmas Revelations

During His birthday season, Jesus was a constant presence in my mind, heart, and meditations. At one point, I began seeing vivid images of the crucifixion, as if viewing it through the eyes of someone who was there. This roused profound grief and a newfound understanding of Jesus' suffering for the salvation of humanity. As I spent hours online reading and learning about Him, I became fascinated by Mary Magdalene. She was with Him during the crucifixion when the male disciples hid, and she was the first person to see Him upon His resurrection.

Like many people who were taught the story in the Bible that was written by men and fails to describe the many women who financially supported Jesus, I believed that Mary Magdalene was a prostitute.

She was not. Some say she was his wife, and some believe she is pictured beside him in Leonardo Da Vinci's painting of *The Last Supper*. Historians say she was a wealthy woman from Magdala, a fishing town on the Sea of Galilee. She was a trusted disciple, and Jesus sought her counsel on many topics, much to the jealousy of Saint Peter.

After Jesus went to heaven, she fled on a boat across the Mediterranean, landing in the south of France, where she retreated for 30 years in a cave in a mountain called La Sainte Baume. People pilgrimage to the cave every summer to celebrate the Feast Day of Mary Magdalene on July 22. Many believers consider this trip third in line after Jerusalem and Rome.

As my crash course on spirituality continued, I learned that the entire body of Christianity is considered The Bride of Christ. And that the church is viewed as the bride, and Jesus is the bridegroom. This metaphor appears in Revelation, which says that the pure souls at the end of the world are symbolized as the bride of Jesus.

Deciphering Bible language is like trying to understand William Shakespeare's writing as a college English major; I was an A student then, and really wanted to comprehend this now. Here's what Revelation 19:7 says:

"Let us be glad and rejoice and give Him glory, for the marriage of the Lamb has come, and His wife has made herself ready." Translation: Jesus is the Lamb and His wife symbolizes all the people He will take to heaven, because they are pure-hearted, as indicated by Revelation 19:7's metaphoric description of her/their clothing: "And to her it was granted to be arrayed in fine linen, clean and bright, for the fine linen is the righteous acts of the saints."

This means that all believers who live in love and peace are the Bride of Christ. What does that mean? I concluded that being in union with the Divine during this lifetime promises connectivity to this infinite power in the physical world, as well as the reward of our souls ascending to the heavenly realm after physical death.

If the word Christ doesn't resonate with you, as it once did not for me, think of it this way: spiritual seekers who live in love and peace are one with the Divine. As such, we embody the love, peace, and power of God/Source/Creator/Universe.

When we do this as a collective of the human race, we can raise the consciousness of the entire planet for all people to live in peace, love, and positive influence, while restoring Mother Earth to her majestic glory for future generations.

These revelations inspired a conclusion that my mission is:

- To serve as an example and a messenger of peace and love;
- To teach how to access and activate the divine power within yourself; and
- To share this message with as many people as possible.

This message is "spiritual, not religious." My experiences with the Divine conveyed a feeling of embracing, celebrating, and loving all people, regardless of religion, race, ethnicity, geographic origin, or other factors that humans use to divide.

God Is H2O

I was also aware that millions of people believe religious leaders who renounce any love-based spiritual practice or belief that does not adhere to their rigid religious doctrine. So I asked Dr. Rama: "How can one religion assert that it's the only pathway to God, and that only believers in its doctrine will go to heaven?"

"God is universal," Dr. Rama answered. "Every religion and spiritual practice is a highway leading to the same destination."

Then he offered another metaphor: "God is H2O. Every language has a different word for water, and every human being needs to drink it. They may not know that it's called H2O, which is the universal language of chemists in reference to water. So you can say 'water' in 100 different languages, but's all H2O."

And you can describe God in 100 different religions and languages, but it's all God.

Celebrating Family & Spiritual Fellowship

Elation electrified my mind, body, and spirit as I sat amidst 40 people, all facing Dr. Rama and an altar adorned with marigolds, candles, and spiritual images. Shaking a tambourine and singing along, I shivered with gratitude, loving the joy and praise emanating from everyone around me.

A vegetarian feast followed, and I savored spicy cauliflower, Mrs. Dwivedi's amazing cilantro chutney, and other Indian cuisine. During this weekend visit to their home with my mother, I expressed profuse gratitude to Dr. Rama for first teaching me how to meditate. I shared updates about what I was learning and experiencing, and he said the secret to my success was putting into practice what he had taught.

Also throughout this period, we enjoyed many fun, happy gatherings with my father's side of the family. These included my mother serving as officiant for two cousins' weddings, and we attended graduations and other celebrations.

Daily Q & A With The Divine

Back at home, meditation often evolved into Question & Answer sessions with the Divine. Here are some Answers:

We should all sit on a symbolic throne. My spirit guides conveyed that we should all sit on a symbolic throne, which means living from a place of love, peace, and spiritual power. Staying on the throne means being centered with God guiding our steps.

Love, Romance, and Solitude. Once, during the summer, I walked to the vibrant shopping district near my home. People were enjoying ice cream, laughing, talking, and enjoying a Friday evening out.

I felt like an alien, observing the scene as if floating above it. I just wanted to buy pineapples and hurry back to my computer and write until bedtime. I didn't feel I was missing out on anything.

But one day during the Christmas season, while driving past extravagant light displays on homes, I felt alone and detached from the world.

"Treat yourself like you're newly in love with someone—you!" said the divine voice within. "Your relationships have become more harmonious. You endured hell with your ex-husband, during the earlier years of your divorce. Now you can help him." Help him? What did that mean? And would I ever meet someone new and enjoy a romantic relationship?

"You will find love again, and it will be glorious, but not now," Jesus said. "You will get double for your trouble."

Discerning Contradictory Guidance. One day during yoga, I heard, "Go to the garage and get the Christmas tree and put it up." Later, during meditation, the message was, "Don't put up the tree yet."

So I asked my spirit guides, "Is this the conscious monkey-mind that jumps from thought to thought causing confusion? How can you trust what you believe is divine guidance if you hear conflicting information?"

"Sometimes free will interferes and changes the outcome," they said.

"Isn't everything preordained?" I asked.

"Yes, but free will can sometimes change the outcome," added my spirit guides. They said that you may receive intuitive guidance, but your human mind may override it, and that fear can "talk" to you in a way that mimics your spirit guides. For example, I heard that I would have a "tumultuous week."

"No," said the voice within, "that is your fear talking." (The week was not tumultuous).

So I prayed, "Jesus, please give me a discerning ear and power to know what is fear talking and what is the Divine talking."

"You have done a superb job at that discernment already, Elizabeth," He said. "You always have the power."

Dr. Rama and I also discussed contradictory guidance.

"Ask your heart," he said, "and you will know the answer." I tried that: with the voice in my mind, I directed a question at my heart, and an answer immediately popped into my head as the truest, purest answer.

Dr. Rama also recommended using "discriminating intellect"— which means follow your intuition while considering all factors that influence a situation.

Back to free will. Jesus gave another example: my friend who died.

"His free will changed the outcome," Jesus said. "It was ordained for him to recover, but he changed his mind. He gave up and he died."

"Because he didn't believe?"

"Yes."

My extremely intelligent, accomplished friend and I had engaged in a lively debate about the Divine. He did not believe in God. In fact, he was among several of my friends who were atheist. Some blamed their disbelief on religious hypocrisy that they had witnessed. Others simply felt no connection to something that you can't see, feel, touch, taste, or smell in the physical world.

My friend insisted that angels had neither the time nor the desire to "micro-manage" his privileged life—even when he was gravely ill—while people were suffering in other parts of the world. At first he was confident about a successful recovery, and I was shown in meditation a laser beam of pure white light healing his body.

"Believing in the Divine," Jesus said, "would have meant believing in his survival."

A few weeks later in my kitchen, I felt my friend's presence. I went into meditation and engaged him in conversation. His voice was as clear as if we were talking on the phone, and his personality was exactly as when he was living in a human body.

"You are so beautiful," he said. "I can't believe you're alone."

"You know I don't want to be with anyone," I answered. "I'm totally focused."

"It seems like you're going to waste in the romance and love department," he said. "You deserve love."

"Okay, when the time is right."

"Take it from me," he said, "don't wait too long."

"I don't want the distraction," I said.

"You'll be a lot happier," he said. This banter continued until I referenced his romantic innuendo the last time I saw him alive.

"A brotha's gotta try," he said playfully. The lively conversations and fun we had together as friends, he said, replayed in his mind while he was in hospice.

"You could think when you were in a coma?" I asked.

"It was a dream-like state," he said. Then he referenced the "life review" that many people describe after Near Death Experiences— they see a filmstrip of their lives as they hover in the space between life and death.

"During the review," my friend said, "you get these video streams of life experiences, good and bad, very vivid. It's amazing how it's all recorded, but you have to be in a coma to really see it clearly."

"Were you in pain?" I asked.

He said no, but "things got fuzzy" toward the end.

"Did you meet my father?" I asked.

"Your dad is cool," he said. "Yes, I knew him before I knew you (in this lifetime). You and I were married." (This was not surprising, even though our friendship was strictly platonic).

Then I asked him about dying: "So did you give up?"

"Yes, I did."

"I was really surprised," I said, "because you were so upbeat."

"That was my life journey. That was my assignment to go when I went."

"Why did you give up?"

"I got tired. Physically tired of fighting."

I reminded him of his athletic prowess. "The guy who could do all that got tired?"

He chuckled. "Yes, as ironic as it sounds."

"What do you see up there?" I asked.

"Mist."

"Did you change your mind about God?"

"Yes, Elizabeth, God is everything. Indescribably beautiful."

"Why do you think you were an atheist in this life?" I asked. "If we come from God, then why choose not to believe when we're going to be reminded that He IS the Almighty when we return to spirit form?"

"Sympathy," he said. "To show other humans why they need to believe."

"If what you know now about God—you had believed while here—would it have affected your outcome?"

"No. My story was my story," he said. "Go to bed, Elizabeth. I will always love you and I will see you a long time from now when you come here. You are in for so many treats. Enjoy it all. You deserve it, my dear."

I answered, "I love you... thank you for making me smile and learn and experience new ideas and feelings."

Releasing Fears & Furniture

During another conversation with Jesus, He told me to review my progress.

"Think about all the fears you have released this year," Jesus said. "You allowed Alexander to attend two sleepover camps and you were not fearful. You trusted the Divine. You trusted what we showed you in meditation: your father, his other grandfather, and Archangel Michael at the door of the dorm. You trusted that and you were able to allow him to go without fear, and to Washington, D.C. as well. That is tremendous."

He added, "This is another huge step in releasing that fear, Elizabeth. It is an important part of your evolution and ascent."

I asked about a disturbing meditation a few days before, when I saw fire burning around me.

"That was to show you, we are burning away the fear," Jesus said.

"Why fire?" I asked.

"Because fire is a very powerful symbol, and it's permanent," Jesus said. "Nothing bad is going to happen, Elizabeth. You are safe." He said leaving fears in the past opens space for happiness. "Allow that celebratory joy inside you right now to come out. Allow yourself to savor this feeling that is welling within you, this feeling of profound relief from fear."

I felt chills.

"Allow yourself to float in this joy and relief and happiness, Elizabeth," Jesus said. "You are a divine being. Only by going through this can you teach others to toughen up in the face of whatever their inner demons of fear are. You are a great teacher, Elizabeth. We have been preparing you all year with daily lessons, daily miracles, and daily blessings. You are going to testify and teach."

Along with fear, I was instructed to get rid of my plants, clothing, and furniture, which included the dresser from when I was a teenager (still in perfect condition) as well as the pretty bedroom set that I'd had since my apartment.

"Get all new furniture," my father added. "The furniture you have holds old energy that's not good for your future. Start fresh, clear of any past people or memories."

That made sense. But I was baffled about giving away my beautiful plants whose leaves seemed to dance, like those at Dr. Rama's house.

"Can you please tell me why I should get rid of my plants?" I asked in meditation.

"They're holding all the energy of your past years," my spirit guides said, explaining that the leaves absorbed and held molecules of air expelled from me while depressed, anxious, troubled over my ex-husband, and struggling. This was confusing, because that energy also included the love and laughter that I had shared with Alexander for the past eight years.

They conveyed that, just as a tree releases its leaves so that new ones can grow, shedding is part of a normal life cycle of growth for both me and my son, who had, indeed, outgrown his furniture, his little-boy bedroom décor, and his clothing.

"You will have nothing that was in your apartment," my spirit guides said. "None of the furniture, bedding, or dishes. You will have all new, because you are all new."

More Messages Through Meditation

One day during meditation, Jesus said, "Teach the world that I always keep my promises."

So I asked, "Jesus, what are your promises?" He answered that the keys to living a fulfilled, peaceful, and successful life are: "Love of God. Love of self. Compassion for fellow man. He that does unto others as he does unto himself also does unto God."

My next question: "Jesus, what is the message for this book?" He said for people to know that:

"We each are the light of the world. The way to fight hatred is not to use violence. It is to shine our own lights so brightly that the darkness disappears. You don't fight darkness. You simply turn on the light and the darkness disappears."

My father then instructed: "When you talk about this book, describe how you discovered your true self with this message to share: We can't fulfill our life missions until we commune with spirit and learn our divine assignments and know that God is making it all unfold, as long as we're obedient to His instructions and guidance."

And how do we know God's guidance? Through prayer—as well as listening to, and obeying, the divine voice within—which you can amplify with the techniques in the last section of this book.

"Remember," Jesus said, "Banish all fear, worry, and doubt. God is the Almighty and God is within you." He said many people are not ready or willing to take this spiritual journey, but many are ready.

Loving A New Lightness Of Being

I laid on the sofa to meditate and instantaneously entered into another dimension where my spirit guides said, "We are going to start incorporating meat back into your diet."

I did not want to eat meat. Would it cause weight gain? My plant-based regimen had melted off fat. They assured me that I would be fine, adding, "Keep writing. Keep following your regimen."

That evening, I stepped on the scale and gasped. "Oh my goodness! I lost 40 pounds!"

A Beautiful Christmas

On Christmas morning, I was overwhelmed with gratitude for Alexander, my mother and sister and extended family, and for this amazing year of spiritual growth.

"Merry Christmas, Mom," Alexander said, calling from his annual Christmas Eve sleepover at his father's house. "I'm going to go play some new games that Dad got me." We said "I love you" a million times and at 8:44, the call ended. I was overwhelmed with thankfulness that Alexander and his father enjoyed a lot of time together and had a great relationship.

After having black coffee, blackberries, and chia seeds, I was about to do yoga when Jesus said, "Turn on *Oprah*, Elizabeth." So I switched on the TV. She was featuring *Super Soul Sunday* guests speaking about spirituality. It was magnificent, and included Marianne Williamson talking about the twentieth anniversary of her book, *Return to Love*.

Then I did yoga while listening to a radio special with glorious church music, a sermon about Jesus and Mary, and *The Lord's Prayer*. I stayed in child pose for a long time, savoring pure peace and joy. As I meditated on the yoga mat, Jesus gave me an assignment for later at an annual gathering at Alexander's father's house, amidst a dozen relatives:

"Say a prayer at Christmas brunch today, about everyone going within and shutting out the noise of the world and knowing that the kingdom of God is within, and focus on the positive, not the negative. Tell everyone to stay in constant contact with God and Jesus, and they will guide you for everything."

This long meditation covered many topics. At one point, Ernest Hemingway appeared and said, "You need to write about race more!"

Another part of the meditation addressed anxiety about maximizing productivity and prosperity. I wanted to ask Jesus about time and money, but He said, "No." Like, *don't even ask*. Then He said, "Know. Your job is simply to KNOW right now."

My inquiry about whether I should buy a lucky Christmas lottery ticket drew a similar response. Apparently, winning millions of dollars was not Elizabeth's path to enlightenment.

"Do not play the lottery," my spirit guides said. "If we wanted you to win, you would have won by now. Your assignment is to know you're infinitely rich. Your obedience will be richly rewarded."

After meditation, Dr. Rama called, and I shared the mystical occurrences of my meditations.

"You are showing others that you can be happy with peace of mind and really enjoy the bliss," he said. "The moment that I heard you are doing the meditation and yoga, you don't know how happy I am. You have great human power, Elizabeth. You have profound love inside you. I'm very happy that you can experience that love."

I told him that I wanted to someday teach what I was learning in a way that others would understand and utilize for themselves.

"You are a very highly elevated soul," he said. "This connection does not happen very easily. Tell people who don't understand, and they will laugh. They will say, 'What?'"

He encouraged me to share these messages.

"Peace, bliss, and joy," he said. "This is what Elizabeth has. They don't have it, because it's not available in the market. You can't go and buy it in the market, even by giving a million or a trillion dollars. You get it when you are connected. I am proud of you."

A short time later, I went to the brunch (which I didn't eat), said the prayer, and felt grateful that for now, the contentious divorce and subsequent conflict were released to the past and I enjoyed nice visits with his family while Alexander played video games with his cousins.

After brunch, Alexander and I visited my mother to share hugs and gifts. She loved the outfit we gave her. We also expressed holiday greetings with Catherine by phone. My Christmas dinner was lentils, a spinach/cilantro salad, and fresh pineapple. I had no desire to eat traditional holiday food. That evening, before my son came home, I meditated again.

"You must teach," Jesus said. "You are ready to teach."

A Divine Healing For Obsessive Compulsive Disorder

As the meditation continued, Jesus commended that I was being "very obedient, despite the fear." The fear was Obsessive Compulsive Disorder. Also known as OCD, it causes overwhelming thoughts that trigger repetitive actions.

While the term often brings to mind people who wash their hands excessively—and I *am* vigilant about hygiene—OCD manifest differently for me. Our home had a gas stove, so I would always check it and say out loud, "The stove is off," before going to bed or leaving home. Prior to departing, even when wearing a bulky coat and winter boots and carrying a big purse, I would also dash upstairs—sometimes several times—to make sure the bathroom sinks were off. Each time, I had to stop and acknowledge the silence and say, "The sinks are off," before I could leave with confidence.

Then as soon as I left, worries whirled: *Did I set the alarm? Did I close and lock the door? Did I leave a sink running? Did I leave the iron on? Did I leave a window open? Is the stove on?*

This overwhelming fear hijacked my ability to trust or remember that yes, I had done all of these things that we normally do on auto-pilot. Rather than know that I had taken care of everything, my mind spun with images of the house flooding or burning or being robbed or filling with toxic, explosive natural gas.

As a result, many days, I drove away, only to turn around after five, ten, or even more minutes, to return and confirm that everything was off and locked. So, on Christmas, as I left for the brunch, I had the strong urge to go home and make sure I had turned off the sinks. My spirit guides spoke through my inner voice, telling me to keep driving, and that *of course* I had turned everything off. During the brunch, I noticed a water stain on the ceiling from a leak in the bathroom upstairs, which reminded me of this worry, but I trusted my inner voice and pushed it out of my mind.

My interpretation of OCD boils down to not trusting yourself. Not trusting that you were smart enough to turn off the sink or the stove. Not trusting that you had the good sense to close and lock the windows and doors. Not trusting that you can remember that of course you turned everything off and locked up before leaving.

If you can't trust yourself, you can't trust anyone else. And you certainly can't trust an invisible entity such as God that you can't see, hear, touch, taste, or smell in the physical realm. This fear, this distrust of self, is the opposite of Hebrews 11:1: "Now faith is the substance of things hoped for, the evidence of things not seen."

Fear is the opposite of faith. Fear renders you powerless. Powerlessness makes you as an easy target. A target for Satan to push you off God-centeredness, off your divine purpose, and into dark places where you are doing the devil's work. If you're not doing God's work, you're doing the devil's work.

"If you're not part of the solution, you're part of the problem," said writer and activist Eldridge Cleaver, quoting an African proverb.

Likewise, both President John F. Kennedy and Dr. Martin Luther King, Jr. made famous the quote: "The only thing necessary for the triumph of evil is that good men should do nothing."

How does this relate to OCD? I didn't allow fear to prevail; I courageously proceeded. If I had allowed fear to paralyze my mind, I couldn't write or execute my divine assignment.

"I am very proud of you today," Jesus said in my evening meditation. "You have been very obedient despite the fear."

It was baffling how I had plunged that morning from profound peace into panic. So I asked Jesus, "What is the fear?"

"It's dark energy," he said, "essentially Satan. And the ego is dark energy. You are a leader and a teacher, so the enemy wants to stop you. Those dark forces are Satan. You must always call in the light and set boundaries and refuse to indulge it, and when it comes, you continue to pray incessantly."

Dark energy. Satan.

I've seen it and felt it in meditation. It's like an evil riptide that creates a suction sensation, like a vacuum of bad energy pulling into a thick, endless, black hole in space. Sometimes this spiritual attack has been so sudden and strong, I have called out loud for Archangel Michael and an army of angels to pull me back, freeing me from its grip.

This evil energy has tried to intercept me during ascents to the Akashic Records, as well as during meditations that are peaceful and beautiful—until suddenly, dark energy ambushes, and I call on all the power of heaven to block it.

Dark energy. Satan.

"You are blessed with a vivid imagination," Jesus said. "That is part of your gift. We are teaching you to use it for the light, not the dark."

Then He reiterated the importance of always asking for divine protection in the spirit realm: "With every meditation, you should set parameters, boundaries. Declare that you are only letting in the light. The higher you rise, the stronger it will try to enter and poison your mind and create fear fantasies. You have to create an atmosphere when you cross into the Divine that feels safe." He added that if you engage fear, it opens a doorway for more fear to enter. Then I realized that if you never open that door, it becomes part of the wall and you lock fear on the other side. You are safe.

When Jesus said the ego is the dark energy of Satan, I finally understood. Until then, the word "ego" in a spiritual context was confusing. In high school psychology class, the "ego" was something that Sigmund Freud defined as the healthy part of our self-image that helps us function confidently in the world.

However, metaphysical teachers define the spiritual ego as: the thinking mind that identifies strictly with the physical world and therefore separates us from God.

Our goal as spiritual beings is to unify with God.

To *know* that God is within us.

To "be still and know that I am God."

To know that each of us is the "I am," and therefore, each of us is "God."

God is pure love and light.

Satan is pure evil and darkness.

God speaks through our spirit.

Satan speaks through our ego in a language of fear, lack, and self-loathing.

God's Answer Is Know.

Satan's answer is No.

The crucial component here is to "be still" in prayer and meditation, so that you can hear your spirit speak God's guidance and wisdom. Hence, Psalm 46:10 says, "Be still and know that I am God."

Dark energy, Satan, works through the ego to inflict spiritual warfare, especially on those called to do God's work, and especially in the form of fear. I concluded that OCD was spiritual warfare. So during this meditation, I called on Archangel Raphael to heal me of Obsessive Compulsive Disorder.

"It is done," Archangel Raphael declared, before he even got started. He took me to a space where I was laying on my back, suspended in the air. The Native American medicine men were around me and Archangel Raphael was standing there, bigger than ever.

A huge pack of wolves—with their beautiful faces and blue eyes— were running toward us and formed an oval around the medicine men. In shamanic tradition, wolf energy has healing power.

"Remove the Obsessive Compulsive Disorder from her," Archangel Raphael told the wolves, which were growling and baring their teeth.

The wolves yanked the OCD with their teeth, growling with ferocity… yanking… pulling this writhing mass of black snakes that was all through me and connected like seaweed. Then the wolves shook it and it became still.

After that, Archangel Raphael showed that removing the mass had left big holes in my being and he filled them with white light, so it was like holes had been punched through me and now they were glowing with light from the inside.

The wolves tossed the OCD carcass onto the lavender flame. Golden dust surged up, fell into me, and filled those holes with golden-white light. I was totally aglow.

"It is done," Archangel Raphael said. "It will still have some residue, but stay in prayer and it will be gone entirely."

"Thank you for this healing, Archangel Raphael," I said, feeling an incredible lightness.

As always, I went into the meditation having no idea what might occur, and not imposing any ideas or visions to influence the outcome. After that, Jesus addressed my anxiety about a person involved in a business relationship that had played out in a disturbing dream.

"You are here to teach him that patience is richly rewarded and that is a lesson for you as well," Jesus said. "You knew him in a past life in Abyssinia. He was a merchant and… felt cheated, but will soon see that what looks like something negative can turn around to become a huge benefit."

Having paid my son's tuition and relying on my ghostwriting projects for income, I also asked about my finances. "You never have to worry about money," Jesus said. "You always have more than enough money."

The meditation ended with Jesus saying, "You are this:" and I saw a huge explosion of orange-gold energy that was light-fire-power.

"Enjoy time with your son every day," Jesus said. "He is growing very fast and will soon be a grown man. Celebrate him. Cherish your time together."

Later, when Alexander came home, we snuggled on the sofa, watched a funny movie, and enjoyed a delightful evening. The day concluded with a journal entry: "Thank you, God, for a beautiful Christmas!"

"You Are An Angel For Them"

The next day, my father spoke about love: "Know that everyone loves you and you make everyone's life better. They don't always show it at the time, but in the end, you are an angel for them with many blessings."

Then he provided guidance for my many ideas and writing projects. "You have nothing to fear," he said. "You have more than enough at all times. God is your employer and your Father. God is not a male entity and is impossible to describe or comprehend in human terms. You will see, after a long life of love and all good things: prosperity, creativity, happiness, joy, and making the world better as the Princess of Peace."

A Healing Teacher

An hour after meditation on December 29, 2013, my stomach hurt so much, I stopped writing and called on Archangel Raphael. He said: "Put your healing hand chakras on your belly, Elizabeth."

I did, and continued sitting with my legs crossed on the sofa. I closed my eyes and asked him to heal my stomach. Archangel Raphael pulled out the discomfort in the symbolic image of a green glob. He said it was from the white beans I had left on the counter all afternoon yesterday then ate in the evening with more heated up, even though I had been hearing, "Don't eat beans."

So he put it in the lavender flame. It crackled, then transmuted into golden sparkles, which he put in his hands and guided back to me. This healing energy swirled into my abdomen, turned solid gold, then expanded outward. I kept my hands on my bloated belly the whole time.

"Within thirty minutes you can go running," Archangel Raphael said. "Don't eat anything before that. When you get back, you may eat black beans and juice and olive oil and an apple. No more coconut oil today."

The pain was gone!

"Thank you, Archangel Raphael!" I exclaimed, crying tears of gratitude.

"Elizabeth, you must teach people how to heal themselves," he said.

You can learn this healing technique in the last section, *Ascend: 8 Steps to an Infinite You.*

Feeling Skinny And Sick

In January of 2014, I started to not feel well. I was really thin (ribs sticking out), pale, and weak. Cravings for salmon and chicken overwhelmed me.

I discovered that my vegan diet lacked two key nutrients that are plentiful in salmon and chicken: vitamin D and the B vitamins. I meditated to receive permission to do what my spirit guides had mentioned the month before. Then I stocked up on salmon and chicken, and ate. It didn't taste good at first, but I started to feel better, and I did not gain weight.

Two Sisters: "A Formidable Team In The Publishing World"

Catherine was eager to transition into being a full-time writer. At the time, I was planning to publish my books through a company that I created and named Sea Kingdom International.

"It's a good name," our father said during meditation. "It's a play on words to 'see' the kingdom within."

I hoped that Catherine and I would someday pool our writing talent to work together.

"You two will be a formidable team in the publishing world!" our father said. "With her financial expertise and business savvy, and your creativity, look out! Your mother will be so proud."

He appeared so clearly, it was like he was 3-D. He held hands with me and Catherine, who was holding books that she wrote: one about finance, and—I wrote in my journal—"a short story compilation and more."

To accomplish this, a sense of urgency always propelled me to work hard. Except, one morning, I hit the snooze button on the alarm clock.

"Get up!" said Martha Jean "The Queen" Steinberg. "Girl, you got a lot of work to do. Every minute counts. Your time on earth is precious and you're already 46 going on 47. You're ready. So now you're about to bolt out of the gate and run the race. You've been training up to this point. Now's the time to go for the gold. Don't waste any time!"

The Divine Prophecizes My New Car

One day in meditation, my spirit guides said, "You're getting a new car next week." Within a few days, I received a voucher for a rebate, and sure enough, found myself driving a brand new, 2014 white Ford Explorer.

One frigid morning, while driving Alexander to school—at 7:44 a.m. with 144 miles to empty on the gas gauge—we saw a glorious pink-gold sunrise over the ice-covered lake. A gold beam was shooting up from the rising sun, and it was like the universe was showing the same image that I used to ascend into the Divine during meditation.

So, later that morning when I meditated, I envisioned that real-life golden beam.

"God is within you," God said. "You know this. Teach, Elizabeth."

My father was also there, and we were surrounded by divine beings, angels, and ancestors.

"Work on your book," Jesus said. "It is all easier than you think."

My spirit guides gave instructions on all the state and federal paperwork I was completing to register the business; it would be a quick process to publish books. I did not want to leave the peace, joy, and knowing that comes in meditation, but it concluded and I got back to work.

"Cherish Your Mother!"

The winter of 2014 was so cold that schools were closed, roads were treacherous, and we stayed inside for days in a row. One night, when it was snowing and the roads were icy, Alexander and his dad went somewhere, and they were late in bringing Alexander home to me. I was very worried.

Finally when his dad dropped him off, I was so relieved and happy to see Alexander! I gave him big hugs and kisses and felt overwhelmed with love. A few days later, my father referenced this as the way to love all the time, especially concerning my mother.

"Cherish her," he said. "Love her. She is your angel. Be hers."

"What should I do?" I asked.

"Spend more time with her," he said. "Express more love. Kiss her. Have more fun together. The three of you—you, her, and Alexander—go out to eat or eat in together. Go to Idlewild more. Sell books at the music festival. Make her proud. Love harder."

Think In Terms Of Divine Assignments, Not Dollars

During this period, my bank balances were far more impressive than you'd guess based on the anxiety that I expressed throughout my journal. All the while, Jesus was trying to reprogram my thinking around money. During one meditation, He said:

"Do not think in terms of numbers. Think in terms of divine assignments. Finish your ghostwriting project as soon as possible. Your other divine assignments are your blog, *God's Answer Is Know*, and (another spiritual book). Do not think in terms of numbers. The human mind is not capable of comprehending the vast resources that God has for you."

Celebrating Spirituality and Sensuality

My intention for this year-long retreat was to complete my novel—which expanded into a trilogy—and relaunch my career as a novelist while expressing my philosophies about marriage and monogamy.

The women of *Husbands, Incorporated* played by society's rules, but ended up disillusioned and divorced, feeling discarded and dissatisfied. Now they're seeking the power and pleasure in romantic relationships, on their terms. So I created a world where that is possible. I believe very strongly in the themes that I worked so hard to illustrate through four couples.

Writing about this during my extraordinary spiritual experiences convinced me that my messages would ultimately integrate society's seemingly polar opposites of a woman's sexuality and her spirituality, into a healthy congruence. This idea reminded me of the age-old, Madonna-Whore Complex that has ranked women at one end or the other. When I became aware of this damning social construct during Women's Studies classes at the University of Michigan, I was infuriated. I felt that the "Virgin Mary" concept only perpetuated this. My new understanding about Mary Magdalene—who was deeply spiritual, intelligent, wealthy, and wrongly portrayed as a prostitute—put her at the other end of the Madonna-Whore scale.

This archaic concept should be abolished altogether. It's all about shaming and controlling women to conform to society's rules. This deeply ingrained and insidious rating scale can still have detrimental consequences for a woman's reputation.

As a deeply spiritual being with strong beliefs in women's equality, I prayed for the courage to someday express this through writing and speaking. For the time being, *Husbands, Inc.* became my literary response to a global society where men typically made the rules about women's lives. In my books, women have the power.

Determined to proceed, I considered publishing with a local printing shop that had produced copies of *Dark Secret*, or Lightning Source, a print-on-demand company that would make my books available on amazon.com and online retail sites around the world.

"Use Lightning Source," my spirit guides instructed. "It has greater distribution. Use Lightning Source because you will be like bolts of lightning over the world. You are building an empire. You will publish many books. You and your sister… are starting a new author-publisher model. You own it. You are doing it all yourself. It's your empire. That is your claim to fame. You do not want all the layers of the agent, the publisher, the editors, the marketing people, the art people. You create your covers, your design, your marketing, and events. You control it all. You are global."

My father added that resources for publishing would be provided, including new computers, new software, and all the financial resources for printing. "Know that," he said.

In February of 2014, I published book one of the *Husbands, Inc.* trilogy. I promoted it on my own. I had some media interviews, and people I know across the country read it and loved it. I was certain that it would be a blockbuster. It wasn't. Yet.

Alexander's 16th Birthday Party

Bowling, pizza, and a surprise visit from his college-age Godbrother. That was Alexander's 16th birthday party as family members joined 32 teenagers celebrating in a fun venue with four bowling lanes, a pool table, air hockey, plus cool lighting and lots of food.

"You have the best parties," said one of our guests. "A pop star impersonator one year, now this."

My Spiritual Retreat Ends Abruptly

During the spring of 2014, the condo I was leasing was sold suddenly, and we moved.

I was guided to give away furniture, along with dresses, blazers, boots, jeans, and shoes. Without means to replenish my wardrobe, I knew that I would bountifully replace everything someday. The art teacher at my son's school adopted my plants to thrive in her atrium-style classroom.

Then we moved in with my mother for the third time since my divorce. I was grateful for her support.

But I felt I had failed, again. I became depressed. I had worked so hard, all year, with all this glorious spiritual devotion and revelation. It had seemed like success was imminent. Spiritual teachings say that time and space are only an illusion, and the work of physicist Albert Einstein proved that. If our existence is not happening in linear time, but simultaneously, what was I supposed to do now?

My novel had yet to draw attention or commercial success. And while the memoir that I had ghostwritten for a client drew tremendous praise, it did not immediately attract new ghostwriting projects.

What was I doing wrong?

"I Don't Know."

As summer began, after so much time alone, I longed for romantic love. So I meditated on this, and Jesus said he would send me a mate. He showed me a man's mouth and hands.

"Why are you only showing me the mouth and hands?" I asked.

"Because he speaks the truth," Jesus said, "and touches your life as you've never been touched."

Ever since, I've met men resembling the man in my meditation, and who seemed to speak truth and touch my life in a special way. More on that later...

Meanwhile, I shared my writing expertise and experience by coaching several individuals who needed help composing their books. I met with clients at restaurants, coffee shops, and libraries; for aspiring authors in other states, I coached by phone.

I loved coaching! Creative synergy is electrifying when talking about writing with someone who's struggling to focus and organize their content. This happened when outlining a book, talking about how to flesh out a chapter, or conceiving the title. It was thrilling to help people write their books!

At the same time, I made YouTube videos about writing and wellness. While this was great practice, the videos failed to boost book sales or attract many views and likes.

"Elizabeth, you dress like a nun," a girlfriend said. "You should wear clothes that show off your curves." Several people said I would sell more books by exposing more skin. This created a profound conflict within me; being classy is important, and I didn't want the attention of gawking eyes and comments if I wore provocative cloth-ing. I wanted to be valued for my talent, not titillating clothes.

But the conversation was definitely provocative during a reunion of Cover to Cover book club, after a dozen members read my new novel. My friend Ormandy hosted a barbecue at a beautiful home where we celebrated sisterhood amidst these accomplished women.

I was suntanned, fit, and very blessed in many ways. My days often sparkled with laughter and fun with family and friends. We had a ball at our cottage in Idlewild, hosting guests, grilling steaks, and bike riding by the lake. My son and his buddies enjoyed jet skiing and taking boat rides. They also loved devouring pancakes and bacon that my mother lovingly prepared in her outdoor cooking area. I often walked on Heavenly Way, praying and expressing gratitude for the joy, health, and bounty that blessed us every day.

What brought me down, however, was feeling that I had failed to garner the career success that I had hoped to attain by age 47.

"I am baffled that you're not a superstar," said a friend who is very intelligent and successful in her own career.

"We are dumbfounded that you haven't hit the kind of success that your talent deserves," another friend said.

These comments made me so sad. Depression began to pull me into a place where I questioned my existence. I felt worthless, two thoughts away from crying. Thinking about ending my life. My sole confidant was my journal. On August 18, 2018, I wrote: "The mes-sage is that, I don't know." *2014*

My Son Is My Salvation

What I did know was that I was blessed with an amazing child, a loving family, writing talent, friends, many accomplishments, and vivid dreams. The joy of being Alexander's mom helped me stay afloat when I risked sinking into the abyss.

Plus, I remembered my meditation teacher talking about how people who took their own lives always regretted it, as soon as they pulled the trigger. And my understanding of the karmic life cycle is that our souls learn lessons each time we come back in human form. If we fail to learn a lesson during one lifetime, we repeat it the next time around. I'd like to get as much right this time, so I can continue to learn, grow, evolve, and ascend into better lives.

Once, these thoughts spun through my head while bike riding on the RiverWalk. I stopped to stare at the water. If I changed the course of my karmic life by choosing not to stay here, my spirit guides warned, "You would have hell to pay."

Vivid Meditations Continue

During this period, I continued to eat healthy, exercise, journal, and meditate daily. Once, during a healing meditation about a contentious relationship, a handsome male spirit showed up and introduced himself as Archangel Daniel. It felt like I was making this up, because he was wearing jeans and his buff upper body was bare. He was a hunk!

"I've never heard of Archangel Daniel," I told him.

"Look me up," he said.

It's hilarious for an angel to tell you to research him online. But guess what? I looked him up, and Archangel Daniel is the Angel of Marriage who helps heal past broken relationships and bring you new, extraordinary ones. I was awed by this affirmation.

A few weeks later during meditation, my spirit guides told me to read Revelation Chapter Four in the Bible as research for something that I was writing. I did as told. An hour later, the doorbell rang. Two Jehovah's Witnesses were on the porch. One lady held up the Bible and said, "I just want to read to you Revelation Chapter Four, Verse 22."

Divine guidance is real.

Another time, an Egyptian goddess came to me in meditation

amidst a huge whoosh, explosion of diamonds and gold light… and this beautiful face of a woman with big cat eyes came into focus. Then her face became more cat-like. She showed me opulent visions about my past life in Egypt, and that I still have that power and richness of spirit today. After the meditation, I went online and discovered that Bast was an Egyptian goddess with a cat face, and she ruled truth, wisdom, enlightenment, and creative talent, including writing.

"What does this mean?" I asked.

"You are Goddess," my spirit guides said. "The goddess spirits are calling out to you, claiming you, making you see and feel your power." During the meditation, the cat goddess lifted me up to a big, golden throne, and I was wearing a bejeweled gold cat mask. As people offered lavish trays of food and drink, she said, "You are one of us. Your time is now."

During another meditation, the Egyptian Goddess Isis appeared and said, "I am you."

When I reflected on these experiences in a later meditation, my father said, "That is the real you, Elizabeth. You are Goddess." I interpreted this to mean female God energy within.

So I asked, "How do I make my life reflect that in 3D?"

"Just do it," he said. "Know it. Believe it. Act like it. It starts with deserving. Think of how amazing and powerful and happy you felt all day. Seize your power."

My next book, *Goddess: Be One,* will share what I have discovered and applied as a result of these insights.

During this meditation, my spirit guides said the key to my success was: "Write. Do the PowerJournal website. Cater to women especially. As you teach them, they will teach you. You are moving in January. That will be pivotal to your self-empowerment. You will be amazed."

They said the home would have "beautiful hardwood floors,

sunshine, and that it would be spacious, private, and safe with upscale, modern everything you desire, Elizabeth. Go to sleep and know this. Meditate more. Do yoga tomorrow. Do your books. That will change your life dramatically."

Celebrating "Anything Is Possible"

Wearing a slinky red evening gown from Italy, I was walking the red carpet at the Saban Theatre in Beverly Hills. Cameras flashed as media outlets snapped my picture, and TV cameras were rolling.

"Tell us about your movie," a reporter said, extending her microphone.

"I'm so proud that *Anything is Possible* is nominated for several awards tonight," I said. "Our movie is about love, faith, and family, with a universal message about hope."

In the crowd filling the lobby with an excited buzz, Lara snapped pictures, capturing the floor-length dress that my dear friend, author and filmmaker Pierette Simpson, had loaned to me. A red flower adorned my hair, placed there by a stylist who had done make-up for Lara and me.

At the event inside this historic, Art Deco theatre, Demetrius introduced me to a producer who was interested in my screenplay, *Redemption*. I met celebrated actors and actresses. Our movie won several Nollywood and African Film Critics Awards. And I loved celebrating with my beloved friend.

During that trip, I cast many prayers over the Pacific Ocean for myself, my family, and my friends. Specifically, I asked God to please help my dear friend in Detroit relocate to California. Six months later, she did so, after securing a great job and a lovely new home.

Getting Ghosted By A Ghostwriting Project

Three days before Christmas, I was consumed by suicidal thoughts, but my father told me to "rejoice."

"Rejoice was like the last feeling on my mind," I wrote in my journal. "I cried myself to sleep last night. Suicide was on my mind. But I can't because I am here to raise Alexander and this morning Daddy said 'rejoice.'"

I prayed for the strength to rejoice when I was feeling so devastated. Here's why. During the Fall of 2014, I met with an accomplished person and their agent about writing a memoir. They agreed to the terms of my contract, including the significant fee that would cover extensive research, travel, interviews, and writing.

"You will have the first installment in hand by November 14," the agent told me. The remainder of the payments would be dispersed throughout the two-year project. But November 14 came and went.

Meanwhile, I enjoyed Thanksgiving dinner with 15 family members at the annual gathering at my cousin's home. Afterward, I meditated.

"Get centered," Jesus said. "You are not centered when your stomach is stuffed and sticking out. There's a reason I fasted in the Bible. Clarity of mind. Lightness of body. Clearness of spirit." He reminded me that my ability to enjoy two-way communication with Him and the heavenly realm resulted from all of the above. Being numbed out on food was a sure-fire block.

So I acknowledged that I had eaten too much and said, "Thank you, Jesus."

"You have nothing to fear, Elizabeth," He said. "All your dreams are yours for the taking. Remember what Anita said last night."

My dear friend had said, "If you're waiting on God, God is waiting on you." That means "faith without works is dead," as James 2:14-26 says.

God provides guidance, but you have to do the work for God by taking action to change things. I thought I was doing the work to secure an amazing writing project that would provide significant income. But by the end of December, I was told that the project would not happen for reasons beyond my control.

I cried myself to sleep that night. The devastation wasn't so much triggered by the book deal going bust. It was that I had put all my eggs in one basket, and had no other income on the horizon. It was Christmas, and were it not for my amazing mother's love and generosity for me and Alexander to live with her, I didn't know what we would have done.

My insides felt like a dark spiral sucking my entire being down into a hot abyss. I just wanted to cry. I knew I was viewing myself through a very twisted lens, because I was extremely blessed. On a positive note, my healthy eating and exercise were keeping me slim and fit.

Yet I was failing to achieve my professional potential. The glorious revelations of the prior year's spiritual retreat seemed like a distant dream; a dream, however, that I knew deep down would all come to fruition. But when? How? How could I "represent" as my spirit guides, ancestors, and The Council of Women Writers had so confidently declared as my mission? And why had their guidance provided no indication that I would be struggling like this?

I decided to seek employment, hoping for a communications position that would utilize my broadcast journalism skills. Some companies have internal TV networks, and I envisioned myself anchoring a corporate newscast. I spoke about this with my mother at her kitchen table, as we discussed why I was having such a tough time.

While I saw no such jobs listed on the employment websites where I was applying for positions, I remained faithful, and immensely grateful for my mother's support and encouragement, as well as the immeasurable joy of being Alexander's mother.

"In 2015," I declared to Alexander, "I'm going to become a leader for women to stay strong. I have been preserved for a reason and I exemplify that what doesn't kill you makes you stronger, and I am the inspiration and example to women around the world to be strong."

"Real Women, Real Issues"

A few days later, I sold books and performed my *White Chocolate* poem at Jungle Juice Bar in Grosse Pointe Park. During this wonderful evening of live music, I saw TV producer Steve Hood, who invited me as a guest on his show called *Real Women, Real Issues* on January 6, 2015.

I rocked the TV interview with host Ardelle Bradley, as we discussed race and women's empowerment in my novels. That night, Steve called and said:

"We're taping a pilot for a TV show in two days and we need a co-host. The show is about mental health. Are you interested?"

Yes! I went to the set the next day to meet the other host. Michael Hunter and I clicked immediately. The Michael Brock Band was performing classic Motown hits live in the TV studio, located in Eastern Market across from where I shopped for fresh produce every Saturday.

Now, as I stepped over the cables and light stands to get seated in front of the cameras, I paused… flashing back to the day at my gym when I had stepped over a film crew's equipment, anxiously wondering, *When is my time?*

"Let's get you mic'd," the producer said as I took my seat facing three cameras under bright lights. I tingled with excitement and gratitude. *Thank you, God!*

The following day, we taped the first edition of MI Healthy Mind, a 30-minute TV show that explores mental health and addiction with the goal of shattering stigmas so that people will seek the help they need. At the time, I had very little understanding of the mental health field. The shocking irony was that no one would have ever guessed that beneath my big smiles and bubbly personality that I was suffering from depression and suicidal thoughts.

And no way was I going to reveal that to anyone.

Because even admitting that word felt egregious. Supremely ungrateful!

First, my understanding of the law of attraction and the power of thought and language to create your physical reality made me fear that speaking about it would attract more and make it worse. I soon learned that not getting help was the worst thing I could do.

"Let's talk about it!" I told our viewers, repeating our show's motto like the mantra that I needed to hear.

Secondly, interpreting my sadness as being ungrateful compounded the depression. It felt like a betrayal of the joy and gratitude that I should have felt. Thinking about how others perceived me only intensified this shameful disconnect.

"You're such a great mom, Elizabeth," people routinely said, "and you look so happy when you're with your son."

"You're so talented!" others praised. "I love your novels! When is your next one coming out?"

"You inspired me to write my first book!"

"You motivated me to lose weight!"

"Do you have another movie role?"

"I saw you out running! You are so fit! Your muscles are just fantastic!"

"You always look the same! You don't age, what's your secret?"

"You look like a goddess," a bride told me at her wedding reception, echoing what a girlfriend had said a month before at a restaurant.

"You live in California, right?"

The world viewed me this way; but on the inside, I was wracked with shame.

Thankfully, as always, God stepped in, gloriously!

Healing While Hosting Guests About Mental Health & Addiction

Divine intervention. We hear the term all the time. I'm here to testify that God flexed His miracle-working powers. I was depressed with suicidal thoughts, with a history of food addiction—and was offered an out-of-the-blue opportunity to co-host a TV show about mental health and addiction.

It gets even better...

Not only was I offered a position as co-host of the MI Healthy Mind TV show that would air every Sunday on a major station across Southeast Michigan, but I was also given a full-time job with benefits as marketing director for the show's sponsor, Team Wellness Center.

The company provides outpatient treatment for mental illness and addiction for tens of thousands of people at three clinics in Detroit and a downriver suburb. I loved spending most of my time at the Eastern Market clinic, where many patients had survived struggles with drugs, mental illness, homelessness, and street life.

"It's Miss America!" exclaimed an older gentleman who often sat outside on a bench with other men. Inside, I could hardly walk the halls without being showered with hugs, smiles, and joyous greetings.

"You don't have to be here," a man in the lobby said. "You could be doing a whole lot of other things with your time, but you being here lights up a lot of people. Every time I see you, I feel like I'm seeing an angel."

Even better, I taught a PowerJournal class to men and women who lived in residential treatment facilities and came to Team for weekly appointments. I gave them notebooks and pens, and encouraged them to write about their life experiences that sounded straight out of a Hollywood movie, but had actually happened in drug houses, jails, and crime-plagued neighborhoods.

"You are survivors, and writing is a way to purge and heal the emotions from your past, and write a new plan for your future," I told the women, including one who appeared totally unreceptive. I kept talking, hoping that my message would sink in.

The next week, she was bent over the table, writing feverishly in a notebook. Her facial expression was intense, and she was totally absorbed in her composition. A few months later, I saw her in the hallway; she was working and living independently. She pulled a journal from her backpack and said proudly, "I keep it with me all the time. It helps me so much. Thank you."

I get chills every time I think of her. The poet Rumi said, "The wound is where the light comes in." Individuals who have overcome unimaginable challenges exude so much light once they come out of the darkness of addiction and street life. It's beautiful to witness, and I cherished the blessing of being surrounded by so many unique and fascinating people at Team Wellness Center.

I was so grateful to CEO Tony Pollicella and President Pam Jastrabek for this opportunity to help people.

Meanwhile, when we taped four episodes of MI Healthy Mind every month, Michael and I interviewed guests about how they sought treatment for mental illness and were recovering from addiction. With these "heroes," we featured mental health experts who discussed the causes, symptoms, treatments, and resources for people experiencing mental illness and addiction. At first, I was booking guests, researching topics, and writing scripts.

MI Healthy Mind premiered on Easter Sunday of 2015. We interviewed Kevin Fischer, who became Executive Director of the National Alliance on Mental Illness' Michigan chapter after his son Dominique's bipolar disorder led to suicide.

The 30-minute show has aired every Sunday since then, now broadcasting across Michigan at stations in Grand Rapids, Lansing, Jackson, Traverse City, and Cadillac. MIHealthyMind.com provides links to all episodes on YouTube.

Thankfully, Executive Producer Millie Elston came on board, along with writer Nancy McKeon, with our stellar production team led by Steve Lovill, owner and Creative Director of Eidos Creative Media. We moved to a new set designed for our show. Topics have included schizoaffective disorder, bipolar disorder, suicide, post traumatic stress disorder (PTSD), anorexia nervosa, opioid addiction, gambling addiction, dissociative identity disorder (multiple personality disorder), and human trafficking. Our many awards include:

- Heroes of Mental Health Award from the National Alliance of Mental Health, Michigan (NAMI) in 2017;
- NAMI Michigan Media Award Nomination in 2019;
- Five honors from the 23rd Annual Communicator Awards;
- Several Telly Awards; and
- The 2018 Jim Neubacher Award from the Michigan Department of Community Health.

Billboards featuring promotional photos of me, Michael, the MI Healthy Mind logo, and sometimes our guests are periodically posted along freeways throughout Metro Detroit. I emailed photos to my Columbia professor, David Klatell, who responded: *"I am very happy for you and proud of your success. Those billboards are rockin'."*

For my work with Team Wellness Center, I attended meetings, organized events, led tours, coordinated job fairs, attracted media, and helped organize the annual golf outing. Michael and I also testified at a legislative hearing in the state capitol. We attended a luncheon where I met a man who was the father of the Okemos woman killed in San Diego when I was there in 1990. What a small world.

My work with Team Wellness Center also included promoting annual luncheons for its nonprofit organization, Team Cares. In 2015, the guest speaker was baseball superstar Darryl Strawberry, who delivered a rousing speech about his recovery from drug addiction, for hundreds of people at Detroit's Charles H. Wright Museum of African American History. It was a delight meeting him and his wife, Tracy, and escorting them to the TV and radio interviews that I scheduled for them.

The next year, I interviewed Academy Award-nominated actress Mariel Hemingway, granddaughter of literary legend Ernest Hemingway, who self-medicated his depression with alcohol and ultimately took his own life. After our MI Healthy Mind interview, Mariel spoke before hundreds of people at the luncheon about her book, *Out Came the Sun: Overcoming the Legacy of Mental Illness, Addiction, and Suicide in My Family.*

For the Team Cares luncheon in 2018, I arranged media coverage and introduced country music superstar Naomi Judd before she shared her dramatic story about recovering from depression and health crises before 333 people at the Roostertail banquet hall.

Over the four years that I have co-hosted MI Healthy Mind, my personal—and until now, secret—struggles with depression and suicidal thoughts made me extremely empathetic while interviewing our guests. Similarly, as I began to understand that food had been my "drug of choice," this realization offered yet another point of empathy while interviewing people about addiction. Meanwhile, it was thrilling to apply my broadcast journalism skills.

"How'd you land a TV show?" people ask.

"God is my agent," I respond. I'm awed that His divine intervention blessed me with this long-term opportunity to heal myself emotionally and financially, while being of service to millions of viewers in Michigan and around the world.

I am so proud of our show, and so grateful and honored to help shatter the stigma around mental illness and addiction with our motto, "Let's talk about it!"

Moving Onward And Upward In Extreme Gratitude

Just weeks after the devastating disappointment of the book deal dissolving, and a heart-wrenching conversation with my mother at the kitchen table about my stalled career, she hugged me and cried tears of joy.

It was mid-January of 2015, and she had just watched me being interviewed on *Street Beat* TV show, and on *Real Women, Real Issues*. She was overwhelmed with pride and hope inspired by these interviews, as well as my new marketing job and TV host position.

"Things are really looking up for you," she said. "A month ago, you were sitting here wondering, 'What the heck?' Now you're on TV with great new opportunities."

I meditated on this, and wrote in my journal on January 16, 2015 this message from Jesus: "Use your imagination, Elizabeth. Rise up and out of your circumstances through the power of your imagination. Let your dreams take flight in your mind first, then they will manifest in the physical world. Do that all the time."

"Get The Princess House," My Father Said

While searching for the perfect home to lease within my budget, I made a list of everything I wanted for myself and Alexander, then prayed and meditated on finding it.

"Get the princess house," my father said.

Well one day, I passed an "Open House" sign at a mini-mansion near the spiritual vortex by the lake; I toured what was definitely a princess house.

Thankfully, I found the perfect place—within my budget—with everything on my list: a three-bedroom bungalow with a private back yard, close proximity to school, hardwood floors, a peaceful feeling, lots of natural light, a modern kitchen, and a family room for Alexander's "man cave."

When we moved in, the owner said, "Your keys are on the kitchen counter." I went into the kitchen and gasped. My house key was pink, adorned with rhinestones, and across the top, it said "Princess."

Two Sisters Writing & Publishing

Catherine and I were both hearing the call to open a business together and become full-time writers.

In early 2015, I began working on a memoir for former coaching client Herman Williams, MD, who died of cardiac arrest at age 31, and lived to tell about it. I loved writing about how the love of his wife and family, the miracles of modern medicine, and his faith enabled him to reinvent himself to teach people how to live a more fulfilling life.

I balanced my full-time job and the TV show with interviewing him and writing in my home office during the evenings and weekends.

During the spring of 2015, it was thrilling to attend a book signing reception for *My American Success Story: Always the First, Never the Last* by Roy S. Roberts. It was an honor to ghostwrite this memoir describing how he rose from poverty through education and hard work to become the highest-ranking African American in the global automotive industry.

"I've read a lot of memoirs," said a prominent business woman whom I have long admired, "but you did an extraordinary job, Elizabeth. My only complaint is that I stayed up so late reading when I had to go to work in the morning! I could not stop reading this book!" As she spoke in the bustling atrium of the Wright Museum while Roy autographed books, I was awed and grateful to again honor my promise to God by using my writing talent to showcase inspiring people.

During this time, I helped my son with the many tasks required of his senior year in high school. He was completing college applications, playing a lead role in the fall theatrical production, preparing to take the ACT, playing starting point guard on the varsity basketball team, and keeping up with an enormous homework load. This, on top of my full-time job and ghostwriting assignments, was exciting, but exhausting and overwhelming at times.

Unfortunately, my former husband's behavior prompted me to obtain a fourth restraining order.

In the midst of this, I edited a book called *The No BS Diet* by Joel Kahn, MD, a cardiologist who advocates vegetarianism and who owns GreenSpace Café in Ferndale. He wanted the book published on amazon's CreateSpace platform, so Catherine orchestrated the process. This flipped the switch on a lightbulb moment! Catherine realized how easy it is to publish books, thanks to the technology that's available via the Internet.

Knowing this, along with my publishing experience, Catherine and I decided that we would both write and publish books.

Two Sisters Writing and Publishing went into official business on February 2, 2016. By August, Catherine and I had left our day jobs (I continue to co-host MI Healthy Mind) and were working full-time on our company (which replaced Sea Kingdom International). Lightning Source presented a print-on-demand platform for independent publishers called Ingram Spark, which provides global distribution for our books to 39,000 online retailers, including amazon and Barnes & Noble.

Catherine and I worked hard, excited that someday people everywhere would read the books we were writing.

Favorite Professor's Death Is A Reminder To Seize The Day

After an invigorating run, I checked the fitness app on my phone to confirm that I had reached four miles. A sudden urge to check email revealed news from Columbia University: "Memorial Service for David Klatell." I froze in my tracks. And burst into tears.

My favorite professor is dead! The last time I saw him, in February of 2013, we enjoyed a wonderful visit in his sunny office, painted robin's egg blue, on the top floor of The Journalism School. *Now Professor Klatell is gone!* The idea that I could not share future career accomplishments with him triggered more tears. I also prayed for his family.

In recent years, he was establishing global outposts as Chair of International Studies for Columbia's Graduate School of Journalism. We kept in touch by email, and he shared happy news about his family and travels: *I am in the Amsterdam airport, en route to Barcelona. Life is good. Best, DK*

He had recently asked me to mentor a young graduate who wanted to host a TV show. He wrote: *In many ways she reminds me of you: very upbeat - and optimistic, with a strong interest in interviews and blog posts about popular culture and mindfulness.*

David Klatell died on August 11, 2016 of pancreatic cancer, days after being diagnosed. He was 68. Everyone is going to die, but it's shocking when death strikes people who were seemingly healthy and living life to the fullest.

Therein lies the silver lining. It made me stop crying. And feel peace. My professor's life was a lesson on using your gifts to help others while celebrating family, friends, and the next generation. This reminds us to savor every second of life, because it can end in a shocking blink. *Life is good.*

A Message From Beyond About College Admissions

Alexander always dreamed of attending his favorite college, so he applied there, as well as nine other schools. He visited campuses in multiple states, and enjoyed overnights in dormitories, meetings with students, faculty, and staff, and attendance in classes.

In April, college acceptance letters were mailed, and his classmates were abuzz with who got in where. But no acceptance letter arrived from Alexander's top choice. We were anxious. Meanwhile, he received acceptance letters from every other college.

One Friday night while Alexander was with his dad for the weekend, I was driving home in a rainstorm. Suddenly I felt the presence of my grandfather, as strongly as if he were physically in the car with me. He said: "Alexander is going to his favorite school."

"Thank you God!" I praised over and over while navigating the slick roads.

When I got home, his dad texted me. A rejection letter had arrived. We were devastated. A short time later, I was proud that Alexander selected a small liberal arts college with a picturesque campus, a nurturing and multicultural atmosphere, and a warm, engaged faculty and staff.

He thrived, and halfway through the school year, received notice that he could apply to transfer to his favorite college. He was accepted to attend in the Fall. I believe my grandfather shared a "supernatural future news flash," so that I would "know" the ultimate result in the midst of our disappointment.

"I Forgive You"

I was on a three-way phone call with Alexander and one of his mentors, talking about his education and future career. My mother knew this, so when she tried to call several times, I knew something was wrong.

A short time later, she joined me at a local hospital's Emergency Room, where a doctor told us that my former husband had a stroke. Emergency brain surgery was required.

Alexander, who was preparing for final exams and writing term papers, flew home immediately and stayed for the surgery. Once he saw that his father was conscious and stable in the ICU, I promised to make sure his dad was okay, and he flew back to school.

Within an hour, his dad stopped breathing and was put on a ventilator.

After the doctors and nurses left the room, I stood at his bedside, listening to monitors beeping and the breathing machine *whooshing*.

The past 15 years of his intermittently terrible treatment of me whirled through my head. Then I thought of Alexander away at college, and my promise to make sure his dad was okay. The only way I could do that was to release my anger and angst toward this man, and focus on getting him well so that our son could come home that summer to a fully functioning father.

"I forgive you," I said aloud, as he lay unconscious at death's door.

Until that moment, I had never understood forgiveness, a huge tenet of spirituality. But it created a physical sensation—as if 100 pounds of rocks were lifted from my shoulders. (The restraining order had expired a few months before, and until now, we had had very little contact).

My ex-husband's friends were shocked that I was at his bedside every day, advocating for his care, observing treatments, and working on my computer while he was sedated. I even cancelled a much-anticipated weekend trip to stay with him.

"My ex-wife would have just said, 'Let him die,'" joked one of his friends.

But it wasn't about him and me. It was about our son. Each day, I held my cell phone to my ex-husband's ear so Alexander could talk to him.

"When will my dad be able to talk back to me?" he asked anxiously.

"Soon, I hope," I said.

But he wasn't getting better. Doctors performed a surgical procedure, but it failed. I demanded a second procedure, but was told it would be a few days to get him on the schedule. I was about to pitch a fit—when a woman showed up at the doorway and said:

"We're here to take him into the OR," she said.

The attending RN looked surprised and said, "There's no surgical procedure on his schedule."

I just smiled, knowing that God doesn't need paperwork to make miracles happen.

"You're being an angel," said several people, echoing my father in meditation. I remembered how, years ago, the spirit of my ex-husband's best friend had come in meditation and said I would help my former husband, but at the time, I had no idea what that meant.

The stroke happened a week before Palm Sunday. On that holy day, he was still on a ventilator. So I wrote out a prayerful declaration that on Good Friday, my son's father would be resurrected—able to breathe on his own and recover fully. Amazingly, on Good Friday, doctors took him off the ventilator! He woke up and started talking right away, expressing gratitude that I was the first person he saw.

I immediately FaceTimed Alexander, who was thrilled. His dad—who had to learn how to walk again—said his next goal was to walk across campus with him. After 69 days in the hospital and rehabilitation, he lived independently in his home and ultimately returned to work.

"You saved my life," he has repeatedly told me. His near-death experience has made him a much nicer, more grateful person who recognizes that God kept him alive for a reason.

Most importantly, Alexander came home from college to a fully-functioning father, and I showed our son what forgiveness looks like. That summer, when they walked on campus together, a rainbow appeared in the sky. It was such a magic moment, I took a picture to prove it.

On the two-year anniversary of his stroke, he texted: "Thank you for saving my life. You and Alexander keep me living and bring me hope. You are my guardian angel." A few days later, he wrote, "I continue to be ever thankful and grateful to you and my existence in life. You are an angel. That's very real."

"Let Food Be Thy Medicine"

Ever since 2013, my daily regimen to cultivate wellness in my mind, body, and spirit has included two daily green drinks. At home, I prepare my prescription for disease prevention by tossing fresh, organic, green plant foods into my blender and whirring up my Green Goddess Smoothie.

"Mom, you have a green mustache," Alexander often says.

When traveling, my mini blender goes in the suitcase and gets filled every morning with fresh ingredients that I either transport or purchase at my destination. I wrote about this ritual on our "Tale of Two Sisters" Blog at TwoSistersWriting.com:

I just chugged my morning green drink, and I'm revved with super-sonic energy! This glass full of green goodness is like rocket fuel from Mother Nature—I'm turbocharged to write from breakfast to bedtime, or tape my TV show, go running, do yoga, and have fun with family and friends—all while feeling great.

So what's in it? Organic kale, jalapeño peppers, avocado, spinach and some kind of herb—today I used parsley and super flavorful basil. Then I whirr it up in the blender 'til it's smooth and creamy, and it tastes so good, I drink the whole glass all at once.

Besides spiking your energy, it boosts your metabolism, packs a power-ful punch of vitamins, minerals and antioxidants, gives you tons of fiber to cleanse you from the inside out, and cranks up your immune system. Your skin will be clear and glowing, and you will look and feel younger.

Since you are what you eat, and what you put into your mouth has a huge impact on your brain and your mental health, eating "clean" natu-ral foods such as fresh greens every day helps to stabilize your mood and cultivate mental wellness all day and night.

Think about it—green leaves bask in the sunlight as they grow. They absorb the sun's rays. So when you eat greens, you are literally consuming sunshine!

The trick is to keep the ingredients on hand. Open my refrigerator, and it looks like a farmer's market. If you think it's too expensive to eat healthy, a bunch of organic kale is 99-cents, whereas a bag of chips will cost you $4! Plus, what you invest in your health now, you'll save on medical bills, prescriptions, and doctor visits later in life.

You can also sweeten your drinks with fruit—but calories really add up, so do what works best for you. Another thing, don't expect your green smoothies to taste like a milkshake. They don't! But they're fueling your mind, body, and spirit to maximize your creativity, productivity, and wellness throughout the day and night, and your longer lifetime! So drink up!

Second Movie Role Is International

Pierette Domenica Simpson was nine years old, traveling with her family in 1956 on a luxury ocean liner from their home in Italy to America. Another ship crashed into the *Andrea Doria*, and Pierette witnessed the terrifying mayhem that claimed 46 lives. The ship sunk near Cape Cod, Massachusetts, and the captain was vilified.

In 2008, Pierette published *Alive on the Andrea Doria!: The Greatest Sea Rescue in History*, then wrote a screenplay. She produced the movie, filming in Ferndale and her native Pranzalito, Italy.

I was honored by Pierette's invitation to play a 1950s journalist. The cast visited a salon where our hair and makeup were given 1950s style, then we filmed outdoors on a rainy day during a sudden blaze of sunshine.

Italian Director Luca Guardabascio created a cinematic masterpiece using historical footage, sound effects, and documentary-style interviews with survivors, including Pierette and Mike Stoller, songwriter for Elvis Presley. The Italian film had English subtitles, and won honors in the Italian Parliament.

Luca—who lives in Rome and specializes in films featuring spirituality and angels—took selfies with me and Pierette. Royal blue and deep purple beams of light appeared in the photos. Angel energy registers in photographs as orbs or beams whose colors represent certain angels. Archangel Michael was making his presence known in the photos with me, Pierette, and Luca. (The yellow orbs on photos on this book's cover signify peace, health, and enlightenment aided by Archangel Jophiel).

What a thrill to attend the black-tie, world premiere of *The Andrea Doria: Are the Passengers Saved?* at the Detroit Film Theatre at the Detroit Institute of Arts. A reception followed a press conference where Pierette spoke beside an actual lifeboat from the shipwreck.

Then hundreds of people packed the theatre. Joining me were Catherine and our mother, who shared a "small world" connection with Pierette. A nun on the *Andrea Doria* jumped to safety in a lifeboat, broke her leg, and limped the rest of her life. She later became my mother's Catholic school teacher.

The film celebrated immigrants, and marked the 60-year anniversary of the shipwreck. The evening was a glorious celebration of Pierette's hard work to bring her dream to life and exonerate the captain of the *Andrea Doria*. I embraced her and exclaimed, "I am so thrilled for you!"

Philosophies on Life

"Oh this is so beautiful!" I exclaimed as my friend toured me around her newly constructed dream home. "I am soooo happy for you!" I hugged her.

My friend later shared that several "friends" had expressed envy and jealousy while visiting her new house. This later inspired a great conversation with my son.

"If something ever makes me feel envy or jealousy," Alexander said, "it's a message that I'm seeing something that I really want. Then I release that feeling and strive to obtain that object or achieve that goal."

I smiled. "Me too! And that God is showing it as an example that we can also have it."

One day, Alexander was talking about "self-mastery."

"What's that?" I asked.

"It means you have the choice to decide how you will react—or not react—to certain situations," he said. "You have the power to have mastery over yourself."

One day when I visited him on campus, he schooled me on stoicism, existentialism, and other philosophies. We even went to Barnes & Noble and perused the philosophy shelves, where he treated himself to several books.

When I'm home and realize he's grown, I remember how Jesus and my spirit guides encouraged me to cherish every moment with him as he was growing up. Now I tell friends: "Enjoy your kids now, because they will be grown and gone to college or work in a blink!"

Writing Is A Family Affair

As an empty nester, I work full-time on our books. I have a home office, as well as new furniture, plants, clothing, and other items that the Divine promised would be replaced.

Catherine handles publishing, which includes coordinating with graphic designers about book covers and interior formatting for photographs and text.

Two Sisters Writing and Publishing released our first publication in May of 2017: the third edition of *Dark Secret*, with a hot new cover.

Then in August of 2017, Catherine became a published author. She pioneers new literary ground by writing the first-ever Young Adult series featuring a biracial girl navigating the tricky world of race, boys, and friends. Inspired by her childhood and teenage experiences, she wrote: *Veronica, I Heard Your Mom's Black, Veronica Talks to Boys,* and *Race Home, Veronica* by Catherine M. Greenspan. Girls of many backgrounds have written letters to Catherine saying they loved the beautifully designed books because they deal with the universal themes of a girl coming of age in a confusing world.

Coming up next? *Grace Under Pressure; Sally's Indoor Fiesta;* and *Hey, Jude, Is That White Lady Your Mom?*

In September of 2017, we published *"CLEAR!" Living the Life You Didn't Dream Of* by Herman Williams, MD. His book has drawn rave reviews, and he has spoken at the Detroit Medical Center, the Harvard School of Public Health, University of California at San Diego, Boston University, and the American Heart Association.

In December of 2017, it was an absolute honor to publish *Let the Future Begin* by Dennis W. Archer. In this 440-page book, the former Detroit mayor shares how he rose from poverty to lead the Motor City's remarkable revitalization and how he became the first person of color elected as president of the American Bar Association. His many book signings and speaking events have included: Cousen Rose Gallery on Martha's Vineyard, Harvard University, and the American Bar Association.

Catherine and I experienced a miracle with publishing this book. Hundreds of guests were expected at a gala release party orchestrated by Ignition Media, owned by former Mayor Archer's son, Dennis Archer, Jr. We ordered 600 copies of the book, but learned that the holiday rush could not guarantee production and delivery of such a large order in time for the party.

We were in a panic. Thankfully, a longtime professional relationship with James Mays of MCS Multimedia resulted in his company quickly producing the hardcover books with excellent quality, just in time for the party. I had not spoken with James for years, but he had called me about a month before this, out of the blue, to say hello and offer deeply spiritual words of encouragement.

Another amazing moment occurred when an intelligent person

whom I interviewed for the book called it "a masterpiece." I am so grateful for the honor of writing Mayor Archer's inspiring story.

Two Sisters Publishing Our Mother's Book

For years, people urged our mother to write her memoir. Well, in December of 2016, she started—and didn't stop until she finished in May of 2017.

"I can't talk right now, I'm writing," she'd say when we phoned. "I got up at four this morning to write."

We are so proud of her! *The Triumph of Rosemary: A Memoir* by Judge Marylin E. Atkins chronicles how she was a biracial foster baby named Rosemary Lupo who was put in foster care by her Italian mother because she was half black. Her adoptive mother was verbally, emotionally, and psychologically abusive. Then she describes meeting our father when she was the church organist, and trying to convince him to stay in the priesthood when he told her that he was contemplating a departure in 1965 because he wanted to marry and have children. The story details: their damnation by the Bishop; their families' disapproval and subsequent acceptance; and their extremely loving, peaceful life together—raising me and Catherine, and working as a team as she attended law school and began her upward trajectory as a lawyer, becoming the longest-serving Chief Judge of Detroit's 36th District Court, ultimately retiring in 2012.

Our dear family friend Lorna Thomas, MD hosted a lovely book signing reception attended by friends, family, and former colleagues in October of 2017. Alexander came home from college for the affair that was featured in a local newspaper. Since then, her book has received five-star reviews from readers, book clubs, and journalists interviewing her for radio programs, podcasts, newspapers, and blogs across America and the world. Her many book signings have been at Cousen Rose Gallery on Martha's Vineyard, as well as with The Sunshine Book Club in Naples, Florida.

Editing and publishing our mother's book has created many unique moments for me and Catherine. First, we don't know of any other such mother-daughter writing and publishing team. Second, we learned so much about our mother and how she overcame terrible abuse. Third, we both feel a much greater appreciation for our mother's determination to become a lawyer with the goal of putting us through college.

We are so proud that she returned to Saginaw Valley State University in 1971. After speaking on campus and having a book signing in February of 2018, she was invited to deliver the SVSU commencement address for two different crowds of 5,000 people each in May of 2018. Around that time, she spoke at The University of Detroit Mercy School of Law, and a year later, her book was given to honor students during the annual Book Awards in the school's chapel.

Now our mother is delivering keynote speeches and writing the screenplay based on her book, after so many people read her story and said, "This sounds like a movie!"

More Books Showcase Against-the-Odds Success

Catherine and I began composing books to heal and affirm our unique experiences as white-looking multiracial women. In doing so, we wrote ourselves into American literature by filling a void where no such books existed. We also wanted to empower ourselves with our own publishing company, so we could publish our books, our way. This meant no more frustrating attempts to impress a literary agent or face rejection letters from New York publishers.

Our personal mission evolved into a professional quest as Two Sisters Writing and Publishing, which—through word-of-mouth referrals—attracted diverse ghostwriting and publishing clients whose stories celebrated against-the-odds success.

In February of 2018, we published *My Name is Steve Delano Bullock: How I Changed My World and the World Around Me Through Leadership, Caring, and Perseverance* by Steve D. Bullock. I ghostwrote this book about how he was a sharecropper's son who rose to become a global humanitarian as the first black interim president of the American Red Cross.

After childhood abuse, and decades of struggling, Lin Day was depressed and dying, until she finally found the solution: hypnotherapy. Now she's about the most joyous person you'll meet, having slimmed down by 50 pounds, and being cured of cancer, with no more walker or fibromyalgia. In *Remembering and Forgetting: A Spiritual Journey* by Lin Day, and a foreword by hypnotherapist Kim Manning, PhD, Lin shares her inspiring story that she wrote herself.

When I was a writer at Detroit's Fox 2 News, everybody loved and respected veteran reporter Al Allen. In August of 2018, we published his memoir, *We're Standing By* by Al Allen, which provides unique insights on 50 years in broadcast journalism. Al wrote it in broadcast journalism style, with vignettes from his career and life.

We have been writing *The Life Story of Julius V. Combs MD* by Julius V. Combs, MD. It describes how Dr. Combs made history as co-founder of the first African American-owned health care company to become publicly traded on the New York Stock Exchange.

We were thrilled to present *The Energy Within Us: An Illuminating Perspective From Five Trailblazers*, by Joyce Hayes Giles, Hilda Pinnix-Ragland, Rose McKinney-James, Carolyn Green, and Telisa Toliver in May of 2019. This collection of their mini-autobiographies showcases how they blazed trails for women and African Americans to shatter the glass and black ceilings as top executives in America's energy industry. Each woman wrote her own story, which we edited.

Working with these powerhouses was truly a delight and inspiration.

As we were growing up, our mother was active with the Black Caucus of Michigan, participating in its Drug-Free Youth Program that included an annual parade. In December of 2018, Catherine and I published two books by the organization's respected founder, Alma G. Stallworth, PhD.

In *Legacy of a Lawmaker: Inspired by Family & Faith*, the retired state representative showcases the power of faith, family, and determination to make a positive impact. And in *Broken Hearts: Like Mother, Like Daughter—A Spiritual Call to Action for Equality in Health Care*, she chronicles two generations of her family coping with congestive heart failure.

Catherine and I ventured to Texas to watch an Ivy League-trained, board-certified plastic surgeon perform procedures live on social media. Then we wrote *Confessions of a Plastic Surgeon: Shocking Secrets about Enhancing Butts, Boobs, and Beauty* by Thomas T. Jeneby, MD, which offers a fascinating peek into his world, and includes his hilarious commentary on the psychology behind plastic surgery.

We're working on *The Dr. Sanchez Books on Raising Healthy Children—Baby's First Year: A Survival Guide For New & Experienced Parents* by Dr. Eduardo Sanchez, who shares everything parents need to know about baby's first year.

Also on the health front comes *A.M. Total Being Fitness Journal* by Anthony Moses. This personal trainer, gym owner, and bodybuilding competitor guides men and women into better thinking, eating, and exercising.

Ghostwriter, Or Writer For Ghosts?

Catherine and I wrote a biography about an amazing woman who died long ago and left a powerful legacy. We have conducted extensive research to chronicle her life, which exemplifies a tremendous *joie de vivre* and ahead-of-her-time progressiveness.

As a ghostwriter, I am invisible, as if the subject is speaking.

One night, after an intense day of work, I was awakened by an influential person who was a significant person in this woman's life. He told me to write something for the book. I opened my laptop and took dictation from this highly revered man who died a long time ago. Meanwhile, I couldn't help laughing about the play on words: *Am I a ghostwriter, or a writer for ghosts?*

A Chilling Message About The Diabesity Epidemic

After watching Michael Wood, MD, perform bariatric surgeries, I composed a book proposal containing his 20 ways that America can embark on a campaign to eat healthier foods, get more exercise, learn about health and nutrition, and change cultural habits that perpetuate obesity and its many health problems.

A literary agent shopped the proposal to New York publishers. Rejected! The book market, they said, was saturated with "policy books" about obesity.

"Let's write a novel instead," Dr. Wood said.

So we wrote *The Enemy Within*, a fast-paced thriller with frightening plot twists designed to wake people from their fog of food and fat. Obesity is the enemy within, and in our fictitious story, terrorists use it against Americans. It's a scary tale, but so is the obesity epidemic.

"Use Your Breaking Point As Your Making Point"

Raised by his mother in a trailer in North Carolina, Master Sergeant Cedric King became an Army Ranger, battling the Taliban in Afghanistan. A bomb blasted off his legs—but two years later, he was running marathons and soon giving motivational speeches across America.

"You need a book!" our mother told Cedric and his wife, Khieda, after hearing him speak in Miami. She put Cedric and Khieda in touch with me and Catherine. We wrote and published *The Making Point: How to Succeed When You're at Your Breaking Point* by US Army Master Sgt. Cedric King, with forewords by former Starbucks Chairman Howard Schultz and Actor Gary Sinise. The book became an amazon #1 New Release with divine timing; it was released the same day as Schultz's book, *From the Ground Up,* in which he praised Cedric as a brave veteran.

Cedric's message is that if he can do the impossible—become a triathlete with no legs—then you can do anything.

Catherine Loves Helping Aspiring Writers

Years ago as an aspiring writer, Catherine sent stories to magazines, hoping to get published. She received a slew of rejection letters or no response at all.

"When I'm in a position to help other writers get published," she decided, "I will." She kept her promise by creating the Two Sisters Writing & Publishing Short Story Contests. Every month, she posted a new theme on TwoSistersWriting.com, judged the submissions, and awarded cash prizes.

In July of 2018, we published the winners in our *First Annual Anthology Featuring International Writers,* showcasing 21 authors from around the world. Our second annual Anthology is coming soon. Another cool twist? Our student interns from the University of Michigan help us create the anthologies.

Two Sisters Laughing & Learning

Catherine and I had "the giddies"—we couldn't stop laughing.

"It's two in the morning!" I exclaimed, laughing harder. "We're in book index delirium!"

We'd been working for hours to complete an index for a thick book. Anxiety and deadline pressure bubbled up in a giggle-fit, just like during our English Major all-nighters at U of M, and when playing cards and eating chocolate with Daddy in the camper as little girls.

Now, Catherine was visiting me and our mother in Metro Detroit. We were working on a dozen books in varying stages of completion, so all that work was looming. Thankfully, we finished the index and got a few hours of sleep. The next morning, we had the honor of speaking to a Creative Writing class at Okemos High School.

"We were once students just like you," we told Jennifer Garmin's class, "and now we write and publish books. We're doing what we love, and it all starts with a passion for writing."

We talked about writing, gave away books, and answered questions. When a student said she was biracial and named Veronica, we gave her one of Catherine's novels. Then, delighted by the diversity of students, we toured the new building; met the librarian; and saw the TV studio.

OHS Alumni Association President Rod Ellis had arranged our visit, and invited a half-dozen alumni who chatted with me and Catherine and bought our books in the café of Schuler's Books at Meridian Mall. We also met the store manager; six months later, we had a triple book signing for Mother's Day! In a lovely fireplace cove, our unique mother-daughter trio discussed and autographed our books.

"This is one of the best moments ever!" I exclaimed as three of my high school teachers walked in! Tears of joy overwhelmed me while hugging Mrs. Hammerle, Mrs. Marsh, and Mrs. Tanner—such influential powerhouses in my education and my life.

Also attending was then-Superintendent Alena Zachery-Ross,

whom we had met earlier when Rod arranged for me, Catherine, and our mother to speak in the OHS auditorium. Our presentation aired on the district's TV station.

Later, we celebrated with Rod and our real estate agent, Nena Bondarenko, at a restaurant near the home she helped our parents buy and later sell. That day was an absolute joy!

Drained, Disappointed, Praying For Divine Intervention

A panic attack jolted me awake, heart pounding, mind racing over a stressful situation. My anxiety exploded in an angry red splotch of eczema on the back of my scalp, and burned in swirls of tension on my back, extending around to my heart.

Then later, as I sat at my desk, with fingertips poised over the keyboard, my body felt like someone had pulled a plug in my feet, causing all my energy to drain out. Fatigue burned my eyes. I stared blankly at the computer screen, unable to extract a single sentence from the fog in my brain.

"We have an author interview in an hour," Catherine said via FaceTime from her home office in New Mexico. "Let's finish writing the photo captions and make sure the places are marked in the manuscript for each picture. But first let's go over our calendar for the week. We have two new client calls and we should be getting the book proof in email today. Did you write the press release yet?"

The fog in my head spun.

I am so exhausted! God please help me!

We were working on so many books! We had interviews and writing and deadlines and proofreading and photographs and back-and-forth emails with our graphic designer. And while grateful for the booming business, the many deadlines and tasks that I needed to meet as soon as possible loomed like ominous boulders threatening to topple down and crush me.

Like the cold, winter gloom outside my home office window, discontent consumed my entire being. I knew I was under attack by spiritual warfare, as many distractions were derailing my focus with tempting or panic-driven situations that pulled me away from work—and from completing this book.

I felt lost. Disappointed. Angry that I was putting others first at my own expense. Exposing myself to certain situations that violated my boundaries—boundaries that I did not defend by speaking up or by avoiding the individuals. This toxic crush of emotions literally made me sick and bloated.

Too many days, I neglected my morning rituals of yoga, chakra-clearing, meditation, and journaling. Instead, I went straight to my desk with a cup of coffee (after a green drink) to work intensely on editing a manuscript or having video conference calls with Catherine and our clients across America.

"What?!" I lamented. "How is it already four o'clock!? I have so much to do!" Pulling all-nighters was no longer an option; I need eight hours of sleep to keep my brain working at optimum capacity, so the five- to six-hours lately were woefully insufficient.

Time—and life—were slipping through my fingers like water. I was trying to paddle toward the island that I dreamed of owning. But I was slipping into an abyss of burnout.

This constant race against time consumed me with guilt and regret. Every hour seemed so precious now; how many hours, weeks, and years had I wasted on struggles with food and fat? How much time I had blown in ManLand—Catherine's word for when I get caught up in the purple haze of romance—where I expended time, energy, and money, while having incredible fun and adventure, but cultivating relationships that sometimes didn't work out and left me feeling distrustful and cynical?

Meanwhile, this angst sharply contrasted with my public image.

"You and your sister are crushin' it with all your books," people praised.

"I'm so amazed at all the things you," longtime friends added.

"Your TV show is really impactful," said a woman at the bank.

"You're a boss!" others declared.

"I saw your workout videos on social media, girl. You are fit!"

I had so much more to do, and now that I was 50, time was ticking fiercely forward. This book remained unfinished because our time and energy were committed to our many clients' projects that were paying bills and Alexander's college expenses.

"Biss!" Catherine exclaimed during a visit to Detroit to meet with our local clients. "It's time for our first video call with Leisa Peterson!"

I glanced at the clock; I just wanted to keep writing to complete our client's book and meet the deadline for publication. Plus my sister and I were doing a crash course about online marketing and sales to promote our writing workshops and webinars, and we were expending a lot of energy to master our huge entrepreneurial learning curve.

"Hurry," Catherine insisted, motioning for me to sit beside her at the computer on my dining room table, where we were working on our many projects.

Agitation and impatience burned through me. I didn't want to take time for a business coaching call that would only put me an hour behind all this work. But I reluctantly sat beside Catherine as Leisa appeared on the screen in her office in Sedona, Arizona. Peace washed through me. My tense muscles relaxed.

No wonder Catherine's been raving about Leisa Peterson! She radiates such calming light! They met years ago through a mutual friend, and Leisa provided helpful guidance for Catherine. A former bank executive, Leisa combined her financial expertise with two decades of spiritual learning to host the Art of Abundance Podcast and to create The Atlas Collective, a mastermind group that instructs how to be a successful entrepreneur by cultivating spiritual principles in oneself.

Catherine believed that Leisa could show how to maximize our potential as business women. So, we summarized our challenges, and Leisa offered helpful guidance during individual and group video calls with entrepreneurs around the world.

Still, something was blocking me from tapping into my most genius writing, my highest energy and personal power, and my most fierce focus. I prayed that attending Leisa's Atlas Collective Retreat in Arizona with Catherine would help me blast past that block and finally achieve all that Jesus and my spirit guides had promised years before.

As I trudged through the airport, my body and spirit were heavy with unrelenting fatigue and overwhelm. In contrast, I'm usually so excited to take a trip, I walk through the airport smiling. Now, tears filled my eyes as I prayed for transformation in the spiritual mecca of Sedona. Once entirely populated by Native Americans, the city surrounded by red mountains sits on crystal beds and iron deposits that create energy "vortexes" that stimulate healing and spiritual ascension.

"I want to return from Sedona feeling like Moses coming down the mountain after he saw the burning bush," I wrote in my journal on the airplane. "God please talk to me loudly and clearly in Sedona, Arizona."

Sedona Inspires Revelations And Action

A short time later, under a clear blue sky, I was hiking in the spectacular, Red Rock mountains...

Doing yoga and meditating with entrepreneurs from across the world...

Hearing speakers share spiritual messages about using the power of crystals, channeling God through writing, and releasing limiting beliefs...

And participating in spiritual rituals in Peace Park.

When we first arrived in Sedona, Catherine and I hiked up a

mountain to the Airport Vortex, amongst people from around the world. I expected the vortexes to make me feel some kind of Holy Spirit moment on the mountaintop. But other than the thrill of an awesome workout while huffing up steep stone paths amidst glorious views, I felt no such jolt.

Until after the hike—at Whole Foods. I was walking through aisles of fresh produce and health products when suddenly chills danced over my skin. I stopped in my tracks, savoring surges of more joy and optimism than I had felt in a long time. "Don't eat meat," my guides said as I met Catherine at the salad bar, where we ate many times and enjoyed delicious greens, hummus, black beans, and brussels sprouts, with pineapple and berries for dessert.

That first night, sleep was serene! The next day, Leisa Peterson's retreat began with yoga and meditation; God blessed me with one of my clearest communications with the Divine in months.

"It's time for liftoff," Jesus told me, along with a directive to leave behind anything that was not serving my highest good. He showed me a rocket, which drops jet propulsion parts as it ascends, to lighten its load and soar higher.

"Jesus, God," I prayed in meditation, "please tell me what to do."

"Find yourself," Jesus said. "Know who you are. You are the Princess of Peace. You are above worldly goods. You are above material gain. You are above the world driven by physical pleasures."

"What do I do?"

"Live from your mind, not your body," Jesus said. "Live from your spirit, which works through your mind."

My spirit guides then explained that our spirit power gets silenced by succumbing to the body's cravings. Both our creativity and our desire for sensual pleasures such as food and romance are ruled by the sacral chakra. But if the energy is squandered there by indulging sensual appetites, then it never rises up to fuel the power-and-action-generating solar plexus chakra, and it does not ascend further into the heart to cultivate love and healing, to the throat to express and live our truth, into the third eye that oversees intuition, or into the crown chakra that connects with the Divine. As a result, this most powerful energy would never surge up into my brain to fuel my writing.

"Cultivate a relationship with yourself, Elizabeth," Jesus said.

I had been forfeiting my power in several situations, seeking external validation, playing myself small, and as a result feeling stuck in certain ways of thinking and behaving. It was time to reclaim my power and step into my most magnificent self.

More guidance on how to do this came from a woman who channels Mother Mary. Her name is Samarah Grace; she spoke at our retreat and later gave me a reading.

To change the way you think and behave, she said, imagine yourself as a computer being upgraded with a new operating system. All you need to activate its power is a new password. That password is a mantra.

Repeating it would "spin away" anything that wasn't serving my highest good, she said, and I would automatically speak up, say no, or say yes, depending upon the circumstances, to make the best decisions—without conforming to a "template" of what society or others want for me.

"You have no need to apologize or explain," Mother Mary said through Samarah. "You're reclaiming yourself. You're claiming for yourself what your father and your mother had to claim for themselves: 'I don't care what other people are telling me is the nature of Jesus. I don't care what the Catholic Church is saying about me. I'm going to go with what my heart is telling me.'"

When seeking love, she said: "What is the maximum kind of relationship you could have on this planet? Jesus and Mary Magdalene! Life is to enjoy!"

Then she added, "I want you to have very clear, specific steps for yourself, because this new operating system is going to free you. From there, what comes is glorious and wonderful and life-affirming and fun. You are so ready, darling."

"Thank you, Mother Mary."

"You're welcome, darling," she said. "Much love and happy creating."

"The Key To Success And Joy Is Unconditional Love"

It was a heavenly moment as Leisa and I cleared our chakras on the mountain—under a blue sky, and over a pristine expanse of pine trees and red rock ridges. The crisp breeze danced over our faces warmed by the Arizona sun in the Kachina Woman Vortex, a wellspring of feminine energy.

As we walked to join the Atlas Collective group amidst international tourists, a white-haired man approached and handed me a flat, heart-shaped rock that he had carved from the region's famed red rock.

"The meaning of life is unconditional love," he said, starting an eloquent speech about God, nature, the heart, and our power to cultivate love and peace in ourselves, other people, and the world.

I just stood there, joyously holding the heart-rock (he had a pocket-full!). His words echoed my spirit guides during a group meditation the night before: "The key to success and joy is unconditional love." He also reiterated my father's definition of the meaning of life: love. Then this man, named Robert, climbed up a 50-foot rock formation to the top of the mountain.

"This song is about peace!" he announced into the sky as his crew filmed him and others meditated around him. He played a beautiful song, moving his flute in the shape of the infinity symbol. Giant black birds soared past. And the pure peace energy of Mother Nature coursed through us, bathing our souls in loving light that we could then radiate forever thereafter.

"Elizabeth First!"

During the retreat, Leisa led many mind-shifting group discussions about creating businesses and attracting clients that are in alignment with our passions and life purpose.

A major focus was on how to identify and dissolve "limiting beliefs" that block our success with fears, bad habits, and small thinking. My "limiting belief" was still that if I speak up, and say what I'm really thinking and feeling, and do what I really want to do—which may contradict what people around me and society expect—then I will suffer negative consequences. How could I teach if I were afraid to speak up? I committed to changes in thinking and behavior, by writing three, single-spaced pages with 60 items, starting with:

1. I speak up!

2. I fiercely guard my time, energy, and resources.

3. I stay fiercely committed to my divine calling as the Princess of Peace… finishing all the projects and promoting them with courage and gusto.

4. I say no.

5. I obey my guidance.

6. I know that I have more than enough time, money, love, abundance, resources, and opportunities.

Later, at home, I recited the list into the audio recording app on my phone, and listened to the 44-minute recording every day while taking action on each point. I also posted a new mantra—"Elizabeth First!"—on sparkly paper over my desk. Putting myself first means doing what's best for me, my family, and my work.

"Wow, you two have really changed!" exclaimed several Atlas

Collective members when Catherine and I returned for our second retreat six months later. They said we seemed more confident, assertive, and empowered. We attributed that to applying to ourselves and to our business what we were learning at the retreats and while working with Leisa on coaching calls and Atlas video conference calls.

Another highlight was when Leisa gave me the honor of doing a PowerJournal presentation for the group, and my sister shared a spiritual breakthrough, which left me in tears.

"I Want To Fly!"

Catherine and I then headed to Santa Fe, New Mexico for our Two Sisters Writing Retreat. Over two days of intensive strategizing about our short- and long-term goals, we decided to transition from ghostwriting to supporting, celebrating, and teaching writers.

Very importantly, we agreed to focus on writing, publishing, and promoting our own books. Catherine planned her next novels in The Veronica Series, and I described the curriculum that accompanies this book.

"I want to fly!" I declared. "I want to travel the world, speaking and sharing how to activate the spirit-power within to create your best self, living your heart's desires, and being a positive influence."

I added that I want to host my own TV show and build our multimedia empire that includes transforming my books into films, and educating people in classes and conferences.

Floating On A Giver's High

When I boarded the plane back to Michigan, my spirit guides said, "Sit in seat 22B."

"Can I sit here?" asked a young woman who must have sensed our kindred spirits, because we had a ball! A fashion designer, she was headed to New York City. I asked her to design clothing for me someday. After sharing insights about her Native American culture, she revealed that it was her birthday, so when we landed, I bought her a coffee, and gave her an autographed copy of *Dark Secret* with an amethyst crystal heart in a pretty bag. She was overjoyed, and my electrifying "Giver's High" was glowing like a big bubble of joy around us in the busy airport.

In Detroit, I floated off the plane. My entire being felt light and radiant, like pure love and light walking through the airport. I was overwhelmed with gratitude while flashing back six months before, when heading to our first Sedona retreat, feeling so gloomy. Weighted down. Anxious. Overwhelmed and exhausted. Now, a grin flashed across my face; I wasn't Moses, but a new power was definitely sparking within me.

"You're glowing," my mother said when she picked me up.

I felt overwhelmed with gratitude toward my mother, for always encouraging and supporting me through life's highs and lows. She and I and Catherine are each other's biggest cheerleaders, and we are more like friends than mother and daughters. She is a powerhouse; we are immensely proud of her accomplishments, and how she has always been our greatest role model. We have so much fun with her at her book signing events, visiting Alexander at college, and spending time at our cottage in Idlewild.

Now after this transformative trip, I was eager to make her proud.

"The Only Cure Is To Write Her Truth!"

A short time later, I was running with my father, down the stairs to the Lower World, after entering a portal in a beautiful tree and asking Jesus for help.

"Get out of my way!" we shouted toward anything blocking me from writing.

"Come on, come on!" my father said. "There's no time to waste!"

This urgency propelled all three Shamanic Journeys that I took during a group meditation with a dozen people led by Lori Lipten, who said our intention was to ask the Divine to "show me my soul's highest path of fulfillment."

During one meditation, my guardian angel Esmerelda appeared, huge and glowing and beautiful. As she wrapped her wings around me and spoke, peace coursed through my body; I was floating in a warm sea of euphoria. Then she reminded me of what my spirit looks like:

A golden geyser of sparks shooting up and spraying in all directions to create a huge, strong energy field that magnetizes goodness and repels, ignites, and incinerates anything negative, toxic, or hurtful that tries to penetrate this divine shield of protection.

Then, while ascending to the Upper World with my father, up through the veil, angel wings sprouted from my back.

"You have your wings now," Daddy said. "You are safe to use them."

We were flying! He already had wings, and was teaching me to fly like a baby bird. I was soaring! So we went up and up and soon we were over a scene of my life in 20 years, fulfilling my life mission as the Princess of Peace.

"Hurry," a spirit guide said, "you have to take action in the physical world!"

To do that, they said I need to "be louder, be bolder, take action." I could do that with the courage of giant lions and the healing of huge bears surrounding me during these meditations. "You have to yell, Elizabeth. Command it!"

To reinforce this message, my father escorted me to the Lower World, to the cottage across the lavender lake. Inside, I was lying in bed, worried sick. Suddenly a giant burst of emerald green light filled the room, and Archangel Raphael appeared in a huge form.

"The only cure is to write her truth!" he announced.

After that, I was sitting at the table, typing and writing. The Council of Women Writers—dozens of them, too many to count—surrounded me. Virginia Woolf and Zora Neale Hurston were there, along with a woman who was introduced as Mary Quaker.

"You don't know my name because I wasn't allowed to write," she said. (Later that night, my online search for "Mary Quaker" revealed that she was Mary Barrett Dyer, an English Puritan in the colonies who was hanged in Boston, Massachusetts in 1660 because she preached the Quaker belief that God speaks directly to individuals, as opposed to only through the clergy).

What!? That's the point of this book, and I am free as a woman writer to teach this—359 years after Mary Barrett Dyer was killed for it!

This martyr underscored The Council of Women Writers' main message: That we as women writers now enjoy freedoms under the United States Constitution, and we must use that freedom!

As the meditation continued, one of the women—whom I did not recognize—knew that I was contemplating a rekindling with a former lover. She leaned over the table, grasped the sides of my face, and commanded: "Do not go back to him!" Her warning was that getting lost in romantic oblivion would leave this book and others unfinished.

She said her name was Naomi, and because I had never heard of a writer named Naomi, she told me to look her up. That evening, an online search revealed a prolific, eccentric British writer named Naomi Jacob—a newspaper journalist, biographer, author of romantic novels, actress, radio broadcaster of uplifting messages during World War II, and a Women's Suffragist. I was stunned by the many parallels to my life! She died in 1964, three years before I was born. Naomi also wore men's suits, something I did—with men's wingtip shoes!—as a newspaper reporter. And yes, I was obedient to her command.

"Cultivate A Relationship With Yourself, Elizabeth"

Breathtaking romance. Hedonistic indulgence. Laughter and love. Wining and dining. Adventurous trips.

I've enjoyed all of the above with wonderful men during the 16 years that I've been divorced. In fact, many moments felt like I was living inside a romance novel or starring in a romantic film.

Unfortunately, every story has a conflict. And mine was about time and energy. Every minute that I enjoyed in ManLand was one less minute that I devoted to completing this book and others. But didn't I deserve companionship to balance my hard work? And Jesus had promised to send a mate. What if I had met him?

Even though I was ghostwriting books, working hard with my TV show, marketing for Team Wellness Center, then running Two Sisters Writing & Publishing with Catherine—and helping my son complete high school and begin college—all while investing daily time for my spiritual practices, exercise, and healthy eating—my own books and screenplays sat unfinished in my computer.

This triggered an undercurrent of creative angst and guilt. With each passing year, I felt an urgency to finally finish these books, get my screenplays made into TV series and movies, and make my own writing a top priority.

Compounding this discontent was that my books are my divine assignment. If you miss a book deadline with a ghostwriting client, you don't get paid. If you don't deliver on an assignment from God—

I don't want to know the answer! Yet this book, 16 years after I started it, was still nothing more than an icon on my computer screen for a file called, "God's Answer Is Know."

It sat unfinished, because the devil's answer is "No."

All kinds of distractions get thrown in the path of a person with a divine purpose, to derail the mission. Only by becoming aware of this can we find the discipline to focus. Once, when a man called to invite me on a hedonistic adventure, I was standing beside my bookshelf, but not touching it. As he talked, a paperback book fell and hit me in the head. I picked it up and gasped. The book was about spiritual warfare against women. God was speaking "No!" loudly and clearly.

After deep soul-searching, I decided to trade time spent on winning, dining, and romantic fun, and invest it into my own writing projects. This commitment to myself gave me the courage to speak up.

"I need to focus on my writing," I announced. "It's more than a job. It's my divine assignment."

"Stop saying weird stuff," one man said.

"You're being selfish," another responded.

"Success is nothing if you don't have someone to share it with," someone warned. "You'll end up alone."

I obeyed what Jesus said in Sedona: "Cultivate a relationship with yourself, Elizabeth."

So I stopped dating and retreated into my writing zone to transmute all my energy into creation. With a lifestyle similar to my spiritual retreat in 2013, I practiced the "Elizabeth First" mantra. That meant no mental overhead of romantic relationships, time and energy commitments, or the fatiguing brain-drain of having too much fun. While my creativity, clarity, and clean living were thrilling, I missed dating.

"If you don't sacrifice for what you want, what you want becomes the sacrifice," says a popular quote posted on my refrigerator. I coined another sobering mantra to resist temptation: "Fleeting pleasure, books forever." That means, pleasure is temporary, but books last forever.

Plus, Jesus promised to bless me with a relationship on par with his union with Mary Magdalene, and Jesus always keeps His promises.

"Find Yourself," Jesus Said. "Know Who You Are."

Jesus said the key to "lift-off" was to: "Find yourself. Know who you are."

I used writing to do that, and the questions guiding my inner journey became the content as I wrote the first *PowerJournal* workbook that Catherine and I published on my birthday. We also launched the PowerJournal.Life online membership community.

Holding our new *PowerJournal* workbook in my hands, and loving the high quality cover and pages, as well as the beautiful logo that we had designed, was mind-blowing! Something that started when I combined journaling with meditation years ago, was now a physical book that was selling online. We even trademarked the name.

The cover is turquoise, representing the throat chakra and truth. The text is indigo, symbolizing the third eye and intuition. I composed the workbook as a writing roadmap to journey within myself, seeking answers and action steps; now we offer this internal quest to you as *PowerJournal: A 28-Day Challenge*. We provide space in the workbook to explore: *Who am I? What do I want? What's blocking me? And what action do I need to take?* A new question every day helps you excavate answers buried deep in your heart and soul.

In January of 2019, we published the *PowerJournal Workbook #2: A 28-Day Challenge for Weight Loss*. It explores why we use food to soothe our emotions, and how to stop self-sabotaging behaviors.

With this book, we are presenting *PowerJournal for Spiritual Awakening*, and *PowerJournal to Know Your Life Purpose*. I will be teaching in-person and online courses to guide you through the PowerJournal experience. Learn more at PowerJournal.Life.

The Summer of Self-Love

As I worked hard to complete this book and many projects, I embarked on a Summer of Self-Love to cultivate a relationship with myself.

"I love Elizabeth!" I repeated to cancel-clear-delete negative self-talk. I had to forgive myself, release guilt, and nurture my mind, body, and spirit before I could lift-off as a spiritual teacher.

One day, after my spirit guides revealed that holding onto guilt and regret was blocking my progress, I spent hours writing out everything for which I wanted to forgive myself. Then I prayed and meditated on releasing it all, and I felt lighter. You can *PowerJournal for Forgiveness* in the last section of this book.

Years ago, when I studied the writings of Hay House Founder Louise Hay, she talked about doing "mirror work," where you look at yourself and say, "I love you," and recite mantras to accept and celebrate who you are. Now I see my reflection and smile as if encountering a beloved friend.

Lavishing yourself with love fills you up, so you can share the overflow with others; the best you as an individual means you bring the ideal person to personal and professional relationships.

So, what is Self-Love? Here's what I believe:

Self-Love means you stop seeking external validation, affirmation, permission, or approval. It means stepping into your own power and using your own internal compass to guide you, every moment of every day.

Self-Love means feeling happy, peaceful, and complete when you're alone.

Self-Love means knowing that you are a powerful spiritual being inhabiting a physical body that you nurture, nourish, exercise, rest, and pamper. It means respecting your body as the temple where God dwells within you.

Self-Love means quieting the inner critic that spews vitriol that you would never tell someone you love. You can reprogram your brain by writing a new script of how you'd like to perceive yourself, then record it into your phone and listen to it—day and night—until your more positive self-talk overrules the inner critic.

Self-Love inspires you to forgive yourself—to release regret, guilt, anger, angst, and sadness, about anything you may have done, or didn't do, or did wrong.

Self-Love happens on the inside, all by yourself. It means investing time to change the things you can control, such as what you eat, whether you exercise, how you think, what you think about, how you present yourself, and how you behave.

Self-Love means putting yourself first, just like on an airplane: secure your own oxygen mask first, because you can't help your kids if you pass out. This is not selfish. A better you benefits them.

Self-Love means doing what's right for you, following your heart, and fulfilling your life's purpose—courageously and unapologetically.

Self-Love means trusting yourself to make decisions based on what you want and need, not what others want for you, and having the courage to speak up, say no, and express what's best for you.

Self-Love means filling yourself up with so much joy and satisfaction that any praise, love, affection, and attention that you receive from others is simply extra icing on an already perfect cake.

I spent the summer praying, journaling, and meditating on these ideas, and most importantly, putting them into practice.

"I am the person that I have been searching for all this time," I recently told Alexander. "I could only get to know her and fall in love with her, by spending a lot of time with her. Alone. Anyone whom I allow into my matrix is merely an enhancement; the price of admission is to add value or multiply value."

When you saturate yourself with love, it flows out toward everyone you encounter. And the more of us who are living in that flow, the better the world will be.

"Thy Will Be Done…"

As I was growing up, our father led me and Catherine in reciting *The Lord's Prayer* every night before bed. I must have said—"Thy will be done, on Earth as it is in Heaven"—thousands of times. As a girl, the meaning of this rote repetition eluded me.

As it did decades later, during the worst moments of my ex-husband's post-divorce antagonism, when someone said, "Let God's will be done." How was I supposed to know what God's will was?

Writing this book has helped me figure this out. First, some of the things I wanted so badly, but never came to fruition, were apparently not God's will, or at least not yet. While other things that came "out of the blue" were clearly gifts from God. When I stopped living for what Elizabeth desires and listened to what God wants for me… then everything flows.

Next, we can know God's will for our lives—which is our life purpose—by asking and receiving answers through prayer, meditation, and writing. God will speak to you through writing when you *PowerJournal to Know Your Life Purpose & Action Plan*. I'll show you how in the next section.

Switching Into Spirit-Teacher Autopilot

"I speak up!" This mantra—and many other action steps on my 44-minute recording of my own voice—became the password to Elizabeth's Operating System. This switched me into spirit-teacher autopilot.

I shed the fear of talking about God, or sounding like someone other than the Elizabeth most people knew. I knew God was speaking through me as the words began to gush from my mouth without forming sentences in my mind first.

"You have to share your miraculous healing story with as many people as possible, to help them believe in God's power," I told a book coaching client while standing in the middle of a restaurant in Detroit's Greektown. This man has known me for decades, and his eyes were wide with awe as he listened.

Wow, I've never talked like this before! I realized afterward.

This was the first of many such experiences that now happen routinely. I met a beautiful, intelligent woman and immediately recognized her mission to write and speak from her unique perspective. She was electrified by this external affirmation that awakened the Godpower that she already knew was within herself. It also emboldened her dream to write books and speak her eloquent messages on stages everywhere.

A short time later, a different friend was so transformed by my speaking God over her about her life purpose and mission, she called me a "shifter." She went from anxious and sad to overjoyed and confident about how to proceed.

Yet another friend asked me to do a meditation to learn what would happen in this person's personal and professional life over the next six months. I visited the Akashic Records on my friend's behalf, and received extremely vivid and clear information. A short time later, the first item came to fruition out of the blue. My friend was awed.

"Elizabeth, you should do this for CEOs and other people to help them shift and know what they should do in business and in life," these friends suggested. "Call yourself A Spiritual Shifter."

Meanwhile, I began teaching friends in other states how to meditate during phone and video calls, and conducted healing meditations for other friends. Then at a banquet where my mother was receiving an award, a state lawmaker asked me to lead her Monday

Mindfulness class to demonstrate meditation—three days later! Rave reviews resulted, and God continued to provide more teaching opportunities.

Peek Into "A Day In The Life"

Today I truly feel reborn. I'm no longer the Queen of Chaos, plagued by fears, an insatiable appetite, fat, self-loathing, depression, conflict with my ex-husband, distraction, or struggles.

"Only by going through this can you teach others to toughen up in the face of whatever their inner demons of fear are," Jesus said in 2013. "You are a great teacher, Elizabeth. We have been preparing you all year with daily lessons, daily miracles, and daily blessings."

Finally, thanks to divine guidance, I became the Princess of Peace within, so that I could share these lessons with you.

"As within, so without," say the famous words originating in The Emerald Tablet, an ancient manuscript containing spiritual secrets.

My life story exemplifies the power of the Divine to transform. I'm proof that you don't have to look like what you've been through, and that you can weather the storms of life with peace and a loving heart, and sail into tranquil waters when you know that God is within you, guiding you to safety and peace. As proof, here's a peek into my spirit-powered lifestyle now...

On the best mornings, I awake in silent prayer: "Thank you God for an excellent night's sleep. Thank you God for health, safety, security, love, prosperity, protection for me and my loved ones, and for inner peace."

If I'm anxious about something, I pray: "Thank you God for helping me resolve this today, better than I ever imagined."

As my feet touch the floor, I thank God for the ability to stand and walk and function with sight, hearing, touch, taste, smell, intuition, and purpose.

Then I head to the kitchen to toss ingredients into the NutriBullet and drink a Green Goddess Smoothie, followed by a steaming cup of coffee with organic half and half. After that, I head to the yoga mat in the living room to do The Five Tibetans with additional Kundalini breathing and movements. Then I clear my chakras and pray.

Next, on the sofa, I meditate for 15 to 30 minutes with shamanic drumming music.

Then I go to my desk to write or host The Two Sisters Writing Club with Catherine; the Club is our online time and space for writers to commit to one hour of focused creativity, four times every week. Later, if I have a business meeting, I dress and go.

After lunch, I return to my desk to write, and later enjoy my second cup of coffee and green drink. Sometime late afternoon, I either go to the gym for weight lifting and/or cardio, or take a walk or bike ride outdoors. Then I eat dinner and get back to work until bedtime.

During breaks, I love talking with relatives, mentors, and friends such as Louise, whose nearly lifelong friendship I cherish dearly.

My daily activities also may include: leading phone- or FaceTime meditations and prayers with friends and people who need it; running errands; visiting our son at college; attending events with my mother or a friend; going on dates; and taking trips such as a week in Florida with my family.

I'm also attending book signing events; teaching classes online and in person; speaking at colleges, conferences, and companies; and traveling to do all of the above.

Making Peace With Food

As I work, I'm grateful for mental clarity, creativity, and stamina that are enhanced by "intermittent fasting." For me, that means not consuming solid food after dinner, and then not eating again until late morning or midday.

My first meal consists of: salmon with health-boosting spices and organic extra virgin olive oil; organic baked sweet potato with organic virgin coconut oil and Himalayan pink sea salt; and organic steamed kale. I artfully arrange a bounteous serving, eat half, and save the rest for dinner. No more cooking or prep-time required. My meals sometimes include broccoli, beets, bananas, and occasionally chicken or other types of fish.

This mainstay meal is rocket fuel for my brain and body, so I eat it consistently. Its protein-carb-fat combo guarantees mental and physical endurance—thanks to a stable blood sugar level—required for long hours of writing.

"God bless Mother Nature for creating this salmon, sweet potato, and kale, and the people who raised it, packaged it, and sold it," I pray over the food. I rub my hands together, activating the healing energy of my hand chakras, then hold my open palms over the plate while saying, "Thank you God for this food that nourishes my mind, body, and spirit so that I can share my gifts with the world to serve as your messenger."

Blessing your food infuses it with energy that aids digestion and makes it an offering to the temple that is your body. Prayer actually makes your food more delicious!

Some days, especially if I'm going to an evening event, I eat only the midday meal, then keep my energy pumped and appetite suppressed with Green Goddess Smoothies.

Here's a miracle that inspires immense gratitude on a daily basis—

I'm at peace with food and my body! It's like I'm on autopilot, thanks to many healing meditations, as well as journaling, reciting mantras, and listening to my thought-shifting recordings. It's almost shocking to suddenly realize a profound lack of desire to snack between meals, veer off this regimen, or overeat at the table.

"Stop eating," the divine voice within commands after I've eaten enough. Obedience is rewarded with sharp focus and sustained energy for writing, as well as an upbeat mood. If I keep eating, I feel bloated, sluggish, and foggy. Discipline while dining has many rewards: an ideal body weight; clear skin; a lightness of being; excellent sleep; and strong connectivity to the Divine.

Knowing

Another dramatic transformation is the extreme kindness and gratitude that my former husband demonstrates toward me every day.

As for my racial identity, I am comfortable with the skin I'm in. Never fitting in has been a blessing, not a curse. It forced me to figure out who I am and know that my unique appearance and experiences are in fact an "instrument" for cultivating understanding and harmony across the lines that divide us.

Another change? I speak up, say no, and fiercely guard my time to maintain optimum wellness and productivity. I put Elizabeth First. I feel elevated into a higher consciousness while simultaneously staying centered and grounded.

I am not perfect. I am still a work in progress. But I am putting in the work to learn more every day. I still have moods. Anxiety, fear, angst, and sadness still come. But rather than wallow in worry or succumb to stress, my daily regimen is an aggressive prophylactic to protect my emotional and physical wellbeing. I use tools to shift my mood and outlook; the other day, I was really edgy as Catherine and I worked to simultaneously complete three book projects. So I took a 45-minute bike ride by the lake, which restored my energy and optimism for an extremely productive evening.

The major difference now compared to earlier decades is that I am finally *owning* the power that the Divine has been saying I had all along. This means thinking, walking, talking, and behaving with confidence inspired by **knowing** that my existence is powered by pure

God energy within. This spiritual GPS provides constant directions to orchestrate my steps and instruct "yes" or "no" every inch of the way. If I ignore it, the consequences are a reminder to be obedient next time. When I listen and obey, the results are glorious.

My life was created by my parents' courageous, colorblind love, and was then anointed by my father's baptismal prayer for God to make me a Princess of Peace. Forty-four years later, I was blessed with a spiritual awakening that led to an immense reverence for the Prince of Peace, and a new knowing that God is within all of us.

Now please allow me to honor my divine assignment to teach Lessons From a Spiritual Life so that you can Ascend with 8 Steps to an Infinite You.

ASCEND

8 Steps to an Infinite You

YOU'RE EMBARKING ON THIS spiritual journey with divine timing, because this is an era of ascension. Something is shifting in the universe that's causing more people like you to awaken to your spiritual power, so you can see beyond the physical world and experience the transformative powers of the invisible world of spirit.

What's blocking you from seeing this now is "The Veil of Illusion"—the barrier between our three-dimensional reality, and the higher, invisible dimensions. Albert Einstein said that time and space are an illusion, and that parallel dimensions exist simultaneously.

"Reality is merely an illusion, albeit a very persistent one," Einstein said.

Yes, your health, your mortgage, your failing relationships, or other problems, *are* reality in your 3D life. However, tapping into the spiritual dimensions can empower you with information and abilities to greatly improve your circumstances—in ways that feel like magic and miracles.

Now, my mission is to teach how to Ascend with 8 Steps to an Infinite You. This information will enhance and accelerate your spiritual awakening and powers. The goal is for your spirit to travel at the speed of light into heavenly realms to heal, learn, manifest your heart's desires, and be a positive influence in the world.

So let's get back to the "veil." You saw me ascend through it—to enter the heavenly realm in meditation. Right now, our planet's evolution is eroding this metaphoric blinder.

Here's an easy way to think of it. Say you're boarding an airplane on a cloudy day. During lift-off, the aircraft flies up through the "veil" of clouds, then ascends into the bright sunshine and a vivid blue sky leading to the limitlessness of the cosmos. As you saw in my story, it is a glorious place full of wonders.

And it's where the immeasurable, golden infinity of God resides. A starburst of that energy is pulsing inside you. It's your spirit. And you're reading this book because you feel a yearning to reconnect to its Source: the peace, love, and power of God in the kingdom of heaven.

Let's go!

Step #1: Chart Your Course.

Before you embark on this spiritual journey, let's chart your course by determining your destination. That will help you navigate how to get there.

Where do you want this information to take you? For example, if you'd like to learn how to establish a daily routine that will help you feel inner peace and enjoy more harmonious relationships, then you can set that as your goal. Perhaps you'd like to master meditation to explore your past lives and learn from the Akashic Records. Maybe you just want to feel better all the way around. For me, I wanted to learn meditation to cultivate supernatural powers; I had no idea that it would lead to the extraordinary experiences that I shared in this book.

Let's take a few minutes to Chart Your Course. This allows you to set your intention, which I view as a goal infused with spiritual energy because achieving it can elevate your thinking, living, and influence.

Why do you want to activate your spiritual power?

_____

_____

_____

_____

_____

_____

_____

How do you want your life to improve by cultivating a spiritual lifestyle?

_____

_____

_____

_____

_____

_____

What would you like to achieve on this journey within one month, one year, and your lifetime?

_____

_____

_____

_____

_____

_____

Write your intention for why you want to ascend into your most infinite You.

_____

_____

_____

_____

_____

_____

What is the consequence if you never do this?

_____

_____

_____

_____

_____

_____

Describe how you will feel, look, and experience life as your most infinite You.

_____

_____

_____

_____

_____

_____

_____

Dedicate Time. When you take a trip, you need to designate time for travel. The same goes for your spiritual journey.

So evaluate your schedule to determine when you can devote time to meditate, journal, clear your chakras, exercise, shop for healthy foods and prepare healthy meals, take yoga classes, attend a retreat, and learn.

You don't have to do all of the above. But you do need to block time on your calendar for your "Spiritual PhMe." Consider rising 30 minutes early, or swapping out a less important activity for meditation, journaling, etc.

Calculate time required for driving to a yoga class, for example. If you're changing your diet, consider how you'll need to shop differently—perhaps at an organic grocer. Also, will you include your partner and/or family in your healthier eating? If not, will you need more time to prepare two meals?

Make Space. Designate a quiet, private space in your home or office for your spiritual practice. For example, I created a plush nook in my home to meditate and journal amidst soft fabrics, big pillows, and strings of lights. It feels so good to nestle into this cozy, pretty space and communicate with Jesus, God, angels, ancestors, and helping spirits.

Clear Clutter. The ancient Chinese principles of feng shui say that clutter zaps energy, as do stuffed drawers and closets, and an unkempt home and office. The time you invest in clearing clutter and creating a clean, simple atmosphere will reward you with focus, calm, and stamina. While you're at it, remove any objects, photos, or other items that make you feel bad. The goal is to clear your launchpad of any debris that can block your lift-off.

Step #2: Plug Into Power.

You can do things every day that activate and expand the starburst of God within you and strengthen your connection to communicate with the Divine. These practices crank your mind, body, and soul to the highest vibrational frequency possible, so you can tune in to your personal video-conference calls with the spiritual realm.

Activating this spiritual power is all about energy. That word gets tossed around so much, but what does it really mean?

Back in science class, we learned that everything is energy. The air, our bodies, and the things we touch are made of molecules, which are made of atoms, which contain electrons around a nucleus of protons and neutrons. These smallest particles of matter are constantly moving, even in solid objects such as your chair that looks like it's not moving. Everything is vibrating with this energy.

Solids are dense and vibrate with the slowest frequency of energy; light is thin and vibrates at the highest frequency. Connecting with the highest frequency energy attunes you to divine power that can fuel your ascent. Everything has this vibrational frequency, including food; meat is low, whereas leafy greens are high. For now, let's talk about light.

That starburst of God energy inside you is your soul, and it's surrounded by an aura of light that extends between nine and 18 feet around you. This is your "light body." It contains "organs of light" along your spine, and each plays a role in your wellness. I'll explain later. While we already have this light within, we need to strengthen it by plugging in to the infinite current of cosmic energy. This section is all about how to do that.

In addition, when you venture into other dimensions, you need to protect yourself by invoking divine light and beings to create a force field around you.

You can call out in your mind or with your voice to God, Creator, Universe, Jesus, Buddha, Quan Yin, angels, Mother Mary, Archangel Michael, deceased loved ones, or any spirit beings you desire. After that, I add, "I'm calling in an army of angels to protect and shield me as I journey into the heavenly realm."

Now it's time to "call in the light" to prime you for chakra clearing and meditation. You can also do this exercise as a way to relax.

Cleansing the Mind, Body, and Spirit in a Light Shower

Sit in a comfortable, private space where you will not be interrupted.

Close your eyes. Imagine you are outdoors. Look up at golden beams shooting down from the sky, into the clouds. Now envision one of these beams coming to the top of your head. Feel its warmth as you imagine a lavender, lotus flower on top of your head, and its thousand petals are opening to allow the light to enter your head.

Imagine this light is so powerful, it's sparkling and pulsing with power. See this golden glow of energy pouring into your head, cascading down your throat, through your chest, your arms and out your fingertips, extending into your abdomen, then surging down your legs and shooting tiny lightning bolts from your feet into the ground. Then envision this light shooting from your tailbone into the earth, through the mud, rocks, and water, and connecting with the core of Mother Earth. Now imagine that the light is surging up from the center of earth, through your body, and up to heaven.

Envision your heart as the connecting point in this luminescent column between heaven and earth. As the light pulses through you, see it illuminating your heart, which rules unconditional love and healing. Now think of someone, something, or someplace that overwhelms you with pure love and joy. Savor that feeling. Allow it to expand outward from your heart, filling your entire body, then bursting out in a joyous bubble around you.

Imagine that this love is brightening the light inside your body, illuminating every cell. See it as a cleansing, crystalline mist that's repairing your DNA to perfection, and shooting like laser beams into your cells to deactivate and destroy any toxins, bacteria, or viruses, restoring every cell to immaculate health.

Imagine this sparkling-bright light from heaven pulsing through your veins and arteries, purifying your blood, your muscles, and your bones. See it rejuvenating every organ for optimum function. Envision this light glowing in your mind to instill emotional balance, creativity, maximum brain function, and excellent mental health. Experience this warm light rejuvenating you from the inside out, from the top of your head to the tips of your toes.

This light is too powerful to contain in your body, so it expands through your skin, glowing around you like an opalescent aura. It heals your skin, restoring its best health, and casting a healthy radiance over you. Then the light fills the room, bursting through the building, across your town, your state or region, your country, and the world. See this heavenly light engulfing Mother Earth, making miracles happen.

Then say, "God please make this healing light and love from heaven make peace prevail where there was war: as healing replaces hurting;

people have food, shelter, clean water, safety, and justice; and governments enact and enforce regulations to stop pollution so that Earth can be restored to her majestic glory and preserved for our children and future generations."

Now see this light swirling back toward you and surrounding your loved ones. Pray for them one at a time, by naming them, and saying a prayer such as: "This beautiful, divine light from heaven is swirling around David today to make him happy, healthy, safe, strong, and successful."

Repeat this prayer for your family members, your friends, your colleagues and clients, your neighbors, and whomever else may come to mind. You can also share this loving light with former friends, lovers, and colleagues, to heal any rift that may linger. This practice is especially helpful when you are having a conflict with someone; envision this healing light swirling around them, allowing you to forgive them and release any anger or disappointment, while they are softening their stance with the goal of resolving the problem in a spirit of harmony and good will.

You can also do this while thinking of political leaders or newsmakers who upset you. You can say, "God please use divine intervention to resolve the conflict involving (name a person) and (name a person or group of people) and bring it to a harmonious conclusion." You can also project this loving light onto news events that trouble you, and envision a positive resolution, even if it seems impossible. I often pray for divine intervention to change the minds and hearts of anyone who was contemplating acts to hurt others, so they stop, and the crime never occurs.

Each of us is a powerful transmission tower, and when we project prayerful intentions to create peace and positive outcomes for ourselves and others, it really works. As more of us do this, we can target our collective prayer-power to make positive changes in any situation.

After casting these prayers with the power of the pure white light from heaven, and bringing the light back to yourself, it's time to clear your chakras.

Brush Your Teeth, Take a Shower, Clear Your Chakras.

Light is invisible—until it shines through a prism, which splits it into colors that appear as a rainbow. The light within you also divides into rainbow colors—in the form of chakras, the organs of light along your spine.

In the sky, if smog is blocking the rainbow, it will look dirty and dim. Likewise, the metaphoric pollution of stress, anger, anxiety, pain, and trauma can dim the power of our seven main chakras. Think of them as lights attached to ceiling fans. You want the fan to spin fast to circulate the energy, and you want the light to glow as brightly as possible. Each chakra rules a different aspect of your being, and you want them all on the highest and brightest settings.

This internal lighting and electrical power system can illuminate your life's best path and regulate your energy for optimum health and happiness. If you don't do regular cleaning and maintenance, you could be holding toxic energy that causes discomfort, disease, and death. You can prevent this when you "cleanse and clear" your chakras.

Let's start by learning the chakra names and corresponding colors, characteristics, prayers, and sounds.

The ruby-red **Root Chakra** at the base of the spine represents physical survival, safety, money, and sexual health.

Prayer: God please cleanse and clear my root chakra, to empower my ability to survive and thrive with courage and success in physical, sexual, and financial health.

Chant: Lam.

The orange **Sacral Chakra** below the navel represents creativity and sensuality.

Prayer: God please cleanse and clear my sacral chakra, so that I may enjoy emotional balance, creativity, and pleasure.

Chant: Vam.

The yellow **Solar Plexus Chakra** above the navel rules personal power and action.

Prayer: God please cleanse and clear my solar plexus chakra, to empower my ability to take action in the world with confidence and knowing.

Chant: Ram.

The emerald green **Heart Chakra** at the center of the chest rules unconditional love and healing.

Prayer: God please cleanse and clear my heart chakra, so that I may give and receive unconditional love and healing.

Chant: Yam.

The turquoise **Throat Chakra** in the neck rules communication.

Prayer: God please cleanse and clear my throat chakra, to empower my ability to express my highest truth with courage and confidence, and to demand honesty from others.

Chant: Ham.

The indigo **Third Eye Chakra** between the eyebrows rules intuition.

Prayer: God please cleanse and clear my third eye chakra, to empower my ability to see into the divine realm and receive wisdom.

Chant: ~~Vam.~~ Sham ♡

The lavender **Crown Chakra** above the head represents divine connection.

Prayer: God please cleanse and clear my crown chakra, to empower my spiritual awakening, self-realization, and unity with God, humanity, and all of the Divine.

Chant: Om.

How to Clear Your Chakras

- Sit comfortably in a private, quiet place.
- Start with the root chakra. Close your eyes and envision a sphere of ruby red light glowing and spinning in your groin.
- Think or say aloud: "God please cleanse and clear my root chakra, to empower my divine right to survive and thrive with courage and success in physical, sexual, and financial health."
- Take a deep breath, and say a loud, "Raaaaaaaaaaaaaaammmm," for as long as possible.
- Savor the vibration as a sound bath for this chakra. Imagine it washing away any thoughts, fears, and memories that might block your physical well-being, sense of safety, and financial security. See cloudiness dissipating as the sound and prayerful intention clears and cleanses the chakra. Envision it glowing brightly and spinning as fast as possible to circulate its energy through you.
- Repeat for each chakra.

When all seven chakras are cleared and cleansed, you will feel peaceful, light, and primed for better health, success, and a stronger connection with God.

Your Pillar of Light is Your Mission Control

One morning as I awakened, Jesus said, "Elizabeth, you are pure white light. You are pure Source."

Then He and my helping spirits showed an image to convey for all of us: a pillar of white light around you, extending up to heaven and down to the core of Mother Earth. At its center are three chakras: the heart, solar plexus, and throat. These represent action and speech powered by love.

"This column of divine light is your control tower," my spirit guides said. "Your heart and soul are mission control, and they are controlling your life mission to teach how to access and activate this Godpower within and cultivate a lifestyle of peace and love."

My spirit guides took this lesson a step further; during sleep, waves of electricity tingled through my body, from my head to my toes, so strongly that it woke me. It was startling, then affirming as physical evidence of the omniscient, supernatural current of God energy that we can plug in to.

In the midst of this, Jesus awoke me by saying that God is within us. God is golden energy like the sun. When we think of God as this golden glow within us, we understand that each of us is the light of the world. And it's our job to radiate.

"Project this pure white light toward individual people, regions of the world, and specific news events," my spirit guides instructed. "Like laser beams of love strategically directed to diffuse hatred and conflict and serve as a transmission tower for peace and love."

Step #3: Explore New Worlds: Meditate.

Prayer and meditation are the best ways to connect to the Divine. Meditation is different than prayer. Prayer involves asking, praising, and thanking. You can pray anytime, anywhere. Meditation is best done in a quiet, safe space. It's an interactive process of asking questions, then receiving responses from God and spiritual beings in the form of feelings, words, sounds, and visions that are like snapshots or movie scenes.

You can hear God speaking to you in the stillness and silence of solitude. Unfortunately, our culture bombards us with messages that being alone is sad and lonely, and that it should be avoided. The opposite is true.

Spending time alone is a gift that you can give yourself. It allows you to go within and discover who you really are. Sometimes we're so programmed by family, friends, and societal expectations that we erase our truth and override our hearts' desires to win approval from external sources. That may feel right for a while, but it may trigger discontent if the self you've become and the life you're living are incongruent with your soul's purpose.

Solitude helps you know this. It's imperative for spiritual discovery. Even if you're meditating with your soul mate, your twin flame, or like-minded people, you can best serve those relationships after you've learned to lavish yourself with so much love that you're in overflow.

What is meditation?

Meditation is your all-access pass to infinity. It's a method for your spirit self to go on a fact-finding mission in other dimensions and return with secrets for your success! It starts with the act of getting still and silent, then disconnecting from the physical world, so you can:

1. Calm the "thinking mind" and dial into a heavenly zone for two-way communication with God, Jesus, and other enlightened beings, angels, ancestors, and helping spirits;

2. Discover your spirit self;

3. Access information about your soul's experiences across all boundaries of time and space, which includes past lives, the present, and the future; and

4. Transform energy to heal yourself and others, and manifest experiences to fulfill your life purpose.

Here are ways to incorporate meditation into your daily life.

Find a teacher. You can learn meditation techniques online through websites and YouTube videos. You can also take classes. Ask

God to connect you with the best teachers. I did not seek my teachers; God brought them through synchronicities.

Set a schedule. Establish a time for your daily meditation. Morning sets the tone for your day. Bedtime is also good; meditation is relaxing and helps you sleep better. If you have a busy life with children, and/or a fast-paced workday in hectic offices and public places, you can wake early to enjoy this powerful self-care.

Create a space. A personal sanctuary will enhance your meditation experience. Designate a place in your home, workplace, garden, or elsewhere for silence, privacy, and no interruptions.

You may find that a particular spot facilitates clear connections to the Divine, whereas another area makes you edgy or sleepy. If your household has blaring TVs, music, traffic, passing trains, or other noise, use headphones with soothing music to block it out.

Disconnect. Ringing, chiming, and streaming devices are the antithesis of peace. So, turn everything off or on silence with no "vibrate." Alert relevant individuals that you're unavailable for however long you devote to your practice.

Don't eat. It's best to meditate on an empty stomach or after a light snack, and when you're not drowsy. Fullness or drowsiness can cause a foggy meditation or even a nap.

Be Obedient. When you awaken your intuition, and you begin to hear guidance from within, it's important to trust it and obey it. It's always working on your behalf for the best possible outcome, even if you can't see that in the moment.

"Take the long way home," you may hear when all you want to do is hop on the freeway and hurry home. Your spirit guides are trying to protect you from danger, so heed the warning and take the long way home. Know that you will be rewarded for following instructions that are intended to provide the best outcome for you.

This is the essence of living a spirit-centered life. Opening your heart, mind, and soul to hear God speak... asking questions... receiving answers... and knowing that every divine download is providing the best blueprint for you, your purpose, and everyone you touch. Why choose to live in a space that's anything less than peaceful and fulfilling?

Your guides will tell you what to do. It's so easy to blow off a spiritual practice. That forfeits a chance for an even better day.

Is Meditation Scary? When I began to meditate, I saw and heard scary images. Years later, I felt a malicious force trying to suck me into a black hole in outer space. I called out loud for my angels and my father and Jesus, and they pulled me to safety. Non-loving entities do exist. That's why it's imperative to call in divine protection prior to venturing into the non-physical realms.

How to Meditate

Breathe! Infuse your brain and body with oxygen by taking several deep belly breaths. Exhale fully and repeat several times.

You can also practice *Pranayama*, or Alternate Nostril Breathing. Press your left thumb to close your left nostril. Inhale deeply through your open nostril, as if you're filling your gut with air. Lift your thumb and press your ring fingertip to close your right nostril. Exhale through your open nostril, until all the air is expelled. With each inhalation, savor the sensation of cool, fresh air entering your body and invigorating you. Also think about expelling the old, stale air and energy with each exhalation. Repeat several times.

Sitting with Om

Here is a simple meditation technique.

- Sit with a straight spine and your legs crossed on a blanket, pillow, or yoga mat to provide a barrier between yourself and the floor or the ground.

- Touch the tips of your thumbs to the tips of your index fingers, as if making the OK sign.
- Rest the backs of your wrists on your knees.
- Close your eyes and focus on the end of your nose or the space between your eyebrows, your "third eye."
- Press the tip of your tongue to the roof of your mouth—between your teeth and that hump in the middle.
- Repeat "Om." Say it in a drawn-out way, like "Ooooooooooo-mmmmmmmmmm." This ancient chant creates a soundwave of pure God energy that attunes you to your spiritual power. Think of Om as the password for direct, clear access to divine wi-fi.
- Enjoy the vibration through your body, washing over you like a sound bath to purify your aura.
- Repeat Om until you feel deeply relaxed.

As you meditate, you may receive guidance, ideas, or psychic flashes that help you "know" something.

Take a Shamanic Journey

A Shamanic Journey is a voyage into another dimension where you can connect with spirit-beings to obtain helpful information. Indigenous healers—"medicine men" and "medicine women"—around the world have used this technique since ancient times.

You can take a Shamanic Journey to the Upper World or the Lower World. You access the Upper World by ascending a golden light beam that passes through the lavender veil separating the earthly realm from the heavenly dimension. The Lower World is an enchanted place, and you enter through an imaginary portal in a tree that leads to a passageway—such as a stone staircase, a root-like chute, or even a crystalline cave.

Ask your spirit guides where you should go. The answer will come faster than you can think; that's how you know it's Spirit speaking, as opposed to you taking time to weigh the pro's and con's in your thinking mind.

During your Shamanic Journeys to the Upper World and the Lower World, you will hopefully enjoy two-way communication with angels, ancestors, power animals, enlightened beings such as Jesus and Buddha, and even God. My very first Shamanic Journey was extremely vivid and impactful.

You will also be totally conscious during this meditation. Doing yoga, calling in the light, and clearing your chakras beforehand will open your intuitive channels to the Divine with awesome clarity and power.

Here's what you need to take a Shamanic Journey: a chair, bed, sofa, yoga mat, pillow, or rug; an eye mask and light blanket (optional); a notebook, journal, or laptop; and earphones and meditation music. Go to your favorite music app and find 30 minutes or more of "shamanic drumming" or "binaural beats." Select one that appeals to you; Native American drumming is excellent. The drum beat serves as a "sonic driver" to induce a trance-like state and has been used by healers since ancient times. The beats alternating in your ears at 4.5 seconds "drive" your brainwaves into the Theta zone, which is just above a dream state and most conducive for meditation. Earphones enhance this effect.

Go to a quiet, private space. Sit or lay down. Cover yourself with a blanket. Listen to the music. Practice *Pranayama*, or Alternate Nostril Breathing. Close or cover your eyes.

Lay still while the music mellows you out. Then call in God, your guardian angel, Jesus, Quan Yin, the archangels, Buddha, ancestors, and other benevolent spirits to protect you as you journey into the spiritual dimension. Do not skip this step! Declare out loud:

"I am calling in an army of angels to surround me in a protective shield of love and light so that only loving spirits can come near me and my family. Archangel Michael, please protect and shield me so that only good can come of this meditation."

For this exercise, let's journey to the Upper World. Imagine a light beam that serves as your supernatural elevator shaft that is your portal to the Divine. You launch into this space via your imagination, but at some point, you will transcend into a multi-sensory experience that doesn't feel like it's coming from your own mind. You may see, hear, and experience things that you *know* you didn't make up. Listen, observe, and allow the experience to unfold.

It may feel like "wishful thinking." I know it's the Divine when I encounter beings, ideas, spoken messages, and visions that are unexpected or totally unfamiliar—nothing I've ever thought about before.

As you enter the light beam to ascend, a spirit guide may appear to escort you. This guide may be Jesus or the Hindu Goddess Lakshmi. An angel may wrap you in her wings. A Pegasus may tell you to get on its back. An ancestor may take your hand. Animal spirit guides may show up. These "power animals" have characteristics that exemplify strengths we can achieve.

Recently when I prayed for courage, many lions roared into my meditation with Jesus and my father. During a Past Life Regression, a giant bear accompanied me; bears symbolize medicine and healing energy. Plus, who wouldn't feel safe traveling to another dimension with your own personal bear for protection?

So, greet and thank your spirit guide or guides. State your intention: "Please show me what will serve my highest good today."

Next, allow your spirit-self to detach from your physical body and ascend up this beam with your guide. As you ascend, you may feel a floaty sensation. Just keep going. Pass through the lavender veil separating the physical world from the heavenly realm. Land in your "power spot" which is your portal back.

This experience is different for everyone, so observe what you see, feel, and hear. Don't worry about doing it right or wrong. If it's not

TWO SISTERS
WRITING & PUBLISHING™

Elizabeth Ann Atkins

18530 Mack Avenue, Suite #166, Grosse Pointe Farms, MI 48236 USA

313-492-5718

Elizabeth@TwoSistersWriting.com

October 11, 2020

Sir Richard Branson
Virgin Management Limited
The Battleship Building
179 Harrow Road
London, W2 6NB
United Kingdom

Dear Sir Branson

Thank you for brilliantly shining your light on the world!

We share a reverence for former South African President Nelson Mandela.

For that, and the many reasons that I admire you and your work, please find enclosed the gift of an autographed copy of my memoir, *God's Answer Is Know: Lessons From a Spiritual Life.*

Please enjoy my life story, which centers on a personal quest for inner peace and a collective mission to cultivate human harmony worldwide.

I'm joining your book club as well. THANK YOU for providing a literary realm to promote inspiration and knowledge for all of us to ascend into higher realms of being.

Wishing you peace & power,

Elizabeth Ann Atkins
Co-Creator
Two Sisters Writing & Publishing

clear, and your "thinking mind" is still churning over worries or your to-do list, don't quit. With practice, meditation can work for you.

Next, allow your spirit-self to call to God, Archangel Michael, Archangel Gabriel, your grandmother, or whomever you decided you would contact. You may see, feel, hear, or sense a presence. Or you just "know" that you are with God and the angels. You can offer a greeting. They may take you somewhere—to a throne, an altar, a forest, a house, or anywhere. Then ask: "Please show me what will serve my highest good today."

You may hear words, see symbols, or be shown visions. Ask questions. Listen. When the interaction concludes, thank God and/or the angels and/or other beings who helped you.

Then your spirit guide will take you back to your power spot, to descend through the veil, down the golden beam, back to your physical body. Observe any more messages or visions that you receive. Like coming to the last page of a great book, you may feel like, "I don't want it to end!" Because this ultra-relaxed state feels phenomenal! Notice the stillness in your body and the slowness of your heartbeat and breathing. Achieving this meditative state regularly has tremendous mental and physical health benefits.

Slowly "come back" by wiggling your fingers and toes. Take some deep breaths and savor the stillness. When you're ready, uncover your eyes and sit up.

What did God and divine beings say to you? Did they answer your questions? Did you receive instructions? Notice how you feel now. Use your journal, notebook, or laptop to record your experience in the divine dimension and refer back to it as you incorporate this guidance into your life.

#4 Chronicle Your Journey: Write.

You can communicate with God and the spirit world through writing. Pressing a pen to paper enables you to embark on an infinite rhythm of asking and answering. As you record God's answers, you deepen your knowing that this omniscient power is a brilliant guiding light within you. Writing can also help you interact with enlightened beings such as Jesus, Yogananda, Mother Mary, angels, ancestors, power animals, and helpful spirits.

Here are three ways that you can use writing to cultivate a spirit-centered life.

Journaling. Some of history's most creative geniuses—including Leonardo daVinci, Virginia Woolf, Albert Einstein, and Maya Angelou—kept journals to record their ideas, feelings, and experiences. A journal can be a plain notebook, a cloth-covered diary, computer files, even voice recordings on your phone if you don't like to write.

A journal is where you can privately write whatever you desire—your fears, your dreams, your traumas, your triumphs—and no other pair of eyes need ever view your words. For that reason, a journal is a deeply personal and therapeutic place to purge your negative emotions, explore questions about yourself, and devote time to spiritual contemplation.

Writing is a sacred act of creation. It enables you to engage in the literary alchemy of transcribing your thoughts into physical form as you experience epiphanies along your spiritual journey. Please keep a journal to chronicle your spiritual evolution, then someday teach what you've learned, start a blog, make videos, even write a book or screenplay.

Intuitive Writing or Automatic Writing. This is the best-kept secret that's literally hiding under your fingertips. Intuitive Writing allows God to speak to you through writing. You become a clear channel to receive divine downloads that can help you live and love to your highest capacity and in alignment with your soul's highest purpose.

These supernatural communications flash into your mind and

through your pen unhindered by your thinking mind, thus bypassing the creativity-crushing minefield of fear, worry, and doubt that lurks in the conscious mind. Then you are literally transcribing messages from the voice of God within you.

You can achieve this when you get into a meditative state prior to Intuitive Writing. Then, while poised to write, ask a question of God. Write whatever comes to mind, and just keep writing. This "stream of consciousness" will open the floodgates of ideas and insights that flash so quickly, your hand will seemingly write automatically, expressing messages that have been locked away in your heart and soul for a long time.

Write for 20 minutes, or for as long as you desire. You can use Intuitive Writing anytime you have a pressing question and need divine guidance.

Meditation + Journaling = Revelation & Transformation

When I combined journaling with meditation, PowerJournal was born. It facilitates supernatural communications that activate life-changing power. Thus, the name.

PowerJournal sounds like a noun, but it's a verb, because it's about action. To PowerJournal is to: set an intention to receive specific information; get into a meditative state; ask questions; write the answers; answer questions with Intuitive Writing; and journal as insights and instructions percolate in your mind.

PowerJournal is an important "how to" aspect of *God's Answer is Know*. It allows you to learn God's Answers, so you will Know how to best live your life.

That's why, to demonstrate how to PowerJournal, I'm beginning with an exercise: PowerJournal to Know Your Life Purpose & Action Plan. You can use this method to answer any question by setting that as your intention. You can also use our workbooks— *PowerJournal for Spiritual Awakening* and *PowerJournal to Know Your*

Life Purpose— available where books are sold online. Please also visit PowerJournal.Life to join our private online community.

Let's PowerJournal to Know Your Life Purpose & Action Plan

Do you feel that you've been pursuing a path that has been unsuccessful, unfulfilling, or worse? What if that's God's way of telling you that you're pursuing the wrong path, and that when you discover your soul's mission during this lifetime, a more fulfilling, prosperous, and impactful life will evolve for you?

Let's find out! We're going to PowerJournal by combining journaling with a Shamanic Journey meditation (see instructions in the previous chapter). Settle into your meditation space, open your journal or laptop, and write:

PowerJournal to Know My Life Purpose & Action Plan

Date, time, location

Intention: "My intention is to ask God to reveal my life purpose and an action plan to make it happen."

Begin this practice in a spirit of gratitude and knowing that it will work. Write: *"Thank you God for revealing my life purpose and action plan."* Do a breathing exercise. Sit or lay down. Cover yourself with a blanket. Listen to meditation music. Close your eyes or use an eye mask. Call in the light and divine protection.

Let's journey to the Upper World. Ponder your intention as you envision a golden beam that you ascend with a spirit guide. Pass through the veil, land in your power spot, and allow your spirit-self to call to God and ask, "God, what is my purpose for this lifetime? And what is the action plan for making it happen?"

You may hear words, feel an impression, or see visions. Ask questions. When the conversation concludes, thank God and any other beings. Then your spirit guide will take you to your power spot, through the veil, down the beam, back to your physical body. Observe any more messages or visions that you receive.

Slowly acclimate to your body. Now write as many details as you can remember. What did God say is your life purpose and action plan? Even if it felt and looked fantastical, as if you were making it up, or like something impossible, write it. Then use Intuitive Writing to allow any more ideas to pour forth from your soul. Know that God is speaking to you, through you, within you. Write everything, even if it seems meaningless. Ask questions and listen for answers to shoot like lightning through your head.

This is your opportunity to continue your one-on-one, private conversation with God! This is about your future, so don't be shy, and don't clam up. God already knows what you're thinking, feeling, and doing, because God is already inside you. Now it's time to start hearing and heeding this wisdom.

If God told you a life mission that seems impossible, continue in future prayers and meditations to ask, "What is the first step I need to take to achieve this great task?" Pray for courage to do it. Trust that God will provide the resources. And know that God's will is always done.

#5: Command Mission Control: Honor your temple.

"Do you not know that your bodies are temples of the Holy Spirit,
who is in you, whom you have received from God?
Therefore honor God with your bodies."
—1 Corinthians 6:19-20.

Your body is your temple, and it includes the space around you, which is your "light body." It's the airspace, grounds, and earth around your temple. As such, we need to treat ourselves with the same reverence as a place of worship.

Would you stand in the middle of the sanctuary and shout insults? Would you litter the altar or lawn with junk food? Would you blast music with vulgar and violent lyrics in the sanctuary? Would you smoke a cigarette? Would you show a horror movie in a temple? Would you host a meeting with the most negative, gossiping people you know inside a chapel? Would you turn up the volume on a newscast about crime, corruption, and chaos inside a spiritual retreat?

No.

So, if your body is the temple where God dwells, why would you subject it to: hateful self-talk; toxic substances; music with negative lyrics; gossip and criticism; and bad news? You wouldn't. So let's explore how to honor your temple.

Eating A Super Natural Diet Creates A Supernatural Life

Call it God's Diet. Mother Earth's Meal Plan. Or Sunshine Foods.

Because the best nutrition comes straight from nature. The goal of spiritual awakening is to raise your vibrational frequency as high as possible, because that—like a strong radio signal or five bars on your cell phone— gives you the strongest connection to God and the spiritual dimension.

Whole, organic foods such as fruits and vegetables raise your vibrational frequency, whereas fake foods that are manufactured— such as candy bars, soda pop, and fluorescent orange snack chips— lower it, clouding your connection.

The key ingredient that creates these whole, organic foods is sunshine. You should eat as much sunshine as possible. What? Leaves on plants and trees absorb the sun's rays, which react with a chemical called chlorophyll, which makes the leaves turn green.

Some of the highest vibrational foods are leafy greens, fruits, vegetables, and herbs. All of which grow on plants and trees that soaked up sunshine. By eating this food, you're consuming sunshine. And what evokes more happiness or exudes more power than the sun? Nothing.

You can get those greens into your body by drinking a vegetable smoothie twice a day. They boost your immunity, your mood, your energy, and your overall well-being. To make a Green Goddess Drink, you'll need: kale leaves, spinach leaves, avocado, a jalapeno pepper (if you like spicy), a garlic clove (optional), a flavorful herb such as basil, spring water, coconut water, or almond milk. Use fresh, organic ingredients when possible, and wash them thoroughly.

"Are you drinking your grass clippings today?" family members tease. Once, my son's buddy said, "Miss Elizabeth, it looks like you dipped your glass in a pond and a frog is going to jump out."

It *will* taste like swamp water without ingredients that create creaminess. They include avocado, chia seeds, hemp seeds, nuts, and Greek yogurt. These ingredients add protein and healthy fats, which suppress your appetite and make your skin glow. Experiment with your favorite ingredients. If you add fruit, it can add hundreds of calories and lots of sugar.

Don't chug a green drink if you're boarding an airplane or leading a presentation. My friends joke that my high-fiber drink sends them to the nearest bathroom for an extended stay. If you've been eating a low-fiber diet, your intestines are probably holding gunk that can weigh you down and make you sick. A clean gut improves your health and heightens your intuition, which speaks through a "gut feeling."

Fresh herbs are a fun way to enhance the taste and health-boosting benefits of your green drink and food. Here are some of my favorites:

Basil. Toss basil leaves with fresh garlic and pine nuts, along with your kale and spinach, and your taste buds will be celebrating this delicious drink. Basil helps your digestion, boosts your mood, helps detoxify your body, and is anti-inflammatory.

Parsley. This natural diuretic can reduce bloating and puffiness from water retention.

Cilantro. Best known as the green specks in salsa, cilantro is a powerful detoxifier that can help remove heavy metal toxins from eating salmon and other foods. It's great in your drink with garlic, tomato, and avocado. Cilantro can help your skin, fight diseases, reduce cholesterol, stabilize your blood sugar, and strengthen your eyes.

Thyme. It can raise your vibrational frequency, reduce stress, help your breathing, boost your heart health and immunity, and prevent infections and diseases.

Mint. It adds a refreshing and delicious kick to your green drinks! It freshens your breath, helps with digestion and weight loss, combats depression and fatigue, and helps your skin glow.

What are your favorite herbs? Experiment with flavors, then give your green drink a personalized name, like Jeannie's Goddess Gulp or Tom's Turmeric Tonic.

Medicinal Spices & Garlic

Open my kitchen cabinet and you'll find spices that I consume every day on beans, meat, poultry, and fish for their taste and medicinal qualities. They are turmeric; cayenne; black pepper; cumin; curry; and Himalayan pink sea salt. Turmeric, for example, reduces inflammation and kills cancer cells, among other benefits (when paired with black pepper). As you incorporate healthier eating into your day, which is a microcosm for your life, experiment with spices and research their health benefits. Or research what spices can help with your specific ailments.

Garlic is a powerhouse for health. Enjoy it in green drinks, in soup, and on food. Add it to olive oil and balsamic vinegar as salad dressing. Sometimes I smash raw garlic into half an avocado on a plate, sprinkle with sea salt and fresh pepper... and it is delicious!

What Should You Drink?

Soda pop has no nutritional value. It's a manufactured substance, mixed on machines with sugar, artificial flavors, and chemicals that make it colorful. Sugar-free soda is even worse; many believe that artificial sweeteners cause cancer.

If you want something fizzy, try carbonated mineral water, and mix it with organic real fruit juice (not punch, which is fake-dyed sugar water).

Also, drink lots of water. Just slight dehydration—before you even feel thirsty—can impair your thinking. And if you can't think clearly, you are not feeling your best or doing your best.

What about alcohol? I've had my share of tequila shots and vodka drinks. While wining, dining, and loving it, headache and fatigue prevented me from working the next day. The indulgence isn't worth it. The choice is yours. The same goes for marijuana. I don't smoke or use intoxicants, and I stopped drinking alcohol because it dulls your intuition. I'd rather have strong spiritual powers than a buzz.

But What About Comfort Foods?

Ice cream and peanut butter were once my favorite comfort foods. Now I don't eat them at all, because they were also binge foods. Still, we all love comfort foods, so what can you eat when you're craving them?

My go-to comfort food is soup. I create delicious concoctions that start with organic, no-sodium tomato sauce, then I may add navy beans, garlic, basil, mushrooms, kale, and olive oil. You can add spices and sea salt. A hearty bowl of homemade soup—which does not take long to prepare—is delicious, hot, steaming, and soothing for the soul. Plus it will fill you up without filling you out.

Another favorite indulgence? Frozen bananas. Peel them, and place in freezer containers. Before eating one, let it thaw on a plate just long enough for your fork to press through it. Then savor the cold, sweet, creaminess. You can also puree bananas in a blender, then freeze the puree and eat it like ice cream.

Get creative to enjoy comfort foods that are healthy.

Excess Sugar Is Toxic

Fearing borderline diabetes during pregnancy, and having consumed excessive sugar in my past, I eat only enough natural sugar to keep my brain and body fueled for my work and workouts.

I've read that refined sugar: feeds cancer cells; increases the risk of diabetes; accelerates aging by weakening collagen; causes weight gain; and clouds your intuition, to name a few. I also don't miss the mood swings inflicted by a sugar binge: super high, then super low, exacerbated by feeling guilty and fat.

If I have a craving—such as for flourless chocolate cake, or dark chocolate—I indulge in moderation. What stops me from pigging out is the threat of consequences that I have known too well in the past. Since we know better, we should do better.

But we don't always. Last summer, I satisfied a craving with an organic dark chocolate bar. It was so creamy and delicious, I ate the whole thing and felt euphoric. The next day I was really sad!

Don't Keep Your Temple Open At All Hours

Some people think it's vogue to sacrifice sleep. I used to stay up all night writing as a college student and new mom. Now I'm very committed to getting eight hours of sleep every night. This makes me feel my best emotionally, physically, and spiritually. If I'm too sleepy, I get drowsy or foggy when attempting to meditate or write.

Sleep is also another way you can connect with the Divine, as dreams often provide messages and your spirit guides may speak clearly in that phase just before you wake up, so you can remember their guidance.

Move Your Body!

A strong body equals a strong mind, both of which provide a powerful vessel for Spirit. Choose exercises and activities that you love.

Yoga opens your channels to your Godpower within. But if you don't like yoga, don't do it. If you've never tried it, experiment with teachers and styles. Use online videos and ask friends to recommend a local studio.

Every morning I do an ancient yoga practice called The Five Tibetans. It's quick, easy, and according to the experts, extends the ends of your DNA called telomeres to reverse aging. This routine wakes me up, soothes my soul, and sets the stage for a better day.

That includes exercise. Do you like to walk, take bike rides, swim? Choose a form of exercise that you enjoy. Fitness will help you feel better by elevating your mood, reducing excess weight, and improving your overall health.

Sex: Do I Have to Live Like a Nun or a Monk?

When you're intimate with someone, you're fusing energy. If they have low vibrational energy, it will bring yours down. If they're promiscuous with low vibration people, they bring all that to you. If your promiscuous partner is male, he's literally inserting his negative energy—and that of his partners—inside you.

Even worse, if he ejaculates inside you, his sperm—his living DNA—is injected into your body. A study showed that women in their 90s had living male DNA in their brains and other body parts. Researchers concluded that the sperm burrowed into spaces where those living cells containing another person's DNA lived for the rest of the women's lives.

"Never have sex with someone you wouldn't want to be," I once read. That study showed why: that person becomes part of you when their living cells take up residence in your body. Do you want that person to become part of your physical and spiritual being?

That is an extremely sobering way to view sexual relations. And don't think a condom will block their bad energy. Once you engage in the act and that person's body part is inside you, their energy permeates you. So be mindful of whose energy field you choose to fuse with your own.

You have the freedom to choose as many partners as you desire. This liberation for women is very important. But it's not all about fun and pleasure. It's about energy. And once you begin to elevate yours, you may decide to only share it with people who are also doing the spiritual work to honor our bodies as the temples that we are.

This sobering revelation inspired me to choose celibacy while staying independent and reveling in self-discovery.

Work with Crystals

You can charge your energy field with the high frequency vibration of crystals.

Crystals have healing powers. These beautiful stones from Mother Earth have properties that can enhance your health, prosperity, romance, protection, peace, communication, creativity, and anything you can think of.

My crystal teacher is Deborah Burton of http://www.meta physicalRealm1.com. The magical energy of 14,000 crystals inside her boutique in Sedona, Arizona made me shiver with joy. On her website, you can learn about each crystal's qualities, and purchase them. You can also email her to ask what crystals are best for what you need.

Catherine gifted me with one of Deb's "Prosperity Kits" which contain eight different crystals. The colorful, powerful crystals on my desk and around my home are delightful. I hold certain crystals while clearing my chakras, meditating, and going about various tasks. I especially love my pink Rose Quartz hearts; this is the crystal for love and peace.

Detox with Salt

Salt has healing and detoxifying powers. Many people with skin ailments and other health problems travel to the Dead Sea between Israel and Jordan to immerse in water saturated with minerals—including sea salt.

Now I exfoliate with pink Himalayan sea salt on an all-natural body brush in the shower. Moisturizing with coconut oil concludes this practice that's especially powerful during a new moon and full moon.

Himalayan salt lamps around my home cast a rosy-peachy glow, and they supposedly charge and purify the air, encouraging serenity and better sleep.

Purify Your Space with Sage

One night, a bad dream woke me. The next day, I felt an energy that made the hairs on the back of my neck stand, and I felt chills, not in a good way.

"Smudge the house," my father said.

Rooted in Native American ceremonies for spiritual cleansing, "smudging" involves using a bundle of sage that's wrapped with string to create a "smudging stick." You burn the end of it, and when the flames subside, you use the smoke to ward off negative and evil energy by carrying it from room to room.

"God please clear this energy so that only loving spirits can enter," I prayed while waving the smoke through my house. "I am calling on all angels and all the power of the Divine to cleanse and clear my home so that only loving spirits may enter."

As I purified my home with sage, I felt the negative energy dissipate; the air around me felt lighter, more clear. It's good to do this if you've hosted guests or experienced something whose energy you'd like to clear.

A small bottle of pure sage essential oil on my desk helps me focus after a distraction or annoyance. The scent is absolutely heavenly! Inhaling sage is a way to take a moment to savor life's simple pleasures.

Be in Nature

Fresh air and sunshine are not just the stuff of poems. Being in nature boosts your mood, your health, and your vibrational frequency to connect with the Divine. You feel better. Sunshine helps your body manufacture Vitamin D, which is crucial to good health. Walking barefoot on the grass, dirt, rocks, and sand grounds you to Mother Earth, and breathing in fresh air is exhilarating.

Step #6: Meet Your Team.

Teamwork makes the dream work, so you need a great team, which has three parts: you, other people, and spirit beings.

Love Yourself

We are God, and God is love, so we are love, right? Not always.

The terms self-hatred and self-loathing exist for a reason. They are a problem for too many of us. Spiritual empowerment enables us to heal, reprogram our minds, and fall in love with ourselves.

This is an inside job. It starts with releasing the need for approval, permission, affirmation, or praise from others. It also requires not filling yourself up with someone else's opinions or preferences or interests.

Love yourself with the same enthusiasm and awe as when you fall in love with another person. You know that feeling, where you want to spend all your time with that person and know everything about them? Apply that same infatuation to yourself! Spend time alone. Earn your PhMe. Become an expert on you. Our *PowerJournal 28-Day Challenge* helps you do that by asking, *Who am I? What do I want? Am I ready for change?* and *What action is required?*

Here are more ways to love yourself.

Do the Mirror Work. This means looking at yourself in the mirror and saying kind things to yourself. If you're not ready to declare,

"I love you," then start with something like, "I promise to treat myself better." Look into your own eyes and say it like you mean it. Imagine you're talking to a beloved friend or relative. If they were feeling bad, think of the compassion and concern you would express.

Even at your lowest point, know that a brilliant, beautiful diamond lies within the jagged rock of self-hatred or disappointment you may feel. Chip away at the rock, and the diamond will sparkle. You can polish the way you perceive yourself with mantras or affirmations, such as, "I am a divine child of God and God loves me," or "Every day I am becoming my best me," or "I am awesome!" Make up your own mantra, and say it to yourself, out loud, as often as possible.

Commit to change what needs improvement and make peace with that which you cannot change.

Give yourself "unconditional love," which is how you feel about a person for whom you would give your last breath. If you are a parent, your child may elicit that feeling. If you have a beloved pet, they may elicit unconditional love. Try to transfer that emotion onto yourself. Does it stick? If not, why? Do this often to strengthen your I-love-myself-unconditionally muscle until it flexes automatically.

Reprogram Your Thinking with Audio and Video. The blessing of two new relationships inspired me to banish the ghosts of failed friendships. When disappointment and doubt from the past tried to cloud the present, I declared out loud, "I refuse" to have these thoughts. Then I made a videotape of myself on my phone, telling myself to stop! I spoke with authority—saying the past is gone, the present is a gift, and I want to experience new relationships with peace and trust.

Here's how to reprogram your thinking.

1. Talk to yourself out loud to stop the thoughts. You can't dwell on something and talk at the same time.

2. Ask for help. I asked my father to help me clear negative thinking, and he told me to ask my guardian angel, David John, to remove the thoughts. It worked!

3. Make audio and video recordings, telling yourself in great detail how you now think and feel—with trust, confidence, and focus on the joy of new relationships, not the fear of what could go wrong or what has not worked in the past.

These techniques work—fast!

They result in spaciousness and expansiveness.

That's how I feel, inside and out.

It's like I emptied cluttered closets whose shelves were straining under heavy bins of anxiety, angst, sadness, guilt, regret, and fear. This toxic storage contaminated my mind with negative thinking, made my chest burn with anxiety, and corroded my scalp with an angry red, scaly eczema outbreak.

My spiritual journey has cleaned the closets and illuminated a pristine space to welcome a whole new life. At first, spaciousness was so dramatic, it startled me.

What's that feeling?

It was the absence of feeling anxious or afraid or sad.

I truly have banished all fear, worry, and doubt.

"Thank you, God!" The change was gradual; the revelation was sudden. And glorious!

Seeking a Soul Mate? Elevate Your Own First!

The answer to finding your soulmate is to first become the person you've been seeking all these years. You want the best possible partner. Make a list of all the qualities you want in a mate. Are you bringing all that to the union? If not, you're not ready.

And if you're seeking another person to "complete" you or "make you happy" or be your "other half," then you're cheating yourself out of the best possible relationship. This mentality gives away your power, by thinking that this person is going to rescue you; that's a set-up for disappointment and resentment when the other person fails to do what you should do for yourself.

Be everything for yourself first.

Alone. From the inside out. It takes work. And discipline. Because it's not fun when you yearn for touch and comfort and love from someone who has yet to show up. But the consequence of settling for someone less than what you deserve is not worth the wasted time, energy, and angst.

Know that your beloved will appear after you go within, seek divine guidance, and do the work to attract your ideal mate.

Find a New Tribe

Once you begin to ascend, you'll be intolerant of people and situations that don't vibe with your spiritual quest. Going out for drinks, eating junk food, gossiping, and dwelling on negativity will no longer interest you.

As you recalibrate your spiritual frequency, you'll attract new teachers, friends, groups, and opportunities to learn. These individuals and groups can be online, and you can join Meet Up groups or go on a spiritual retreat to connect with like-minded people.

Some of my teachers are online astrologers whom I've been watching for years. My father loved astrology, and ever since my roommate in San Diego did my chart, I've been hooked on how planets affect us as individuals, as the collective and the earth. My sun sign is cancer, which is ruled by the moon. I get "full moon insomnia." Understanding Mercury Retrograde, eclipses, and planetary cycles can help you plan and maximize success.

I also discovered several online tarot readers who often seem like they're doing the reading just for me, because they're so accurate with my circumstances about career, self, and relationships.

Your Spiritual Team

Who is your guardian angel? Who are your spirit guides? You can get acquainted with them by going into meditation and setting the intention to meet your spiritual team.

Notice Messages in Signs & Symbols All Around You

One day while driving, my mind was whirling with worries. As I looked left to merge, a hand-written sign taped to a street sign said: Trust Jesus.

I laughed out loud! Could a message get any more clear than that? This is a perfect example of how the Divine is always communicating with us. But we only get the messages if we're paying attention and noticing the synchronicities all day and night.

Another time, I was baffled about how to accomplish a certain goal. Then a big yellow bus whizzed past and its side said Trinity Transportation. The message? The Divine will get you there, quickly.

When you know that nothing is a coincidence, and that everything is divinely orchestrated to help you awaken to your spirit self, you will notice messages from the Divine everywhere. You may overhear a snippet of conversation in public, or see a billboard, or pick up a book.

You may be wondering whether you should go on a date with the person you just met. As you're thinking, you hear police sirens. Perhaps that's a warning. On the other hand, you may be thinking of this person when you glance up and see the word "celestial" on a poster or street sign.

Sometimes the message comes through a dilemma. You're about to leave for an event, and you can't find your car keys. You search everywhere, but they're lost. You miss the event. Perhaps that's the

Divine saying you weren't supposed to go. You may even learn that something happened at the event where you could have been hurt; in hindsight you're grateful that the Divine was protecting you.

Here are common ways that divine messages show up:

Number Sequences. When my spiritual awakening began, 44 and 444 appeared on the clock, my car's odometer, receipts. Then I discovered that repeating numbers are the Divine's way of communicating with us. And 444 means "angels are around you." What number sequences are you seeing?

Birds & Insects. Hummingbirds, blue jays, cardinals, butterflies, and spiders appear frequently, and I look up their spiritual meaning. Sometimes they "whisper" a message. Pay attention to what these messengers are telling you.

Animals. We all have at least one spirit animal whose characteristics reflect your personality and can teach you something. So when a spirit animal comes to you in meditation, or you see it in dreams, movies, magazines, online, and on TV, look up "spiritual meaning of bear," for example. What is that animal conveying to you?

Coins. Sometimes the glimmer of a coin catches my attention right when I'm thinking about something. Often the coin is in an odd place. A message comes to mind that I needed to hear. Our loved ones in heaven often speak through coins, which may have special meaning for you.

Song Lyrics. Have you ever been thinking about something or someone, and suddenly song lyrics express something you need to hear? That's no coincidence! Are the lyrics an affirmation or a warning?

Feathers. Feathers are a symbol from the Divine that you are safe. You may be worried about something, and at the exact moment of thinking about it, you glance down and see a feather. Once, I was anxious about a trip and took a jog. As my mind churned with questions, I glanced up at the sunset sky and saw a cloud that looked like a giant pink feather! I took that as affirmation that the trip would be safe and full of love, and it was.

Nature. One day I was standing on the dry cement slab of a lighthouse pier on Lake Michigan. It was a beautiful summer day, and I was casting prayers over the calm blue waters. I had a long list of prayers and wishes, gazing at the calm-as-glass water for a while. No boats were going by; I prayed silently: "God please help me someday win an Oscar for best screenplay for the movie based on *Dark Secret*."

Splash! Water splashed up on my face! Out of nowhere! I took that as affirmation.

Dreams. Dreams are a powerful way for the Divine to speak to us. Keep a notebook by your bed and write them down when you awaken, then look up the spiritual meaning of the animal, object, or action in your dream.

Step #7: Lighten Your Load.

Whatever has been holding you down has actually helped propel you to the launchpad. But shooting into the next stratosphere requires you to drop extra weight. That can be people, bad habits, addictions, fat, fears, anxieties, time-drains, and more. Let's lighten your load to prepare for lift-off.

Release Past Pain and Past Life Traumas

Your load might be ancient. It may result from events in past lives that scarred your soul and came into this life. Now this fear, habit, or belief system is stopping you from being your best. But how do you determine the root of the problem?

You can visit the Akashic Records. This archive in the spiritual dimension is an enormous book containing information about your past lives, along with records of everything that ever was, is, and will be.

You can access the Akashic Records via meditation. Follow my instructions for a Shamanic Journey, and use the PowerJournal technique to set your Intention as this: *"I intend to visit the Akashic Records to discover what happened in a past life that caused my terrible fear of _____, so that I can forgive the experience and release the fear in this lifetime."*

You can fill in the blank with anything: water, fire, heights, a type of food, trains, or whatever is troubling you.

When you meet your spirit guide, state your intention. Your guide will escort you up the beam, to the Akashic Records. Be open to observing how this unfolds for you. My experience is that we travel through the purple-blackness of outer space, up to a place surrounded by gold gates. The keeper will let you in with your guide, who will state your name, date, time, and location of your birth, and the knowledge you're seeking. The keeper will then turn to the giant book on a stone table behind him and open it. Video-type images may rise from the open book, to show you answers.

You may even feel transported inside the scene. Listen, observe, and remember everything. When it's over, thank the keeper and your guide, who will escort you back into 3D reality.

Now write everything you experienced and hold the intention of releasing the fear.

Past Life Regression

Another way to resolve traumas, addictions, and other hindrances is through Past Life Regression, the technique that Dr. Brian Weiss described in *Many Lives, Many Masters*. In this process conducted by a trained professional, you're led into a hypnotic, meditative state where you visit your past lives to identify a trauma that plagues you today. If you're afraid of water, you may have drowned in a past life. When you discover this, the professional guides you through a process of understanding what happened, then forgiving and releasing it.

I underwent this process with the goal of resolving anything blocking prosperity. The experience took me back hundreds of years to a European convent. I was a nun. My food, shelter, and clothing were provided by the church. I never touched money. Never made a budget, bought a house, went to the market, or negotiated a deal. I had no relationship with financial matters. And I had taken a vow of poverty, then—and I already knew—in several lives as a nun. I then nullified those vows during a healing meditation.

Release Attachments

Life brings suffering when we crave what we don't have, and when we feel attachments to people, things, and experiences. This premise of the Buddhist philosophy is based on the idea that suffering is part of life, and that it's exacerbated by our desires and attachments. You can find the remedy—joy and spiritual enlightenment—by following a path that has two lanes: first, refusing to be a slave to our desires; and second, releasing attachments. Easier said than done! However, when you commit to these principles and do the work, the rewards are extraordinary.

What are your cravings and attachments? How are they holding you back? How can you release them?

Would you rather stay stuck in a pleasure-seeking lifestyle at the expense of ascending into a higher realm of creating, prospering, and influencing? It's your choice.

You can push your reset button when you activate the Godpower within. It will put you on autopilot to ascend. This will lift you out of your comfort zone—a very toxic place. It feels cozy in the moment, but it's trapping you from going out into the world to take chances and maximize your potential. Are you ready to step into an infinite you?

Step #8: Heal Your Vessel.

What's hurting you—physically, emotionally, and spiritually? Are you struggling with addictions, bad habits, and physical pain? You can heal your mind, body, and spirit by connecting to the Divine through meditation and journaling.

"The wound is where the light comes in," said the ancient poet Rumi. But before we can let the light come in, we need to heal the wound with the help of God and Archangel Raphael.

> *Disclaimer: I am not a physician or a psychologist. If you have a serious mental or physical medical condition, please continue with your doctor's prescribed medical regimen.*

Give Yourself the Gift of Forgiveness

Forgiveness means healing yourself by releasing hurtful feelings caused by something that you or someone else did. To forgive is "to cease to feel resentment against" an offender, according to Merriam-Webster's dictionary. Notice that forgiveness is an inside job. It's a shift in feelings.

"Resentment is like drinking poison and then hoping it will kill your enemies," Nelson Mandela said.

Failing to forgive only hurts you more, well after the offense was committed. Forgiveness is a major tenet of spirituality. In fact, *The Lord's Prayer* says, "Forgive those who trespass against us." But how? I did not understand how to truly forgive until I was 49 years old, standing at my ex-husband's bedside in the ICU while a breathing machine kept him alive.

"I forgive you," I said aloud. My motivation was love for our son. The power of forgiveness lifted a heavy weight from my shoulders and enabled me to help him, and to bless our son with a fully functioning father. Plus his near-death experience made him a much nicer person and we finally achieved "the harmonious resolution" that I had scripted years before.

I have since applied my PowerJournal technique to forgive myself for things that gnawed at me with guilt and anger. Releasing bad feelings toward myself opens space for love and peace to pour in, which make me feel and function better. Forgiveness is a gift that we give ourselves.

So let's PowerJournal for Forgiveness, by combining meditation and journaling. For this emotional healing, we're calling on God's healing angel, Archangel Raphael, to perform his powerful alchemy to transform negative emotions into peace and love. To start, write:

PowerJournal to Forgive Myself.

Date, time, location

My intention is to ask Archangel Raphael for a healing to forgive myself for _____ so that I can replace guilt and regret with peace and love.

List reasons why you want to forgive yourself. I recently listed everything for which I needed to forgive myself, then released it. For example: *My Intention is to forgive myself for wasting years of time, energy, money, and productivity on my struggles with food, fat, and the misery that accompanied it.* Feel grateful and confident that this healing will rid you of bad feelings toward yourself. Write: *"Thank you God that I forgave myself."*

Do a breathing exercise, then follow the instructions for a Shamanic Journey.

Let's journey to the Lower World. Think of your favorite tree or any beautiful tree and imagine a small door at its base. This is your entrance to the Lower World. As you approach, you will encounter your spirit guide, who will accompany you into the divine realm by entering the tree trunk. There, imagine a giant root that you can slide down. You may also envision a stone staircase or even a crystalline tunnel.

At the end, land in your "power spot," which is your portal for returning to the physical world. You may experience the Lower World as an enchanted forest, a mountainside, an Atlantis-type underwater wonderland, a rocky terrain, or something else. Simply observe what you hear, see, and feel. Your spirit guide will remain with you.

Next, allow your spirit-self to call to Archangel Raphael, whom you may see, feel, or simply know that he is there. God's healing angel performs his healings amidst the emerald green light of the heart chakra, which symbolizes pure love. So you may notice flashes of emerald green, or you may see a giant angel, or the outline of wings.

Tell him your intention to forgive yourself. Archangel Raphael may take you to a particular place or lay you on a bed. Other beings may appear. My healings with Archangel Raphael sometimes include Native American medicine men, as well as wolves and bears.

Since the Divine communicates through metaphors, you may envision that he's removing an object representing the offense for which you're seeking forgiveness. For example, if you want to forgive yourself for something that has manifest as guilt, he may pull a slimy net from your body, symbolizing how the negative emotion had permeated you. Every healing meditation with Archangel Raphael is different, depending on the nature of the ailment. Sometimes, no physical object is removed.

His healing power is all about transmutation. In physics class, we learned the Law of Conservation of Energy: Energy can be neither created nor destroyed. It just changes form. Well Archangel Raphael takes the energy that's hurting you and transmutes it into healing energy. He does this by removing your affliction and putting it in a lavender flame that activates metaphysical alchemy. The lavender flame appears to me as a shallow gold cauldron of vibrant purple fire, similar to the one that holds the Olympic flame. It may appear differently for you.

Your ailment crackles, transforms, and shoots up from the flame in golden sparkles or an emerald green mist, which he directs back into your body as healing energy.

"It is done," he says, which indicates your healing is complete. Thank him and listen for instructions.

Next, your spirit guide will return you to your power spot and escort you through the tree to your body. After you adjust, write as many details as you remember. Use Intuitive Writing to answer more questions.

Forgiveness doesn't mean forgetting. It's important to remember what caused the need for forgiveness. Remembering our own mistakes helps us avoid repeating them.

> *Disclaimer:* **I am not a physician.** *If you have a serious medical condition, please continue with your doctor's prescribed medical regimen.*

PowerJournal for Healing

Meditation and journaling can accelerate your healing, ease your symptoms, and relieve pain. Activating the Godpower within you can change your body on a cellular level. To start, write:

> *PowerJournal for Healing.*

> *Date, time, location*

> *My intention is to ask Archangel Raphael to heal my _____ and restore me to perfect health.*

Then express your gratitude and knowing that it will work: *"Thank you God for making me feel excellent. And thank you for this healing that reveals to me what is causing this pain, so that I can prevent it forever."*

Metaphysics 101 teaches that pain is the manifestation of negative energy; when we discover what that energy is, we can clear it and heal it. Write anything else that pours from your heart and soul regarding the ailment.

Do a breathing exercise, then follow instructions for a Shamanic Journey.

Let's journey to the Lower World as described in PowerJournal for Forgiveness. Your spirit guide will meet you at the tree portal to escort you down to your power spot. Express your intention. Next, allow your spirit-self to call to Archangel Raphael, who may show up with flashes of emerald green, or you may see a giant angel, or the outline of wings.

Tell him your intention to heal; he may take you to a particular place or lay you on a bed. Other beings may appear. Observe and listen as Archangel Raphael takes the energy that's hurting you and transmutes it into healing energy. He does this by removing the affliction and putting it in a lavender flame that activates metaphysical alchemy.

The ailment transforms in the fire, shoots up in golden sparkles or an emerald green mist, which he directs back into your body as healing energy.

"It is done," he says. Your healing is complete. Thank him and listen for instructions. Now your spirit guide will return you to your power spot and escort you through the tree to your body. Write as many details as you can remember. Use Intuitive Writing to answer any questions. Follow his instructions to ensure your best recovery. You can use this technique to heal and dramatically transform yourself.

With this, and everything in this book, I wish you peace and love as you Ascend and become an Infinite You.

"Oh that my words were now written!
oh that they were printed in a book!
That they were graven with an iron pen
and lead in the rock forever!"
—Job 19:23-24 (KJV)

Biography Elizabeth Ann Atkins

ELIZABETH IS A BEST-SELLING author, actress, TV host, and an award-winning journalist who uses a multimedia platform to inspire people to unlock their infinite potential and live with passion, prosperity, health, and happiness. Her 2019 spiritual memoir is *God's Answer is Know: Lessons from a Spiritual Life*.

Elizabeth's desire to empower others springs from a trailblazing matrix of colorblind love and courage from her mother, an African American and Italian judge, and her father, a former Roman Catholic priest who was English, French Canadian, and Cherokee. They taught her to challenge the status quo by writing innovative ideas to *edu-tain* people.

With a master's degree in Journalism from Columbia University and a bachelor's degree in English Literature from the University of Michigan, Elizabeth has written over 20 books, including novels *White Chocolate, Dark Secret* and *Twilight* (with Billy Dee Williams).

Elizabeth has ghostwritten books for executives, prominent government and civic leaders, physicians, a surgeon, an intuitive medium, a family that triumphed on NBC's The Biggest Loser, an insurance agent, and a quadriplegic man who lived his dream to become a record company CEO. Her novellas about empowering women to overcome abuse and identity crises were published in *My Blue Suede Shoes: An Anthology* and *Other People's Skin: An Anthology*.

Elizabeth runs Two Sisters Writing and Publishing with her sister, the young adult author Catherine M. Greenspan. Together they have published more than twenty books, including an annual anthology of short stories by international writers who won the Two Sisters' ongoing short story writing contests.

Elizabeth is a health and fitness enthusiast whose 100-pound weight loss was featured on *Oprah*. Elizabeth co-hosts a weekly television show, *MI Healthy Mind*, which explores mental illness, addiction, and abuse.

She is a popular writing coach whose PowerJournal™ program teaches people to enrich their lives with journal-writing. She has taught writing at Wayne State University, Oakland University, Wayne County Community College District, and at national conferences.

As a speaker who promotes human harmony, Elizabeth rouses ovations by reciting her autobiographical poem, "White Chocolate," and has spoken at Columbia University, the University of Michigan, GM's World Diversity Day, Gannett, 100 Black Men, the NAACP, and many other venues.

As an actress, Elizabeth plays a major role in the feature-length film *Anything Is Possible*, nominated for "Best Foreign Film" by the Nollywood and African Film Critics Association. She composed an original screenplay, *Redemption*, a gritty drama about a Detroit gangster and a writer. And Elizabeth plays a 1950s journalist in the international shipwreck drama, *The Andrea Doria: Are The Passengers Saved?*

Elizabeth has been a guest on Oprah, Montel, NPR, Good Morning America Sunday, The CBS Evening News, and many national TV shows. After writing her master's thesis about mixed-race Americans, her work appeared in *The New York Times*, *The San Diego Tribune*, *Essence*, *Ebony*, and many publications.

Her *Detroit News* articles on race were nominated for the Pulitzer Prize, and she wrote a biography for the Presidential Medal of Freedom tribute for Rosa Parks.

Elizabeth runs, cycles, lifts weights, does yoga, journals and meditates to cultivate a joyous and peaceful mind, body and spirit.

Books Published By Two Sisters Writing and Publishing

A.M. Total Being Fitness Journal: A different kind of journal
Anthony Moses

Broken Hearts: Like Mother, Like Daughter—A Spiritual Call For Equality In Health Care
Alma G. Stallworth, PhD

"CLEAR!" Living the Life You Didn't Dream Of
Herman Williams, MD

Confessions of a Plastic Surgeon: Shocking Stories about Enhancing Butts, Boobs, and Beauty
Thomas T. Jeneby, MD

Dark Secret (Previously published by Forge)
Elizabeth Ann Atkins

The Dr. Sanchez Books on Raising Healthy Children—Baby's First Year: A Survival Guide For New & Experienced Parents
(Forthcoming)
Eduardo M. Sanchez, DNP

*The Energy Within Us: An Illuminating Perspective from Five
Trailblazers*

Joyce Hayes Giles

Carolyn Green

Rose McKinney-James

Hilda Pinnix-Ragland

Telisa Toliver

God's Answer is Know: Lessons from a Spiritual Life

Elizabeth Ann Atkins

Legacy of a Lawmaker: Inspired by Faith & Family

Alma G. Stallworth, PhD

Let the Future Begin

Dennis W. Archer

Lifted: A Journey from Trauma to Triumph

Mike Ritter

The Making Point: How to succeed when you're at your breaking point

Master Sgt. Cedric King

*My Name is Steve Delano Bullock: How I Changed My World and the
World Around Me through Leadership, Caring, and Perseverance*

Steve D. Bullock

The PowerJournal™ Series

PowerJournal: A 28-Day Challenge - Workbook #1

PowerJournal: A 28-Day Challenge for Weight Loss - Workbook #2

PowerJournal: A 28-Day Challenge for Making Big Decisions - Workbook #3

PowerJournal: A 28-Day Challenge for Spiritual Awakening - Workbook #4 (Forthcoming)

PowerJournal: A 28-Day Challenge for Discovering Your Purpose - Workbook #5 (Forthcoming)

Elizabeth Ann Atkins

Catherine M. Greenspan

Remembering and Forgetting: A spiritual journey

Lin Day

The Triumph of Rosemary: A Memoir

Judge Marylin E. Atkins

The Veronica Series

    Veronica, I Heard Your Mom's Black

    Veronica Talks to Boys

    Race Home, Veronica

    Grace Under Pressure (Forthcoming)

    Sally's Indoor Fiesta (Forthcoming)

    Hey, Jude, Is that White Lady Your Mom? (Forthcoming)

    A Girl Named George (Forthcoming)

    Have You Seen Debbie? (Forthcoming)

Catherine M. Greenspan

Two Sisters Writing and Publishing Short Story Anthologies

Two Sisters Writing and Publishing First Annual Anthology: Featuring International Writers

Two Sisters Writing and Publishing Second Annual Anthology: Featuring International Writers (Forthcoming)

Catherine M. Greenspan

Elizabeth Ann Atkins

We're Standing By

Al Allen

CPSIA information can be obtained
at www.ICGtesting.com
Printed in the USA
LVHW031147300719
625788LV00001B/4